Scott C. Jones
Rumors of Wisdom

Beihefte zur Zeitschrift für die alttestamentliche Wissenschaft

Herausgegeben von
John Barton · Reinhard G. Kratz
Choon-Leong Seow · Markus Witte

Band 398

Walter de Gruyter · Berlin · New York

Scott C. Jones

Rumors of Wisdom

Job 28 as Poetry

Walter de Gruyter · Berlin · New York

♾ Printed on acid-free paper which falls within the guidelines of the ANSI
to ensure permanence and durability.

ISBN 978-3-11-021477-2

ISSN 0934-2575

Library of Congress Cataloging-in-Publication Data

A CIP catalogue record for this book is available from the Library of Congress.

Bibliographic information published by the Deutsche Nationalbibliothek

The Deutsche Nationalbibliothek lists this publication in the Deutsche Nationalbibliografie;
detailed bibliographic data are available in the Internet at http://dnb.d-nb.de.

Printed in Germany

Cover design: Christopher Schneider, Laufen
The TranslitPalaU font used to print this work is available from Linguist's Software, Inc.,
PO Box 580, Edmonds, WA 98020–0580 USA, tel (425) 775 1130, www.linguistsoftware.com

For Jessica, who knows where wisdom is to be found.

For Abigail, Isaac, and Clara: May they find it.

Table of Contents

Acknowledgements

This book represents a substantial revision of my doctoral thesis at Princeton Theological Seminary. After the oral defense in 2007, I took to reading through Luckenbill's old edition, *Ancient Records from Assyria and Babylonia*, in which I stumbled upon a way of re-conceiving Job 28 in light of Neo-Assyrian royal inscriptions. Unable to resist the urge to effect the changes I felt that vision demanded, I re-wrote much of the work. The present volume is the result.

I am enormously grateful for the wise guidance and unflagging encouragement of Professor Leong Seow, who supervised my thesis and has continued to lend his learned voice to its revision. This is but a small token toward a debt that cannot be repaid. Sincere thanks are also due Chip Dobbs-Allsopp who served on the dissertation committee and taught me, above all, to read Biblical Hebrew poetry as a part of the larger human enterprise of poetic expression. Finally, I thank Professor Jim Roberts for his gracious willingness to read parts of the manuscript and offer his expert advice.

Many colleagues have been perceptive and encouraging conversation partners along the way. I think especially of Bruce Waltke, Ray Van Leeuwen, Kelly Kapic, Jeff Dryden, Brennan Breed, Scott Redd, Casey Strine, Jeremy Schipper, and Peter Altmann. John Muether prepared most of the indices. My student, Carlo Saulzallido, proofread the manuscript. Finally, I wish to extend my gratitude to the editors of BZAW for accepting this manuscript for publication and to the staff of Walter de Gruyter for their assistance in the process.

The production of this book would not have been possible without the support of my colleagues at Covenant College and the staff of Kresge Memorial Library, who went out of their way to make available the resources I needed to bring this project to completion. While I am exceedingly grateful for the contributions of all those named above, I alone am responsible for the mistakes and wrongheadedness that remain.

Sigla and Abbreviations

<	develops from
>	develops into
< >	Correction to consonantal text preserved in MT
{ }	Letters or words added by the scribe
*	Unattested form
⁎	LXX additions to the Old Greek with counterparts in the Hebrew
√	Root
AASOR	Annual of the American Schools of Oriental Research
AB	Anchor Bible
ABL	*Assyrian and Babylonian Letters belonging to the Kouyunjik Collections of the British Museum*. Robert Francis Harper. Chicago, 1892-1914
ABD	*Anchor Bible Dictionary*. Edited by D. N. Freedman. 6 vols. New York, 1992
AfO	*Archiv für Orientforschung*
AfOB	Archiv für Orientforschung: Beiheft
AGJU	Arbeiten zur Geschichte des antiken Judentums und des Urchristentums
AHw	*Akkadisches Handwörterbuch*. W. von Soden. 3 vols. Wiesbaden, 1965-1981
AJSL	*American Journal of Semitic Languages and Literature*
Akk.	Akkadian
ALASP	Abhandlungen zur Literatur Alt-Syren-Palästinas und Mesopotamiens
ALUOS	*Annual of the Leeds University Oriental Society*
ANEP	*The Ancient Near East in Pictures Relating to the Old Testament*. Edited by J. B. Pritchard. Princeton, 1954
ANESSup	Ancient Near Eastern Studies: Supplement
ANET	*Ancient Near Eastern Texts Relating to the Old Testament*. Edited by J. B. Pritchard. 3d ed. Princeton, 1969
AnOr	Analecta orientalia
AnSt	*Anatolian Studies*
AOAT	Alter Orient und Altes Testament
Aq	Aquila
Arab.	Arabic
ARAB	*Ancient Records of Assyria and Babylonia*. Daniel David Luckenbill. 2 vols. Chicago, 1926-27. Cited by volume and paragraph number.
Aram.	Aramaic
ArBib	The Aramaic Bible

AS	*Assyriological Studies*
ASOR	American Schools of Oriental Research
ASTI	*Annual of the Swedish Theological Institute*
ATANT	Abhandlungen zur Theologie des Alten und Neuen Testaments
Aug	*Augustinianum*
b.	Babylonian Talmud
BA	Biblical Aramaic
BA	*Biblical Archaeologist*
BaF	Baghdader Forschungen
BAR	*Biblical Archaeology Review*
BCAW	Blackwell Companions to the Ancient World
BDB	Brown, F., S. R. Driver, and C. A. Briggs. *A Hebrew and English Lexicon of the Old Testament*. Oxford, 1907
BETL	Bibliotheca ephemeridum theologicarum lovaniensium
BGE	*The Babylonian Gilgamesh Epic: Introduction, Critical Edition, and Cuneiform Texts*. A. R. George. 2 vols. Oxford, 2003
BH	Biblical Hebrew
BHAW	Blackwell History of the Ancient World
BHK	*Biblia Hebraica*. Edited by R. Kittel. Stuttgart, 1905-1906, 1925^{2}, 1937^{3}, 1951^{4}, 1973^{16}
BHS	*Biblia Hebraica Stuttgartensia*. Edited by K. Elliger and W. Rudolph. Stuttgart, 1983.
BHT	Beiträge zur historischen Theologie
BI	Biblical Interpretation Series
Bib	*Biblica*
BibOr	Biblica et orientalia
BJS	Brown Judaic Studies
BKAT	Biblischer Kommentar, Altes Testament. Edited by M. Noth and H. W. Wolff
BLH	Biblical Languages: Hebrew
BM	British Museum
BR	*Biblical Research*
BRev	*Bible Review*
BT	*The Bible Translator*
BTM	*Before the Muses: An Anthology of Akkadian Literature*. 3d edition. Benjamin Foster. Bethesda, 2005
BWL	*Babylonian Wisdom Literature*. W. G. Lambert. Oxford, 1960
BZ	*Biblische Zeitschrift*
BZAW	Beihefte zur Zeitschrift für die alttestamentliche Wissenschaft
C-stem	causative stem (Hebrew Hiphil)
CAD	*The Assyrian Dictionary of the Oriental Institute of the University of Chicago*. 21 vols. Chicago, 1956-
CANE	*Civilizations of the Ancient Near East*. Edited by J. Sasson. 4 vols. New York, 1995
CBQ	*Catholic Biblical Quarterly*
CBQMS	Catholic Biblical Quarterly Monograph Series
ch(s).	chapter(s)

COS	*The Context of Scripture*. Edited by W. W. Hallo. 3 vols. Leiden, 1997-2003
CT	*Cuneiform Texts from Babylonian Tablets &c. in the British Museum*
CTA	*Corpus des tablettes en cuneiforms alphabétiques découvertes à Ras Shamra-Ugarit de 1929 à 1939*. Edited by A. Herdner. Mission de Ras Shamra 10. Paris, 1963
CTU	*The Cuneiform Alphabetic Texts from Ugarit, Ras Ibn Hani, and Other Places*. Edited by M. Dietrich, O. Loretz, and J. Sanmartín. Münster, 1995
CBR	*Currents in Biblical Research*
CThM	Calwer Theologische Monographien
D-stem	doubled stem (Hebrew Piel)
DCH	*Dictionary of Classical Hebrew*. Edited by D. J. A. Clines. Sheffield, 1993-
DDD	*Dictionary of Deities and Demons in the Bible*. Edited by K. van der Toorn, B. Becking, and P. W. van der Horst. 2d ed. Leiden, 1999
DJD	Discoveries in the Judean Desert
DN	divine name
DNWSI	*Dictionary of the North-West Semitic Inscriptions*. J. Hoftijzer and K. Jongeling. 2 vols. Leiden, 1995.
Dp-stem	D-passive (Hebrew Pual)
DUL	*A Dictionary of the Ugaritic Language in the Alphabetic Tradition*. 2d ed. Gregorio del Olmo Lete and Joaquín Sanmartín. 2 vols. Edited and translated by Wilfred G. E. Watson. Leiden and Boston, 2004
EA	El-Amarna tablets. According to the edition of J. A. Knudtzon, *Die el-Amarna-Tafeln*. Leipzig, 1908-1915. Reprint, Aalen, 1964. Continued in A. F. Rainey, *El-Amarna Tablets, 359-379*. 2d revised ed. Kevelaer, 1978
EB	Early Bronze
EBib	*Études bibliques*
EdF	Erträge der Forschung
Ee.	*Enūma eliš*
Eg.	Egyptian
EHAT	Exegetisches Handbuch zum Alten Testament
EncJud	*Encyclopaedia Judaica*. 16 vols. Jerusalem, 1972
ErIsr	*Eretz-Israel*
ETCSL	The Electronic Text Corpus of Sumerian Literature: http://etcsl.orinst.ox.ac.uk
Eth.	Ethiopic
ExpTim	*Expository Times*
fig(s).	figure(s)
G-stem	*Grundstamm* (Hebrew Qal)
Gilg.	Gilgamesh epic or Gilgamesh
Gk.	Greek

GKC	*Gesenius' Hebrew Grammar*. Edited by E. Kautzsch. Translated by A. E. Cowley. 2d ed. Oxford, 1910
HALOT	*The Hebrew and Aramaic Lexicon of the Old Testament*. L. Koehler, W. Baumgartner, and J. J. Stamm. Translated and edited under the supervision of M. E. J. Richardson. 5 vols. Leiden, 1994-1999
HAR	*Hebrew Annual Review*
HAT	Handbuch zum Alten Testament
HBS	Herders Biblische Studien
HBT	*Horizons in Biblical Theology*
Heb.	Hebrew
Hen	*Henoch*
HI	*Hebrew Inscriptions: Texts from the Biblical Period of the Monarchy, with Concordance*. F. W. Dobbs-Allsopp, J. J. M. Roberts, C. L. Seow, and R. E. Whitaker. New Haven, 2004
HKAT	Handkommentar zum Alten Testament
HO	Handbuch der Orientalistik
HS	*Hebrew Studies*
HSM	Harvard Semitic Monographs
HSS	Harvard Semitic Studies
HTS	Harvard Theological Studies
HUCA	*Hebrew Union College Annual*
IBC	Interpretation: A Bible Commentary for Teaching and Preaching
IBHS	*An Introduction to Biblical Hebrew Syntax*. B. K. Waltke and M. O'Connor. Winona Lake, 1990
ICC	International Critical Commentary
IDB	*The Interpreter's Dictionary of the Bible*. Edited by G. A. Buttrick. 4 vols. Nashville, 1962
impv.	imperative
inf.	infinitive
infc.	infinitive construct
infa.	infinitive absolute
IRT	Issues in Religion and Theology
JANESCU	*Journal of the Ancient Near Eastern Society of Columbia University*
JAOS	*Journal of the American Oriental Society*
JB	Jerusalem Bible
JBA	*Jewish Book Annual*
JBL	*Journal of Biblical Literature*
JBQ	*Jewish Bible Quarterly*
JCS	*Journal of Cuneiform Studies*
JJS	*Journal of Jewish Studies*
JNES	*Journal of Near Eastern Studies*
JNSL	*Journal of Northwest Semitic Languages*
Joüon	Joüon, P. *A Grammar of Biblical Hebrew*. Translated and revised by T. Muraoka. 2 vols. Subsidia biblica 14/1-2. Rome, 1991
JPS	Jewish Publication Society Version
JQR	*Jewish Quarterly Review*

JR	*Journal of Religion*
JSem	*Journal for Semitics* (= *Tydskrif vir Semitistiek*)
JSJ	*Journal for the Study of Judaism in the Persian, Hellenistic, and Roman Periods*
JSP	*Journal for the Study of the Pseudepigrapha*
JSOT	*Journal for the Study of the Old Testament*
JSOTSup	Journal for the Study of the Old Testament: Supplement Series
JSS	*Journal of Semitic Studies*
JTS	*Journal of Theological Studies*
KAI	*Kanaanäische und aramäische Inschriften*. H. Donner and W. Röllig. Wiesbaden. 1962-1964. Cited according to text number and line.
KAR	*Keilschrifttexte aus Assur religiösen Inhalts*. Edited by E. Ebeling. Leipzig, 1919-1923
KAT	Kommentar zum Alten Testament
Ken.	Kennicott
KHC	Kurzer Hand-Commentar zum Alten Testament
KJV	King James Version
l(l).	line(s)
LAI	Library of Ancient Israel
LAS	*The Literature of Ancient Sumer*. Jeremy Black, Graham Cunningham, Eleanor Robson, and Gábor Zólyomi. Oxford, 2004
LB	Late Bronze
LBH	Late Biblical Hebrew
LCL	Loeb Classical Library
LD	Lectio divina
LUÅ	Lunds universitets årsskrift
LXX	Septuagint
LXX^{A}	Septuagint Codex Alexandrinus
LXX^{B}	Septuagint Codex Vaticanus
LXX^{C}	Septuagint Codex Ephraem
LXX^{S}	Septuagint Codex Sinaiticus
m.	Mishnah
MA	Middle Assyrian
Mand.	Mandaic
marg.	marginal reading
MARI	*Mari: Annales de recherches interdisciplinaires*
MB	Middle Babylonian
MC	Mesopotamian Civilizations
MCG	*Mesopotamian Cosmic Geography*. Wayne Horowitz. Mesopotamian Civilizations 8. Winona Lake, 1998
MDOG	*Mitteilungen der Deutschen Orient-Gesellschaft zu Berlin*
MGWJ	*Monatschrift für Geschichte und Wissenschaft des Judentums*
Midr.	Midrash
MS(S)	manuscript(s)
MT	Masoretic Text
NA	Neo-Assyrian
NAB	New American Bible

Nab.	Nabatean
NAS	New American Standard Bible
NB	Neo-Babylonian
NCB	New Century Bible
NEB	New English Bible
N.F.	neue Folge (= new series)
NIBC	New International Biblical Commentary
NICOT	New International Commentary on the Old Testament
NIDB	*The New Interpreter's Dictionary of the Bible.* Edited by K. D. Sakenfeld. 5 vols. Nashville, 2006-2009
NIDOTTE	*New International Dictionary of Old Testament Theology and Exegesis*. Edited by W. A. VanGemeren. 5 vols. Grand Rapids, 1997
NIV	New International Version
NJB	New Jerusalem Bible
NJPS	*Tanakh: The Holy Scriptures: The New JPS Translation according to the Traditional Hebrew Text*
NKJV	New King James Version
n.p.	no pagination
n.pub.	no publisher
NPEPP	*The New Princeton Encyclopedia of Poetry and Poetics*. Edited by Alex Preminger and T. V. F. Brogan. New York, 1993
NPNF[2]	*Nicene and Post-Nicene Fathers*, Series 2
N.S.	new series
OA	Old Assyrian
OAkk	Old Akkadian
OB	Old Babylonian
obv.	obverse
OBO	Orbis Biblicus et Orientalis
ÖBS	Österreichische Biblische Studien
OEANE	*The Oxford Encyclopedia of Archaeology in the Near East*. Edited by E. M. Meyers. 5 vols. New York, 1997
Off. Aram.	Official Aramaic, also known as "Imperial Aramaic," or "Reichsaramaisch"
OG	Old Greek
OL	Old Latin
OLP	Orientalia lovaniensia periodica
Or	*Orientalia*, new series
OSA	Old South Arabian
OT	Old Testament
OTE	*Old Testament Essays*
OTL	Old Testament Library
OtSt	*Oudtestamentische Studiën*
p(p).	page(s)
PEQ	*Palestine Exploration Quarterly*
PG	Patrologia graeca [= Patrologiae cursus completus: Series graeca]. Edited by J.-P. Migne. 162 vols. Paris, 1857-1886
Phoen.	Phoenician

PSB	*Princeton Seminary Bulletin*
RA	*Revue d'assyriologie et d'archéologie orientale*
Rab.	Rabbah
RB	*Revue biblique*
ResQ	*Restoration Quarterly*
rev.	reverse
RIMA	Royal Inscriptions of Mesopotamia, Assyrian Periods
RlA	*Reallexikon der Assyriologie und Vorderasiatischen Archäologie.* Edited by Erich Ebeling et al. Berlin, 1928-
RS	Ras Shamra
RSV	Revised Standard Version
SAACT	State Archives of Assyria Cuneiform Texts
SAAS	State Archives of Assyria Studies
SAK	*Die Sumerischen und Akkadischen Königsinschriften.* François Thureau-Dangin. Vorderasiatische Bibliothek 1/1. Leipzig, 1907
SB	Standard Babylonian
SBB	Soncino Books of the Bible
SBFLA	*Studii biblici Franciscani liber annus*
SBLDS	Society of Biblical Literature Dissertation Series
SBLSCS	Society of Biblical Literature Septuagint and Cognate Studies
SBLSymS	Society of Biblical Literature Symposium Series
SBLWAW	Society of Biblical Literature Writings from the Ancient World
SBT^2	Studies in Biblical Theology, second series
SBTS	Sources for Biblical and Theological Study
ScrHier	Scripta Hierosolymitana
SJOT	*Scandinavian Journal of the Old Testament*
SFSHJ	South Florida Studies in the History of Judaism
SHBC	Smyth & Helwys Bible Commentary
SR	*Studies in Religion*
SRSup	Studies in Religion Supplement
SSN	Studia semitica neederlandica
SubBi	*Subsidia biblica*
Sum.	Sumerian
s.v.	*sub verbo*
Syh.	Syro-hexaplar
Sym	Symmachus
Syr.	Syriac *or* the Syriac Peshitta
t.	Tosefta
TCL	Textes cuneiforms du Louvre. TCL 3 = *Une relation de la huitème campagne de Sargon (714 av. J.-C.).* François Thureau-Dangin. Musée du Louvre—Département des antiquités orientales. Paris, 1912
TDOT	*Theological Dictionary of the Old Testament.* Edited by G. J. Botterweck and H. Ringgren. Translated by J. T. Willis, G. W. Bromiley, and D. E. Green. 16 vols. Grand Rapids, 1974-
Text	*Textus*

Tg(s).	rabbinic Targum(s). The siglum Tg. often refers specifically to the critical edition of the rabbinic Targum to Job prepared by David M. Stec, *The Text of the Targum of Job*. Leiden, New York, and Köln, 1994
Tg^{C}	rabbinic Targum manuscript Cambridge, University Library Ee. 5.9
Tg^{M}	rabbinic Targum manuscript Madrid, Biblioteca de la Universidad Complutense 116-Z-40, transcribed in Luis Díez Merino, *Targum de Job: Edición Principe del Ms. Villa-Amil n. 5 de Alfonso de Zamora*. Madrid, 1984
Tg^{L}	rabbinic Targum of Job in Paul de Lagarde, *Hagiographa Chaldaice*. Leipzig, 1873
Tg^{S}	rabbinic Targum manuscript Salamanca, Biblioteca Universitaria M-2
Th	Theodotion
TNIV	Today's New International Version
TOTC	Tyndale Old Testament Commentaries
TRu	*Theologische Rundschau*
TS	*Theological Studies*
TSAJ	Texte und Studien zum Antiken Judentum
TSSI	*Textbook of Syrian Semitic Inscriptions*. John C. L. Gibson. 3 vols. Oxford, 1971-1982. Cited by volume and page number.
TVers	*Theologische Versuche*
UAVA	Untersuchungen zur Assyriologie und vorderasiatischen Archäologie
UF	*Ugarit-Forschungen*
Ug.	Ugaritic
UVST	*Ugaritic Vocabulary in Syllabic Transcription*. John Huehnergard. Harvard Semitic Studies 32. Atlanta, 1987
v(v).	verse(s)
VAB	Vorderasiatische Bibliothek. VAB 4 = *Die Neubabylonischen Königsinschriften*. Stephen Langdon. Translated by Rudolf Zehnpfund. Leipzig, 1912
Vg.	Vulgate
VT	*Vetus Testamentum*
VTSup	Vetus Testamentum Supplements
WBC	Word Biblical Commentary
WUNT	Wissenschaftliche Untersuchungen zum Neuen Testament
YNER	Yale Near Eastern Researches
YOS	Yale Oriental Series
ZAH	*Zeitschrift für Althebraistik*
ZAW	*Zeitschrift für die alttestamentliche Wissenschaft*
ZTK	*Zeitschrift für Theologie und Kirche*

Chapter One: Job 28 as Poetry

[A]ll study of literature must emerge from and return to reading.[1]

1.1 Job 28 as Problematic Masterpiece

The poem in Job 28 suffers from a rather confused reputation.[2] On the one hand, the nature of the poem itself is disputed. As Peter Zerafa comments, "The text is a masterpiece of poetry and rhetoric."[3] Yet he goes on to say, "An intriguing masterpiece, to be sure, that artfully camouflages its poetic structure, seeing that the critics do not agree about its strophic disposition."[4] The ending of the poem is perhaps the most contested piece, commonly seen as the lowest form of platitude that must be excised from the more transcendent and seemingly philosophical meditations[5] of its beautiful body.

To the difficulties of poetic structure one must add the problems of the conceptual background of Section One (vv. 1-11). Though commonly thought to be descriptive of the expedition of a lone miner out in the Sinai or the ʿArabah, hanging suspended from ropes in dark shafts on a search for precious ore, interpretations along these lines often rest on little more than assumption. As Edward Greenstein states, "It is striking… that one does not find in this passage a single verb or derived noun that refers to digging, excavating, or mining… Moreover all the paraphernalia of mining that crop up in the commentaries are only im-

---

1 Robert Alter, *The Pleasures of Reading in an Ideological Age* (New York: Simon and Schuster, 1989), 21.

2 See the recent survey of opinions on Job 28 in Carol A. Newsom, "Re-considering Job," *CBR* 5 (2007): 161-64. As she states, "Few parts of the book have been as contested" (ibid., 162).

3 Peter Paul Zerafa, *The Wisdom of God in the Book of Job* (Studia Universitatis S. Thomae in Urbe 8; Rome: Herder, 1978), 130.

4 Ibid., 130.

5 Édouard Dhorme calls vv. 1-27 "a fine metaphysical flight" (*A Commentary on the Book of Job* [trans. Harold Knight; Nashville, Tenn.: Thomas Nelson, 1984], li). Originally published as *Le Livre de Job* (*EBib*; Paris: J. Gabalda, 1926).

plicit, in the minds of the interpreters."[6] More recently, some scholars have even questioned whether a human is the subject of these lines at all. They suggest returning to the ancient view[7] that *God* is the subject of vv. 3-11, as he searches out deep wisdom.[8]

On the other hand, the place and function of Job 28 within the Book of Job is also problematic. Michael Coogan colorfully describes it as "altogether anomalous."[9] Though previous generations of scholars largely assumed the unity of the Book of Job, the rise of historical criticism radically questioned this assumption, replacing it with another: that the Poem of Job is a piecemeal pastiche, not the work of a single author.[10] Chief among the corpus of supposedly secondary additions to the original Poem of Job is the poem on wisdom in ch. 28. Gillis Gerleman's comment is representative: "The poem is quite independent and it is difficult to find any immediate connection with what is otherwise dealt with in the Job dialogue."[11] Many assume that the whole of ch. 28 is an interpolation of a later editor who could not help but inject his opinion on the dialogues to this point. A typical description of the poem is actually a contextual judgment in the guise of a form-critical category: "interlude." But despite such suspicions, some scholars still insist that Job 28 is "the climax of the third dialogue—and perhaps the whole

6 Edward L. Greenstein, "The Poem on Wisdom in Job 28 in its Conceptual and Literary Contexts," in *Job 28: Cognition in Context* (ed. Ellen van Wolde; BI 64; eds. R. Alan Culpepper and Rolf Rendtorff; Leiden and Boston: Brill, 2003), 267. Compare the comments of Zerafa: "The text itself does not contain any incontrovertible reference to mining or tunneling or to any precious metal" (*Wisdom of God*, 157).

7 This view is evident in LXX-Job as well as in the Peshitta and in the rabbinic Targums.

8 See especially Greenstein, "The Poem on Wisdom in Job 28," 268-69; John F. Elwolde, "Non-Contiguous Parallelism as a Key to Literary Structure and Lexical Meaning in Job 28," in *Job 28: Cognition in Context* (ed. Ellen van Wolde; BI 64; eds. R. Alan Culpepper and Rolf Rendtorff; Leiden and Boston: Brill, 2003), 103-18; and N. H. Tur-Sinai, *The Book of Job: A New Commentary* (rev. ed.; Jerusalem: Kiryat Sepher, 1967), 396.

9 Michael D. Coogan, "The Goddess Wisdom—'Where Can She Be Found?': Literary Reflexes of Popular Religion," in *Ki Baruch hu: Ancient Near Eastern, Biblical and Judaic Studies in Honor of Baruch A. Levine* (eds. R. Chazon, W. W. Hallo, and L. H. Schiffman; Winona Lake, Ind.: Eisenbrauns, 1999), 205.

10 See especially Carol A. Newsom, *The Book of Job: A Contest of Moral Imaginations* (Oxford and New York: Oxford University Press, 2003), 4-7; and Katharine Dell, *The Book of Job as Sceptical Literature* (BZAW 197; ed. O. Kaiser; Berlin and New York: Walter de Gruyter, 1991), 29-56.

11 Gillis Gerleman, *Studies in the Septuagint, I. Book of Job* (LUÅ N.F. 1; 43/2; Lund: C. W. K. Gleerup, 1946), 29.

book..."[12] In sum, Job 28 is "a brilliant but embarrassing poem for many commentators."[13] It is a scintillating work of art whose resumé of scholarly inquiry might nevertheless read: "the object hidden; the text and its interpretation enigmatic."[14]

The problems surrounding Job 28 are no doubt facilitated by the difficulty of the Book of Job itself. In the preface to his late 4th century C.E. Vulgate translation of Job, Jerome highlighted the elusiveness of the book by likening it to an eel, which, when squeezed, slips out of the hands.[15] Yet many attempts to mine the meaning of the poem have only contributed to this difficulty by focusing too narrowly on either the language of the chapter or on its poetic structure. Such a dichotomy between the literary and the philological—whether philosophically or practically motivated—has, I believe, steered interpreters away from the "pattern of resolutions and balances and harmonizations" in Job 28 that Cleanth Brooks calls "the essential structure of a poem."[16]

1.2 Philology and Literature in the Study of Biblical Poetry

Comparative philology is a long-standing discipline, and it has proved its staying power in the fields of ancient Near Eastern and Biblical studies over the last two centuries. Unfortunately, the philological method has often carried with it a positivistic strain that "treats 'literary texts' exactly as any other form of historical 'text', discarding as too subjective and unscientific any attempt to account for precisely those distinctive

---

12 Alan Cooper, "Narrative Theory and the Book of Job," *SR* 11 (1992): 42. From a structural perspective, Ernst Wendland suggests that Job 28 is the fulcrum of the entire book (" 'Where in the world can wisdom be found?' [Job 28:12, 20]: A textual and contextual survey of Job 28 in relation to its communicative setting, ancient [ANE] and modern [Africa]," *JSem* 12 [2003]: 1-33, here 16-21).

13 Norman C. Habel, *The Book of Job: A Commentary* (OTL; Philadelphia, Pa.: Westminster, 1985), 391.

14 So Jürgen van Oorschot: »Verborgen die Sache, enigmatisch der Text und seine Auslegung« (»Hiob 28: Verborgene Weisheit und die Furcht Gottes als Überwindung einer Generalisierten חכמה,« in *The Book of Job* [ed. W.A.M. Beuken; BETL 114; Leuven: Leuven University Press, 1994], 183).

15 "Obliquus enim etiam apud Hebraeos totus liber fertur et lubricus et quod graece rethores vocant ἐσχηματισμένος, dumque aliud loquitur aliud agit, ut si velis anguillam aut murenulam strictis tenere manibus, quanto fortius presseris, tanto citius elabitur" ("Incipit Prologus Sancti Hieronymi in Libro Iob," in *Biblia Sacra iuxta Vulgatem Versionem. Tomus I: Genesis-Psalmi* [ed. Robert Weber; 3d, corrected ed.; 2 vols.; Stuttgart: Deutsche Bibelgesellschaft, 1985], 731). See the English translation in his "Preface to Job," *NPNF*[2] 6:491.

16 Cleanth Brooks, "The Heresy of Paraphrase," in *The Well Wrought Urn: Studies in the Structure of Poetry* (San Diego, New York, and London: Harcourt Brace, 1942), 203.

qualities that make literature 'literary': the meaning and effect of the experience of reading."[17] As a result, much of the work of philologists and text-critics remains largely unaffected by the literary nature of the texts which are the object of their study. Aesthetic considerations too rarely impinge upon judgments about the nature of these works as texts and about the meaning and history of their words.[18] Yet philology, which Auden once called "the most poetical of all scholastic disciplines,"[19] can surely serve no greater purpose than to provide avenues into "the impulses and reflexes of awakened language."[20]

Since the explosion of literary approaches to the Bible in the 1960's, a newer guild has rightly emphasized the need to read biblical poems as works of art, but often without taking full account of the problems of language or the various philological motivations for poetic diction. Many such "literary" analyses show little regard for philological and textual criticism. As an illustration of this, John Elwolde speaks of a current "structured shift away from comparativism, reflected..., at the level of biblical interpretation, in the move away from text-criticism and philology to a new emphasis on the Bible as a literary document—

17 Jeremy Black thus describes the typical mode of scholarship in Assyriology in *Reading Sumerian Poetry* (Ithaca, NY: Cornell University Press, 1998), 7. See also the comments of Piotr Michalowski, who speaks of "a strongly anti-theoretical philological tradition" in Assyriology ("Presence at the Creation," in *Lingering Over Words: Studies in Ancient Near Eastern Literature in Honor of William L. Moran* [eds. Tzvi Abusch, John Huehnergard, and Piotr Steinkeller; Atlanta, Ga.: Scholars, 1990], 381). Baruch Halpern has also noted the overriding deterministic and quantitative philological strain in historical methodology as applied to ancient Israel ("Erasing History: The Minimalist Assault on Ancient Israel," *BRev* 11/6 [1995]: 25-35, 47).

18 Joseph Blenkinsopp's comments regarding late 19th century Pentateuchal criticism also obtain to the philological method as applied elsewhere in the Old Testament: "The standard approach, therefore, was decidedly referential, diachronic, and objectivist, and relatively little attention was paid to the purely literary and aesthetic qualities of the texts in question" ("The Pentateuch," in *The Cambridge Companion to Biblical Interpretation* [ed. John Barton; Cambridge: Cambridge University Press, 1998], 181).

19 W. H. Auden in an Inaugural Lecture as Professor of Poetry delivered before the University of Oxford on June 11, 1956 (published as "Making, Knowing and Judging," in *The Dyer's Hand and Other Essays* [New York: Vintage International, 1989], 35).

20 Seamus Heaney, "The Redress of Poetry," in *The Redress of Poetry* (New York: The Noonday Press / Farrar, Straus, and Giroux, 1995), 10.

or series of documents—to be valued and analysed in its own right."[21] In response to a similar tendency in his own day, C. S. Lewis remarked,

> I am sometimes told that there are people who want a study of literature wholly free from philology; that is, from the love and knowledge of words. Perhaps no such people exist. If they do, they are either crying for the moon or else resolving on a lifetime of persistent and carefully guarded delusion... If we reject as 'mere philology' every attempt to restore for us [the author's] real poem, we are safeguarding the deceit.[22]

One cannot truly understand poems as works of art without accounting for the intricacies of language and text with which they are woven. As Terry Eagleton states, "[T]he language of a poem is *constitutive* of its ideas."[23] The poet of the Book of Job in particular seems to have been very intentional about choosing language that enhances meaning.[24] Any aspect of a word may be the basis for play, be it semantics, phonology, or morphology, in both diachronic and synchronic perspectives.

1.3 Job 28 in Current Research: A Selected Survey

1.3.1 Commentaries

A dichotomy between the literary and the philological has carried over into the study of the poem in Job 28 as well. A brief survey of prominent commentaries on the Book of Job in the last one hundred years reveals an intense focus on philology and textual criticism without as much concern for how the language and text contribute to the overall message and aesthetic achievement of the poem. The substantial vol-

---

21 John F. Elwolde, "The Use of Arabic in Hebrew Lexicography: Whence? Whither?, and Why?," in *William Robertson Smith: Essays in Reassessment* (JSOTSup 189; ed. W. Johnstone; Sheffield, U.K.: Sheffield Academic Press, 1995), 372. Compare the discussion of J. A. Emerton, "Comparative Semitic Philology and Hebrew Lexicography," in *Congress Volume, Cambridge 1995* (VTSup 66; ed. J. A. Emerton; Leiden, New York, Boston, and Köln: Brill, 1997), 10, who also cites this passage in almost precisely the same form.

22 C. S. Lewis, *Studies in Words* (2d ed.; Cambridge, New York, and Melbourne: Cambridge University Press, 1960), 3.

23 Terry Eagleton, *How to Read a Poem* (Malden, Mass.; Oxford, United Kingdom; and Carlton, Victoria: Blackwell Publishing, 2007), 2 (emphasis his).

24 See Edward L. Greenstein, "Features of Language in the Poetry of Job," in *Das Buch Hiob und seine Interpretationen. Beiträge zum Hiob-Symposium auf dem Monte Verità von 14.-19. August 2005* (ed. T. Krüger et al.; ATANT 88; ed. Erhard Blum et al.; Zürich: Theologischer Verlag Zürich, 2007), 81-96, especially 86; and idem, "The Language of Job and its Poetic Function," *JBL* 122 (2003): 651-66.

umes of Dhorme,[25] Driver and Gray,[26] Pope,[27] Tur-Sinai,[28] and Gordis[29] focus intently on philological and textual matters, often relegating literary and theological issues to introductory sections or appendices. In addition to philological commentary, the shorter classic treatments of Duhm[30] and Budde[31] also focus on the diachronic growth of the poem. These foci are likewise prominent in the moderate volume by De Wilde[32] and in the larger commentary of Fohrer.[33]

The Book of Job remains—with good reason—a playground for textual critics[34] and specialists in comparative Semitic philology.[35] Some who have employed these methods seem to suppose that objective and

25 Dhorme, *Commentary on the Book of Job.*

26 Samuel Rolles Driver and George Buchanan Gray, *A Critical and Exegetical Commentary on the Book of Job* (2 vols.; ICC; Edinburgh: T & T Clark, 1921).

27 Marvin H. Pope, *Job, Translated with an Introduction and Notes* (3d ed.; AB 15; Garden City, NY: Doubleday, 1973).

28 N. H. Tur-Sinai, *The Book of Job* (rev. ed.; Jerusalem: Kiryat Sepher, 1967). This is also true of his earlier commentary, published under his previous name, Harry Torczyner, *Das Buch Hiob. Eine Kritische Analyse des Überlieferten Hiobtextes* (Wien and Berlin: R. Löwit Verlag, 1920).

29 Robert Gordis, *The Book of Job: Commentary, New Translation, and Special Studies* (New York: Jewish Theological Seminary of America, 1978).

30 Bernhard Duhm, *Das Buch Hiob erklärt* (KHC XVI; Freiburg im Breisgau: J.C.B. Mohr, 1897).

31 Karl Budde, *Das Buch Hiob* (HKAT 2/1; Göttingen: Vandenhoeck & Ruprecht, 1896).

32 A. De Wilde, *Das Buch Hiob: eingeleitet, übersetzt und erläutert* (*OtSt* 22; ed. A. S. van der Woude. Leiden: E.J. Brill, 1981).

33 Georg Fohrer, *Das Buch Hiob* (KAT 16; Gütersloh: Gerd Mohn, 1963).

34 Note especially the contributions of Georg Beer (*Der Text des Buches Hiob untersucht* [Marburg: N. G. Elwertsche Verlagsbuchhandlung, 1897]) and Martijn Theodor Houtsma (*Textkritische Studien zum Alten Testament I: Das Buch Hiob* [Leiden: E. J. Brill, 1925]).

35 Note the work of Mitchell Dahood and his students. Especially pertinent are the studies of Anton Blommerde (*Northwest Semitic Grammar and Job* [BibOr 22; Rome: Pontifical Biblical Institute, 1969]) and Anthony Ceresko (*Job 29-31 in the Light of Northwest Semitic: A Translation and Philological Commentary* [BibOr 36; Rome: Pontifical Biblical Institute, 1980]). In the same vein is Walter Michel's monograph, *Job in the Light of Northwest Semitic* (BibOr 42; Rome: Pontifical Biblical Institute, 1987), which was based on his 1970 University of Wisconsin dissertation supervised by Menahem Mansoor, entitled "The Ugaritic Texts and the Mythological Expressions in the Book of Job." See the review of the Dahood school in Peter C. Craigie, "Job and Ugaritic Studies," in *Studies in the Book of Job: Papers Presented at the Forty-ninth Annual Meeting of the Canadian Society of Biblical Studies, May 1981* (ed. Walter E. Aufrecht; SRSup 16; Waterloo, Ontario: Wilfrid Laurier University Press / Canadian Corporation for Studies in Religion, 1985), 28-35. For an attempt to establish a more controlled method for comparative philology in the exegesis of the Book of Job, see Lester L. Grabbe, *Comparative Philology and the Text of Job: A Study in Methodology* (SBLDS 34; eds. Howard C. Kee and Douglas A. Knight.; Missoula, Mont.: Scholars Press / The Society of Biblical Literature, 1977).

quantitative solutions could be put to the riddles of philology and text which, in turn, would serve as a secure foundation upon which to build up higher levels of meaning of the text as a literary work. Yet one woners whether this rather one-sided focus has contributed as much to the "Job problem"[36] as it has done to solve it.

On the other hand, Job scholars of recent decades have begun to focus more on the literary or theological structure of the canonical Job (as opposed to the reconstructed Job) and its internal resonances and dissonances. In this vein are the commentaries of Habel,[37] Janzen,[38] Good,[39] Newsom,[40] and Wilson,[41] as well as the brief treatment by Whybray.[42] Samuel Balentine's important volume, whose hallmark is Job's reception history, also tends to emphasize literary interpretation of the final form of the book.[43] Each of these is quite different in its approach, but all succeed in bringing to light numerous aspects of the Joban poet's (or poets') sophistication in composing or editing the poem. However, none of the aforementioned works gives sustained attention to the problems of language and text in Job. To be sure, this lack may simply be a practical limitation of a commentary series or a matter of emphasis. Nevertheless, the point remains that the cogency of such literary or theological readings of Joban poetry must be determined, at least in part, by the degree to which they find roots in the language and text of which it is comprised.

Of all the treatments of Job 28 in the commentaries, the recent volume by David Clines devotes the most substantial attention both to philological matters and to a reading of the poem as a whole.[44] Remarkably, however, he gives very little attention to the problems of textual

---

36 Echoing the title of Hans-Peter Müller's monograph, *Das Hiobproblem: Seine Stellung und Entstehung im Alten Orient und im Alten Testament* (EdF 84; Darmstadt: Wissenschaftliche Buchgesellschaft, 1978).

37 Habel, *The Book of Job*.

38 J. Gerald Janzen, *Job* (IBC; Atlanta: John Knox Press, 1985).

39 Edwin Good, *In Turns of Tempest: A Reading of Job with a Translation* (Stanford: Stanford University Press, 1990). As the title suggests, Good's volume is not a commentary *per se*, but a reading of Job. Nonetheless, the point still obtains.

40 Carol A. Newsom, "The Book of Job: Introduction Commentary, and Reflections," in *The New Interpreter's Bible, Volume IV: 1 & 2 Maccabees; Introduction to Hebrew Poetry; Job; Psalms* (ed. Leander Keck et al.; Nashville, Tenn.: Abingdon, 1996), 319-637.

41 Gerald H. Wilson, *Job* (NIBC 10; Old Testament Series; Peabody, Mass.: Hendrickson; Milton Keynes, UK: Paternoster, 2007).

42 Norman Whybray, *Job* (Readings: A New Biblical Commentary; ed. John Jarick; Sheffield: Sheffield Academic Press, 1988).

43 Samuel E. Balentine, *Job* (SHBC 10; Macon, Ga.: Smyth & Helwys, 2006). See Scott C. Jones, review of Samuel E. Balentine, *Job, Koinonia* 19 (2007): 110-14.

44 Clines, *Job 21-37* (WBC 18A; Nashville, Tenn.: Thomas Nelson, 2006), 889-926.

transmission and interpretation in the ancient versions. Both the Aleppo Codex and the important "targum" from Qumran (11Q10) are completely ignored.

1.3.2 Essays and Monographs on Job 28

Scholarship on Job 28 has been governed largely by questions of its implied authorship and its controversial place and function in the Book of Job. These larger questions have also precipitated discussions of the chapter's genre and its presentation of wisdom.

Many interpreters have set out to solve these problems at a macro-structural level, often employing various generic rubrics for the whole of Job and then situating Job 28 within that generic framework. Such studies may have radically different results. The work of Clara Settlemire,[45] for example, begins with the typical assumptions that (1) the third cycle has been disarranged[46] and (2) that ch. 28 is incompatible with Job's attitude at this point in the dialogues. Her proposed solution is to re-locate ch. 28 at the end of the book, following Job 42:6.[47] This arrangement follows Claus Westermann's proposal for the structure of the Book of Job as an individual lament,[48] though unlike Westermann, she views Job 28 as a song of praise, functioning much like a salvation oracle.[49]

Alison Lo explains the oddity of Job 28 in Job's mouth as part of the author's rhetorical strategy. According to Lo, the Book of Job is a continuous narrative of incongruities which are intentionally juxtaposed to draw in the audience with the goal of correcting their traditional view of retributive justice. Within the context of chs. 22-31, Job 28 serves as a "pseudo-climax" which moves the book toward its true resolution. Af-

---

45 Settlemire, "The Original Position of Job 28," in *The Answers Lie Below: Essays in Honor of Lawrence Edmund Toombs* (ed. Henry O. Thompson; Lanham, New York, and London: University Press of America, 1984), 287-88. See also her earlier dissertation, "The Meaning, Importance, and Original Position of Job 28" (Ph.D. diss., Drew University, 1969).

46 On this assumption, see especially the remarks of Alan Cooper, "Narrative Theory and the Book of Job," 42 and n. 29.

47 Settlemire, "The Original Position of Job 28," 288, 299-300.

48 Claus Westermann, *Der Aufbau des Buches Hiob. Mit eine Einführung in die neuere Hiobforschung von Jürgen Kegler* (2d, expanded ed.; CThM: Reihe A, Bibelwissenschaft, 6; eds. Peter Stuhlmacher and Claus Westermann; Stuttgart: Calwer Verlag, 1977). The first edition was published as *Der Aufbau des Buches Hiob* (BHT 23; Tübingen: Mohr Siebeck, 1956).

49 Settlemire, "The Original Position of Job 28," 299-305.

ter the collapse of the debates, Job seeks out wisdom, and in ch. 28 he offers "second-hand knowledge" about God. But his reflections on wisdom (especially in 28:28) only fuel his determination for personal vindication (chs. 29-31). The Yhwh speeches in chs. 38-41 provide the book's answer by offering "first-hand experience." It is not until Job submits to Yhwh in 42:1-6 that he "actualizes and internalizes the true meaning of wisdom."[50] Thus both Job and the audience move "from less to more adequate perspectives."[51]

The views of Settlemire and Lo are only two of a myriad of proposals regarding the place and function of Job 28 within the entire Poem of Job. It is not my intention to judge or to survey all of these in the present study.[52] The point here is simply to note that such observations

---

50 Alison Lo, *Job 28 as Rhetoric: An Analysis of Job 28 in the Context of Job 22-31* (VTSup 97; ed. H. M. Barstad et al.; Leiden and Boston: E. J. Brill, 2003), 231.

51 Lo, *Job 28 as Rhetoric,* 20 and n. 84. As she states, she borrows this phrase from Newsom, "The Book of Job," 337.

52 For a very useful listing of various views on the place and function of Job 28 up to about 1970, see Excursus III in Gary Martin's Ph.D. dissertation, "Elihu and the Third Cycle in the Book of Job" (Ph.D. diss., Princeton University, 1972), 265-269.

Among the literature devoted to the subject, see H. H. Grätz, »Die Integrität der Kapitel 27 und 28 im Hiob,« *MGWJ* 21 (1872): 241-50; Carl Budde, »Die Capitel 27 und 28 des Buches Hiob,« *ZAW* 2 (1882): 193-274; George Barton, "The Composition of Job 24-30," *JBL* 30 (1911): 66-77; P. Dhorme, "Les Chapitres XXV-XXVIII du Livre de Job," *RB* 33 (1924): 343-56; A. Regnier, "La Distribution des Chapitres 25-28 du Livre de Job," *RB* 33 (1924): 186-200; Curt Kuhl, »Neuere Literarkritik des Buches Hiob,« *TRu* N.F. 21 (1953): 257-317; R. Tournay, "L'Ordre primitif des Chapitres XXIV-XXVIII du Livre de Job," *RB* 64 (1957): 321-34; Robert Laurin, "The Theological Structure of Job," *ZAW* 84 (1972): 86-89; M. Prakasa Reddy, "The Book of Job—A Reconstruction," *ZAW* 90 (1978): 59-94; John F. A. Sawyer, "The Authorship and Structure of the Book of Job," in *Studia Biblica 1978: I. Papers on Old Testament and Related Themes* (Sixth International Congress on Biblical Studies, Oxford, 3-7 April 1978; ed. E. A. Livingstone; JSOTSup 11; Sheffield: JSOT Press, 1979); Yosef Tsamodi, "The Wisdom Hymn (Job 28): Its Place in the Book of Job," *Beit Mikra* 28 (1982-83): 268-77 (in Hebrew); Ruben Zimmerman, »Homo Sapiens Ignorans: Hiob 28 als Bestandteil der ursprünglichen Hiobdichtung,« *BN* 74 (1994): 80-100; and Markus Witte, *Vom Leiden zur Lehre: Der dritte Redegang (Hiob 21-27) und die Redaktionsgeschichte des Hiobbuches* (BZAW 230; ed. Otto Kaiser; Berlin and New York: Walter de Gruyter, 1994), 173-175, 205-211.

Both Edward Greenstein and David J. A. Clines have independently re-located ch. 28 to the end of the Elihu speeches. See Greenstein, "The Poem on Wisdom in Job 28," 271-272; and David J. A. Clines, "Putting Elihu in his Place: A Proposal for the Relocation of Job 32-37," *JSOT* 29 (2004): 243-53; idem, " 'The Fear of the Lord is Wisdom' (Job 28:28)," in *Job 28: Cognition in Context* (ed. Ellen van Wolde; BI 64; eds. R. Alan Culpepper and Rolf Rendtorff; Leiden and Boston: Brill, 2003), 80-83; idem, Job 21-37, 905-909, 925-26. While Greenstein suggests moving ch. 28 to the end of the Elihu speeches in chs. 32-37, Clines re-positions chs. 32-37 between chs. 27-28.

Clines suggests that he and Greenstein are the only scholars of which he is aware that assigned ch. 28 to Elihu ("Putting Elihu in his Place," 248 n. 22). Though

about the function of Job 28 within the larger Poem of Job must take account of the layers of exegetical issues within the chapter itself. Unfortunately, neither Settlemire nor Lo gives any sustained attention to the language, text, or poetics of Job 28.[53] As Alan Cooper rightly points out, "The integrity of a literary work of art—and above all, its meaning—can only be perceived by close reading of the text itself, without recourse to external unity imposed by genre requirements."[54]

A volume dedicated to Job 28 collects essays presented at a colloquium at the Royal Academy of Arts and Sciences in Amsterdam in 2002.[55] Several of these essays impact the exegesis of Job 28 either directly or indirectly. The opening piece by Ellen van Wolde offers a lexicographical analysis of Job 28:1-11, archaeological background information, and a cognitive exploration of the passage which commends re-reading these verses from the point of view of the material taken from the earth.[56] Albert Kamp draws on a cognitive model of world building and suggests that Job 28 opens up three successive sub-worlds which impact its readers to perform similar acts of world building in order to understand the text's conceptual logic.[57] David Clines focuses on the meaning of the "fear of the Lord" in Job 28:28.[58] Carol Newsom's brief contribution also treats v. 28, but she attends primarily to the "dialogic" relation between that verse, the book's prose introduction, and third cycle of dialogues.[59] John Elwolde is concerned with how large-scale parallelism contributes to the structure of Job 28 and to the readers' understanding of the meaning of its words.[60] Norman Habel distinguishes "codes" for the elements of God's creation and concludes that

---

somewhat different in details, in 1972 Gary Martin had already suggested that ch. 28 was a late incorporation by the Elihu author between the Elihu speeches and the speeches of Yhwh ("Elihu and the Third Cycle in the Book of Job"). Martin himself cites Horace Meyer Kallen (*The Book of Job as a Greek Tragedy Restored* [New York: Moffat, Yard & Co., 1918]), who assigned ch. 28 to Elihu at the beginning of the twentieth century ("Elihu and the Third Cycle in the Book of Job," 174).

53 Lo's reading of the poem is confined to eight pages (*Job 28 as Rhetoric*, 197-205). Settlemire's exegesis in her dissertation totals forty pages ("The Meaning, Importance, and Original Position of Job 28," 35-75).

54 Cooper, "Narrative Theory and the Book of Job," 39.

55 *Job 28: Cognition in Context* (ed. Ellen van Wolde; BI 64; eds. R. Alan Culpepper and Rolf Rendtorff; Leiden and Boston: Brill, 2003).

56 van Wolde, "Wisdom, Who Can Find It?: A Non-Cognitive and Cognitive Study of Job 28:1-11," 1-36.

57 Kamp, "World Building in Job 28: A Case of Conceptual Logic," 307-20.

58 Clines, " 'The Fear of the Lord is Wisdom' " 57-92.

59 Newsom, "Dialogue and Allegorical Hermeneutics in Job 28:28," 299-306.

60 Elwolde, "Non-Contiguous Parallelism as a Key to Literary Structure and Lexical Meaning in Job 28," 103-18.

God's finding wisdom in the earth suggests a reading of Job 28 from the perspective of the earth and recognition of its inherent value.[61] Edward Greenstein outlines two ancient Near Eastern conceptualizations of the search for wisdom, applies them to the exegesis of Job 28, and concludes that the rhetoric of the poem fits best with the Elihu speeches.[62] Finally, essays by James Aitken and Pierre van Hecke investigate the meaning of *ḥāqar* in Job 28 using cognitive semantics.[63]

While Job 28 is the central text of investigation, these papers are dedicated primarily to cognitive linguistics and to BH lexicography. On the whole, there is little sustained attention to textual criticism, comparative philology, or the poetics of Job 28. Despite some questionable conclusions drawn from his analysis, Elwolde's contribution is the most significant for the structure and lexicon of Job 28. Greenstein's presentation of the ancient Near Eastern background of the search for wisdom is indispensable for understanding the poem rightly within its *conceptual* context, even if one does not ultimately accept his arguments about the original *literary* context of the poem.

Other studies of Job 28 focus on its theology or presentation of wisdom.[64] Paul Fiddes argues that Job 28 takes the form of a riddle and that wisdom is objectified rather than personified.[65] Only one kind of wisdom is in view throughout the poem—the wisdom of apportioning the world's elements. The wisdom of humans and the wisdom of God are not different in kind, but in scope and extent. Job 28 ultimately commends cautious humility when confronted with the boundlessness of wisdom and the limitations of humanity.

Jürgen van Oorschot also concentrates on the presentation of wisdom in the poem, suggesting, however, that there is a tension between

---

61 Habel, "The Implications of God's Discovering Wisdom in Earth," 281-98. Compare also the earth-centered reading of Katharine Dell, "Plumbing the Depths of Earth: Job 28 and Deep Ecology," in *The Earth Story in Wisdom Traditions* (eds. Norman C. Habel and Shirley Wurst; The Earth Bible 3; Sheffield: Sheffield Academic, 2001), 116-25.

62 Greenstein, "The Poem on Wisdom in Job 28 in Its Conceptual and Literary Contexts," 253-280.

63 Aitken, "Lexical Semantics and the Cultural Context of Knowledge in Job 28, Illustrated by the Meaning of *ḥāqar*," 119-138; van Hecke, "Searching and Exploring Wisdom: A Cognitive-Semantic Approach to the Hebrew verb *ḥāqar* in Job 28," 139-62.

64 I leave aside the studies dedicated to the afterlife of the poem in its history of interpretation and reception. These are vast and important but are not the point of focus here.

65 Fiddes, " 'Where Shall Wisdom be Found?': Job 28 as a Riddle for Ancient and Modern Readers," in *After the Exile: Essays in Honour of Rex Mason* (eds. John Barton and David J. Reimer; Macon, Ga.: Mercer University Press, 1996), 171-90. On Job 28 as a riddle, compare also Clines, *Job 21-37*, 906, and see my brief discussion in chs. 6.6-6.7.

hidden wisdom in vv. 1-27 and wisdom as the fear of God in v. 28.[66] According to van Oorschot, v. 28 is not an example of orthodox wisdom theology but reflects theocentric skepticism as a challenge to traditional, aphoristic wisdom, since cosmic wisdom is presented as being ultimately out of human reach.

William McKane's essay outlines the contribution of the poem to the theology of the Book of Job as a whole.[67] He points out that ch. 28 has affinities especially with the speeches of Elihu and God. While the friends and Job are similarly invested in the doctrine of theodicy, they reach different conclusions. McKane believes that ch. 28 presents wisdom as a hypostasis of God, which proves that the friends have overstepped human boundaries by claiming to know too much about wisdom.

Ansfridus Hulsbosch focuses on wisdom in Job 28:23-28.[68] After an exegesis of vv. 23-27, he suggests that wisdom in this passage is a demiurge who takes part in the work of creation and who is the object of God's knowledge in v. 27. As an attribute of God which is at the same time immanent in creation, it serves as an intermediary between God and humanity. Though the addition of v. 28 suggests that human wisdom can be found in the fear of God, divine wisdom itself remains inaccessible. Nonetheless, humans can perceive traces of this wisdom in creation.

Christfried Bauldauf's essay begins in review of Helmut Wilsdorf's attempt to interpret Job 28:1-11 in terms of mining technology.[69] Baldauf suggests that while some of the language in these verses may be understood against such a technological background, the description in vv. 1-11 ultimately makes a larger theological point. Language used of God elsewhere in the OT is in Job 28:1-11 applied to humans, who are portrayed as being capable of divine works. Nevertheless, these seemingly divine actions do not produce divine wisdom, which God alone possesses. As v. 28 emphasizes, true wisdom is submitting oneself to God's wisdom, fully aware of both the possibilities and the limitations of human wisdom.

66 van Oorschot, »Hiob 28,« 183-201.

67 McKane, "The Theology of the Book of Job and Chapter 28 in Particular," in *Gott und Mensch im Dialog: Festschrift für Otto Kaiser zum 80. Geburtstag* (ed. Markus Witte; BZAW 345/II; Berlin and New York: Walter de Gruyter, 2004), 711-22.

68 Hulsbosch, "Sagesse créatrice et éducatrice. I. Job 28," *Aug* 1 (1961): 217-35.

69 Baldauf, »Menschliches Können und göttliche Weisheit in Hiob 28,« *TVers* 13 (1983): 57-68. Wilsdorf's monograph is *Bergleute und Hüttenmänner im Altertum bis zum Ausgang der römischen Republik* (Freiberger Forschungshefte, Beihefte zur Zeitschrift »Bergakademie,« Reihe D, Heft 1; Berlin: Akademie-Verlag, 1952).

Ilse Müllner considers the poem's contribution to the question of epistemology in the Book of Job.[70] She expounds the bulk of the poem through cognitive-metaphorical study, focusing on the structuring semantic fields of "space" and "value." The cognitive dissonance created by the juxtaposition of these two fields in vv. 1-20 is eventually resolved in vv. 23-28, which stress God's access to wisdom. Verse 28 is integral to the message of the chapter, since it presents a synthesis between the poem's two-fold description of wisdom being hidden from humans on the one hand and accessible to God on the other. In uttering this poem, Job pulls out of the bombastic *ad hominem* discourses about the justice of God and brings up what is, in fact, the key theme of the whole book: human knowledge and access to wisdom.

In many respects, Alviero Niccacci's essay is one of the most comprehensive and insightful.[71] Noting the tendency of scholars to repeat typical arguments against the authenticity of the poem without much personal examination,[72] he first treats the philological difficulties in the poem and offers useful insights. In the second section, he analyzes the poem's composition, dividing it into three sections (vv. 1-11, 12-19, 20-28), each of which repeats the motifs of "place," "limits," and "activity."[73] One important conclusion from this analysis is that v. 28 is the necessary ending to the poem. In the third section, he points out the divine overtones of the language of human activity in vv. 1-11 and the simultaneously spatial and directive language used to describe God's perfect knowledge of wisdom in vv. 23-27. He moves on to consider the use of the term "wisdom" in the poem and concludes (concurring largely with von Rad) that it is incarnated in the created order[74] but revealed to humanity through fearing God and turning from evil. Finally, after comparing chs. 26-31 with Job's replies in the first cycle, Niccacci suggests that Job 28 should be read as a part of Job's final response to his friends in the third cycle.

---

70 Müllner, »Der Ort des Verstehens: Ijob 28 als Erkenntnisdiskussion des Ijobbuchs,« in *Das Buch Ijob: Gesamtdeutungen— Einzeltexte— Zentrale Themen* (eds. Theodor Seidl and Stephanie Ernst; ÖBS 31; ed. Georg Braulik; Frankfurt am Main: Peter Lang, 2007), 57-83.

71 Niccacci, "Giobbe 28," *SBFLA* 31 (1981): 29-58.

72 Ibid., 29.

73 Compare the thematic analysis of Habel, *The Book of Job*, 394-95.

74 Von Rad states, »Diese ›Weisheit,‹ ›Vernunft‹ muß also etwas wie den von Gott der Schöpfung eingesenkten ›Sinn,‹ ihr göttliches Schöpfungsgeheimnis bedeuten...« (*Weisheit in Israel* [Neukirchen-Vluyn: Neukirchener, 1970], 193-94).

1.3.3 Job 28 in Monographs on the Book of Job

Several monographs on the Book of Job give significant attention to Job 28, despite being dedicated primarily to describing the structure and message of the book as a whole. In his monumental two-volume work, *Job et son Dieu*,[75] Jean Lévêque asserts that that ch. 28 is, after the Elihu speeches, the second major addition to the original Book of Job. He bases this judgment primarily on the problematic nature of certain verses in the chapter and on the difficulty of the poem's strophic division. Rather than engaging in a reading of the poem itself, he proceeds to inquire after the role of ch. 28 in the Book of Job and its theology. He follows Dhorme in thinking that a redactor inserted the poem as a judgment on the previous dialogues and that it asserts the impossibility of a human discovering divine wisdom. The addition of v. 28 as "une exégèse du poème,"[76] moves the piece toward a still later stage in Israelite wisdom theology in which God's wisdom is granted to Israel in the Torah (Bar 3:37-4:4).

Peter Zerafa believes that the Book of Job was addressed to exilic returnees to Yehud to remind them that their restoration was not due to their obedience or wisdom, but to God's gracious acts.[77] In ch. 2 of his book, Zerafa attends to issues of exegesis surrounding Job 28 and its theology. According to Zerafa, this poem embodies the message of the book as a whole with its radical theology which attributes wisdom to God alone and thus removes it from the grasp of humans altogether.

Bruce Zuckerman's 1991 monograph attempts to dig up the complex tradition history of the Book of Job.[78] He believes that the core of the Book of Job (chs. 3-41) was originally a parody in which disparate pieces were read in counterpoint to one another. This parody was intended as an attack on traditional assumptions about the relation between God and humanity. However, it was misinterpreted by later contributors to the book who supplied various additions which shaped the book back toward orthodox theology. Zuckerman believes that Job 28 was the first of such supplements but that "the Hymn's intent is not so much to oppose the Poem of Job as to derive a traditional insight from it."[79]

75 Jean Lévêque, *Job et son Dieu: Essai d'exégèse et le théologie biblique* (2 vols.; EBib; Paris: Gabalda, 1970), 2:593-606.

76 Ibid., 2:648.

77 Zerafa, *Wisdom of God*. For his treatment of Job 28, see 126-84.

78 Zuckerman, *Job the Silent: A Study in Historical Counterpoint* (New York and Oxford: Oxford University Press, 1991).

79 Ibid., 145. On Job 28, see 138-45.

In *A Blemished Perfection*, Yair Hoffman sets out to determine the aesthetic problem that the Book of Job was created to resolve.[80] In doing so, Hoffman is particularly concerned with its genre, poetic conventions, mimetic devices, and language.[81] Following his analysis of ancient Near Eastern literary conventions, Hoffman concludes that the Joban poet draws upon literary forms from his milieu in order to create a new, eclectic, and non-traditional work of art which collectively addresses various aspects of the doctrine of theodicy. This eclectic and unique form of the book matches its eclectic and unique content. Job 28, however, is among later additions. It is a "closed intellectual literary unit"[82] and part of a block in chs. 25-28 which breaks what Hoffman believes to be the anticipated structure of the third cycle of debates.

Carol Newsom reads the Book of Job as a polyphonic text.[83] Using Bakhtinian theory as her primary theoretical lens, she commends the "heuristic fiction" that the book's multiple voices were put together by a single author who wished to set their perspectives in an unresolved and open-ended dialogue.[84] These voices, in fact, reflect distinct modes of conceptualizing the world—"moral imaginations"—which are expressed in distinct genres within the book (the prose frame tale [chs. 1-2, 42]; the wisdom dialogue [chs. 3-27]; the speculative wisdom poem [ch. 28]; and Job's final soliloquy [chs. 29-31] and the Yhwh speeches [chs. 38-41], neither of which is created according to a generic model). She views ch. 28 as an interlude between the wisdom dialogues on the one hand and Job's final soliloquy and the God speeches on the other.[85] In her dialogic analysis, however, the poem becomes an allegorical critique of the preceding wisdom dialogues (chs. 3-27) *as a genre*.[86] Job 28 interprets these dialogues which were concerned with the existence of moral order in the cosmos in terms of a quest for transcendent wisdom.[87] She argues that Job 28 participates in a distinctive wisdom

80 Hoffman, *A Blemished Perfection: The Book of Job in Context* (trans. J. Chipman; JSOTSup 213; eds. David J. A. Clines and Philip R. Davies; Sheffield: Sheffield Academic Press, 1996). Originally published as *Sh'lemut p'gumah: sefer Iyyob we-riqʿo* (Biblical Encyclopedia Library 12; Jerusalem and Tel Aviv: Bailik and Hayim Rosenburg, Tel Aviv University, 1995).

81 See also idem, "Ancient Near Eastern Literary Conventions and the Restoration of the Book of Job," *ZAW* 103 (1991): 399-411.

82 *A Blemished Perfection*, 278.

83 Newsom, *Moral Imaginations*; idem, "The Book of Job as Polyphonic Text," *JSOT* 97 (2002): 87-108; idem, "Bakhtin, the Bible, and Dialogic Truth," *JR* 76 (1996): 290-306.

84 See especially Newsom, *Moral Imaginations*, 17, 23-42.

85 See her descriptions in ibid., 26, 80, 169, 170.

86 Ibid., 26, 175-77.

87 Ibid., 19, 26, 88-89, 169-82; idem, "Dialogue and Allegorical Hermeneutics," 299-306.

genre—the "speculative wisdom poem"—together with Prov 8; Sir 1, 24; Bar 3:9-4:4; and possibly *1 Enoch* 42.[88]

1.3.4 Studies on the Poetry of Job 28

Given the universal appeal of its poetic genius, scholarly treatments of the poetry of Job 28 are surprisingly sparse. Pieter van der Lugt[89] and J. P. Fokkelman[90] have dedicated monographs to the prosody, rhetoric, and structure of the poem. While these works are at many points provocative, the fact that they often generate remarkably "neat" reconstructions based upon highly formal conceptions of Biblical Hebrew stylistics at both macro- and micro-structural levels leaves their validity open to question and their analyses inorganic.

Ernst Wendland's study of the poem is likewise governed by a strong formal sense, attentive particularly to discourse structure and rhetorical dynamics.[91] Wendland's division of the poem into three strophes is further subdivided into an incredible array of concentric structures of lexical and semantic patterning. Furthermore, Wendland argues that the entire Book of Job is patterned on such concentric structures and that Job 28 is the structural fulcrum of the book.

The most sophisticated and sensitive engagement with the poetry of Job 28 is Stephen Geller's 1987 essay, " 'Where is Wisdom?'."[92] Two-thirds of the essay is devoted to a close reading of the poem, attending

88 Newsom, *Moral Imaginations*, 171-72.

89 Pieter van der Lugt, "The Form and Function of the Refrains in Job 28: Some Comments Relating to the 'Strophic' Structure of Hebrew Poetry," in *The Structural Analysis of Biblical and Canaanite Poetry* (JSOTSup 74; eds. Willem van der Meer and Johannes C. de Moor; Sheffield: Sheffield Academic Press, 1988), 265-93; idem, *Rhetorical Criticism and the Poetry of the Book of Job* (*OtSt* 32; ed. A. S. van der Woude; Leiden, New York, and Köln: E. J. Brill, 1995), 309-24, 521-36.

90 J. P. Fokkelman, *Major Poems of the Hebrew Bible: At the Interface of Prosody and Structural Analysis, Volume IV: Job 15-42* (trans. Ch. E. Smit; SSN 47; ed. W. J. van Bekkum et al.; Assen, The Netherlands: Van Gorcum, 2004), 146-62. See also Fokkelman's brief structural analysis in *Reading Biblical Poetry: An Introductory Guide* (Louisville, Ky.: Westminster John Knox Press, 2001), 132-40.

91 Wendland, " 'Where in the world can wisdom be found?' " 1-33.

92 Stephen A. Geller, " 'Where is Wisdom?': A Literary Study of Job 28 in its Settings," in *Judaic Perspectives on Ancient Israel* (eds. Jacob Neusner, Baruch A. Levine, and Ernest S. Frerichs; Philadelphia, Pa.: Fortress, 1987), 155-88. Reprinted in a slightly condensed form in idem, *Sacred Enigmas: Literary Religion in the Hebrew Bible* (London and New York: Routledge, 1996), 87-107.

to form, meaning, and effect.[93] Fundamental to his exposition is his delineation of "realistic" and "metaphorical" planes of meaning in vv. 1-11, with the realistic ultimately being submerged into the figurative.[94] Geller is particularly harsh on what he considers to be "pietistic wisdom" that has made its way into the final edition of the poem—especially v. 28, which, according to him, was added to distract readers from the poem's unorthodox message.[95] He believes that Job 28, with its message of human ignorance of wisdom (especially v. 13), is intended as a polemic against traditional wisdom, which based itself on observing natural order.[96]

1.4 The Aims of this Study

On the whole, this brief survey of literature on Job 28 illustrates a common divide between literary, philological, and theological questions and a remarkable paucity of studies dedicated to how Job 28 builds up meaning as poetry. If scholars are to begin to give Job 28 its due as "...one of the incomparably great poems in the Bible, and... in world literature,"[97] the poem's layers of meaning must be described from multiple angles with the hope that such eclecticism can achieve more in interpretation than any one of its parts.[98]

---

93 Ibid., 155.

94 Ibid., 158 and 158-64.

95 Ibid., 175. For his comments on v. 28, see 168-69, 174-75. Note the language he uses: "pietistic," "deadening effect," "banal," "bland."

96 Ibid., 173-74. See his expanded reconstruction of the polemic of Old (nature-) Wisdom against the newer Deuteronomic (torah-) Wisdom in "Nature's Answer: The Meaning of the Book of Job in its Intellectual Context," in *Judaism and Ecology: Created World and Revealed Word* (ed. Hava Tirosh-Samuelson; Publications of the Center for the Study of World Religions, Harvard Divinity School; ed. Lawrence E. Sullivan; Religions of the World and Ecology; ed. Mary Evelyn Tucker and John Grim; Cambridge, Mass.: Harvard University Press, 2002), 109-132.

97 Victor E. Reichert, *Job. Hebrew Text & English Translation with an Introduction and Commentary* (SBB; London, Jerusalem, and New York: Soncino, 1946), 139.

98 In this regard, compare the study of David Damrosch on biblical narrative in *The Narrative Covenant: Transformations of Genre in the Growth of Biblical Literature* (Ithaca, NY: Cornell University Press, 1987). Damrosch states, "...I believe it is high time to begin the work of integrating the fields of comparative, text-historical, and literary study. The chapters to follow will attempt to show that a unified use of the three approaches can produce valuable results that cannot be achieved by isolated study within one approach alone" (7-8).

The overriding goal of this monograph is a "deep exegesis" of the poem in Job 28 that weds the philological and the literary modes.[99] In highlighting how the poem achieves its meaning, the study is attentive to elements "in the poem" (linguistic, textual, structural, etc.), "behind the poem" (cognitive background), and "in front of the poem" (aesthetic and rhetorical effects, reader response) without any illusions of being exhaustive or objective.[100]

While I have for purposes of organization separated the section on philology and textual criticism (ch. 4) from the section on poetic phenomena in Job 28 (ch. 3), these two angles of vision are, in reality, interdependent, and each of these sections has been written and re-written in light of the other. The movement is hardly linear in either direction, as if one could simply begin with text and philology and move forward toward poetic structures, metaphors, and rhetoric; or begin with broad literary context while subordinating diachronic elements of historical linguistics or textual development.[101]

I have fronted my translation and text of Job 28 in ch. 2 as an embodiment of my interpretation of the poem. A reading of the poem follows in ch. 3, with special focus on poetic phenomena and sustained attention to vv. 1-11. This reading precedes the philological and textual study in ch. 4 largely because it is shorter and more accessible. However, both the translation in ch. 2 and the reading in ch. 3 presume the philological and textual work in ch. 4. Finally, ch. 5 is an analysis of what I have called the "structured commentary" in Job 28:15-19, which, for reasons stated there, I believe to be an early exegetical comment that has become a part of the canonical poem. The reader would do well to

---

99 On the goals of interpretation as being synthetic and sympathetic "deep exegesis," see Geller, *Sacred Enigmas*, vii-3. He draws particularly on Hermann Gunkel, but he also terms this kind of exegesis "total interpretation," which seems to owe to Meir Weiss' *The Bible From Within: The Method of Total Interpretation* (Jerusalem: Magnes, 1984), though he does not cite it. However, while Weiss' "total interpretation" is more strictly New Critical in stressing the autonomy of the piece of literature (see *Weiss, Bible from Within*, 63, 65-66, 72, etc.), Geller's use of the term is not so limited. I employ this phrase in Geller's broader sense.

100 I recognize the problems with these metaphors—especially the false implications that the "poem" is something static and that these aspects of interpretation are distinct from each other. Nevertheless, I believe it is still a useful way of speaking.

101 The latter seems to be the view of John Elwolde, at least with regard to lexicography: "[L]iterary analysis must precede lexicographical, the macro- must take priority over the micro-" ("Non-Contiguous Parallelism," 103 n. 1). Yet as Mary Kinzie points out, "One of the most devilling things about the unities of poems is that they cannot be treated as if one clear thing could be laid, like a transparent crystal, on a second clear thing until the perfect visionary temple was complete" (*A Poet's Guide to Poetry* [Chicago Guides to Writing, Editing, and Publishing; Chicago, Ill.: University of Chicago, 1997], 10).

approach chs. 3, 4, and 5 as cross-referencing pieces of work. I have tried whenever possible to provide cues in ch. 3 to relevant philological and textual discussion in chs. 4 and 5. The study closes in ch. 6 by drawing some conclusions from the analysis of the poem in the preceding chs., including a prospectus regarding its place and function in the Book of Job.

Though every interpretation undoubtedly reflects an underlying ideology, or even a whole collection of them, the present study is not intended to be theoretically or ideologically driven in any self-conscious sense.[102] The method that governs this study is largely descriptive, and the criteria by which I have judged the adequacy of the interpretations here are essentially pragmatic. I operate under the assumption that the cogency of an interpretation is, in large part, proved by what it produces. If the reading works, it can be seen as sufficient; but this does not mean that other readings will not work.[103]

My approach is akin to the "eclectic pragmatism" that informed Jeremy Black's reading of the Sumerian narrative poem *Lugalbanda and the Anzud Bird* in his monograph *Reading Sumerian Poetry*.[104] There he described it as "a pragmatic approach led by elements of any theory which seem[s] pregnant and responsive to that literature's special character..."[105] Black formulated this method in response to lack of information regarding text, date, and authorship in Sumerian poetry. Such a method is equally appropriate in studying the poem in Job 28—also a piece whose authorship, textual integrity, and larger literary function are matters of dispute.

If, as Lewis believes, "Imagination is the organ of meaning,"[106] then any attempt to get at the meanings of poems requires as much imaginative effort in reading them as their authors expended in writing them.[107] Yet that which has its origin in the imagination often produces a range of imaginative and emotional effects that cannot be encompassed by attempting to sort out a single, rational meaning.[108] The greatest poetry

102 Cf. Geller, *Sacred Enigmas*, 2; Black, *Reading Sumerian Poetry*, 20.

103 Edward Greenstein, "Writing a Commentary on the Book of Job," n.p.

104 Black, *Reading Sumerian Poetry*, 20, 43, 67, 170.

105 Ibid., 43.

106 C. S. Lewis, "Bluspels and Flalansferes: A Semantic Nightmare," in *Selected Literary Essays* (ed. Walter Hooper; Cambridge: Cambridge University Press, 1969), 265. My thanks to Doug Miller for drawing this essay to my attention.

107 Auden comments, "Whatever its actual content and overt interest, every poem is rooted in imaginative awe" ("Making, Knowing and Judging," 60).

108 Wallace Stevens, "Poetry and Meaning," in *Opus Posthumous* (revised, enlarged, and corrected edition; ed. Milton J. Bates; New York: Vintage Books, 1990 [orig. pub. 1957]), 249-50.

transcends the logic of its own language. Even without accounting for all their elements, the best works still communicate and draw us into their world.[109]

And yet a reader must nonetheless give an accounting, a way in to the poem as a "constant symbol."[110] There remains the necessity of a kind of "applied reading" which "skips nothing" but is after the "layering of significance," as Barthes puts it.[111] Though falling fathoms short of being exhaustive, the reading offered here aims to open a window into the poetic brilliance of Job 28 that has evoked the praises of its interpreters for centuries.

This work, I believe, is a necessary first step toward addressing the pressing problems of the poem's implied authorship and its place and function in the Book of Job. It likewise has ramifications for considerations of the poem's genre and its presentation of wisdom. Solutions to these problems can hardly be cogent if they are founded on mere impressions of the poem's meaning. In order to make real progress toward interpreting Job 28 on the horizontal plane of its broader literary context, it is necessary first to dive into its center and sound its depths to describe its genius from within.

1.5 A Note on Poetic Terminology

The study of Hebrew poetry has become a specialized sub-discipline within the field of Old Testament studies, and, as such, it has generated a good deal taxonomy that is basically unique to that field. While it has been common in the past for scholars to use poetic terminology typically employed in the analysis of Greek and Latin prosody (such as "stich" or "colon"), there is now little consensus about such terminology. Rather than adopting one of the myriad of taxonomies developed by scholars of Biblical Hebrew poetry, I have simply used the terminology typical in analysis of English verse.

---

109 See Giorgio Buccellati, "On Poetry—Theirs and Ours," in *Lingering Over Words: Studies in Ancient Near Eastern Literature in Honor of William L. Moran* (eds. Tzvi Abusch, John Huehnergard, and Piotr Steinkeller; Atlanta, Ga.: Scholars, 1990), 108.

110 Robert Frost, "The Constant Symbol," in *Selected Prose of Robert Frost* (eds. Hyde Cox and Edward Connery Lathem; New York, Chicago, and San Francisco: Holt, Rinehart and Winston, 1966), 23-29 (first published in *The Atlantic Monthly*, October 1946).

111 Roland Barthes, *The Pleasure of the Text* (trans. Richard Miller with a note on the text by Richard Howard; New York: Hill and Wang, 1975), 12. Compare the comments of Good, *In Turns of Tempest*, 180.

The basic unit is the line. In accord with the tendency toward parallelism in Biblical Hebrew poetry, a line is typically one half of a couplet. Lines may also build up larger units, such as a triplet, consisting of three lines, or a quatrain, consisting of four lines. I use "verse" as a word either for the medieval verse numbers or as a synonym for "poetry."

All translations are my own unless otherwise noted. Verse citations follow the Hebrew.

Chapter Two: Translation and Vocalized Text

[P]oetry is what is lost in translation.[1]

2.1 Introduction

All poetry seems to defy translation, to resist the dissolution of the intimate relation between phonetics and feelings.[2] Shelley expounds upon the vanity of this exercise in his *Defence of Poetry*: "[I]t were as wise to cast a violet into a crucible that you might discover the formal principle of its colour and odour, as seek to transfuse from one language into another the creations of a poet."[3] The Italian adage, "Traduttore, traditore," finds an ancient antecedent in Rabbi Judah's warning recounted in the Babylonian Talmud: "If one translates a verse literally, he is a liar; if he adds thereto, he is a blasphemer and a libeler."[4] Such warnings are particularly germane to translating the Book of Job. Indeed, as Edward Greenstein states, "It is difficult to imagine a more formidable task of translating than that of restating the Hebrew text of Job in other words."[5] Despite the challenges of the task, I present a translation of the

1 Robert Frost, as recounted by Louis Untermeyer in a lecture entitled "Robert Frost: A Backward Look," delivered on March 23, 1964. Now in Louis Untermeyer, *Robert Frost: A Backward Look. Lecture Presented Under the Auspices of the Gertrude Clarke Whittall Poetry and Literature Fund, with a Selective Bibliography of Frost Manuscripts, Separately Published Works, Recordings, and Motion Pictures in the Collections of the Library of Congress* (Washington, D.C.: Reference Dept., Library of Congress, 1964), 18.

2 See Seamus Heaney, "The Impact of Translation," in *The Government of the Tongue: Selected Prose 1978-1987* (New York: The Noonday Press / Farrar, Straus and Giroux, 1988), 39.

3 Percy Bysshe Shelley, *A Defence of Poetry*, first published in idem, *Essays, Letters from Abroad, Translations, and Fragments* (2 vols.; ed. Mary Shelley; London: Edward Moxon, 1840). Cited here from *Shelley's Poetry and Prose: A Norton Critical Edition* (ed. Donald H. Reiman and Sharon B. Powers; Authoritative Texts Criticism; New York and London: W. W. Norton, 1977), 484.

4 *b. Qidd.* 49a. Translation of H. Freedman, *Hebrew-English Edition of the Babylonian Talmud: Kiddushin* (ed. I. Epstein; London: Soncino, 1990). See also *t. Meg.* 3:41B in Jacob Neusner, *The Tosefta. Translated from the Hebrew with a New Introduction* (2 vols.; Peabody, Mass.: Hendrickson, 2002), 1:653.

5 "The Job of Translating Job," in *Essays in Biblical Method and Translation* (BJS 92; ed. Jacob Neusner, et al.; Atlanta, Ga.: Scholars Press, 1989), 119.

poem in Job 28 here as an embodiment of my interpretation of it and as a window into its rich language.

2.2 Translation

Section One

1 There is indeed a source for silver,
a place for gold which is refined.
2 Iron is taken from dirt,
copper from hard rock.
3 Setting a bound for darkness,
he probes every limit
for the stone of deepest gloom.
4 He breaches course<s> far from dwellers,
ones forgotten by passers-by.
They are bereft of humans. {they wander}
5 A land from which food springs forth,
beneath transformed as fire.
6 A place of lapis is its stones,
which has dust of gold.
7 A path no bird of prey knows,
upon which no falcon's eye has gazed.
8 Serpents have not thrashed upon it.
No lion has moved over it.
9 He assaults the hard rock,
overturns summits at the roots.
10 He splits streams in the mountains.
His eye sees every precious thing.
11 He binds up the sources of the rivers,
brings the dark thing to light.

Section Two

12 But wisdom—where is it found?
Where is the place of understanding?
13 No human has knowledge of its abode.
Nor is it found in the land of the living.
14 Deep says, "It is not in me."
Sea says, "It is not with me."

{ }[6]

20 But wisdom—from where does it come?
Where is the place of understanding?
21 It is darkened from the eyes of all beasts,
obscured from the birds of the heavens.
22 Destruction and Death say,
"Our ears have heard its rumor."

Section Three

23 *God* perceives its path.
He knows its place.
24 Because he gazes at the edges of the earth,
sees beneath all the heavens.
25 When he made a weight for the wind,
apportioned the waters by measure,
26 when he made a groove for the rain,
and a track for the thundershower,
27 then he saw it and numbered it,
established it and even probed it,
28 and he said to the human,
"Behold, awe of the Lord, *that* is wisdom,
to turn from evil, understanding."

---

6 For a translation, text, commentary, and brief discussion of verses 15-19, see ch. 5.

2.3 Vocalized Text

Section One

1 *kî yēš lakkesep môṣāʾ*
ûmāqôm lazzāhāb yāzōqqû
2 *barzel mēʿāpār yuqqāḥ*
wĕʾeben yāṣûq nĕḥûšâ
3 *qēṣ śām laḥōšek*
ûlĕkol-taklît hûʾ ḥôqēr
ʾeben ʾōpel wĕṣalmôt
4 *pāraṣ nĕḥāl<īm> mēʿīm-gār*
hanniškāḥîm minnî-rāgel
dallû mēʾĕnôš {nāʿû}
5 *ʾereṣ mimmennāh yēṣēʾ-lāḥem*
wĕtaḥtêhā nehpak kĕmô-ʾēš
6 *mĕqôm-sappîr ʾăbānêhā*
ʿaprōt zāhāb lô
7 *nātîb lōʾ-yĕdāʿô ʿāyiṭ*
wĕlōʾ šĕzāpattû ʿên ʾayyâ
8 *lōʾ-hidrîkūhû bĕnê-šāḥaṣ*
lōʾ-ʿādâ ʿālāyw šāḥal
9 *baḥallāmîš šālaḥ yādô*
hāpak miššōreš hārîm
10 *baṣṣûrôt yĕʾōrîm biqqēaʿ*
wĕkol-yĕqār rāʾătâ ʿênô
11 *mabbĕkê nĕhārôt ḥibbēš*
wĕtaʿălūmâ yōṣīʾ ʾôr

Section Two

12 *wĕhaḥokmâ mēʾayin timmāṣēʾ*
wĕʾê zeh mĕqôm bînâ
13 *lōʾ-yādaʿ ʾĕnôš ʿerkāh*
wĕlōʾ timmāṣēʾ bĕʾereṣ haḥayyîm
14 *tĕhôm ʾāmar lōʾ bî-hîʾ*
wĕyām ʾāmar ʾên ʿimmādî

{ }

20 *wĕhaḥokmâ mēʾayin tābôʾ*
wĕʾê zeh mĕqôm bînâ
21 *wĕneʿelmâ mēʿênê kol-ḥayyā*
ûmēʿôp haššāmayim nistārâ
22 *ʾăbaddôn wāmāwet ʾāmĕrû*
bĕʾoznênû šāmaʿnû šimʿāh

Section Three

23 *ʾĕlōhîm hēbîn darkāh*
wĕhûʾ yādaʿ ʾet-mĕqômāh
24 *kî-hûʾ liqṣôt-hāʾāreṣ yabbîṭ*
taḥat kol-haššāmayim yirʾeh
25 *laʿăśôt lārûaḥ mišqāl*
ûmayim tikkēn bĕmiddâ
26 *baʿăśōtô lammāṭār ḥōq*
wĕderek laḥăzîz qōlôt
27 *ʾāz rāʾāh waysappĕrāh*
hĕkînāh wĕgam-ḥăqārāh
28 *wayyōʾmer lāʾādām*
hēn yirʾat ʾădōnāy hîʾ ḥokmâ
wĕsûr mērāʿ bînâ

Chapter Three: A Reading of Job 28

It is only au pays de la métaphore / Qu'on est poète.[1]

Poetry is language in which the signified... is *the whole process of signification itself.*[2]

3.1 Introduction

The task of this chapter is to develop a reading of Job 28 as poetry, with an interest in how the poem achieves meaning.[3] It attends particularly to its formal linguistic structures, its conceptual metaphors,[4] and its aes-

---

1 Wallace Stevens, "From Miscellaneous Notebooks," in *Opus Posthumous* (revised, enlarged, and corrected edition; ed. Milton J. Bates; New York: Vintage Books, 1990), 204. Originally published in 1957.

2 Eagleton, *How to Read a Poem*, 21 (emphasis his).

3 My hope is that this chapter contributes to filling the need pointed out by Adele Berlin, among others. She states, "I would argue that we need to attend more to biblical poetry *qua* poetry—to give more attention to the *meaning* of a poem and to how a poem achieves its meaning. That is, to develop ways of reading poetry" ("On Reading Biblical Poetry: The Role of Metaphor," in *Congress Volume, Cambridge 1995* [ed. J. A. Emerton; VTSup 66; Leiden, New York, and Köln, 1997], 26 [emphasis original]). The comments of F. W. Dobbs-Allsopp are germane in this connection: "Poetry... is ultimately all about reading. Readings (always in the plural) are the stuff out of which all construals of prosody and poetics are necessarily made and at the same time are what complete these construals (i.e., a prosody is only as good as the reading it helps to generate). Readings of poems are the ultimate justification of poetry, they are the gift of poetry. And readings of biblical poems (especially close, deep, lusciously savored, highly imaginative readings) are still rare and desperately needed" ("Poetry, Hebrew," *NIDB* 4:556).

4 In my application of cognitive metaphor theory, I am particularly indebted to Andrew Goatly, *The Language of Metaphors* (London and New York: Routledge, 1997), as well as to Pierre van Hecke, who has applied cognitive metaphor theory to numerous biblical texts (see essays by van Hecke in the Bibliography). Both Goatly and van Hecke draw on cognitive metaphor theory as set forth by George Lakoff, Mark Johnson, and Mark Turner, though each author advances the discussion in significant ways (e.g., Goatly in light of relevance theory).

It should also be noted that the view that metaphors are figures of thought and not simply figures of speech is not novel to Lakoff, Johnson, or Turner, as is often implied by biblical scholars who draw from their works. Poets have been advocating

thetic effects, all of which have earned the poem its well-deserved reputation as an exquisite work of art. The following reading takes as its starting point the "standard description" of biblical poetry, focusing on scientific description of verse by employing the linguistic method. Yet it is also an attempt to root this description within the aesthetic "logic" of the poem's extralinguistic elements, including the conceptual framework of its metaphors and its impact on its implied readers.[5] In other words, the concern here is both with classification and evocation, description and perception. While formal elements in the poem are an essential part of poetic composition, the nature of poems can hardly be reduced to form. As Wallace Stevens states, "Poetry, as an imaginative thing, consists of more than lies on the surface."[6] Meaning accrues through the dynamic interaction of all poetic phenomena in a network of relations, including both form and effect.[7] As Giorgio Buccellati has stated of Akkadian poetry, "[W]e must develop a sensitivity for the original as if it were a living organism, since mere dissection can only be performed on corpses, and it is life we seek in the ancient cultures."[8] Indeed, as Wendell Berry says, "Works of art participate in our lives; we are not just distant observers of *their* lives."[9]

---

this view for decades. See especially Robert Frost, "Education by Poetry," in *Selected Prose of Robert Frost* (eds. Hyde Cox and Edward Connery Lathem; New York, Chicago, and San Francisco: Holt, Rinehart, and Winston, 1966), 32-46; and C. S. Lewis, "Bluspels and Flalansferes," 251-65, esp. 265.

5 Cf. Stephen A. Geller, Theory and Method in the Study of Biblical Poetry," *JQR* 73 (1982): 65-77. Michael V. Fox, who cites Robert M. Fowler ("Who is 'The Reader' in Response Criticism?," *Semeia* 31 [1985]: 5-21, esp. 10, 12), notes that the implied reader is "a literary construct that is projected by the assumptions and aims of the texts and that is constructed in the process of reading. The author seeks to induce the actual reader to identify with this construct but does not necessarily succeed" ("Job the Pious," *ZAW* 117 [2005]: 351 n. 2).

6 Wallace Stevens, "Adagia," in *Opus Posthumous* (revised, enlarged, and corrected edition; ed. Milton J. Bates; New York: Vintage Books, 1990), 188. Originally published in 1957.

7 Stephen A. Geller, "Through Windows and Mirrors into the Bible: History, Literature, and Language in the Study of the Text," in *A Sense of Text. The Art of Language in the Study of Biblical Literature: Papers from the Symposium at the Dropsie College for Hebrew and Cognate Learning, May 11, 1982* (ed. Stephen A. Geller; JQR Supplement 1982; Winona Lake, Ind.: Distributed for the Dropsie College by Eisenbrauns, 1983), 27-28. See also idem, *Sacred Enigmas*, vii-3.

8 Buccellati, "On Poetry—Theirs and Ours," 105. Compare also the remarks of Terry Eagleton: "Poetry is something which is done to us, not just said to us. The meaning of its words is closely bound up with the experience of them" (*How to Read a Poem*, 21).

9 Wendell Berry, "Style and Grace," in *What are People For? Essays by Wendell Berry* (New York: North Point Press, 1990), 64 (emphasis original).

Any reading of biblical poetry must attend extensively to its figurative dimension.[10] Robert Frost was an advocate of the view that poetry is, in essence, metaphor: "There are many other things I have found myself saying about poetry, but the chiefest of these is that it is metaphor, saying one thing and meaning another, saying one thing in terms of another, the pleasure of ulteriority. Poetry is simply made of metaphor."[11] Metaphors build up a way of seeing, and thus a way of reading, that holds figures of speech and figures of thought together. As both cognitive and linguistic phenomena, metaphors themselves demonstrate that formal description and aesthetic perception are integrated parts of a whole. Likewise poems, as extended metaphors, achieve meaning by tapping into the cognitive metaphorical domains in which their images are rooted, while expressing themselves in the material of language.

The interaction of images provides structure and meaning to poems. As Edward Greenstein has noted, in Joban poetry in particular, metaphors are not simply rhetorical; they are embodiments of the argument.[12] This is certainly true of Job 28. The argument of the first eleven verses of the poem is highly dependent on the accretion of images that eventually converge to impress their symbolic value upon the reader. As John Elwolde has rightly noted, the poet "slowly reveal[s] his central focus by the use of metaphor."[13]

Yet the interaction of linguistic and non-linguistic elements within metaphors, as well as the interaction between various metaphors among themselves, cannot be understood without an attempt to engage the conceptual framework in which these figures resonate and signify.[14] This requires the reader to enter into the symbolic world of the text. In attempting to clarify the larger conceptual background against which the symbols of Job 28 may be understood, I will draw on both biblical and extrabiblical texts that employ similar images to those found in Job 28, thereby setting the biblical poem and its intertexts in a dialogue that

10 See especially the concerns stated by Patrick Miller, "Meter, Parallelism, and Tropes: The Search for Poetic Style," *JSOT* 28 (1984): 103-104.

11 Robert Frost, "The Constant Symbol," 24. Cf. Weiss, *The Bible From Within*, 132; and the comments of Luis Alonso Schökel, *A Manual of Hebrew Poetics* (SubBi 11; Rome: Pontifical Biblical Institute, 1988), 95.

12 Edward Greenstein, "Some Remarks on Metaphors in the Book of Job" (paper presented at the annual meeting of the SBL, Atlanta, Ga., November 2003).

13 Elwolde, "Non-Contiguous Parallelism," 111. See also Clines, *Job 21-37*, 916.

14 This is the task of William P. Brown in *Seeing the Psalms: A Theology of Metaphor* (Louisville and London: Westminster John Knox Press, 2002). He outlines his project for the Psalter in the preface (ix-x) and the introduction (1-14), thereafter applying his approach to images in the Book of Psalms.

itself creates a large-scale metaphor.[15] This large-scale metaphoric process of intertextuality will highlight numerous aspects common to both pieces of literature (i.e., in their embedded narratives) while simultaneously creating a new, encompassing narrative within which these might fruitfully be interpreted.[16]

3.2 Planes of Meaning in Job 28: Realistic and Symbolic

The language of Job 28 is beautiful and evocative, often dense, and loaded with significance. Stephen Geller correctly discerns two levels of meaning in the poem which he expounds in dialectic throughout his essay: "[T]here is a 'realistic,' narrative plane comprising a description of how jewels are found and mined; ...there exists also the poetically dominant plane of metaphor and associations."[17] While these two planes are both integral parts of a fuller whole, the literal and figurative senses are not equally dominant within the linear movement of the poem. The comments of Barbara Herrnstein Smith on the perception of poetic structure apply well to the relationship between each of these planes of meaning in Job 28:

> [T]he reader's experience is not only continuous over a period of time, but continuously changes in response to succeeding events. As we read, structural principles, both formal and thematic, are gradually deployed and perceived; and as these principles make themselves known, we are engaged in a steady process of readjustment and retrospective patterning.[18]

In this vein, the interpretation of Job 28 that follows focuses particularly on mapping the relative prominence of the "realistic" (or "material") and the "symbolic" (or "figurative") planes in the act of reading and re-

15 Paul Ricoeur, "The Bible and the Imagination," in *Figuring the Sacred: Religion, Narrative, and Imagination* (trans. David Pellauer; ed. Mark I. Wallace; Minneapolis, Minn.: Fortress, 1995), 160-61. Originally published in *The Bible as a Document of the University* (ed. Hans Dieter Betz; Chico, Calif.: Scholars Press, 1981), 49-75.

16 Ricoeur, "The Bible and the Imagination," 150.

17 Geller, " 'Where is Wisdom?' " 158.

18 Barbara Herrnstein Smith, *Poetic Closure: A Study of How Poems End* (Chicago and London: University of Chicago Press, 1968), 10. By poetic "structure," Smith does not mean only the poem's formal elements. Rather, she defines structure as "the product of all the principles, both formal and thematic, by which a poem is generated..." (ibid., 6). Note also the similar comments of Robert Alter on perception of structure in *The Pleasures of Reading*, 141.

reading Section One of the poem.[19] Continuing Geller's spatial metaphor, it is helpful to think in terms of foreground and background. While both planes are ever present, the realistic plane bears more weight in the early portion of the poem. Yet the symbolic plane slowly surfaces throughout its movement, spurring a re-reading of the preceding lines in that light.

The two planes of meaning perceived by Geller correspond to two different accounts of the poem's conceptual background. On the one hand, the large majority of interpreters read vv. 1-11 in a material sense, as a technical description of ancient mining technology. On the other hand, a few modern interpreters have begun to take account of the more symbolic, and particularly cosmic, connotations in these lines—returning to an interpretive stream already in place in antiquity. Both of these models for reading Job 28 will be re-examined in this study.

3.3 Job 28 and the Deeds of Ancient Mesopotamian Kings

The reading of Job 28 proffered here interprets the biblical poem in light of the famous achievements of ancient Mesopotamian kings. The historically rooted accounts of foreign expeditions in Akkadian royal inscriptions provide a helpful lens through which to view the more realistic plane of meaning in Section One of the biblical poem.[20] On the other hand, the more universal Mesopotamian epic[21] traditions—and

---

19 I say "relative prominence" because, despite the rather linear presentation of these two planes of meaning in the following reading of Job 28, the "realistic" and the "symbolic" are not entirely separable. Borrowing Jeremy Black's comments on the opening lines of a *balbale* to Suen: "Literal and figurative meanings intermingle as different levels of expression appear to flow in and out of each other, like the currents of water at different temperatures where two rivers meet" (*Reading Sumerian Poetry*, 12).

20 By "realistic," I do not mean to imply that the Akkadian royal inscriptions are simply historical. Rather, the term "realistic" emphasizes their more conventional (and less figurative) reference. There is a continuum between literal and metaphorical meaning. See Goatly, *The Language of Metaphors*, 15, 38-39.

21 The definition of "epic" is contested. Karl Hecker's is remarkably broad, including all narrative poetry (*Untersuchungen zur akkadischen Epik* [AOAT 8; eds. Kurt Bergerhof, Manfried Dietrich, and Oswald Loretz; Kevelaer: Butzon and Bercker; Neukirchen-Vluyn: Neukirchener, 1974]). The definition assumed here revolves around the centrality of a hero. However, this should not be limited to poetic narrative; it includes the "*narû* literature" or "fictional autobiographies" as well. For a similar definition, see Joan Goodnick Westenholz, "Heroes of Akkad," *JAOS* 103 (1983): 327-28.

the Gilgamesh epic in particular—illustrate well the resonance and significance of the more symbolic plane of meaning in Job 28.[22]

3.3.1 Akkadian Royal Inscriptions

The corpus of Akkadian royal inscriptions and the poetry of Job 28 are surely as dissimilar as they are similar. Most often composed in lengthy first person narratives containing stereotypical boasts of foreign conquests or domestic construction, the Akkadian texts are generically set apart from the condensed poetic expedition in Job 28:1-11 with its fragments of action told in the third person. Their "biased, exaggerated, bombastic, and self-celebrative"[23] quality stands in stark contrast to the Joban poem, which is more subtle and allusive, telling its tale primarily through a dense juxtaposition of symbols.[24]

Yet modes of conceptualizing the world and their expression in literary metaphors often cut across generic boundaries.[25] In spite of their differences, the symbolic worlds of the Akkadian royal inscriptions and the Joban poem overlap significantly. Two fundamental motifs connect the biblical poem with the Mesopotamian material. The first is the hero's epic journey[26] and its cosmic geography.[27] The second is the motif of the "first discoverer."[28]

---

22 For this classification of "historical epic" and "universal epic" as sub-types of "heroic epic," see Adele Berlin, "Ethnopoetry and the Enmerkar Epics," *JAOS* 103 (1983): 18-19. Berlin is here influenced by Heda Jason's study of ethnopoetic genres in idem, *Ethnopoetry: Form, Content, Function* (Bonn: Linguistica Biblica, 1977).

23 Mario Liverani, "The Deeds of Ancient Mesopotamian Kings," in *CANE* 4:2359.

24 Granting these generic differences, it is instructive to note that two types of accounts about Shalamaneser III's campaign to Urartu in 856 survive. A more typical annalistic account is recorded in the Kurkh Monolith inscription, among others, while a more focused poetic account (still in first person) has also been found. For a comparison of these two, with text and translation, see W. G. Lambert, "The Sultantepe Tablets: VIII. Shalmaneser in Ararat," *AnSt* 11 (1961): 143-158; and RIMA 3 A.0.102.17 (A. Kirk Grayson, *Assyrian Rulers of the Early First Millennium BC II (858-745 BC)* [RIMA 3; Toronto, Buffalo, and London: University of Toronto Press, 1996], 84-87). Cf. *ARAB* 1, §§602-607.

25 This point is well made by Raymond C. Van Leeuwen, "Cosmos, Temple, House: Building and Wisdom in Mesopotamia and Israel," in *Wisdom Literature in Mesopotamia and Israel* (ed. Richard J. Clifford; SBLSymS 36; ed. Christopher R. Matthews; Atlanta, Ga.: Society of Biblical Literature, 2007), 79-80 and n. 61.

26 See especially Sabrina Favaro, *Voyages et voyageurs à l'époque néo-assyrienne* (SAAS 18; Helsinki: The Neo-Assyrian Text Corpus Project of the University of Helsinki, 2007), 93-136.

27 On Mesopotamian cosmic geography pertinent to this reading, see especially Horowitz, *MCG*, 20-42, 67-106; John H. Walton, *Ancient Near Eastern Thought and the*

In commenting on the journey motif in ancient epics, Jack Sasson states,

> In lore as in monumental inscriptions, the activities of kings that are most often deemed heroic and worthy of emulation are those that recount many voyages of conquest termed unique or never previously attempted. ... The most elaborate narratives can be built around a simple notion: someone goes far from home and then comes back. So, we might consider grist for our mill any imaginative narrative (prose, lyrical, or poetic) in which someone ... undertake[s] [a] distant journey... through which they acquire status, wisdom, or insight.[29]

Beginning in the Old Akkadian period, Akkadian royal inscriptions typically feature boasts of campaigns to distant regions far outside the civilized world.[30] These accounts assume an inner-outer spatialization of center and periphery, culture and chaos.[31] The treacherous peaks, dry steppes, and massive bodies of water of the outermost regions provide daunting physical challenges which the king meets with heroic might. While such forceful promotion of "culture" in the barbaric regions is undoubtedly meant to demonstrate political and economic control,[32] Sargon II's *Letter to Assur* detailing his eighth campaign also casts such achievements in terms of wisdom. He attributes his acumen in breaking

---

Old Testament: Introducing the Conceptual World of the Hebrew Bible (Grand Rapids, Mich.: Baker Academic, 2006), 165-178; and Favaro, *Voyages et voyageurs*, 124-29.

28 Mario Liverani, "The Deeds of Ancient Mesopotamian Kings," in *CANE* 4:2362-63.

29 Jack M. Sasson, "Comparative Observations on the Near Eastern Epic Traditions," in *A Companion to Ancient Epic* (ed. John Miles Foley; Malden, Mass., Oxford, UK, and Carlton, Victoria: Blackwell, 2005), 228.

30 Marc Van De Mieroop, *A History of the Ancient Near East ca. 3000-323* (BHAW; Oxford, UK; Malden, Mass.; and Carlton, Victoria: Blackwell, 2004), 63.

31 Liverani, "The Deeds of Ancient Mesopotamian Kings," in *CANE* 4:2362-63. See also Berlin, "Ethnopoetry and the Enmerkar Epics," 21-22; and Favaro, *Voyages et voyageurs*, 124-29, 110 n. 365 and 98 n. 333 (there citing Piero Zanini, *Significati del confine: I limiti naturali, storici, mentali* [Milan: Bruno Mondadori, 1997], 11). The brief discussion of Mark Smith on such spatialization in the Ugaritic literature is also helpful (*The Origins of Biblical Monotheism: Israel's Polytheistic Background and the Ugaritic Texts* [Oxford and New York: Oxford University Press, 2001], 27-40).

A wonderful example of such spatialization in 14th century English epic is found in *Sir Gawain and the Green Knight*. As Gawain heads northward to the domain of the Green Knight, the narrator remarks: "He faltered not nor feared, / But quickly went his way: / His road was rough and weird, / Or so the stories say" (*Sir Gawain and the Green Knight*, xxix; translation in *Sir Gawain and the Green Knight: Translated with an Introduction by Brian Stone* [Middlesex, England: Penguin Books, 1959], 51). Stone comments in the introduction, "Thus all is warm and Christian where the courtly writ runs, as at Camelot, but the north, where Gawain goes for his ordeal, is cold and mysterious" (ibid., 12).

32 E.g., Michelle I. Marcus, "Geography as an Organizing Principle in the Imperial Art of Shalmaneser III," *Iraq* 49 (1987): 81.

open a passageway through the side of the cosmic Mount Simirriya to "the wisdom and breadth of understanding" given to him by Ea and Bēlet-ilī.[33] Wise kings embody not only agility and strength, but skill derived from the Lord of the Deep himself.

These dangerous journeys also provide opportunity for new discoveries that impact the cultured world. Akkadian annals report not only what was done "out there" in the periphery, but the exotic plunder that accompanies them back to the city. Assyrian rulers return to the civilized center boasting cedars from the Amanus, precious stones, or a pride of mountain lions. Famously, Shalmaneser III claims even to have discovered the sources of the Tigris and Euphrates rivers.[34] Modern excavations at the Tigris Tunnel in eastern Turkey bear out his claim: "At the source of the Tigris I wrote my name."[35]

These achievements contribute to what Mario Liverani calls "the motif of the 'first discoverer'." He states,

> Here the celebration of some positive achievement by the king is underscored by counterposition to a past when such an achievement did not exist. The achievement can be of any kind: the opening of a new road or reaching of a remote land, the possession of an exotic product or the introduction of a technological improvement, even the building of a new temple or the establishment of a new festival.[36]

As first discoverers, these rulers joined the ranks of kings and sages of old.[37] While drawing a line of continuity between their contemporary reign and epic heroes before them, their foreign conquests and domes-

---

33 TCL 3:i 23 (=*ARAB* 2, §142). Translation of Ronald F. G. Sweet, "The Sage in Akkadian Literature: A Philological Study," in *The Sage in Israel and the Ancient Near East* (eds. John G. Gammie and Leo G. Perdue; Winona Lake, Ind.: Eisenbrauns, 1990), 53. I have consistently checked Thureau-Dangin's edition against the more recent edition of Walter Mayer, »Sargons Feldzug gegen Urartu – 714 v. Chr. Text und Übersetzung,« *MDOG* 115 (1983): 65-132, here 70-71.

34 See the Black Obelisk in RIMA 3 A.0.102.14:69, 92 (=*ARAB* 1, §§564, 572), a Bull Colossus from Nimrud in RIMA 3 A.0.102.8:27-28 (=*ARAB* 1, §641), and the Statue from Assur in RIMA 3 A.0.102.25:12-13 (=*ARAB* 1, §674). For a study of the historical geography of this region, see H. F. Russell, "Shalmaneser's Campaign to Urartu in 856 B.C. and the Historical Geography of Eastern Anatolia According to the Assyrian Sources," *AnSt* 34 (1984): 171-201.

35 *ina* SAG IGI *šá* ÍD *idiqlat* MU *al-ṭu-ur*. Tigris Tunnel inscription III in RIMA 3 A.0.102.21:17 (=*ARAB* 1, §692). For the slightly different formulation of the contemporary inscription V, see RIMA 3 A.0.102.22:13.

36 Liverani, "The Deeds of Ancient Mesopotamian Kings," in *CANE* 4:2361.

37 See ibid., 2362.

tic building projects were also meant to afford them fame that would endure for generations to come.[38]

Applied to Job 28, this Mesopotamian model turns the typical interpretation of the biblical poem on its side. The majority of interpreters have conceived of vv. 3-11 as painting a picture of a miner descending into dark, vertical mine shafts to gain precious stones. But read against the exploits of Mesopotamian kings out to the borders of the world into treacherous and uninhabited regions full of wealth, Job 28:3-11 is dominated by a horizontal, not a vertical, focus. Job 28 thus portrays its explorer as travelling through a dark peripheral zone beyond the limits of culture and out toward the mountains at the edges of the earth. It is only when he comes to the far-reaches of the world that the vertical dimension becomes prominent (i.e., in vv. 9-11).

3.3.2 The Standard Babylonian Gilgamesh Epic

While the more realistic plane of meaning has commonly been expounded in essays and commentaries on Job 28, the symbolic values of the metaphors in vv. 1-11 have received less attention in modern scholarship until recently. Alviero Niccacci has correctly noted the "strong mythological coloration of Job 28."[39] Stephen Geller and Carol Newsom have likewise expounded the divine overtones in the poem's first section.[40] Most recently, Edward Greenstein has argued that the entire poem is best situated within the conceptual background of the Mesopotamian (divine) search for cosmic wisdom in the depths of the earth and the heights of the heavens.[41]

These symbolic dimensions of Job 28 require fuller explication. While Greenstein has helpfully pointed a way forward by highlighting ancient Near Eastern cognates to the search for wisdom figured in Job 28, his views that the subject of Section One (vv. 3-11) is God rather than a human[42] and that the poem should be re-located to the end of Elihu's speeches[43] are not necessary conclusions from his investigation.

---

38 On the temporal dimension of the heroic journey which ties the monarch both to the past and the future, see Favaro, *Voyages et voyageurs*, 103.

39 "...la forte colorazione mitologica di Giob 28" ("Giobbe 28," 46 n. 45).

40 Geller, " 'Where is Wisdom?' " 155-88; Newsom, "The Book of Job," 530.

41 Greenstein, "The Poem on Wisdom in Job 28," 253-63.

42 Greenstein believes that the actions described in this first section only "have pale reflections in certain human activities." ("The Poem on Wisdom in Job 28," 269). On his view of God as the subject of vv. 3-11, see especially 272-273 and n. 44.

43 Ibid., 269-76. See also Clines, *Job 21-37*, 907-909; idem, "Putting Elihu in His Place," 243-53.

I believe that the cosmic overtones in the poem may be understood quite differently.

In attempting to spin out the implications of these symbolic reverberations for the interpretation of Job 28, the following reading sets the biblical poem in conversation with the heroic feats and failures of Gilgamesh in the SB epic (*ša naqba īmuru*), which purports to be a royal inscription of mythic proportions (see I. 10, 24-28). The comparison between these two masterpieces of ancient Near Eastern didactic Wisdom Literature[44] assumes no genetic connection between Gilgamesh and Job.[45]

Job 28 and Gilgamesh each present a heroic *Grenzgänger* who breaks divine-human boundaries and thus challenges the created order.[46] As Giorgio Buccellati points out, "Gilgamesh is presented as rejecting given embodiments of the established system... and as setting out on a

---

44 On this generic designation for Gilgamesh, see W. L. Moran, "Gilgamesh," in *The Encyclopedia of Religion* (15 vols.; ed. Mircea Eliade; New York and London: MacMillan, 1987), 5:559; idem, "The Gilgamesh Epic: A Masterpiece from Ancient Mesopotamia," in *CANE* 4:2331-32; Andrew George, *The Epic of Gilgamesh: The Babylonian Epic Poem and Other Texts in Akkadian and Sumerian* (London: Penguin Books, 1999), xxxii-xxxvii; Joseph Blenkinsopp, "Gilgamesh and Adam: Wisdom through Experience in Gilgamesh and in the Biblical Story of the Man, the Woman, and the Snake," in *Treasures Old and New: Essays in the Theology of the Pentateuch* (Grand Rapids, Mich.: Eerdmans, 2004), 86; Karel van der Toorn, "Why Wisdom Became a Secret: On Wisdom as a Written Genre," in *Wisdom Literature in Mesopotamia and Israel* (ed. Richard J. Clifford; SBLSymS 36; ed. Christopher R. Matthews; Atlanta, Ga.: Society of Biblical Literature, 2007), 21; and Paul-Alain Beaulieu, "The Social and Intellectual Setting of Babylonian Wisdom" in *Wisdom Literature in Mesopotamia and Israel* (ed. Richard J. Clifford; SBLSymS 36; ed. Christopher R. Matthews. Atlanta, Ga.: Society of Biblical Literature, 2007), 6.

In a later essay, George clarifies this designation by suggesting that the SB epic is an *anthology of genre* that is cast in the *wisdom mode* ("The Epic of Gilgameš: Thoughts on Genre and Meaning," in *Gilgameš and the World of Assyria: Proceedings of the Conference held at Mandelbaum House, the University of Sydney, 21-23 July 2004* [eds. Joseph Azize and Noel Weeks; ANESSup 21; eds. Antonio Sagona and Claudia Sagona; Leuven, Paris, and Dudley, Mass.: Peeters, 2007], 51-54).

45 To my knowledge, extended comparisons between Gilgamesh and portions of Job are rare. The most recent essay of which I am aware is Georg Sauer, »Der Mensch vor der Aporie des Todes: Gilgamesh—Hiob,« in *Gott und Mensch im Dialog. Festschrift für Otto Kaiser zum 80. Geburtstag* (ed. Markus Witte; 2 vols.; BZAW 345/II; Berlin and New York: Walter de Gruyter, 2004), 655-65.

46 Though the texts are more fragmentary and difficult to interpret, Adapa and Etana might also be named as examples of such boundary-crossers in the Mesopotamian tradition. See the brief discussion of epic boundaries by Bruce Louden, "The Gods in Epic, or the Divine Economy," in *A Companion to Ancient Epic* (ed. John Miles Foley; Malden, Mass.; Oxford; and Carlton, Victoria: Blackwell, 2005), 98-99.

personal quest in defiance of established norms."[47] But while Gilgamesh develops in the lengthy narrative fashion typical of epic, the first section of Job 28 gives the impression of being condensed heroic poetry.[48] After two introductory couplets (vv. 1-2), it details in the remaining twenty lines (vv. 3-11) a brash venture to the edge of the world to obtain precious objects from the watery depths. The remarks of Stella Revard on epic poetry are in many ways fitting for Job 28:3-11 as well: "E[pic] often focuses on a hero, sometimes semi-divine, who performs difficult and virtuous deeds; it frequently involves the interaction between human beings and gods."[49]

Both Job 28 and the standard Gilgamesh epic are governed by the "violent search" trope, and their quests culminate at distant rivers in remote lands (Job 28:11; SB Gilg. XI). However, the objects of these expeditions are initially different. In Job 28, the focus of the opening couplet is material and realistic. However, as the symbolic plane moves to the fore throughout Section One, it becomes clear that wisdom is the ultimate object of the search. Gilgamesh's quest, on the other hand, is two-fold: first for eternal fame, and then for eternal life. But while Gilgamesh fails to escape his mortality (at least in life), the prologue to the standard version of the epic nevertheless attributes to him wisdom, which was gained through his exploration of the Deep (*naqbu*, SB Gilg. I. 1, 3).

Finally, the conceptualizations of wisdom in Job 28 develop along lines analogous to the various conceptualizations of wisdom in the OB and SB Gilg. epics. Karel van der Toorn has argued for a thematic shift from wisdom based on personal experience in the OB Gilg. epic to wis-

47 Giorgio Buccellati, "Wisdom and Not: The Case of Mesopotamia," *JAOS* 101 (1981): 37.

48 Niccacci rightly suggests that the language of the poem at places has an "epic coloring" ("una tonalità epica;" "Giobbe 28," 44). Remarkably, patristic interpreters considered the whole of the Poem of Job to be a (spiritual) epic according to Aristotelian categories of genre (see Carol A. Newsom, "Dramaturgy and the Book of Job," in *Das Buch Hiob und seine Interpretationen. Beiträge zum Hiob-Symposium auf dem Monte Verità von 14.-19. August 2005* [ed. T. Krüger et al.; ATANT 88; ed. Erhard Blum et al.; Zürich: Theologischer Verlag Zürich, 2007], 375). Milton also classified Job as a "brief epic" (see C. S. Lewis, *A Preface to Paradise Lost* [London: Oxford University Press, 1942]), 3-4. On entirely different bases (and with quite a different meaning), Nahum Sarna has compared the prose tale with Ugaritic literature and has suggested that the extant prose narrative was derived from an original Joban epic ("Epic Substratum in the Prose of Job," *JBL* 76 [1957]: 13-25).

49 Stella P. Revard, "Epic: I. History," in *NPEPP*, 362.

dom as a secret that is proper only to the gods in the SB epic.[50] Within the poem in Job 28, wisdom also becomes increasingly abstracted and de-objectified. Though the poem does not initially state that wisdom can be gained through human experience, the first section of the poem (vv. 1-11) tantalizingly suggests as much through symbolic association with metals and hidden stones. Nevertheless, as the rhetoric of the second section (vv. 12-14, 20-22) makes clear, this association ultimately proves to be false. The depiction of God's exploration of the inner content of wisdom during his creative acts in the third section (vv. 23-28) meshes in large part with the depiction of wisdom as divine prerogative in the SB Gilg epic. This inner exploration of wisdom during a world-forming creative act cannot be replicated by humans. Yet with the climax of the poem in Job 28:28, the poet locates wisdom within human grasp, diverging from the trajectory of the SB Gilg. epic and returning to a conception similar to that which is set forth in the OB version. What Gilgamesh learns in the SB epic is stated outright in Job 28:28: humans must learn their place in the divine scheme of things. They may nevertheless approximate the wisdom of the gods by acting and ruling wisely. The effects of this divine encounter on the course of human history are left up to those who are spectators of this narrative epiphany.

3.4 The Movement and Structure of the Poem

Though the symbolic values of the poem's imagery are hinted at early on by the employ of divine creation language in describing heroic expedition (e.g., v. 3), they remain in the background to their apparent realistic referents toward the beginning of the first section. These connotations thicken in the subsequent lines, and eventually the deeper, figurative senses burst through the literal, surface meanings. As Section One peaks with an assault on the mountains and an expedition into the underground fount (vv. 9-11) that was thought to have bubbled out below the cosmic mountain of the wise Creator god in the ancient Near East, the reader is suddenly immersed in a cosmic landscape. This gradual foregrounding of the symbolic and cosmic referents of the poem's imagery forces a re-reading of Section One in this light. In Sections Two and Three, the poem operates almost exclusively on this

50 van der Toorn, "Why Wisdom Became a Secret," 21-29; idem, *Scribal Culture and the Making of the Hebrew Bible* (Cambridge, Mass., and London: Harvard University Press, 2007), 213-214.

cosmic level, the high point of which is the poem's final section on the creation of the cosmos and the revelation of wisdom (vv. 24-28).

The poem in Job 28 is clearly divided into three main sections, the seams of which are marked with two interrogative refrains.[51] The first section begins with two closely related couplets that introduce the poem's root metaphors of source and place (vv. 1-2) and then continue by detailing actions of binding and splitting (vv. 3-4, 10-11) which envelop a description of the domain in which these actions are undertaken (vv. 5-8).

Section Two begins with the poem's crucial question (v. 12), which is matched by an almost exact repetition of this refrain toward the end of that section (v. 20). Both are followed by two couplets declaring the ignorance of humans, birds, beasts, and the powers of the Deep and Death concerning the source and place of wisdom.[52]

The beginning of Section Three is marked by fronting its subject (God) together with emphatic personal pronouns (*hûʾ* in vv. 23b, 24a). This section moves to the primordial scene of creation in preparation for God's answer to the question posed by the poet in the refrains (vv. 12, 20), which is given at the end of Section Three (v. 28).

The frame of the poem as a whole is epigrammatic. Its basic rhetoric is perceived by reading vv. 1a, 12a, and 28aβ together: "There is indeed a source for silver... / But wisdom—where is it found? / ...awe of the Lord, *that* is wisdom..." Between these proverbial statements and probing questions, the poet expands these themes in short narratives about human attempts to obtain wisdom (vv. 3-11) and God's perceiving wisdom during the process of creation (vv. 23-27).

3.5 Reading Section One (vv. 1-11)

The focus of the poem's introductory couplets (vv. 1-2) is unambiguously material and realistic. The pair *môṣāʾ* // *māqôm* in v. 1 initiates the source // place parallel that is picked up in vv. 12 (*timmāṣēʾ* // *māqôm*) and 20 (*tābôʾ* // *māqôm*), and these metaphors remain dominant through-

51 As Robert Alter points out, this fairly neat division is unusual in BH poetry ("The Characteristics of Ancient Hebrew Poetry," in *The Literary Guide to the Bible* [eds. Robert Alter and Frank Kermode; Cambridge, Mass.: Belknap, 1987], 621). Elsewhere he comments specifically on the refrains in Job 28: "[S]uch explicit symmetry of form is not observable elsewhere in the poetry of Job" (*The Art of Biblical Poetry* [New York: Basic Books, 1985], 92). There are, however, numerous other "refrains" in BH poetry. See, e.g., 2 Sam 1: 19, 25, 27; Pss 42: 6, 12, with 43:5; Pss 46:8, 12; 49:13, 21; 56:5, 12; 57:6, 12; 59:7, 15; 62:2, 3, 6, 7; 67:4, 6; 80:4, 8, 15, 20; 107:1, 8, 15, 21, 31; etc.

52 For a treatment of vv. 15-19, see ch. 5.

out the remainder of the poem. The large-scale parallelism between vv. 1, 12, and 20 sets in place the framework for re-reading Section One in light of the fuller figurative senses relegated now to the background.

The initial emphatic assertion (see *indeed* in ch. 4.3) of the availability of precious metals in v. 1 and the use of predictable poetic structures in the introduction as a whole intimate that the rest of the poem will be equally as predictable. The construction *kî yēš* ("indeed there is")—applied in these lines to silver (*kesep*), gold (*zāhāb*), iron (*barzel*), and copper (*nĕḥûšâ*)—suggests that these precious goods are attainable, despite the fact that ancient Israelites ultimately acquired such objects from foreign lands.[53] The far-distant land projected by these opening lines serves as the domain in which the images of vv. 1-11 resonate and signify.

The formulation of the poem's first line is thoroughly proverbial. In fact, the structure has parallels in the Book of Proverbs, where the rhetoric pits perception against reality. Prov 14:12 (= 16:25) highlights human limits: "There is a way that seems right to a person, / but its end is the ways of death." The sharp contrast depends on setting misperception over against true comprehension with the phrasing *yēš... wĕ...* Applied to the initial line in Job 28:1, one is left with only a half-proverb and thus also half-meaning. The proverbial rhetoric continues at the boundaries of the first section in v. 12.

Proverbs typically produce meaning through pithy juxtaposition, forcing the reader to "read between the lines" to draw out their implications.[54] But in Job 28, such juxtaposition is expanded in vv. 3-11, which comprise the poet's own "reading in between the lines," perhaps. Until the proverb begun in v. 1a closes in v. 12a, the reader is forced into a narrative that itself lies in the center of an aphorism.

Taken together, the four metals listed in the poem's introductory couplets signify great wealth.[55] Since copper, gold, and silver served as payments for commodities before the invention of minted coinage, they are realistically effective here both as objects in themselves and as currency with which to acquire other objects.[56] As Carol Newsom has

---

53 Philip J. King and Lawrence E. Stager, *Life in Biblical Israel* (LAI; ed. Douglas A. Knight; Louisville, Ky.: Westminster John Knox, 2001), 194.

54 See Raymond C. Van Leeuwen, "In Praise of Proverbs," in *Pledges of Jubilee: Essays in Honor of Calvin G. Seerveld* (eds. Lambert Zuidervaart and Henry Luttikhuizen; Grand Rapids, Mich.: Eerdmans, 1995), 314 n. 14. Some of my wording above is paraphrased from Van Leeuwen.

55 The same four metals—silver, gold, copper, and bronze—are named together in Josh 22:8 as items of "great wealth" (*rab-mĕʾōd*).

56 King and Stager, *Life in Biblical Israel*, 194. Silver was typically used as money in the ancient Near East, but gold became prominent in some periods. At Ugarit, prices

pointed out, objectification is one of the main rhetorical strategies of the first section of the poem.[57] This trope is underscored by a chiastic construction in the center of v. 1, which suggests a close connection between precious metal and an attainable physical location (for silver : a source :: a place : for gold). This is precisely the point in the first two lines: these precious and base metals do, in fact, have a "source" (*môṣāʾ*) and a "place" (*māqôm*), be they ever so distant.

The typical word pair *kesep* // *zāhāb* in v. 1 highlights the concept of value and is mimicked in the initial couplet of vv. 15-19, where another pair of synonyms is presented in reverse order: "fine gold" // "silver" (*sāgûr* [MT *sĕgôr*] // *kesep*; v. 15).[58] The repetition of these terms in vv. 15-19 underscores the realistic plane of meaning foregrounded in the poem's opening couplet and expounds upon it in terms of trade and commerce.[59] Taken together, vv. 1-2 introduce the riches ("silver," "gold," "iron," and "copper") that represent the objects of the poem's search, and intimate the loci in which that search will be carried out in vv. 3-11 ("source" [v. 1a] : "channels" [v. 4a] : "streams" [v. 10a]; "dirt" [v. 2a] : "(gold) dirt" [v. 6b]; "rock" [v. 2b] : "hard rock" [v. 9a] : "mountains" [v. 10a]).

Another word pair, *môṣāʾ* // *māqôm*, is unique in the OT, and the first term in particular highlights a key domain into which the unnamed explorer of vv. 3-11 will venture. This pair also phonologically anticipates both *māqôm* in vv. 12b and 20b (also vv. 6a, 23b) and *timmāṣēʾ* in vv. 12a and 13b. This pair thus binds the poem's two introductory couplets (vv. 1-2) to the remainder of the first section (vv. 3-11) and to the second section in vv. 12-14, 20-22. The concepts of "source" and "place" are effectively the preoccupation of the entire poem, and they lead the reader on a search for a discrete physical locus.

The pairing of *môṣāʾ* and *māqôm* creates a play with the roots YṢʾ (vv. 5a, 11b) and MṢʾ (vv. 12a, 13b) throughout the poem. If the orthography of the original poem was, indeed, conservative, this would have

were given in silver, but also in gold and copper. See Daniel C. Snell, *Life in the Ancient Near East* (New Haven and London: Yale University Press, 1997), 73-74, 94, 129.

57 Newsom, *Moral Imaginations*, 179.

58 Clines correctly points out that the word pair is more typically "gold" // "silver" in the Book of Job (as in 3:15; 22:24-25; 28:15), despite the fact that throughout the OT, the order "silver" // "gold" is more productive (*Job 21-37*, 910). It is possible that this has chronological implications (i.e., "gold" // "silver" being more typical of LBH), but it may also be only a matter of style or poetic license. On this word pair, see Ian Young, "Late Biblical Hebrew and Hebrew Inscriptions," in *Biblical Hebrew: Studies in Chronology and Typology* (ed. Ian Young; JSOTSup 369; eds. David J. A. Clines and Philip R. Davies; London and New York: T&T Clark, 2003), 291.

59 Elwolde, "Non-Contiguous Parallelism," 111.

facilitated a visual connection between *môṣāʾ* in v. 1a and *timmāṣēʾ* in vv. 12a, 13b (see ch. 4.2.6). In v. 1, this connection suggests a source (MṢʾ) where silver and gold can be *found* (TMṢʾ).

Scholars' preoccupation with the poem's realistic sense has greatly influenced the interpretation of *môṣāʾ* in Job 28:1a. Many have been quick to assume that *môṣāʾ* is a technical term, reflected in the common translation "mine."[60] To be sure, it is no large leap to construe a "*môṣāʾ* for silver" as a "mine," a common find-spot of precious metals. The rhetoric of the poem's two introductory couplets rests, in fact, on the assumption that the precious and base metals listed there are the products of some place, just as Rib-Hadda's requests to the pharaoh and to the official Amanappa in the Amarna archive understood grain to be the product (*mūṣû*) of Yarmuta.[61]

Yet the poem now refuses to answer where. The generality of this initial image of a "source for silver" is suggestive and evocative, drawing the reader in to solve the problem of meaning. This lack of specificity regarding an exact find-spot is important in the poem's rhetoric. Wealth is simply figured as lying outside the viewpoint of the poet. The effect is consonant with a similar point of view in Mesopotamian literature, where such projections are based on a lack of natural wealth in the Mesopotamian alluvial plain. To build Inanna's temple in Uruk, Enmerkar must traverse seven mountain ranges to reach Aratta in the east, which is rich in gold, silver, and lapis lazuli.[62]

The poem's second couplet (v. 2) shifts the focus from the precious metals, silver and gold, to the base metals, iron (*barzel*) and copper (*nĕḥûšâ*). While *barzel* and *nĕḥûšâ* frame the couplet, their loci, dirt (*ʿāpār*) and rock (*ʾeben*), lie at the core. Though the preposition *min* is gapped in the second line, v. 2 exhibits a tight structure (A B C / B' A'), carrying through the effect of predictability in the search for these metals.[63]

---

60 Aside from the commentaries, see NJPS, NJB, NEB, RSV, NRSV, NAS, NAB, NIV, NKJV.

61 EA 86:33. See also EA 85:35. Both cited in *CAD* M/2, 249 s.v. *mūṣû* A. Translation in William L. Moran, The Amarna Letters (Baltimore and London: The Johns Hopkins University Press, 1992), 156-59. Originally published as *Les Lettres d'El-Amarna* (Paris: Les Éditions du Cerf, 1987).

62 See *Enmerkar and the Lord of Aratta* in Thorkild Jacobsen, *The Harps that Once…: Sumerian Poetry in Translation* (New Haven and London: Yale University Press, 1987), 280-319. For text (and translation), see Herman Vanstiphout, *Epics of Sumerian Kings: The Matter of Aratta* (ed. Jerrold S. Cooper; SBLWAW 20; Atlanta, Ga.: Society of Biblical Literature, 2003), 49-96. Note also the similar projections in *Gudea Cylinder A* in Jacobsen, *Harps*, 406-408.

63 Syr. and Tg[M,S] also understand *min* to be gapped from the first line. For this chiastic structure, see also Niccacci ("Giobbe 28," 29-30) and Dahood ("Chiasmus in Job: A

The pair *ʿāpār* // *ʾeben* offers contrast of surface and depth. While copper lies deep inside "hard rock" (*ʾeben yāṣûq*), iron ore deposits are found on the surface, that is, in the loose earth here called *ʿāpār*.[64] These terms identify the ostensive environs of the "source" (*môṣāʾ*) and "place" (*māqôm*) mentioned in the first line: the surface of the earth (*ʿāpār*) and its core (*ʾeben yāṣûq*). The parallel *ʿāpār* // *ʾeben* in v. 2 matches the reverse parallel *ʾeben* // *ʿaprōt* in v. 6. The movement of the couplet from the locus of iron (i.e., "dirt") to that of copper (i.e., "rock") anticipates the movement of the whole first section of the poem, as the explorer travels toward the "hard rock" (*ḥallāmîš*, v. 9a), and even the base of the "mountains" (*ṣûrôt*, v. 10a; *miššōreš hārîm*, v. 9b) in search of dark treasure (*ʾeben ʾōpel wĕṣalmôt*, v. 3b [MT *ṣalmāwet*]).

Copper/bronze (*nĕḥûšâ*) and iron (*barzel*), along with gold and silver, were used to make jewelry and ornaments in the ancient Near East.[65] Yet these materials were also commonly desirable for temple-building projects. Among other texts, this is clearly depicted in *Gudea Cylinder A*, as Gudea builds a new version of the temple Eninnu for Ningirsu:

> To the ruler building Eninnu / great things offered themselves: / from Kimash a copper mountain / revealed itself to him, / and he mined its copper / from its pockets. / To the ruler, as man in charge of building his master's house, / gold was brought / in dust form from its mountains; / to Gudea they were bringing down / refined silver from its mountains...[66]

While Job 28 is not concerned with building projects, the image of expedition for precious metals from distant mountain rock is a pregnant parallel as the reader attempts to imagine the undisclosed locus of silver, gold, iron, and copper that figure prominently within the first four lines of Job 28.

Such an expedition, it seems, is depicted in the remaining twenty lines of Section One (vv. 3-11). After establishing its root metaphors in two introductory couplets (vv. 1-2), the poem shifts in v. 3 to detail a

---

Text-Critical and Philological Criterion," in *A Light Unto My Path. Old Testament Studies in Honor of Jacob M. Myers* [Gettysburg Theological Studies 4; ed. Howard N. Bream, Ralph D. Heim, and Carey A. Moore; Philadelphia: Temple University Press, 1974], 125).

64 King and Stager, *Life in Biblical Israel*, 167.

65 Ibid., 164.

66 *Gudea Cylinder A*, xvi:13-21, translated in Jacobsen, *Harps*, 408. Text in Thureau-Dangin, *SAK*, 106. Note also the precious metals associated with the foothills in the epic myth *Lugal-e*. Ninurta blesses his newly built foothills and names them Ninhursaga in honor of his mother, Ninlil, who has arrived for a visit: "...may gold and silver be mined for you, ... may it smelt copper and tin for you..." (Jacobsen, *Harps*, 255).

search within this metaphorical world. This compact narrative is foregrounded with triplets in vv. 3-4 against the background of couplets in the introduction (vv. 1-2) and the balance of the poem (vv. 5-27). The formal variation is hardly "incomprehensible," as Wolfers suggests.[67] The numerous emendations of Job 28:3-4 on such grounds are, as Michael Dick says, based on little more than "a strong but unwarranted prejudice of some scholars against the tricolon in Job."[68]

But the difficulties of v. 3 are more than simply formal. This triplet is mixed with both positive and negative imagery. On the one hand, the actions suggest a binding, and thus ordering, of the darkness in the first line (*qēṣ śām laḥōšek*). On the other hand, the search undertaken in this verse has an object of darkness as its explicit goal (*ʾeben ʾōpel wĕṣalmôt* [MT *ṣalmāwet*], v. 3b).

The search for this dark stone has perhaps been anticipated by *ʾeben* in the poem's second line. But while *ʾeben* was a source for copper in v. 2b, here the *ʾeben* itself is the object of the quest—mysteriously described as the "stone of deepest gloom" (*ʾeben ʾōpel wĕṣalmôt*, v. 3b). This lapidary expedition requires not only technical skill, but the audacity to probe to the very limits of civilization (*lĕkol-taklît hûʾ ḥôqēr*, v. 3aβ). To do so the explorer creates a new horizon,[69] circumscribing the domain in which the search will be carried out and travelling beyond the more limited circle of "culture" through the wilderness, toward the mountains at the edges of the world (see esp. vv. 9-10) and the sources of the rivers at their base (see v. 11).[70] The horizontal orientation of the jour-

---

67 David Wolfers states, "[T]he two tristiches, read as tristiches, not only disappoint our expectations of parallelism, the essence of Hebrew poetry, but they are truly incomprehensible as tristiches. The absence of proper parallel in certain verses of Hebrew poetry is, of course, no anomaly in itself; there are scores of verses in the Book of Job which have no trace of parallel. But when we have a poem of 29 [*sic*; read: 28] verses in which almost every verse exhibits the simplest form of parallel, the anomaly becomes a real one, as if we were reading a rhymed poem and encountered a verse without rhyme. We should suspect a scribal error, as we are entitled to do here" ("The Volcano in Job 28," *JBQ* 18 [1989-90]: 234-35).

68 M. B. Dick, "Job xxviii 4: A New Translation," *VT* 29 (1979): 219 n. 3. Note especially De Wilde in this regard, who suggests that the entirety of vv. 1-4 is a later addition and proposes that the remainder of the poem consists of three similar parts, each with four strophes of quatrains, and each being concluded by a refrain (*Das Buch Hiob*, 269).

69 Niccacci, "Giobbe 28," 42. In Mesopotamian cosmic geography, the horizon is roughly where the lower part of the sky meets the edges of the earth (see Horowitz, *MCG*, 234).

70 See the Mesopotamian conception of the cosmos portrayed in Michael B. Dick, "The Neo-Assyrian Royal Lion Hunt and Yahweh's Answer to Job," *JBL* 125 (2006): 244, fig. 1a (adapted from Beate Pongratz-Leisten). The cosmic geography of the Babylonian Map of the World (BM 92687) is also consonant with the geography of the ex-

ney is important. The poem's darkening imagery at this point in the poem is due not to a descent into the depths of the earth, but to a trek outward into the dark regions at the periphery of existence.[71]

The polarization of a cultivated, civilized center over against the dangerous, even barbaric, periphery is clearly evident in the literature of ancient Mesopotamia.[72] In the *King of Combat* (*šar tamḫāri*) legends of Sargon of Akkad, his journey to foreign lands is shrouded in darkness: "Sargon had (barely) ventured into / the land of Uta-rapaštim, / (When) as if he were hostile, the forest waged war against him. / It set darkness / in place of the light of the heavens. / The sun dimmed, / the stars sallied forth against the enemy."[73] Yet it is the illuminated end of this dangerous and gloomy expedition which is memorialized in an OB omen apodosis: "...the omen of Sargon, who went through the darkness and a light came out for him."[74] As Jean-Jacques Glassner remarks, "Il accomplit un exploit héroïque, à travers un universe hostile et asocial..."[75]

In Job 28, too, is figured a hero who conquers the darkness in his quest. As the following verses (vv. 4-7) illustrate, the human's task will be undertaken far away from civilization at the edges of the world, in a land that is uninhabited by and uninhabitable to most living creatures. But the final note of this journey is not darkness but light (*ʾôr*, v. 11b).

---

pedition in Job 28:3-11. At the northernmost limit of the disc of earth is a mountain (*šadû*), where the source of the Euphrates is also found. See discussion in Horowitz, *MCG*, 20-21, 27-29.

71 By way of comparison, note the description in the caption next to the northern *nagû* beyond the ocean (*marratum*) in BM 92687: "Great Wall 6 leagues in between where the sun is not seen" (Horowitz, *MCG*, 21-22). Horowitz believes that this was a region of perpetual darkness (ibid., 33, 100).

72 Beate Pongratz-Leisten comments on such polarization in ancient Mesopotamia: »Im Gegensatz zu dem Raumverständis des modernen Zeitalters ist die mesopotamische Vorstellung von einer starken Differenzierung zwischen Innen und Außen, Sakralem und Profanem, ›eigenem Land‹ und ›Ausland, Fremdland, Feindesland‹ Wüste und kultiviertem Land, geordnetem und ungeordnetem Bereich geprägt, ähnlich dem *urbs* und *ager* des frühen Rom. Die Stadt ist gleichbedeutend mit einer Zone der Sicherheit, die die ›Kultivierung menschlichen Verhaltens und Leistungsvermögens,‹ die Zivilisation, ermöglicht« (*Ina šulmi īrub: Die kulttopographische und ideologische Programmatik der akītu-Prozession in Babylonien und Assyrien im I. Jahrtausend v. Chr.* [BaF 16; Mainz am Rhein: Phillip von Zabern, 1994], 18). See also Dick, "The Neo-Assyrian Royal Lion Hunt," 243-70, esp. 243-44, 259-60.

73 Text and translation of *Sargon, the Conquering Hero*, ii. 57-64, in Joan Goodnick Westenholz, *Legends of the Kings of Akkade: The Texts* (MC 7; ed. Jerrold S. Cooper; Winona Lake, Ind.: Eisenbrauns, 1997), 68-71. See also J.-J. Glassner, "Sargon 'roi du combat' " *RA* 79 (1985): 122.

74 Text and translation in Horowitz, *MCG*, 33. See also another OB omen apodosis as well as NA and NB sources in Glassner, "Sargon 'roi du combat' " 124.

75 Glassner, "Sargon 'roi du combat' " 124.

Despite the dangers lurking in distant lands, gemstones were often thought to be abundant in remote and dark places. This idea is well illustrated by traditions concerning the journeys of Alexander the Great to far-off regions of the world:

> For four months they had not seen the sunlight or moonlight or their own faces. They marched on gravel not knowing what was under their own feet. They tasted and smelled the stones, but because of the darkness they could not tell what they were. Therefore all who had gone to the Land of Darkness were filled with remorse because of these stones. For when they left they discovered that the stones were all precious gems, rubies, and chrysolite.[76]

In the Amarna recension of the *King of Battle* epic, Akkadian merchants resident in Purušḫanda tell Sargon of the exotic treasures of that far-off eastern land: "[Puruš]ḫanda where you wish to travel—the road of which I groan is a task of seven double-miles. [(But there is)] the Mighty Mountain whose boulders are lapis lazuli, (and) gold is in its circumference."[77]

The foregrounding of action (vv. 3-4) against environment (vv. 1-2, 5-8) continues with the triplet in v. 4. While a conquering of the darkness was effected through binding in v. 3a (*qēṣ śām laḥōšek*), this action is paralleled by an ability to split passageways (*pāraṣ nĕḥālīm* [MT *naḥal*]) in remote regions in v. 4a. These dual actions in vv. 3-4 of binding (*qēṣ śām*) and splitting (*pāraṣ*) parallel those of splitting (*biqqēaʿ*) and binding (*ḥibbēš*) in vv. 10-11 and thus hold the bulk of Section One together. While the explorer sets bounds for darkness in order to search out "the stone of deepest darkness" (*ʾeben ʾōpel wĕṣalmôt* [MT *ṣalmāwet*]) in v. 3, he binds up the sources of the rivers (*mabbĕkê* [MT *mibbĕkî*] *nĕhārôt ḥibbēš*) in v. 11 to bring a dark thing to light (*wĕtaʿălūmâ* [MT *taʿălūmāh*] *yōṣīʾ ʾōr*). The two triplets in vv. 3-4 and the three couplets in vv. 9-11 convey the action of this condensed narrative and frame the central description of the land in which the quest is undertaken in the four couplets in vv. 5-8.

The journey motif continues in this notoriously difficult triplet,[78] whose burden is to emphasize the lack of human inhabitants—presumably as the explorer moves outside the bounds of civilization. In the overall structure of the verse, the initial object (*nĕḥālīm* [MT *naḥal*])

---

76 Pseudo-Callisthenes, *Iskandarnama* (trans. Minoo S. Southgate; New York: Columbia University Press, 1978), 58, as cited in Horowitz, *MCG*, 102.

77 Line 28. Text and translation in Westenholz, *Legends of the Kings of Akkade*, 118-119.

78 Leroy Waterman states, "Nearly every word in the verse raises a problem either as to its meaning or its construction or both" ("Note on Job 28 4," *JBL* 71 [1952]: 168).

is expounded upon in the following two lines (v. 4aβ and 4b). The syntactic parallels created by the repetition of prepositional phrases with *min* in each line (*mēʿim-gār*, v. 4aα; *minnî-rāgel*, v. 4aβ; *mēʾĕnôš*, v. 4b) are matched by a semantic heightening. The *nĕḥālīm* [MT *naḥal*] are first said to be remote from dwellers (*mēʿim-gār*, v. 4aα). In v. 4aβ, they are not merely outside the realm of settled existence; they are forgotten even to travelers (*hanniškāḥîm minnî-rāgel*). But not only are these regions so remote that wayfarers would not pass by; they are altogether bereft of human habitation (*dallû mēʾĕnôš*, v. 4b). This is truly a frontier zone.

The use of the term *naḥal* in this line has been a special point of difficulty in the interpretation of the poem, though it seems clear enough that it is a passageway of some sort (see *He breaches course<s> far from dwellers* in ch. 4.3). In the OT, *naḥal* most commonly denotes a dry ravine or a flowing stream. The latter sense fits well with the large-scale parallel in v. 10a, where the explorer splits streams in the mountains (*baṣṣûrôt yĕʾōrîm biqqēaʿ*). Yet the images in the near context of moving out toward the dark edges of the world (v. 3) suggest that the action in v. 4 has to do with breaking open a passageway to traverse these regions. The term *naḥal*, then, may suggest something like a "hole" or "furrow" as Sumerian sidug, an equivalent of Akkadian *naḫallu*, in the opening hymnic portion of *Enki and the World Order*:

> Enki, from whom a single glance is enough to unsettle the heart of the mountains; wherever bison are born, where stags are born, where ibex are born, where wild goats are born, in meadows ......, in hollows (si-dug$_4$-ga) in the heart of the hills, in green ...... unvisited by man, you have fixed your gaze on the heart of the Land as on split reeds.[79]

At any rate, it is not necessary to connect the breaking open of a *naḥal* in v. 4a with the creation of a vertical mine shaft, as many interpreters have supposed.

Given the repeated emphasis on lack of human habitation in v. 4, the setting for such action may be either the steppe or the mountains—both thought to be regions at the periphery of existence. Shemaryahu

---

79 Lines 11-16. Text and translation of *Enki and the World Order* (ETCSL 1.1.3) online: http://etcsl.orinst.ox.ac.uk. Sum. sidug is also used of a "hole" or a "pit" in its four occurrences in *Lugalbanda in the Mountain Cave* (ETCSL 1.8.2.1). Other Sum. equivalents of Akk. *naḫallu* include aruba ("pitfall"), piš ("bank"), and uhrum ("stream") (glosses from the Pennsylvania Sumerian Dictionary online: http://psd.museum.upenn.edu/epsd/index.html). While Akk. *naḫallu* normally means "wadi" or the like, the editors of *CAD* comment: "It is possible, therefore that the refs. in which *naḫallu* is not connected with water refer in fact to a pitfall, ambush, or cave" (*CAD* N/1, 125, s.v. *naḫallu*).

Talmon comments on the conceptualization of the wilderness in Israelite literature:

> The "wilderness" is a place of utter desolation: a vast void of parched earth, with no streams or rivers to provide sustenance for plants and wildlife, except for a very few species ... It is a place not fit for human habitation ... the few wandering nomads ... being the only exception ... It is perilous to enter the vast tracts, which are traversable by only a few paths or byways, often barely recognizable.[80]

Talmon's observations mesh remarkably well with the imagery in the two triplets in Job 28:3-4. The wilderness—a "land of deep gloom" (*ʾereṣ maʾpēlĕyâ*), as Jeremiah figures it (Jer 2:31, // *midbār*)—would be a fitting locus for the object of the search in Job 28, that is, the "stone of deepest gloom" (*ʾereṣ ʾōpel wĕṣalmôt* [MT *ṣalmāwet*], v. 3).

Reference both to wilderness and mountains are included in Assyrian royal inscriptions touting the king as the "first discoverer," who travelled where no king before had been.[81] Esarhaddon's description of Patusharra is illustrative: "Patusharra, a land bordering the salt-desert which is in the midst of the distant Medes, on the edge of Mount Bikni, the lapis-lazuli mountain, the ground of its land which none among my royal ancestors has trodden..."[82]

The king's ability to open up passes in treacherous mountain regions also contributes to the picture of monarch as hero in numerous Assyrian annals. The Zagros Mountains to the east and the Taurus Mountains to the north were considerable barriers for travelers, which could only be accessed through the river valleys.[83] Shalmaneser III boasts in the Kurkh Monolith:

> Shalmaneser, king of all people, ... who has seen remote and rugged regions, who has trodden upon the mountain peaks in all the highlands, ... who opens paths above and below ... magnificent king of lands, who has kept progressing by difficult ways through mountains and seas.[84]

---

80 Talmon, "The 'Desert Motif' in the Bible and in Qumran Literature," in *Biblical Motifs: Origins and Transformations* (ed. Alexander Altmann; Philip W. Lown Institute of Advanced Judaic Studies, Brandeis University: Studies and Texts 3; Cambridge, Mass.: Harvard, 1966), 42.

81 See Favaro, *Voyages et voyageurs*, 124-129.

82 Nineveh Prism A, IV:46-48. My translation with an eye to Riekele Borger, *Die Inschriften Asarhaddons König von Assyrien* (AfOB 9; ed. Ernst Weidner; Graz: Ernst Weidner et al., 1956), §27 (p. 55, "Episode 16" = *ARAB* 2, §540).

83 Van De Mieroop, *A History of the Ancient Near East*, 9.

84 RIMA 3 A.0.102.2:i 5-10 (cf. *ARAB* 1, §596). Translation adapted from Grayson. This theme is ubiquitous in Assyrian royal inscriptions. See also lines 15-17 of the *Sargon Birth Legend* (Westenholz, *Legends of the Kings of Akkade*, 40-43); *ARAB* 1, §165 (Tu-

These remote mountain regions are often characterized by darkness, especially due to the dense forests which allow no sun to pass through to the ground below.[85] If such heroic feats in the highlands are not in fact figured in Job 28:4, the final three couplets of Section One undoubtedly set their narrative in the mountains (vv. 9-11).

Whether the steppe or the mountains, it is clear that the region depicted in vv. 3-4 lies beyond the civilized world. It is dark, bereft of life, and thought to be virtually impassable. The creatures named in the couplets in vv. 7-8 underscore the depiction of danger in vv. 3-4. Yet, as the couplets in vv. 5-6 make clear, it is also paradoxically a land of sustenance and wealth.

The first pair of couplets (vv. 5-6) in vv. 5-8 details the topography of the land in which the explorer undertakes this bold search. The second pair (vv. 7-8) portrays this place as lying beyond the reach of animals of the air and ground. The beginning of each pair of couplets is signaled by the fronting of its topic: first *ʾereṣ* (v. 5a), and then *nātîb* (v. 7a).

Though somewhat different in focus, these lines are clustered around metaphors central to the poem's aesthetic logic: "place" (*māqôm*, v. 6a; also vv. 1b, 12b, 20b, 23b) and "path" (*nātîb*, v. 7a; cf. *derek* in vv. 13a, 23a and the verbal *hidrîkūhû* in v. 8a)—figures which are prominent again in Job 38:19-20 (*derek* – *mĕqōmô* – *nĕtîbôt*). There is a noticeable shift in perspective within and between these lines as well, which alternate above and below/on the surface of the earth (vv. 5a, 6, 7: above; v. 5b: below or on the surface; v. 8: on the surface). The key terms from the opening lines of the poem are repeated or played upon here: *yēṣēʾ* in v. 5a is a root play on *môṣāʾ* in v. 1a; *māqôm* in v. 1b is repeated in v. 6a; *ʿāpār* in v. 2a appears in the plural in v. 6a (*ʿaprōt*); and *zāhāb* in v. 1b is repeated in v. 6b. All the above correspondences suggest that the land spoken of in vv. 5-6 *is the place* where the precious metals detailed in the opening lines of the poem may be found.[86]

The description in v. 5a of "a land from which food springs forth" (*ʾereṣ mimmennāh yēṣēʾ-lāḥem*) finds echoes in the Deuteronomic description of the Promised Land in which there is food (*leḥem*) without end (Deut 8:8-9). The symbolism is even clearer in the perfectly ordered

---

kulti-Ninurta I), §§225, 236 (Tiglath-Pileser I), §370 (Adad-Nirari II), §598 (Shalmaneser III); *ARAB* 2, §§54, 118, 142, 152, 170 (Sargon II).

85 See the description of the jungle-like surfaces of Mount Nikippa and Mount Upa in Sargon II's *Letter to Assur* in TCL 3:i 15-16 (= *ARAB* 2, §142; cf. Mayer, »Sargons Feldzug,« 68-69); and the traditions of Sargon the Great in *Sargon in Foreign Lands* (iv: 9'-11') (Westenholz, *Legends of the Kings of Akkade*, 90-91).

86 Geller, " 'Where is Wisdom' " 161.

creation of Ps 104—a "creation without opposition."[87] Here, too, *leḥem* is brought forth from the earth (*lĕhôṣîʾ leḥem min-hāʾāreṣ*, v. 14b). It seems, in fact, that the generalized designation *leḥem* in Job 28:5 is a metonym for various kinds of herbage and trees such as those which spring forth (YṢʾ) from the ground in Gen 1:12 (*dešeʾ ʿēśeb, zeraʿ, ʿēṣ pĕrî*) or Deut 8:8-9 (*gepen ûtĕʾēnâ wĕrimmôn*). In the triplet in Ps 104:14, *leḥem* is set in parallel with "grass" (*ḥāṣîr*) and "herbage" (*ʿēśeb*).

Once again the cosmic geography that informs Akkadian traditions about royal expeditions to the earth's borders is germane. Those distant lands are filled not only with precious stones, but also with exotic plants and trees. Sargon the Great's *King of Battle* epic relays that along the road to distant Purušḫanda "[...] the apple tree, the fig tree, the boxwood, the *urzinnu*-wood are of a depth of seven abzu."[88] The letter of Sargon II to Assur describes his conquest of lush mountain regions during his campaign in Eastern Anatolia: "(The mountains) are covered with all kinds of desirable trees, fruit trees, and vines, as dense as reeds, and full of dread for the one who approaches their passes, where no king had crossed and whose innermost region none of my princely predecessors had seen. Their great tree-trunks I cut down..."[89]

The image of fire dominates the second line of v. 5. Interpreters have often tried to explain the line in relation to technical prospecting practices.[90] Some believe that fire-setting is in view here as a mining technique.[91] Others can only explain v. 5 as a "geological aside, ...an overemphasis on the literal imagery of the immediately preceding material that has dulled sensitivity to its figurative intent..."[92]

---

87 On the whole psalm, see Jon D. Levenson, *Creation and the Persistence of Evil: The Jewish Drama of Divine Omnipotence* (Princeton, NJ: Princeton University Press, 1988), 53-65. The phrase "creation without opposition" is his.

88 Obv., line 29. Text and translation in Westenholz, *Legends of the Kings of Akkade*, 118-121. See also rev., lines 24'-26' in ibid., 128-129.

89 TCL 3:iii 327-329 (=*ARAB* 2, §170). My translation after Mayer, »Sargons Feldzug,« 100-101. See also TCL 3:i 15-16 (=*ARAB* 2, §142) and *ARAB* 2, §823 (Assurbanipal's Rassam Cylinder).

90 H. H. Rowley understands v. 5a as detailing what takes place on the earth's surface and v. 5b as underground mining activity (*The Book of Job* [rev. ed.; NCB; Grand Rapids, Mich.: Eerdmans, 1976], 181).

91 Gordis suggests that the fire in v. 5b "may refer to an ancient prehistoric technique still in use in the Middle Ages for dislodging hard rocks by kindling wood in a shaft, or the verse may be describing the natural heat of the volcano as evidenced by the burning lava pouring forth" (*The Book of Job*, 306). See also Artur Weiser (*Das Buch Hiob, übersetzt und erklärt* [Göttingen: Vandenhoeck and Ruprecht, 1951], 198); and De Wilde (*Das Buch Hiob*, 271).

92 Elwolde, "Non-Contiguous Parallelism," 118. Cf. his comments at 111.

The couplet, however, is hardly a technical gloss. In fact, it is the highly imagistic nature of the second line that causes the most difficulty in interpretation. The depiction of the place spoken of in the preceding lines now rests on the ambiguous simile "like fire" (*kĕmô-ʾēš*)—an ambiguity matched by that of the landscape itself. Yet this is what one expects of a peripheral zone.

On the one hand, the line could be interpreted as depicting a place destroyed (*nehpak*) as if it were burned with fire (*kĕmô-ʾēš*)—a simile used elsewhere in the OT (see Lam 2:3, 4). Such a description might apply well to the steppe, commonly thought of as a place of desolation and danger (see, e.g., Deut 8:15; cf. Deut 29:22). The description of Mount Ishrun in the annals of Tukulti-Ninurta II as "a region of destruction" suggests that the mountains might also be in view.[93]

On such an interpretation, however, the whole couplet in v. 5 would depict a place that is much like the Israelite Promised Land (v. 5a) and paradoxically also like the wilderness (v. 5b). While the nature of the region depicted in Job 28:4-6 is undoubtedly conflicted, could it really be, to put it in Deuteronomic terms, a place of food (Job 28:5a; Deut 8:9) and a place of no food (Deut 29:6) at the same time?

It is more congruent with the positive description of a life-sustaining land in v. 5a to understand *nehpak kĕmô-ʾēš* in v. 5b as a simile describing the brilliant appearance of precious stones lying in the lower regions of the earth's surface which glow like flames (see *beneath transformed as fire* in ch. 4.3). Though seemingly fantastical, such a conception lies behind the figuring of the first human and his abode in the mountain-garden of God in Ezek 28:12-14. Ancient descriptions of stones as having the appearance of fire undoubtedly underlie the phrase "stones of fire" (*ʾabnê-ʾēš*) in Ezek 28:14, which are said in that account to have been present in Eden.[94] A similar idea may also be attested in Ugaritic literature in the context of a discussion about Baal's mountain, Ṣapān, in which *abn brq* are mentioned—most likely as a reference to "lightning stones" which could also be understood as precious stones (*CTU* 1.3 iii 26 and 1.3 iv 17).[95] The cogency of such an in-

93 *ARAB* 1, §406.

94 See Pope, *Job*, 201; Janzen, *Job*, 193, 199-200; Habel, *The Book of Job*, 396; cf. Rowley, *The Book of Job*, 181. Pope points out elsewhere that the Akk. phrase *aban išāti* occurs in an Akk. lexical text, where it is listed as a synonym of *ḫipindû*, a multi-colored kidney (-shaped stone bead) (Pope, *El in the Ugaritic Texts* [VTSup 2; Leiden: E. J. Brill, 1955], 100), and *CAD* Ḫ, 195-96 s.v. *ḫipindû*). On the phrase *aban išāti*, see reference cited in *CAD* I/J, 228 s.v. *išātu*, 1; and *AHw* 1:6 s.v. *abnu(m)*, 3.

95 Alternatively, Mark S. Smith prefers to translate *abn* in these texts as a verb from √BYN, "I understand" ("The Baal Cycle," in *Ugaritic Narrative Poetry* [ed. Simon B. Parker; SBLWAW 9; Atlanta, Ga.: Scholars Press, 1997], 110, 113). Even if granting

terpretation in Job 28 is strengthened by the images which immediately follow in v. 6.

The couplet in v. 6 continues the description of the land begun in v. 5, though the *ʾereṣ* of v. 5a is here called a "place" (*māqôm,* v. 6a). By this paradigmatic substitution, *māqôm* becomes the subject of the whole couplet, though it is gapped in the second line. More importantly, however, the language of "place" (*māqôm*) in v. 6a is used to recall the initial goal set forth in the poem's opening line (*māqôm,* v. 1b), while it also anticipates the question of v. 12b: "Where is the place of understanding?" (*ʾê zeh mĕqôm bînâ*).

Verse 6 focuses on yet another aspect of the land described in v. 5: not only is it fertile and life-giving (v. 5); it is also full of wealth and beauty (v. 6). But it is not just that treasure is to be found there; rather, the topography of that land *is* a horde of treasure. It is described as a place of lapis stones (*mĕqôm-sappîr ʾăbānêhā*) and gold dust (*ʿaprōt zāhāb lô*) (thus *ʾăbānêhā* // *ʿaprōt*; cf. v. 2: *ʿāpār* // *ʾeben*).

In Mesopotamian literature, lapis and gold are quite commonly said to be products of the mountains. In *Enmerkar and the Lord of Aratta,* such materials—found in the distant mountains in the East—are acquired to build a splendid "mountain" (i.e., temple) for Inanna in the cultural center of Uruk.[96] Akkadian royal epics and annals also feature mountains which are made of azure-blue stones. Esarhaddon's Nineveh Prism A describes Mount Bikni as "the lapis-lazuli mountain" and Mount Hazu as "a mountain of *saggilmud*-stone."[97] Lapis and gold are also clearly juxtaposed—as in Job 28:6—in the description of Puruš-

---

the reading "lightning stones," against Smith's interpretation, there is still a good deal of ambiguity as to what this phrase would mean. F. C. Fensham is on the right track, as he suggests that these "lightning stones" are hurled from Ṣapān by Baal in the thunderstorm ("Thunder-Stones in Ugaritic," *JNES* 18 [1959]: 273, as cited in Walther Zimmerli, *Ezekiel 2: A Commentary on the Book of the Prophet Ezekiel Chapters 25-48* [trans. James D. Martin; eds. Paul D. Hanson with Leonard Jay Greenspoon; Philadelphia, Pa.: Fortress, 1983], 93 and n. 33). However, this does not rule out that these could also be understood as precious stones. Note a similar ambiguity between cognates in Heb., Ug., and Akk., in which Heb. *ʾelgābîš* means either "hail stones" or "lumps of ice," while Ug. *algbṯ* and Akk. *algamešu* are used of precious stones (*HALOT* 1:51, s.v. *ʾelgābîš*). See also literature cited in *DUL*, 1:54-55, s.v. *algbṯ*.

96 See lines 18-19, 39-42. Text and translation in Vanstiphout, *Epics of Sumerian Kings*, 56-59. See also translation in Jacobsen, *Harps*, 281-82.

97 A, IV:47 in Borger, *Inschriften Asarhaddons*, §27 (p. 55, "Episode 16"; cf. *ARAB* 2, §540), and A, IV:57 in Borger, *Inschriften Asarhaddons*, §27 (p. 56, "Episode 17"; cf. *ARAB* 2, §537). On the lapis-like blue *saggilmud* stone, see *CAD* S, 23-24, s.v. In Mesopotamian cosmic geography, it was also thought to be the material with which the Middle Heavens were composed (Horowitz, *MCG*, 11).

ḫanda in the *King of Battle* epic of Sargon the Great, where there is a Mighty Mountain with boulders of lapis and foothills of gold.[98]

Gold is so closely connected with mountain regions in Assyrian royal inscriptions that it is commonly described as the "dust of [the] mountains."[99] In a building inscription, Esarhaddon claims to have provided for his artisans "Dark gold (KÙ.GI SA5), the dust of its mountain (*epir šadīšu*), which no one had yet used for ornamental work; precious stones... without number, the product of the mountains..."[100] In Sumerian literature, too, Gudea is said to have supplied his craftsmen with gold "in dust form (saḫar-ba) from [the] mountains."[101] Such idioms undoubtedly inform the description of the land in Job 28:6. More than simply a mineralogical or geological description,[102] the images of v. 6 evoke a mountainous region with lapis boulders and gold dust.

The two couplets in vv. 7-8 contribute to the projection of a remote region by focusing on its inaccessibility to birds (v. 7) and beasts (v. 8). As such, the two verses are merismatic (cf. also v. 21).[103] The object of both couplets is the "path" (*nātîb*, v. 5a), which is imperceptible to all creatures named there. *Nātîb*, which elsewhere in the Book of Job is clustered with *ʾereṣ* (18:10) and *māqôm* (38:19-20), is in vv. 5-8 parallel to both terms (*ʾereṣ*, v. 5a; *māqôm*, v. 6a). It also anticipates *derek* as a synonym for "path" in v. 23a.

In the Assyrian royal inscriptions, birds are typically employed as markers of distance. Though topography would seem to pose little challenge to creatures of the air, monarchs claimed status as "first discoverer" of a distant land by boasting that their expedition reached farther than any winged creature. In his *Letter to Assur*, Sargon II describes "...Mount Uaush, the great mountain, whose summit reaches the struc-

98 *Sargon, King of Battle*, line 28. See the translation of Foster in *BTM*, 341. Text and alternate translation in Westenholz, *Legends of the Kings of Akkade*, 118-119. Note also the juxtaposition of these two materials in line 251 of the Sum. *Praise Poem of Ishme-Dagan* (*Ishme-Dagan* A+V): "I am gold dust; I am lapis lazuli in its lode" (translation of ETCSL text 2.5.4.01 at http://etcsl.orinst.ox.ac.uk).

99 On this designation, see *CAD* E, 189 s.v. *eperu*, 5.b; *AHw* 1:223, s.v. *eperu*, 3.c.

100 AsBbA:rev. 30-33. My translation with an eye to Borger, *Inschriften Asarhaddons*, §53 (p. 83; cf. *ARAB* 2, §672). Text as cited in *CAD* E, 189 s.v. *eperu*, 5.b. See also AsBbA: rev. 36 in Borger, *Inschriften Asarhaddons*, §53 (p. 84; cf. *ARAB* 2, §673); *ARAB* 1, §806 (Tiglath-pileser III); *ARAB* 2, §907 (Assurbanipal).

101 *Gudea Cylinder A*, xvi:20. Translation in Jacobsen, *Harps*, 408. Text in Thureau-Dangin, *SAK*, 106.

102 Leroy Waterman, for example, supposes that supposes that the verse speaks of "lapis lazuli spangled with iron pyrites, that look like specks of gold" ("Note on Job 28 4," 168). Cf. also Beer, *Der Text des Buches Hiob*, 178; Gordis, *The Book of Job*, 306; Rowley, *The Book of Job*, 181.

103 Cf. Geller " 'Where is Wisdom?' " 163.

ture of clouds in the midst of the heavens, whose land since primeval days no living being has crossed, ... and over which no winged bird of heaven flies..."[104] The Babylonian Map of the World—likely created to locate and describe distant regions—also states that the third *nagû* across the ocean is a region where "A winged [bi]rd cannot safely comp[lete its journey]."[105]

The effect in Job 28:7 is similar, though here the focus is more specifically on the "path" (v. 7a) and the failure of the birds in locating it (v. 7b). There is a sharpening in the couplet, moving from a bird of prey's general ignorance with regard to the path (*nātîb lōʾ-yĕdāʿô ʿāyiṭ*) to the more specific ophthalmic deficiency of the falcon (*lōʾ šĕzāpattû ʿên ʾayyâ*). In the Joban poem, the point is not simply a question of distance, as seems to be the case in the Assyrian inscriptions. Rather, the issue is painted more in terms of a lack of knowledge (*lōʾ-yĕdāʿô*, v. 7a) and visual perception (v. 7b). The irony in v. 7 is great, since it is precisely these birds' power of vision and their familiarity with the habits of their earth-bound prey that make them accomplished hunters and scavengers. They depend on these faculties to survive; and yet not even *they* can discern the path.

Like the birds of prey in v. 7, both the serpent and the lion are often associated with domains outside of the center of civilization.[106] In the OT, serpents are said to be found in the wilderness (Deut 8:15; cf. Num 21:6), while lions make their homes in the forest (Jer 5:6; 12:8; Amos 3:4; Mic 5:7) and in thickets outside of controlled pasture land (Jer 4:7; 49:19; 50:44; Ps 10:9). They also feature in deserted regions in the campaigns of Assyrian kings, as illustrated by Esarhaddon's Prism A from Nineveh:

> The far-distant land Bazu, a forgotten piece of dry land, a region of salt, a place of thirst—120 double-hours region of sand with thistles and magnetite, where serpents and scorpions cover the field like ants, 20 double-hours into Mount Hazu, the mountain of *saggilmud*, I left behind me and I moved on. Into that land to which since distant days none of the kings who ruled

---

104 TCL 3:i 96-98 (=*ARAB* 2, §152). My translation after Mayer, »Sargons Feldzug,« 77. See also the annals of Adad-nirari II (*ARAB* 1, §370), Tukulti-Ninurta II (*ARAB* 1, §406), Assurnasirpal II (*ARAB* 1, §440), and the Rassam Cylinder of Assurbanipal (*ARAB* 2, §823). Other sources for Assurbanipal and Shamshi-Adad V listed in Horowitz, *MCG*, 37-38.

105 BM 92687 rev. 8'. Text and translation in Horowitz, *MCG*, 23-24. On the purpose of the Map, see ibid., 40.

106 Compare the description of the Zabu mountains in *Lugalbanda and the Anzud Bird* as "the mountains where no cypresses grow, where no snake slithers, where no scorpion scurries..." (lines 36-37). Translation in *LAS*, 23. Transliteration in Vanstiphout, *Epics of Sumerian Kings*, 138.

before me has passed, I advanced victoriously into its midst at the behest of my lord, Assur.[107]

In his annals, Esarhaddon even claims to have encountered two-headed serpents between Egypt and Meluhha.[108]

The lion was the epitome of the animal of the wilderness, as is evident in Akkadian descriptions of the king of beasts as "a raging lion of the wilderness" (*nēšu* (UR.MAḪ) *ezzu ša ṣērīšu* (EDIN-*šú*)).[109] This phrase is quite common in the famous reliefs depicting Assurbanipal's lion hunts.[110] In Slabs A-B portraying the rescue of the Elamite king Urtak from attacking lions, the caption describes them as offspring of the mountains: "I went out to the plain, a wide expanse, raging lions, a fierce mountain breed, attacked..."[111] Both the viper (*bašmu*) and the lion (*nēšu* (UR.MAḪ)) are listed among the fauna of distant lands in the Babylonian Map of the World,[112] and Assyrian kings often boasted about mastering such exotic creatures in their expeditions. Assurnasirpal II claims to have captured fifteen lions and fifty lion cubs in the Lebanon, among a litany of "all the beasts of plain and mountain" which he brought back as spoil to Nimrud.[113]

Though they are natives of these frontier zones, the couplet in Job 28:8 claims that neither the king of beasts nor the wily serpent has even moved along the path (*nātîb*, v. 7a) leading to the source of silver or the place of gold. Juxtaposing the craftiest and sleekest animal of the ground with the strongest and fiercest beast of the wilderness, the couplet underscores that such characteristics are of no effect in locating the place of the dark stone (v. 3b). In this light, the explorer's success in superceding the abilities of the keen-eyed carrions (v. 7), the wise serpent (v. 8a), and the mighty lion (v. 8b) in the three couplets that follow in vv. 9-11 is truly remarkable. Given this implicit contrast, it would

---

107 Nineveh A, IV:53-60 ("Episode 17"). My translation after Borger, *Inschriften Assarhaddons*, §27 (p. 56), with slight modification. See also *ARAB* 2, §537.

108 Annals fragment f: rev. 4-7 in Borger, *Inschriften Assarhaddons*, §76 (p. 112; cf. *ARAB* 2, §558).

109 Dick, "The Neo-Assyrian Royal Lion Hunt," 255 and n. 74. See also the description of the wilderness (*ṣēru* (EDIN)) and the lion, lioness, and lion cub as residents of this region who devour blood in lines 57-64 in the *Sargon Birth Legend* (Westenholz, *Legends of the Kings of Akkade*, 46-47 and 47 nn. 62.-64.).

110 See *ARAB* 2, §§1021-26.

111 *ú-ṣi ina* EDIN *áš-ri rap-ši la-ab-bi na-ad-*[*ru-u*]*-ti i-lit-ti ḫur-šá-a-ni* ḪUŠ.MEŠ *it-bu-u*. Slabs A-B in Room S1 of the North Palace. Translation and text in Pamela Gerardi, "Epigraphs and Assyrian Palace Reliefs: The Development of the Epigraphic Text," *JCS* 40 (1988): 26. See also ibid., 14-15, 25.

112 BM 92687 obv. 5'-8'. See Horowitz, *MCG*, 22-23, 35-36.

113 *ARAB* 1, §519.

seem that readers are to attribute these animals' sight, might, sinuosity, and wisdom to him.

The couplets in vv. 9-11 resume the narrative action begun in vv. 3-4 against the environment painted in vv. 5-8. The envelope of binding and splitting begun in the two triplets in vv. 3-4 is closed by repeating the themes in the two couplets in vv. 10-11 (splitting—binding). The pinnacle of achievement in this expedition is symbolized by the explorer's ability to plunge beneath the base of the mountains to tear out treasure from the depths and bring it into the gaze of the sun (see v. 11). Despite the brightening imagery, the explorer's heroic acts are also deeply colored by a violent fever to possess the object that has possessed him.

Though the first two words of v. 9—*ḥallāmîš* and *šālaḥ*—continue the sound patterning dominant in v. 8 with the repetition of the consonants *šîn*, *ḥêt*, and *lāmed*, the couplet is also bound to vv. 10-11 by their interwoven images, themes, and syntax.[114] Verses 9-10 both enumerate similar objects of action ("hard rock," "summits," and "mountains"), being bridged by the stereotypical pair *ḥallāmîš* // *ṣûrôt* (both marked with *bêt*). Yet vv. 10-11 are also bound by parallels between each line. The first two lines in each couplet (vv. 10a, 11a) are grammatically matched with two Piel verbs (*biqqēaʿ* and *ḥibbēš*), and the objects of these verbs are watercourses (*yĕʾōrîm* and *nĕhārôt*). The second lines of each couplet (vv. 10b, 11b) focus on the achievement of reversing the darkness and seeing with the eye what the keenest carrions have not perceived with theirs: *kol-yĕqār* ("every precious thing") and *taʿălūmâ* ("the dark thing" [MT *taʿălūmāh*]). These two verses, and the first section as a whole, climax with light (*ʾôr*, v. 11b).

The acts of violence evoked in the first two lines are signaled by the phrase *šālaḥ yādô bĕ*... in v. 9a, which in every case in the OT is used of murder, war, theft, or plunder (see *He assaults* in ch. 4.3). While in the prologue to Job, God stretched out his hand against Job and all that belonged to him, the explorer in Job 28 stretches out his hand to perpetrate an act of violence against the "hard rock" (*ḥallāmîš*, v. 9a).

The conquest of mountains is also a *topos* in Assyrian royal inscriptions, where monarchs repeatedly claim to have overcome their strength, permanence, and treachery. The "annals" of Assurnasirpal II recount his conquest of enemies who took refuge among the mountain peaks:

> The mountain was as jagged as the point of a dagger and therein no winged bird of the sky flew. They had placed their fortress like the nest of

---

114 Cf. Geller, " 'Where is Wisdom?' " 164.

> the *udīnu*-bird within the mountain which none of the kings my fathers had ever approached. For three days the hero explored the mountain. His bold heart yearned for battle. He ascended on foot (and) overwhelmed the mountain.[115]

The famous inscriptions of Shalmaneser III on a rock face at the source of the Tigris likewise portray him as "the fierce (and) merciless king who has gone after [his] enemies and victoriously swept over rivers and difficult mountains (leaving them) like ruin hills left by a deluge."[116]

Yet here again, the slight contrast between the images evoked by the Assyrian royal inscriptions and the poem in Job 28 is important. The Joban poem, like the Assyrian inscriptions, employs the vocabulary of war. Yet in Job, it is the "hard rock" (v. 9a) and the "summits" (v. 9b) themselves which are the enemy. And in the Joban poem such violent acts against the mountains are ultimately aimed at getting beneath them—to their very roots (v. 9b).

A mountain with roots is a striking image that may well be related to ancient conceptions of a primeval hill which grew like a plant out of the cosmic waters (note also the "birth" of mountains in Ps 90:2).[117] Though the OT nowhere else speaks of the roots (*šōreš*) of the mountains,[118] such an expression is quite common in Akkadian descriptions of a cosmic mountain, with its summit in the heavens and its roots in the Underworld. Sargon II's *Letter to Assur* describes Mt. Simirriya as a mount whose "summit reaches to the heavens above, whose root (*šuršūša*) strikes downward into the midst of Arallu."[119] Richard Clifford rightly points out that not everything with peaks in the heavens and roots in the Underworld has cosmic significance,[120] but the mythical overtones of the imagery in each of the three couplets in Job 28:9-11 certainly suggests more than simple prosaic description.

---

115 RIMA 2 A.0.101.1:i 50-51. Grayson's translation (cf. *ARAB* 1, §440). See also *ARAB* 1, §483 (Assurnasirpal II) and §609 (Shalmaneser III).

116 RIMA 3 A.0.102.23:9-13. Grayson's translation (cf. *ARAB* 1, §685).

117 This is especially evident in Egyptian conceptions of the cosmic mountain (Richard J. Clifford, *The Cosmic Mountain in Canaan and the Old Testament* [HSM 4; Cambridge, Mass.: Harvard University Press, 1972], 26-27), though Clifford believes that "Egypt seems to have influenced Canaan in the area of mountain symbolism not at all" (ibid., 28). Elsewhere in the OT, the creation of the mountains is figured much like temple-building, where their foundations are sunk into the ground from above (e.g., Prov 8:25a; cf. Job 38:6).

118 See, however, the plaster inscription from Kuntillet 'Ajrud, which may well mention the uprooting of mountains (note *šrš* [*šērēš* ?] in line 4 of *KAjr* 15 in *HI*, 287-88).

119 TCL 3:i 19. Translation of Luckenbill in *ARAB* 2, §142. Cf. Mayer, »Sargons Feldzug,« 69.

120 Clifford, *The Cosmic Mountain*, 21.

The term used for "hard rock" (*ḥallāmîš*) in the first line of v. 9 may well contribute to such cosmic overtones by evoking a quasi-mythical precious stone prized in Mesopotamia (*elmešu*) (see *hard rock* in ch. 4.3). Yet the poem's narrative suggests that the true prize lies beneath the rock (v. 9b). Could it be that the dark stone named as the object of the quest in v. 3b, like the ruddy gold *ṣāriru*-stone in Mesopotamia, is thought to lie at the roots of the mountains as a precious object of the Underworld?[121] Niccacci's intuitions about the assault on the mountains in this couplet are no doubt correct: "One gains the impression of it as an activity that... somehow touches the sphere of the divine and the infernal."[122]

The sequence of lines in vv. 10-11 becomes increasingly difficult to explain in any "realistic" sense. The more figurative and symbolic dimensions that have bubbled beneath the realistic plane throughout the poem here begin to burst through its literal surface. While *yĕʾōr* in the first line of v. 10 could perhaps be explained as a term for dry channels into the mountains (cf. v. 4a), the associations with water in the following couplet (v. 11a) undoubtedly activate the watery imagery most naturally suggested by the use of *yĕʾōr* in the OT (see *He splits streams in the mountains* in ch. 4.3). In fact, vv. 9a and 10a are loaded with terminology associated with the Water from the Rock tradition. The Egyptian loan word *yĕʾōr*, also connected contextually to this tradition (see Exod 17:5-6), contributes doubly to the imagery of the poem by evoking water while punning on "light" (*ʾôr*; see v. 11b).[123]

The second line in the couplet peaks with the efficiency of vision—an eye which "sees every precious thing" (*kol-yĕqār rāʾătâ ʿênô*). The water imagery begun in the first line is carried through, however, as *ʿayin* also puns on the meaning "spring." Seeing is an important concept in the poem, and that faculty is highlighted here, as in v. 7b, with mention of the "eye." Despite the fact that the falcon is renowned for penetrating sight (v. 7b), the explorer's vision outstrips it (v. 10b). Human success in sight is also set against the mere rumor heard by Destruction and Death in Section Two of the poem, who have only heard with their

---

121 See the description of the *ṣāriru*-stone in Borger, *Inschriften Asarhaddons*, AsBbA:rev. 36 (§53; p. 84); AsBbE:obv. 14 (§57; p. 88) See also *ARAB* 2, §673; *CAD* Ṣ, 111-12 s.v. *ṣāriru* A; *AHw* 3:1085-86 s.v. *ṣāriru* I.

122 Niccacci, "Giobbe 28," 44 (my translation).

123 Geller, " 'Where is Wisdom?' " 164. The term *yĕʾōr* is a good illustration of the poetic function of Joban diction (See Greenstein, "The Language of Job and its Poetic Function," 655 n. 21). A phonological pun is evident in the Masoretic text (*yĕʾōr* and *ʾôr*), though the original vocalization of YʾR is uncertain (< Eg. *ἰtrw*). Note, however, the vocalization of "Nile" in Akk. as *iaruʾu* (*HALOT* 2:381, s.v. *yĕʾōr*; see *ARAB* 2, §901). Whatever the vocalization, the visual pun is transparent: ʾR and YʾR.

ears (v. 22).[124] There wisdom as the object is more explicit, but it is the ocular failure of these cosmic forces which is the fundamental point of emphasis. Finally, the visual achievement portrayed in v. 10b anticipates God's ability to "look out" beneath all the heavens in v. 24b and to "see" wisdom in v. 27a.

The eye's object is "every precious thing" (*kol-yĕqār*), an apostrophe for a common phrase for precious stones in the OT: (*kol-*)*ʾeben yĕqārâ* (see *His eye sees every precious thing* in ch. 4.3). Having arrived at the cosmic mountain, he can now master with his eyes every treasure that it affords. Especially precious among these jewels, however, is the "dark stone" that has been the object of his quest. To find this stone, he must plunge into the deep at the mountain's base.

While vv. 9-10 have detailed actions in or against mountains (*hārîm* and *ṣûrôt*), in v. 11 the explorer demonstrates mastery over the "sources of the rivers" (*mabbĕkê nĕhārôt* [MT *mibbĕkî*]) which emanate from their roots (see v. 9b). Having already "bound" the darkness at the outset of this quest (v. 3a), the hero now binds the waters (v. 11a) in order to draw out the dark thing from their depths (v. 11b). The first line in the couplet continues the imagery of water highlighted in v. 10a, but, like *yĕʾōr* in that line, *nĕhārôt* in v. 11a evokes water while punning on "light" (*nĕhārâ*; see Job 3:4).[125]

The sources of the rivers are, like the mountains in v. 9-10, objects of conquest in Assyrian royal inscriptions. Though Naram-Sin and Tiglath-Pileser I had preceded him, Shalmaneser III is the king *par excellence* "who has seen the sources of the Tigris and Euphrates."[126] Shalmaneser's annals report his advancement to the sources of these great rivers during the campaigns of his seventh and fifteenth years to Urartu in eastern Anatolia.[127] As discoverers of the source of Mesopotamian life that lay in the virtually impenetrable eastern Taurus mountain range, both Tiglath-Pileser I and Shalmaneser III carved their royal im-

---

124 Note that the Poem of Job itself ends by pitting hearsay against sight, as Job proclaims, "With the hearing of the ear I had heard of you / but now my eye sees you!" (42:5; cf. 13:1; 19:27).

125 Geller, " 'Where is Wisdom?' " 164 and 184 n. 63.

126 Stone statue from Assur, RIMA 3 A.0.102.25:12-13. Translation Grayson (cf. *ARAB* 1, §674, there called the "Throne Inscription"). Though there are no inscriptions of Naram-Sin at the sources of the Tigris, as there are with Tiglath-Pileser I and Shalmaneser III, it seems that Naram-Sin also reached them, since he named a year "The year that Naram-Sin reached the sources of the Tigris and Euphrates" (translation and text in Horowitz, *MCG*, 92).

127 See Black Obelisk, RIMA 3 A.0.102.14:69, 92-93; monumental bull from Nimrud, RIMA 3 A.0.102.8: 47'-49'; annals on clay tablets from Assur, RIMA 3 A.0.102.6:ii 37-38, iii 34-38.

ages in its cliffs, along with inscriptions praising their heroic accomplishments.[128] A monumental bull from Nimrud describes the campaign of Shalmaneser III's fifteenth year:

> *ina* 15 BALA.MEŠ-*ia ana* KUR *na-i-ri al-lik ina* SAG ÍD *e-ni šá* ÍD.ḪAL.ḪAL *ṣalam* MAN-*ti-ia ina* KUR *ka-a-pi šá* KUR-*e ina ṣi-it na-ga-bi-šá ab-ni ta-na-ti kiš-šu-ti-ia al-ka-kát qur-di-ia ina qé-reb-šú al-ṭùr*
>
> In my fifteenth regnal year I marched to the land Nairi. I created at the source of the Tigris, on a mountain cliff where its water comes out, my royal statue. I wrote thereon praises of my power (and) my heroic deeds.[129]

As he says elsewhere, he reached the fount, "the place of the outflow (*mūṣû*) of the water."[130] Through such a feat, these rulers made an enduring name, securing their position among heroic kings of yore.

Yet mention of the "sources of the rivers" in Job 28:11 is surely meant to transport the reader still farther "beyond the explored world, in[to] the realm of fantasy."[131] In fact, the phrasing here (*mabbĕkê nĕhārôt* [MT *mibbĕkî*]) is an abbreviated reflex of the standard Ugaritic epithet for El's abode,[132] who is said to dwell "at the sources of the two rivers, amidst the streams of the double-deep" (*mbk nhrm qrb ʾapq thmtm*; see

---

128 For the inscriptions, see RIMA 3 A.0.102.21—A.0.102.24. See photographs and descriptions of the reliefs and inscriptions from the 2004 University of Munich expedition to the Tigris Tunnel on the web: http://www.vaa.fak12.uni-muenchen.de/Birkleyn/html_englisch/frameset_englisch.htm. See also the discussion of the terrain and maps with modern and ancient toponyms in Russell, "Shalmaneser's Campaign to Urartu," 171-174, 199.

129 RIMA 3 A.0.102.8:47'-49'. Translation Grayson (cf. *ARAB* 1, §684).

130 RIMA 3 A.0.102.14:69 (*a-šar mu-ṣu-u šá* A.MEŠ *šaknu*). Translation Grayson. Compare the almost identical formulation in RIMA A.0.102.6:iii 38.

131 These are the comments of George on the *pî nārāti* in SB Gilg. XI. 205-206 (*BGE*, 1:521).

132 There is some dispute over the locus of El's mountain. It is perhaps to be located in modern Khirbet Afqa in the heart of the Lebanon Mountains, at the source of the Nahr Ibrāhīm (so Marvin H. Pope, *El in the Ugaritic Texts* [VTSup 2; eds. G. W. Anderson et al.; Leiden: E. J. Brill, 1955], 75-80). It is not difficult to imagine this impressive site as consonant with ancient descriptions of El's abode (for a photograph, see Olivier Binst, ed., *The Levant: History and Archaeology in the Eastern Mediterranean* [Köln: Könemann, 2000], 11). F. M. Cross, however, disagrees, preferring to locate the mountain of El in the Amanus ("אֵל," in *TDOT* 1:248). But realistic topography is hardly the focus in this text; the point is that it El's abode lies *beyond* the explored world. Like the standard version of Gilgamesh, Job 28:11 shows a penchant "for the romantic, for the strange—faraway lands, hidden knowledge, and ancient lore" (Thorkild Jacobsen, "The Gilgamesh Epic: Romantic and Tragic Vision," in *Lingering Over Words: Studies in Ancient Near Eastern Literature in Honor of William L. Moran* [eds. Tzvi Abusch, John Huehnergard, and Piotr Steinkeller; HSS 37; Atlanta, Ga.: Scholars, 1990], 247).

the sources of the rivers in ch. 4.3).[133] The explorer has somehow stepped beyond the boundaries of *this* world into a cosmic landscape.[134] The "realistic" meaning is ultimately outstripped by the mythical and symbolic, and the explorer is transformed into a universal epic hero[135]—a kind of Everyman[136] whose superhuman accomplishments have brought him to the watery domain of the wise Creator god.

From these depths the explorer brings the mysterious "dark thing" (*taʿălūmâ*, v. 11b [MT *taʿălūmāh*]) to light. The second line of v. 11 depicts the hero laying hold of the obscure stone and stripping it of the darkness that characterized it at the onset of the expedition (v. 3b).[137] Though metaphors of gloom overshadowed the first half of Section One, at its close all is water and light—a reversal effected by a heroic show of power and sight. It seems that the "dark thing" the explorer obtains from El's fount is, in fact, a form of wisdom itself.

This equation is confirmed by the correspondences between the pieces of the proverbial "frame" at the borders of Section One in vv. 1 and 12:

> There is indeed a *source* for silver, / a *place* for gold which is refined.
> "But wisdom—*where is it found*? / Where is the *place* of understanding?"

The structural similarities between the two couplets are remarkable. The parallel "source" (*môṣāʾ*) and "place" (*māqôm*) of v. 1 is recalled by

133 Habel rightly notes the connection with El in vv. 9-11: "The exploits of mortals in their search for precious metals compares with the deeds of El in might and ingenuity... Mortals even have the capacity to block the 'deep sources of the rivers,' which according to ancient Canaanite tradition is the abode of El himself" (*The Book of Job*, 397). For the Ug. sources, see citations under *the sources of the rivers* in ch. 4.3.

134 One might use the comments of David Damrosch about Gilgamesh's encounter with Utnapishtim to describe the explorer's encounter with the cosmic locus of El in Job 28: "When Gilgamesh visits Utnapishtim, history visits myth" (*The Narrative Covenant*, 114).

135 See Bendt Alster, "The Paradigmatic Character of Mesopotamian Heroes," *RA* 68 (1974): 51.

136 Compare the comments of Andrew George on Gilgamesh in the SB epic: "The mortal Gilgamesh represents the individual Everyman, though one who has been singled out for an extraordinary experience" (*BGE*, 1:528).

137 The identification of the "stone of deepest darkness" in v. 3b and the "dark thing" in v. 11b is suggested by the imagery of the poem. However, in light of the distinct possibility of inter-dialectical mixing, the roots ʿLM (*taʿălūmâ*, v. 11b) and ṢLM (*ṣalmôt*, v. 3b) may be etymologically connected as well. See discussion under *brings the dark thing to light* in ch. 4.3.

MṢʾ (*timmāṣēʾ*) and *māqôm* in v. 12.[138] Though in v. 1, this was a "source" and "place" for silver and gold, in v. 12 it is a locus for wisdom and understanding. The *yēš... wĕ...* construction of the proverb in vv. 1a and 12a also matches those common in the Book of Proverbs (see 14:12; 16:25; and 20:15). Like Job 28:1, 12, Prov 20:15 sets the valuable against the priceless: "There is gold and an abundance of corals, / but a precious vessel are lips that speak knowledge."[139]

These symbolic and structural associations color the whole of Section One with a new hue. The silver spoken of in v. 1 *is* wisdom, and the gold *is* understanding.[140] The half-proverb in v. 12 thus suggests a re-reading of Section One against these associations and in light of the strongly cosmic connotations of the poem's symbols in vv. 10-11. The condensed narrative in vv. 3-11 which lies "between the lines" of this epigram is now exposed as the parable that it is. As van Hecke points out, "By the juxtaposition of verses [1-11 and 12], the digging of the earth is implicitly presented as a metaphorical model with which the searching for wisdom can be understood."[141]

3.6 Re-reading Section One (vv. 1-11)

Conditioned with suspicion of a quest for wisdom in the watery depths, one may now re-interpret *môṣāʾ* in the first line of the poem as the "fount"—in fact the most common meaning of the word in Iron Age Hebrew (see *source* in ch. 4.3). The silver which flows from it is a symbol of wisdom; gold is a metaphor for understanding. The cosmic connotations of the final lines of Section One may thus be seen as having been intimated even in its first line—now perceived as a symbolic introduction to the quest for wisdom in the poetic parable of Job 28:3-11.

---

138 This association between wisdom and understanding with silver and gold is also strengthened by the generic definite article with "wisdom" in v. 12 (*haḥokmâ*) as with "silver" (*lakkesep*) and "gold" (*lazzāhāb*) in v. 1.

139 For translation and commentary, see Bruce K. Waltke, *The Book of Proverbs: Chapters 16-31* (NICOT; Grand Rapids, Mich., and Cambridge, U.K.: Eerdmans, 2005), 138, 143-44.

140 Elwolde, "Non-Contiguous Parallelism," 111. Compare Pio Fedrizzi: "In the course of the poem, the theme of wisdom is made the object of dispute" (*Giobbe* [La Sacra Bibbia: Antico Testamento; ed. Salvatore Garofalo; Rome and Turin: Marietti, 1972], 198 [my translation]).

141 van Hecke, "Searching for and Exploring Wisdom," 158 n. 42. Compare the comments of Albert Kamp in the same volume: "One could even say that within the activated conceptual space, Job 28:12 opens a new sub-world in which the modal reality of the question is the central theme" ("World Building in Job 28," 313).

Both jewels and founts serve as metaphors for wisdom in the ancient Near East. In the Book of Proverbs, wisdom is figured as a "fountain of life" (Prov 10:11; 13:14; 14:27; 16:22; esp. Prov 18:4!), even as it is commonly connected with earthly wealth (Prov 2:4; 3:14-15; 8:10-11, 18-21; 16:16; Eccl 7:12). Wisdom and wealth are also prominent in narratives concerning the Garden of God, which is fertilized with life-giving streams (Gen 2:6, 10-14; Ezek 28:13-14).[142] In Mesopotamian literature, Enki/Ea, the god of wisdom, makes his home in the cosmic fount (*naqbu*).[143] As the god of wisdom, he is also the god of artists and craftsmen, including bronze casters, stone cutters, and jewelers—the basis for his Sumerian epithet, Nudimmud ("image fashioner").[144]

142 Precious stones are also found frequently in Assyrian and Neo-Babylonian building inscriptions as foundation deposits. In re-excavating temple foundations, Mesopotamian kings often claimed to have reached the Apsu. See the inscription of Shalmaneser I in Richard S. Ellis, *Foundation Deposits in Ancient Mesopotamia* (YNER 2; New Haven and London: Yale University Press, 1968), 141, and the inscriptions of Sargon, Esarhaddon, and Sennacherib listed in *CAD* N/1, 110, 2.b, s.v. *nagbu* A. See also the association of precious stones with city foundations in Isa 54:11-12 and Rev 21:11-12, 18-21.

There is also a suggestive parallel in the Ugaritic Kirta text. Throughout the narrative, King Pabuli attempts to bribe Kirta with silver and gold from the royal treasury, along with their "place," and a perpetual servant: *qḥ . ksp . wyrq . ḫrṣ / yd . mqmh . wʿbd . ʿlm* (*CTU* 1.14 iii 22-23; see also v 34-36; vi 4-6): "Take silver and yellow gold / together with its place, and a perpetual servant... " (My translation. Contrast Dennis Pardee, "The Kirta Epic," [*COS* 1.102:335]; and Edward Greenstein, "Kirta," in *Ugaritic Narrative Poetry* [SBLWAW 9; ed. Simon B. Parker; Atlanta, Ga.: Scholars Press, 1997], 16). Though the text is fragmentary, this is presumably the same offer of royal wealth that El makes to Kirta in an attempt to assuage his grief in *CTU* 1.14 i 43-51, just after he offers Kirta kingship (*mlk*) and dominion ([*drk*]*t*) in *CTU* 1.14 i 41-43. In each case, Kirta's response is the same: *lm . ʾank / ksp . w yrq ḫrṣ / yd . mqmh* (*CTU* 1.14 iii 33-34; see also i 51-ii 1; vi 19-20): "What to me is silver or yellow gold, together with its place...?" (translation slightly modified from Greenstein, "Kirta," 13, 17, 22). Thus Kirta rejects El's offer of wealth from his royal treasury, and he will be satisfied only with progeny, of which he is bereft. The preoccupation of the opening line of Job 28 is also a place (*māqôm*) for gold (*zāhāb*) and silver (*kesep*), but I believe the correlations are too general to push a connection.

143 Though the *naqbu* is not exactly synonymous with the Apsu, the term *naqbu* does sometimes refer to waters commonly associated with the Apsu (see Horowitz, *MCG*, 314-15). In glyptic representations, Ea is often seated on his throne in the midst of his secret chamber, which is surrounded by channels of water. See Dominique Collon, *First Impressions: Cylinder Seals in the Ancient Near East* (rev. ed.; London: British Museum Press, 2005), # 760 (p. 164); Rainer Michael Boehmer, *Die Entwicklung der Glyptik während Akkad-Zeit* (UAVA 4; Berlin: Walter de Gruyter, 1965), tables XLII-XLIV, esp. 501, 502, 503, and table XLI, 488; and Hannes D. Galter, *Der Gott Ea/Enki in der Akkadischen Überlieferung. Eine Bestandsaufnahme des vorhanden Materials* (Dissertationen der Karl-Franzens-Universität Graz 58; Graz: Verlag für die Technische Universität Graz, 1983), 111-115.

144 Thorkild Jacobsen, *The Treasures of Darkness: A History of Mesopotamian Religion* (New Haven and London: Yale University Press, 1976), 111. See his appearance with

Crafty wisdom thus resides with Enki/Ea in the sweet, underground waters.

The prologue to the SB Gilg. epic is likewise dominated by images of water and wisdom, and it highlights the two fundamental motifs already noted in the Assyrian royal inscriptions and heroic narratives: (1) the epic journey and its cosmic geography[145] and (2) the motif of the "first discoverer." In fact, the epic recounts *two* journeys beyond the cultured center of Uruk—one to the mountainous Cedar Forest and the other to the "mouth of the rivers" near Utnapishtim's island. It is his second journey, however, for which Gilgamesh is praised as the "first discoverer" of antediluvian wisdom.[146]

The prologue of the SB epic opens with a paean of Gilgamesh's incomparable wisdom gained through his daring adventure to the far-distant cosmic fount: "He who saw the Deep, the country's foundation / Who knew everything, was wise in all matters! (...) / He learnt the sum of wisdom of everything. / He saw what was secret, discovered what was hidden, / He brought back a message from before the flood" (I. 1-2, 6-8).[147] As Stefan Maul points out, the "Deep" (*naqbu*) in the incipit *ša*

craftsmen on seal # 762 in Collon, *First Impressions*, 164. He is called the "carpenter (nagar) of Eridu" in line 38 of *A Hymn to Nisaba (Nisaba A)*. See text and translation of ETCSL 4.16.1 at http://etcsl.orinst.ox.ac.uk/ (="The Blessing of Nisaba by Enki," translated by W. W. Hallo in *COS* 1.163).

145 On the cosmic geography of the Gilg. epic, see especially Horowitz, *MCG*, 96-106.

146 There is some debate over the content of this discovery. The Sum. composition *Death of Bilgames* suggests that it was the rituals and customs of Sumer—specifically hand-washing and mouth-washing. See Andrew George, *The Epic of Gilgamesh: The Babylonian Epic Poem and Other Texts in Akkadian and Sumerian* (London: Penguin, 1999), 198-99; also SB Gilg. I. 43-44.

147 Translation of van der Toorn, "Why Wisdom Became a Secret," 22. Text in George, *BGE*, 1:538. As George points out, Akk. *naqbu* may mean either the "deep body of underground water believed to supply springs and wells, that is, the cosmic realm of Ea better known as the Apsû" or "totality." Both meanings are implied in this instance, but the meaning "wellspring," or, as George translates it, "the Deep," is likely primary (*BGE*, 1:444-45). The latter interpretation is also evident in the most recent scholarly translation of the epic by Stefan Maul, who translates line 1 as »Der, der die Tiefe sah, die Grundfeste des Landes« (*Das Gilgamesch-epos: Neu übersetzt und kommentiert* [Munich: C. H. Beck, 2005], 46).

CAD, however, lists two homonyms, *nagbu* A ("spring, fountain; underground water;" *CAD* N/1, 108-111, s.v.) and *nagbu* B ("totality, all [poetic term];" *CAD* N/1, 111, s.v.), reservedly asserting that its use in the catch-lines of Gilgamesh should be read as *nagbu* B. Von Soden, by contrast reads »Grundwasser, Quellenbereich« in these same catch-lines (*AHw* 2:710, s.v. *nagbu(m)*). As Maul asserts, the ambiguity of the concept of "the Deep" in this line is intentional in the original text (see *Das Gilgamesch-epos*, 153).

naqba īmuru is not only deep water; the water is also a form of deep wisdom.[148]

Set in dialogue with the SB Gilg. epic, the introductory couplets in vv. 1-2 may be seen as a kind of "prologue" to Job 28:3-11. Even as the Sin-liqe-unninni version sets the geographical end of Gilgamesh's journey at the poem's beginning (I. 1-28), the opening couplets in Job 28:1-2 also anticipate the climax of Section One at El's "sources of the rivers" (*mabbĕkê nĕhārôt* [MT *mibbĕkî*], v. 11a) by symbolically projecting a distant place from which a fount of wisdom flows (v. 1). Though this place lies, as Utnapishtim's island does, beyond the known world,[149] the outcome of this exploration may indeed impact the stability of world order.[150] Such paradisiacal projections in the poem's opening couplets are reinforced by their resonance with paradise themes in Israelite literature as well. The clustering of iron (*barzel*), copper (*nĕḥûšâ*), and rock (*ʾeben*) with a fount (*môṣāʾ*) in Job 28:1-2 is remarkable when compared to the Deuteronomic mythic ideal of a promised land "whose rocks (*ʾăbānêhā*) are iron (*barzel*), and from whose hills you may mine copper (*nĕḥōšet*)" (Deut 8:9), in which there are "streams of water, springs, and deeps flowing (*yōṣĕʾîm*) in the valley and in the hills" (8:7).[151]

Attuned now to the poem's more symbolic plane of meaning, the material objects in the first two couplets of Job 28 are figures for the immaterial: wisdom and understanding. This figurative association between wisdom and precious metals is not unique in the ancient Near East. The cuneiform lexical text *CT* 18 29 from the series "*šarru*" contains numerous metaphorical equations in its group vocabulary of valuables. Among these are wisdom, silver, gold, and iron:

148 Maul, *Das Gilgamesch-epos*, 153. Cf. Van Leeuwen: "Here *nagbu* refers not only to the deep waters which Gilgamesh plumbs but also to the wisdom he achieves through his quest" ("Cosmos, Temple, House," 73).

149 Tzvi Abusch, "The Development and Meaning of the Epic of Gilgamesh: An Interpretive Essay," *JAOS* 121/4 (2001): 622 n. 12.

150 Compare the "foundations of the country" (*išdī māti*) in SB Gilg. I. 1, 3, and the comments of George, *BGE*, 2:778-779.

151 The language of mining in the Deuteronomy passage seems to have influenced the OG of Job 28 in v. 2b (λατομέω) and has also likely asserted influence on modern scholars who read the Joban poem in terms of mining technology. See note on *hard* in ch. 4.3.

48. zu ("to know") : *ni-me-qu* ("wisdom")
49. zu ("to know") : KÙ.BABBAR ("silver")
50. zu ("to know") : KÙ.GI ("gold")
51. bar-gal ("great side") : *par-zi-lu* ("iron")[152]

As a result of this association in the Joban poem, the immaterial wisdom and understanding become material, even objectified—a trope that is crucial to the rhetoric of the poem. As Carol Newsom points out, "For the wisdom poem, the 'possession' of wisdom and understanding is the highest value. The governing trope of the poem, which plays on this desire, is the trope of wisdom as object."[153] But what the poem's introduction leaves open at this point (and the prologue to the SB Gilg. epic does not) is the success of the explorer in gaining this "object." In fact, in Job 28:1-2, no explorer or journey is named. That remains for the start of the narrative in the following triplet in v. 3.

For all its romantic vision and projections of epic success, the prologue to the SB Gilg. epic does not completely mask the tragic vision of the OB version to which it was appended.[154] As the last lines of the prologue recount, his journey was laden with dangers[155] (I. 28), and these have been inscribed in lapis lazuli for subsequent generations to read (I. 10, 27). Similarly, a dark subtext whispers around the cosmic fount in Job 28:1-2, even before the journey has begun. The surface of this place is called *ʿāpār* (v. 2a). While the term *ʿāpār* denotes "loose earth" or "dust" in the poem's more realistic plane, in its symbolic plane, it may well connote the Netherworld (see Job 7:21; 17:16; 20:11).[156] At the same

---

152 *CT* 18 29 (= K. 2054 obv.) i 48-51. See Antoine Cavigneaux, »Lexikalische Listen,« *RlA* 6:638. For the autograph copy, see R. Campbell Thompson, *Cuneiform Texts from Babylonian Tablets, &c. in the British Museum. Part XVIII* (London: British Museum, 1904), plate 29. Compare also the friend's description of the sufferer in *The Babylonian Theodicy* as one who is "endowed with all wisdom (*nagab nēmeqi*), jewel of [gold] (*il-lūk li*[*qti*])..." (line 57). See text and translation in Lambert, *BWL*, 74-75, and *CAD* I/J, 86, s.v. *illūku*.

153 Newsom, *Moral Imaginations*, 179.

154 These two "visions" for the OB and SB versions of the Gilg. epic were set forth by Jacobsen, "Romantic and Tragic Vision," 231-249.

155 The phrase here, *ittallaku kalu marṣāti*, recurs in the body of the epic in connection with the travails shared by Gilgamesh and Enkidu, which ended in Enkidu's death (see George, *BGE*, 2:782, and references there).

156 Also noted by Geller, " 'Where is Wisdom?' " 159. On the term *ʿāpār* used in such contexts, see Nicholas J. Tromp, *Primitive Conceptions of Death and the Nether World in the Old Testament* (BibOr 21; Rome: Pontifical Biblical Institute, 1969), 85-91; Delbert R. Hillers, "Dust: Some Aspects of Old Testament Imagery," in *Love and Death in the Ancient Near East: Essays in Honor of Marvin H. Pope* (eds. John H. Marks and Robert M. Good; Guilford, Conn.: Four Quarters Publishing Company, 1987), 105-109; and *HALOT* 2:862 s.v.

time, the phonological similarity of *nĕḥûšâ* ("copper") to *nāḥāš* ("serpent") obliquely anticipates the danger posed by a journey into the realm of the serpentine *bĕnê-šaḥaṣ* of v. 8.[157] If the explorer, like Gilgamesh, is to be successful in becoming wisdom's "first discoverer," he may well have to conquer death to do so.

The journey begins in v. 3, being signaled formally by the introduction of a triplet, in contrast with the poem's two opening couplets. The object of this search is "the stone of deepest gloom" (v. 3b). The emphatically dark imagery in the first and last lines of the triplet may be explained in part by the ideological polarity of a bright, cultivated center and a dark, barbaric periphery in ancient Near Eastern cosmic geography. Yet the final note of "deep gloom" is descriptive not only of the environs beyond the civilized world (see v. 3aβ), but also of the stone itself (v. 3b). Though in a realistic sense, this "stone" may be interpreted as a precious stone, in a symbolic sense, it, like the silver and gold of v. 1, may be understood as wisdom itself. Its obscurity is, perhaps, a by-product of its abode in the watery Apsu at the edge of the world—a deep, dark lair where light does not penetrate.[158]

The loading of the triplet with words for darkness is more than simply descriptive, however. Again the poem whispers of failure, and its etymologizing diction suggests the deadly danger of the search (see *stone of deepest gloom* in ch. 4.3). As Jon Levenson points out, "The Hebrew word *ṣalmāwet*... surely suggests death to the attentive hearer, even if that etymology is unscientific, as many scholars now believe."[159]

---

157 If the orthography of the original poem was conservative, the pun between "copper" (*nĕḥūšā*) and "serpent" (*nāḥāš*) may have been graphic as well. In the most conservative orthography (lacking final *matres lectionis*), both would have been written as NḤŠ. See discussion of the orthography of Job in ch. 4.2.6.

158 Samuel Noah Kramer and John Maier state, "Just as Enki is hidden away in his Sea House, where light does not penetrate, the wisdom that emerges from the waters, carried to humans by the fish-men sages, for example, is 'dark' " (*Myths of Enki, the Crafty God* [New York and Oxford: Oxford University Press, 1989], 201). On the ancient Near Eastern model of depth in the search for wisdom, see Greenstein, "The Poem on Wisdom in Job 28," 258-63, esp. 262-63. Note the connections between depth and wisdom in the Book of Job (11:7-8; 12:22) and the semantic relation between Akk. *nēmequ* ("wisdom") and *emēqu* ("to be deep"), as well as in BH ʿMQ I, which may mean "to be deep" or "to be wise."

159 Jon D. Levenson, *Resurrection and the Restoration of Israel: The Ultimate Victory of the God of Life* (New Haven and London: Yale University Press, 2006), 45. Such an interpretation is clearly evident in the comments of Olympiodorus of Alexandria as preserved in the Syrh. to Job 28 (there attributed to "*ʾlympndrws*"). I paraphrase the Syr.: "He says these stones which are cut off from the mine are placed somewhere in the depth of the earth as though underneath the shadow of death, so that he may say, 'In the depths and in a very deep darkness.' " These comments are taken from Olympiodorus' commentary on Job in Greek. See his "Commentarium in Beatum Job," in

The search for what the rabbinic Targum calls the "chaotic stone"[160] indeed takes place at the earth's horizon,[161] both beyond and beneath civilization.[162] The language of the triplet in v. 3 strongly suggests that it is a search carried out in "death's shadow," where the line between the world and the Underworld is almost indistinguishable.[163]

The two journeys of Gilgamesh in the SB version likewise take the hero beyond the civilized realm of Uruk: first to the Cedar Forest in the West[164] and then to the mouth of the rivers (*pî nārāti*; SB XI. 205-206) near the head of the Persian Gulf to the southeast.[165] The objects of these journeys are not merely precious materials, as in many Sumerian and Akkadian epic narratives. Rather, they are eternal fame and eternal life.

The dangers of the first journey to Humbaba's lair are so daunting that Enkidu advises the elders of Uruk to dissuade Gilgamesh from going. "That journey," he says, "is not one for the making."[166] Nonetheless, Gilgamesh is intent on "travelling the distant path" (SB III. 47-48), even crossing numerous mountain ranges (IV. 234) to meet the ogre in the Forest of Cedar. As he bids farewell, the officers and young men of Uruk are left to plead for Gilgamesh to rely on his more experienced comrade:

> The officers stood there paying him homage,
> in a crowd the young men of Uruk were running behind him,
> and the officers were kissing his feet:
> 'Come back in safety to the quay of Uruk!
> Do not trust, O Gilgamesh, in the fullness of your strength,

---

Hesychii hierosolymitani presbyteri, Olympiodor Alexandrini, Leontii Neapoleos in Cyro Episcopi, Opera omnia (PG 93; ed. J.-P. Migne; Paris: Migne, 1860), col. 287.

160 *ʾbnym mpwlmn*. See Marcus Jastrow, *A Dictionary of the Targumim, the Talmud Babli and Yerushalmi, and the Midrashic Literature* (2 vols; London: Luzac; New York: G. Putnam's Sons, 1903), 2:1183, s.v. *pālam*.

161 See Newsom, "The Book of Job," 529.

162 In Mesopotamian cosmic geography, this would be the *erṣētu qablītu*. See Horowitz, *MCG*, 18-19, 274, 334-347.

163 Compare William McKane: "[T]he 'uttermost end' (28,3b) of their excavation is where the world becomes the underworld, where the earth ends and Sheol is reached" ("The Theology of the Book of Job," 715).

164 In earlier Mesopotamian traditions (including the Sum. Gilg. compositions), the Cedar Forest was figured as lying outside of Mesopotamia in the mountains of western Persia. By the time of the SB epic, however, the location of the forest had moved to the Amanus or the Lebanon in the West, due to gradual deforestation in the East (David Damrosch, *The Buried Book: The Loss and Rediscovery of the Great Epic of Gilgamesh* [New York: Henry Holt and Company, 2006], 206-208).

165 For a discussion of the location of the *pî nārāti*, see George, *BGE*, 1:519-21; and Horowitz, *MCG*, 104-105.

166 SB Gilg. II. 275. Translation in George, *BGE*, 1:569.

let your eyes be satisfied, strike a blow to rely on!
"He who goes in front saves (his) comrade,
he who knows the road should [protect] his friend."
Let Enkidu go in front of you,
he knows the way to the Forest of Cedar!
He is tried in battle and [experienced] in combat,
to the mountain passes [......]...'[167]

Journeying for three days at a time for fifteen days, Gilgamesh and Enkidu traverse a distance that would normally take seven and a half months (Tablet IV).[168] Finally reaching the abode of the gods, they crawl through the forest's dense undergrowth in darkness (V. 1-15).[169]

Gilgamesh's second journey takes him to the edge of the world, to the boundary between darkness and light. Leaving Uruk once again and making his way "around the mountains, [to] the hidden road where the sun rises,"[170] he outruns Shamash (IX. 170) through the dark entrails of Mt. Mashu. The repetition of "darkness" and "no light" throughout Tablet IX (83, 140-165) strongly suggests that this impenetrable gloom *(ekletum)* is the Underworld itself, the nocturnal course of the sun.[171]

Despite all of its dark symbolism, the language of "binding the darkness" in the first line of the triplet in the Joban poem (v. 3a) attributes to the explorer success of cosmic proportions. As Alviero Niccacci states, "the language with which the human work is described is loaded with divine reverberations. That is to say, the search for metals is presented in a magnificent light. The man here ... seems to take part in the omnipotence of God."[172] This separation of light and darkness recalls God's creative acts in Gen 1:4—one who can stand outside the limits that confine created things (cf. Ps 119:96; 104:9) and give form to the formless (cf. Job 28:26a). The verbal echoes in v. 3a of Zophar's

167 SB Gilg. III. 212-223. Translation in George, *BGE*, 1:585.

168 George, *BGE*, 1:463.

169 Though in SB Gilg. V. 8 the shade (*ṣillu*) is said to be pleasant (*ṭābu*), note similar imagery connected with ventures into the forest in *Sargon, the Conquering Hero* (ii. 59-64) and *Sargon in Foreign Lands* (iv. 9'-11') in which such darkness represents the opposition of the forest to the king's expedition. See Westenholz, *Legends of the Kings of Akkade*, 68-71 and 90-91.

170 OB Gilg. VA+BM iv. 10-11. Translation in George, *BGE*, 1:281.

171 See Maureen Gallery Kovacs, *The Epic of Gilgamesh. Translated, with an Introduction, and Notes* (Stanford, Ca.: Stanford University Press, 1985), 77 n. 2. The term *ekletum* is often used as an epithet for the Underworld. See *CAD* I/J, 60-61, s.v. *ikletu*. Contrast George, *BGE*, 1:494.

172 Niccacci, "Giobbe 28," 42-43 (my translation).

mocking query in Job 11:7 suggest that the dark land to be explored in this journey is the terrain of God: "Would you find out the depth (*haḥēqer*) of Eloah? / or would you attain to the boundary (*taklît*) of Shaddai?

The role of such divine imagery in v. 3 and throughout Section One is a crucial but disputed point of interpretation. Is the subject of this search divine, or is it a human poetically invested with divine powers? The difficulty of the question is exacerbated by the grammatical construction of v. 3aα, in which the subject is oddly marked by the independent pronoun *hûʾ* with no antecedent (see *he* in ch. 4.3). This creates a sort of cryptic riddle which requires solution.[173] The difficulty in solving this riddle is illustrated well by Samuel Balentine's interpretation in which he encourages readers to imagine *three* subjects searching for three objects: miners for metals, Job for meaning, and God for wisdom.[174]

Most ancient interpreters, however, understood the subject to be God. The translators of the Old Greek interpreted the text in this way[175] before 100 B.C.E.[176] and were followed centuries later by the Peshitta and rabbinic Targums. Modern interpreters, however, are divided on the issue. On the one hand, Stephen Geller states, "The subject of the verse is certainly man."[177] Yet Martijn Houtsma asserts with equal confidence, "[Das] Subjekt von שׂם ist selbstverständlich Gott..."[178] Though most would understand a human (miner) to be the subject in vv. 3-11, the "divine imagery" in these verses has led some to return to the ancient view that *God* is the subject, as he searches out deep wisdom.[179]

---

173 See also the comments of Hoffman, *A Blemished Perfection*, 279; Clines, *Job 21-37*, 911; and Fiddes, " 'Where Shall Wisdom be Found?' " 172.

174 Balentine, *Job*, 418-21.

175 See Markus Witte, "The Greek Book of Job," in *Das Buch Hiob und seine Interpretationen. Beiträge zum Hiob-Symposium auf dem Monte Verità von 14.-19. August 2005* (ed. T. Krüger et al.; ATANT 88; ed. Erhard Blum et al.; Zürich: Theologischer Verlag Zürich, 2007), 47; Greenstein, "The Poem on Wisdom in Job 28," 267-269 and nn. 32-33; Hartley, *Job*, 27 n. 20.

176 100 B.C.E. is a *terminus ad quem* for LXX-Job, since the historian Aristeas knew the appendix, as suggested by Eusebius' comments in *Praeparatio Evangelica* 9.25 (see Dhorme, *Book of Job*, xviii, cxcvi). However, if one takes the appendix as secondary, there is nothing to prevent dating the OG to the mid-3rd to mid-2nd century B.C.E. On a date in the mid-2nd c. B.C.E., see Witte, "The Greek Book of Job," 53.

177 Geller, " 'Where is Wisdom?' " 178 n. 8.

178 Houtsma, *Textkritische Studien*, 63.

179 See Greenstein, "The Poem on Wisdom in Job 28," 268-69; Elwolde, "Non-Contiguous Parallelism," 103-18; Tur-Sinai, *The Book of Job*, 396; and Michel, "The Ugaritic Texts," 408. For Ibn Ezra, Rashi, and Kimchi, see Hoffman, *A Blemished Perfection*, 280 n. 28.

Greenstein states, "[I]t seems to me highly doubtful that any Biblical author, even the iconoclastic poet of Job, would attribute the prerogatives of the divine creator to mere mortals."[180]

However, superhuman feats are part and parcel of ancient Near Eastern epic patterning. Among such patterns is the "mythicizing of the protagonist," who is at once a historical figure and a mythic hero.[181] As Scott Noegel points out, "[T]he hero undertake[s] quests to distant and dangerous places... which distinguish him from ordinary men."[182] He is, as Favaro states, "un être surhumain qui traverse la condition humaine..."[183] While Job 28:3-11 falls far short of typical epic form, the twenty poetic lines in vv. 3-11 undoubtedly exhibit numerous "mythic patterns" found in Mesopotamian epics and Assyrian royal narratives. The explorer in these lines is mortal; but he is not a *mere* mortal.

Considered along these lines, the poem in Job 28 may once again be fruitfully compared with the Gilgamesh epic, where Gilgamesh's accomplishments of heroic feats normally attributed to the gods are famously prominent. The claim of what was originally the incipit to the OB epic, "Surpassing all other kings" (*šūtur eli šarri*, SB I. 29), is given content by recounting his parentage: "Wild bull of Lugalbanda, Gilgamesh, perfect of strength, / suckling of the exalted cow, Wild-Cow Ninsun!" (I. 35-36). Gilgamesh is, impossibly, two-thirds god and one-third human (I. 48), a fact later recognized both by the scorpion-men guarding Mt. Mashu (IX. 49-51) and by Utnaptishtim (X. 268-69). With these superhuman powers, he is twice able to accomplish the divine prerogatives of Shamash as no human before him had done (IX. 80-170; X. 79-82).

The journey motif continues with the triplet in v. 4, informed by the epic theme of the "difficult road," which Mesopotamian monarchs claim to have overcome time and again with their heroic might.[184] This is not a prosaic description of a miner's descent into a dark vertical shaft (see *He breaches course<s> far from dwellers* in ch. 4.3). Rather, these lines extend the horizontal dimension set out in v. 3aβ—the probing of a geographical frontier (*lĕkol-taklît*). In the construction of what Sabrina Favaro calls "heroic space,"[185] ancient Near Eastern epics and royal narratives commonly depict the peripheral region beyond civilization as

180 Greenstein, "The Poem on Wisdom in Job 28," 269.

181 See Favaro, *Voyages et voyageurs*, 107-108, then 104.

182 Scott Noegel, "Mesopotamian Epic," in *A Companion to Ancient Epic* (ed. John Miles Foley; Malden, Mass.; Oxford; and Carlton, Victoria: Blackwell, 2005), 243.

183 Favaro, *Voyages et voyageurs*, 104.

184 See ibid., 110.

185 Ibid., 124-129.

one of treacherous mountains, scorching deserts, and massive expanses of water. The space is only "heroic," however, insofar as the explorer is able to overcome the obstacles it poses to his becoming "first discoverer." To do so, he must breach courses in the formless steppe or in the impenetrable mountains—an action depicted in the first line of the triplet in v. 4aα (*pāraṣ nĕḥāl<īm>*). The second and third lines of the triplet (vv. 4aβ-b) which underscore the lack of human habitation might be understood as an Israelite echo of a boast common in Mesopotamian epics and royal inscriptions, touting the king as the one who, by reaching the world's end, has accomplished what none of his ancestors before him had been able to achieve.[186] He is the lone human in a land without residents or itinerants.

The conquest of heroic space is also prominent in the opening of the Gilgamesh epic, which emphasizes Gilgamesh's feats as world explorer, enacted through his might:

> Gilgamesh so tall, perfect and terrible,
> who opened passes in the mountains (*petû nērebēti ša ḫursāni*);
> who dug wells on the hill-flanks (*ḫerû būrī kišād* (GÚ) *šadî* (KUR))
> and crossed the ocean, the wide sea, as far as the sunrise;
> who scoured the edges of the world (*kibrāti*) ever searching for life,
> and reached by his strength Uta-napishti the Far-Away.[187]

This is the vaunted recollection of the exploits of a hero who has come home. But the Gilgamesh we find in tablets IX and X does not rise above the perils of the epic's heroic space; rather, he slowly becomes more and more like the wilderness in which he wanders—a fact painfully evident to his three conversation partners at world's end.[188] Gilgamesh responds to the queries of Utnapishtim in Tablet X: "...I went journeying through all the lands. / I passed time and again over arduous mountains, / and I crossed time and again all the seas. / My face did not have enough of sweet sleep, / I scourged myself by going sleepless.

186 See the phrase "where no [one] among the kings my forefathers had passed" (*a-šar ina* MAN.MEŠ-*ni* AD.MEŠ-*i*[*a mamma*] *ina lìb-bi la-a e-te-qu*) in the annals of Tukulti-Ninurta II from Assur (RIMA 2 A.0.100.5:33-34). Similar heroic boasts are conveniently collected in Favaro, *Voyages et voyageurs*, 113-24.

187 SB Gilg. I. 37-42. The translation here is a modification of George, *BGE*, 1:541, in light of the translation of Stephanie Dalley in *Myths from Mesopotamia: Creation, the Flood, Gilgamesh, and Others* (rev. ed.; Oxford: Oxford University Press, 2000), 51. Dalley translates *kibrāti* as "edges of the world," while George translates with "world-regions." See *CAD* K, 331-33, s.v. *kibrāti* and 334-36 s.v. *kibru*.

188 See SB Gilg. X. 40-45 (ale-wife); X. 113-118 (Ur-Shanabi); X. 213-18 (Utnapishtim).

/ I kept filling my sinews with pain; / what have I achieved by my toil?[189]

The form and diction of v. 4 of the Joban poem intimate the same end for the explorer there. The terseness of the last line in v. 4b (as restored: *dallû mēʾĕnôš*; see *They are bereft of humanity* in ch. 4.3) is more than simply descriptive of the environment beyond civilization. It also suggests that the hero may finally be "cut off" from humanity as he succumbs to the dangers of this peripheral zone. The term *naḥal*, too, foreshadows a dark end to this adventure, being used in the OT not only of a passageway through the earth, but also of Sheol (2 Sam 22:5 // Ps 18:5), the grave (Job 21:32-33), and possibly shaft-tombs (Isa 54:5).[190] From this perspective, the explorer in Job 28:4 may not only be breaking open a corridor in the mountains; he may also be digging his own grave. The words of Lugalbanda's comrades to him before his return to Unug from Aratta are perhaps fitting here: "You will not come back from the great mountains, where no one goes alone, / whence no one returns to mankind!"[191]

Despite these dark undertones, the divine imagery begun in v. 3 is carried through in the triplet in v. 4. The ability to breach *nĕḥālīm* outside of the civilized world (v. 4aα) strongly connotes the creation of watercourses in deserted regions—an action commonly attributed to God in the OT (Isa 11:15; Hab 3:9; Ps 74:15; 78:20; 104:10; cf. Exod 17:6; Josh 3:16). J. J. M. Roberts comments, "Yahweh's splitting open of the earth with rivers recalls the motif in which the cosmogonic warrior, after having subdued the waters of chaos, reorders them as manageable sources of water for the benefit of his structured world."[192] The term *naḥal* in v. 4 thus contributes to the water imagery prominent throughout Section One (vv. 1a, 10a, 11a) and to the poetic depiction of an explorer who, by mastering the formless forces of darkness and water (vv. 3-4), may well take part in creating the strange but beautiful landscape through which he ventures.

The two couplets in vv. 5-6 describe a lush paradise thick with vegetation and precious stones. Dense overgrowth figures prominently in ancient accounts of highland adventures by Mesopotamian kings.

---

189 SB Gilg. X. 251-57.

190 On the connection with the cult of the dead and shaft tombs in Isa 54:5, see Theodore Lewis, *Cults of the Dead in Ancient Israel and Ugarit* (HSM 39; Atlanta, Ga.: Scholars, 1989), 157.

191 *Lugalbanda and the Anzud Bird*, lines 335-336. Translation in *LAS*, 29. Transliteration in Vanstiphout, *Epics of Sumerian Kings*, 152.

192 Roberts, *Nahum, Habakkuk, and Zephaniah: A Commentary* (OTL; Louisville, Ky.: Westminster John Knox, 1991), 155-56.

Sargon II's *Letter to Assur*, for example, describes fantastic fruit-bearing trees in the mountains of Urartu.[193] Most commonly, however, these expeditions are set in a cedar forest either in the Lebanon or the Amanus in the West,[194] and by felling and bringing home cedars as an exotic product of the mountains, the monarch is depicted as "king of the wood" (cf. Isa 14:8; 37:24).[195]

Journeys both to Cedar Mountains and to groves of fruit-bearing trees figure prominently in the SB Gilg. epic. Gilgamesh's first heroic venture beyond Uruk takes him and Enkidu to the Cedar Mountain, whose marvels are described in Tablet V:

> "They were gazing at the Cedar Mountain, the dwelling of the gods, the throne-dais of the goddesses, / [on the] very face of the mountain the cedar was proffering its abundance, / sweet was its shade, full of delight. / [All] tangled was the thorny undergrowth, the forest was a thick canopy..."[196]

In the SB epic, the lush beauty of the mountain forest speaks to its cosmic status as the "secret abode of the Anunnaki."[197]

---

193 See *ARAB* 2, §§142, 170. These are likely meant to echo the famous journey of his namesake, Sargon the Great, to Purušḫanda, as recounted in the *King of Battle* epic (obv., line 29; rev., lines 24'-26'; text and translation in Westenholz, *Legends of the Kings of Akkade*, 118-121, 128-29).

194 This is a common *topos* from the OAkk period onward. For inscriptional evidence pertaining to Sargon the Great, Yaḫdun-Lim, Shamshi-Adad I, and others, see Abraham Malamat, "Campaigns to the Mediterranean by Iaḫdunlim and Other Early Mesopotamian Rulers," in *Studies in Honor of Benno Landsberger on his Seventy-Fifth Birthday, April 21, 1965* (eds. Hans G. Güterbock and Thorkild Jacobsen; *AS* 16; Chicago: University of Chicago, 1965), 365-75. See also *Gudea Cylinder A* xv 19-22 in Thureau-Dangin, *SAK*, 104-107 (translation in Jacobsen, *Harps*, 407); *The Sargon Geography* in Westenholz, *Legends of the Kings of Akkade*, 69; "Naram-Sin in the Cedar Mountain" in *ANET*, 268; Assurnasirpal II's annals in *ARAB* 1, §479; Shalmaneser III's annals in *ARAB* 1, §633; and references in Manfred Weippert, »Libanon,« *RlA* 6:644.

195 The phrase "king of the wood" is from Aaron Shaffer, "Gilgamesh, the Cedar Forest, and Mesopotamian History," *JAOS* 103 (1983): 307. This is well illustrated by the foundation inscription of Yaḫdun-Lim from the Shamash temple at Mari, ii 1-9: "To the Cedar and Boxwood Mountain, the great mountains, he penetrated, and boxwood, cedar, cypress, and *elammakum* trees, these trees he cut down. He stripped (the forest) bare, established his name, and made known his might" (translation of Malamat, "Campaigns to the Mediterranean," 367 and n. 12; text in Georges Dossin, "L'inscription de fondation de Iaḫdunlim, roi de Mari," *Syria* 32 [1955]: 13).

196 SB Gilg. V. 6-9. Translation in George, *BGE* 1:603. This journey in the SB epic has a Sumerian predecessor in *Bilgames and Huwawa* (see George, *The Epic of Gilgamesh*, 149-66).

197 This phrase is found in the OB fragments from Iščali (tablet A 22007, or the "Bauer tablet"), line 38' (George, *BGE*, 1:264-65), and in the OB fragment in the Iraq Museum (OB IM), line 18 (*BGE*, 1:268-71).

The two Joban couplets, however, are concerned more with the precious stones that this paradise affords (vv. 5b-6) than with its foliage (v. 5a). In this respect, it is Gilgamesh's second journey that best illustrates the symbolic dimensions of the imagery in vv. 5-7. Having traversed the darkness beneath Mt. Mashu, he reaches a brilliant jeweled garden at the edge of the world "where trees and shrubs produce precious stones instead of foliage and fruit."[198] The narrator recounts in Tablet IX: "...there was brilliance: He went forward, seeing [...], the *trees of the gods.* / The carnelian bore its fruit, / Like bunches of grapes dangling, lovely to see, / The lapis bore foliage, / Fruit it bore, a delight to behold."[199] This magical depiction, like that in Job 28:5-6 which figures a land with lapis stones and gold dust, is certainly meant to transport the reader beyond the world of ordinary experience. Even if the divine status of this garden is not clear in the text of the epic itself, it is surely of cosmic import, as it lies between the cosmic Mt. Mashu (see IX. 37-41) and the seaside tavern of Shiduri, "a mysterious goddess of wisdom."[200]

The two precious stones named in the Joban text—lapis and gold—are connected both with the mountains and with the divine in Ugaritic mythic texts. El in his wisdom declares that Baal should have a house like the other gods (*CTU* 1.4 iv 62 – v 1), and Athirat concurs: "Let it be told to Mightiest Baal: ... 'Let the mountains bring you abundant silver, The hills, the choicest gold (*ḫrṣ*); Let the best ore be brought to you. And build the house with silver and gold (*ḫrṣ*), The house with purest lapis lazuli (*iqnim*).' "[201] After commissioning Kothar wa-Hasis for the task, the precious materials are set aflame, and the silver and gold become plates and bricks, fused together into a resplendent palace (*hkl*)[202] atop Mt. Ṣapān.

The language and imagery of Job 28:5-6 may similarly conjure up a mountainous dwelling place of the gods, studded with precious stones. In this respect the two couplets resonate with the biblical traditions which fuse the cosmic mountain and the garden of God motifs, such as

198 Horowitz, *MCG*, 100.

199 SB Gilg. IX. 171-176. Translation of line 171 is from George, *BGE*, 1:673. See also discussion in ibid., 2:867 n. 171. Translation of lines 172-76 is from Benjamin R. Foster, ed., *The Epic of Gilgamesh: A New Translation, Analogues, Criticism* (New York and London: W. W. Norton, 2001), 70 (my italics indicate difficulty with the text). Part of line 172 is broken and requires restoration. See discussion on the textual difficulties of line 172 in George, *BGE*, 2:867 n. 172, and contrast the reading of Dalley, *Myths from Mesopotamia*, 99 and 131 n. 104.

200 George, *BGE*, 1:498.

201 *CTU* 1.4 v 15-19. Translation of Smith, "The Baal Cycle," 130.

202 *CTU* 1.4 vi 22-38. See also Pope, *El in the Ugaritic Texts*, 100-101.

those in Ezek 28:13-14 and Gen 2:10-14.[203] Their diction (YṢʾ, *māqôm*, *ʾeben*, *zāhāb*, and ʿPR) also repeats the language of the two introductory couplets in vv. 1-2, suggesting that this magical landscape of precious stones is also the locus of the cosmic fount (*môṣāʾ*, v. 1a) for silver or, in the poem's more symbolic plane, for wisdom. The place depicted in Job 28:5-6 is, perhaps, like the Solomonic temple, "a mythopoeic realization of heaven on earth, of Paradise, the Garden of Eden." [204] Indeed, the rabbis understood v. 6 precisely in this way, as the Targum specifies that this place of sapphire stones (*šbzyzʾ*, translating *sappîr*) and gold dust is the Garden of Eden (*gntʾ dʿdn*).[205]

Yet as with the preceding lines, a deep duality characterizes the more symbolic plane of meaning in vv. 5-6, as their language and imagery reverberate with negative as well as positive connotations. Though transparently a reference to the land in which the superhuman venture in Section One is undertaken, *ʾereṣ* in v. 5a may simultaneously connote the realm of the dead, as it does elsewhere in the Book of Job (10:21-22; 3:14; possibly 18:17 et al.).[206] The same is true for *taḥtît* in v. 5b (Job 26:5; 40:12; 34:26). In fact, the two terms *ereṣ* // *taḥtît* in v. 5 are collocated in the phrase *ʾereṣ taḥtît* in Ezek 31:14, which clearly refers to the Netherworld.[207] As Stephen Geller points out, *nehpak* in v. 5b is used elsewhere "almost as a technical term for the overthrow of Sodom."[208] The simile "like fire" in that line, interpreted here as a description of the appearance of precious stones, may also resonate with Mesopotamian descriptions of evil demons who roam the steppe, "scorching the country like fire" (see *beneath transformed as fire* in ch. 4.3). The positive

---

203 Some scholars believe that the association of Eden and the mountain of God is late and peculiar to the work of the Ezekielian school (see Clifford, *Cosmic Mountain*, 103, 159). Contrast especially Gary A. Anderson, "The Cosmic Mountain: Eden and Its Early Interpreters in Syriac Christianity," in *Genesis 1-3 in the History of Exegesis: Intrigue in the Garden* (Studies in Women and Religion 27; ed. Gregory Allen Robbins; Lewiston and Queenston: The Edwin Mellen Press, 1988), 187-224; and Levenson, *Sinai and Zion*, 131.

204 On this Eden-temple homology, see Lawrence Stager, "Jerusalem and the Garden of God," *ErIsr* 26 (1999): 191*; idem, "Jerusalem as Eden," *BAR* 26/3 (May-June, 2000): 36-47, 66.

205 The identification of Job with Adam provided the basis for some of the Targum's expansions, as Céline Mangan points out ("The Interpretation of Job in the Targums," in *The Book of Job* [ed. W.A.M. Beuken; BETL 114; Leuven: Leuven University Press, 1994], 276). However, these expansions are rooted in the strongly suggestive Garden of God imagery of its Heb. *Vorlage* in vv. 5-6, even if the Tg. ultimately moves well beyond it.

206 See *HALOT* 1: 90-91 s.v. *ʾereṣ*, and Tromp, *Primitive Conceptions*, 23-46.

207 The Ezekielian phraseology is semantically parallel to an Akk. epithet for the Netherworld, *erṣētu šaplītu*. See Horowitz, *MCG*, 18-19, 274.

208 Geller, " 'Where is Wisdom?' " 162 and references there.

metaphor GOLD IS DUST, found in LB age international correspondence with Egypt,[209] is reversed to DUST IS GOLD with *ʿaprōt zāhāb* in the second line of v. 6, focusing more on the physical makeup of the land than on the vast amount of precious objects that are found there (for the latter, see Zech 9:3; Job 27:16). Yet *ʿaprōt* also contributes to the couplet's dark subtext by connoting the dusty place of death.[210] In fact, in Ugaritic literature *ʿpr* and *ʾrṣ* are a formulaic pair used to designate the Underworld (see *CTU* 1.161:21-22). Finally, the disjointed syntax of v. 6 thrusts the resumptive *lô* to the end of the couplet where it hangs awkwardly but phonetically anticipates the negative particle *lōʾ* in every line of the two couplets in vv. 7-8 (see *which has dust of gold* in ch. 4.3), perhaps as a warning to those who would try to reach this magically dangerous place.

This dark subtext is recognized already in the rabbinic Targum, which interprets the phrase *nehpak kĕmô-ʾēš* in v. 5b as a reference to Gehenna (*gyhnm*, Tg. 1), lying just below the Garden of Eden. In Tg. 2, Gehenna is identified with Sodom, a reading reflected also in rabbinic midrash[211] and in the Babylonian Talmud.[212] This association with Sodom is based on its reputation as a fertile paradise like the Garden of God (Gen 13:10) and its destruction by fire (Gen 19:24-25). However, in ancient Near Eastern terms, it is the cosmic mountain that, as the axis of the world, joins heaven and hell.[213] Having travelled beyond space and time, it seems that the human has reached a dwelling place of the gods, in all its beauty and danger.

The description of this magical but potentially perilous landscape continues in the two couplets in vv. 7-8, which narrow the focus now to a "path" (v. 7a). In the poem's symbolic plane, this is a path not only to silver and gold, but to wisdom and understanding. However, these two couplets repeatedly declare the ignorance of both birds and beasts in locating wisdom's way, with the negative particle *lōʾ* present in each one of their four syntactically matched lines (*lōʾ*-VERB-OBJECT-SUBJECT).

---

209 See EA 16 from Assyria and EA 19 from Mittani. Translation in Moran, *Amarna Letters*, 39, 44. EA 16 was pointed out by Geller, " 'Where is Wisdom?' " 162. This metaphor was apparently generated out of envy for Egypt's ready supply of gold as an exotic luxury (on which see Van De Mieroop, *A History of the Ancient Near East*, 132-33).

210 Again see *ʿāpār* in Job 7:21; 17:16; 20:11; Tromp, *Primitive Conceptions*, 85-91; Hillers, "Dust," 105-109; and *HALOT* 2:862 s.v.

211 Midr. Rab. Lev 4:1; 5:2; Num 9:24 (Midr. Rab. Lev 5:2 noted by Geller, " 'Where is Wisdom?' " 162).

212 See *b. San.* 109a.

213 Clifford, *Cosmic Mountain*, 6-8, 21.

While the birds in v. 7 function poetically as keen-eyed creatures of the heavens who are nevertheless ignorant of the path to wisdom, as predators they are at the same time above-ground signs of death on the surface of the earth, contributing to the sense of danger lurking within the magical topography of this distant place. The phonology of both couplets provides an audible warning of this danger, with the onomatopoeic *ʾayyâ*, mimicking the sound of the falcon's cry (v. 7b),[214] and the serpentine hiss created by the repetition of *šîn*, *ḥêt*, and *ṣādê* (v. 8).

The poetic function of the serpents in v. 8a is more than simply about distance or danger. The serpent is notoriously adept at slithering through the most difficult passageways, and, as a "creature of the dust" (Gen 3:14; Deut 32:24; Mic 7:17), it would seem well suited to locate the paradisiacal place of lapis and gold dust (*ʿaprōt zāhāb*, v. 6). The wisdom of serpents, which was virtually axiomatic in the ancient Near East (Gen 3:1; Matt 10:16; SB Gilg. XI. 305-14), would seem to afford them a distinct advantage as well.[215] But despite their physical fitness and their famed shrewdness, the serpents in Job 28:8a have not thrashed upon wisdom's path. The earth-bound *šaḥal* in the parallel line is notoriously difficult to identify (see *lion* in ch. 4.3). Despite the fact that the term is used in the Book of Job of lions, the phonology of vv. 8a-9a strongly suggests that the *šaḥal*, like the serpent in v. 8a, exhibits reptilian qualities: ... *bĕnê-šaḥaṣ* ... / ... *šaḥal* ... / *baḥallāmîš šālaḥ*.

The animals of the two couplets in vv. 7 and 8 are, like those in Job 38:39-39:30, "associated with places outside of and opposed to the human cultural sphere."[216] The danger posed by these chaotic creatures, however, may be more than simply "realistic."[217] Even their identity challenges modern zoological conceptions.[218] In the poem's symbolic

---

214 *HALOT* 1:39, s.v.; G. R. Driver, "Birds in the Old Testament I: Birds in Law," *PEQ* 87 (1955): 11; idem, "Birds in the Old Testament II: Birds in Life," *PEQ* 87 (1955): 140.

215 As noted by Geller, " 'Where is Wisdom?' " 163-64.

216 Carol A. Newsom, "The Moral Sense of Nature: Ethics in Light of God's Speech," *PSB* N.S. 15 (1994): 22. She cites Othmar Keel, *Jahwes Entgegnung an Hiob* (Göttingen: Vandenhoeck & Ruprecht, 1978) in ibid., 21 n. 7. See also Dick, "The Neo-Assyrian Royal Lion Hunt," 265-66.

217 In the biblical worldview, demons were often thought to inhabit deserted regions beyond civilization (Lev 16:8-10, 21; Tob 8:3; Matt 12:43; Lk 11:24; and imagery in Job 30:1-8). See also Favaro, *Voyages et voyageurs*, 128, on the demonic in NA inscriptions.

218 Such ambiguity is also evident in terms which may mean either "lion" or "serpent" in Akk. (*nēšu*, *bašmu*, and also *labbu*) and possibly also in Sum. (ušum-gal). Jacobsen comments on the ušumgal in line 351 of *Enmerkar and the Lord of Aratta*: "Mentions of it would make one think of a lion or a tiger, but the ancients classed it with serpents" (*Harps*, 303 n. 51). Jacobsen translates with "basilisk," while Vanstiphout translates with "dragon" (*Epics of Sumerian Kings*, 77). The simile in lines 348-51 of *Enmerkar and the Lord of Aratta* suggests that the ušumgal had powerful legs: "...the envoy going to

plane, the clustering of birds of prey, serpents, and lions may well evoke composite creatures common in Mesopotamian epic traditions, such as lion-serpents and lion-eagles. The catalogue of fauna of distant lands in the Babylonian Map of the World illustrates well the fact that the lines between more "realistic" creatures and more fantastic ones was not very sharp in ancient Near Eastern thought, as it lists the "horned viper" (*bašmu*) and "sea-serpent" (*mušḫuššu*)[219] together with the Anzu-bird, the scorpion man, and the lion (*nēšu*).[220] The zoological ambiguity in the Joban text has also influenced the translations of the rabbinic Targum in vv. 7-8. In Tg. 1, Heb. *ʿayiṭ* in the first line of v. 7 is identified with Sammael (*smʾl*), and the *ʾayyâ* of the second line is translated with "serpent" (*ḥwyh*).[221] In v. 8, Heb. *šaḥal* is translated as "snake" (*ḥywyʾ*) in one tradition (Tg. 1) and "lion" (*lywnʾ*) in another (Tg. 2).

While lions feature in the Gilg. epic, as in Assyrian royal inscriptions, as creatures of the wild found outside of the civilized world (SB Gilg. VIII. 16; cf. X. 259), more prominent in the Mesopotamian narrative are mythical monsters which bar the hero's way on each of his epic voyages.[222] In his first journey it is Humbaba who stands in the path to the secret abode of the gods. Enkidu fearfully describes the demon of the Cedar Mountain: "Humbaba, his voice is the Deluge, / his speech is fire, his breath is death. / He hears the forest's murmur for sixty leagues; / who is there who would venture into his forest?"[223] In his

---

Aratta / plunged his foot into the dust of the road, /sent rattling little stones / of the mountain ranges, / like a [ušumgal] prowling its desert, / he had none opposing him" (translation in Jacobsen, *Harps*, 303). The Akk. *ušumgallu* (< Sum. ušum-gal), in fact, is another name for the *mušḫuššu*.

219 The *mušḫuššu* is a composite lion-eagle-serpent (on which, see especially F.A.M. Wiggermann, "mušḫuššu," *RlA* 8:455-462). A classical representation of the *mušḫuššu*-dragon is on the Ishtar gate from Babylon, now partially reconstructed in the Vorderasiatisches Museum in Berlin. See sketch in Dalley, *Myths from Mesopotamia*, 316; glyptic representations in Collon, *First Impressions*, ## 896 (p. 185), 785-86 (p. 168). For a review of iconographic evidence, see W. G. Lambert, "The History of the muš-ḫuš in Ancient Mesopotamia," in *L'animal, l'homme, le dieu dans le proche orient ancient* (ed. P. Borgeaud et al.; Leuven: Peeters, 1985), 87-94.

220 BM 92687, obv. 5'-8'. See Horowitz, *MCG*, 22-23, 33-36. For the reading *girtablullû* for "scorpion-man," see ibid., 22 n. 3; sketch in Dalley, *Myths from Mesopotamia*, 316.

221 See discussion under *bird of prey* and *falcon* in ch. 4.3.

222 Though lions are not cosmic guardians in the Gilg. literature, it is clear that they served in such a function in ancient Mesopotamian culture. Note, for example, the two large basalt lions from Eridu that guarded Enki's temple, Eengura, during the Neo-Sumerian period, now housed in the Iraq Museum (IM 60981). See photograph in Adam Falkenstein and Wolfram von Soden, *Sumerische und akkadische Hymnen und Gebete* [Zürich and Stuttgart: Artemis-Verlag, 1953], 192.

223 SB Gilg. II. 221-24. Text and translation in *BGE*, 1:566-67.

second journey, terrible scorpion-men guard the pass beneath the cosmic Mt. Mashu, this time in the East: "[T]here were scorpion-men guarding its gate, / whose terror was dread and glance was death, / whose radiance was terrifying, enveloping the uplands..."[224]

While the Gilg. epic does not employ birds to a similar effect, they are prominent in the Sumerian narratives about Gilgamesh's father, Lugalbanda.[225] Marching under Enmerkar's command from Unug to Aratta, Lugulbanda falls ill and is left by his troops in a cave "on the unknown way at the edge of the mountains."[226] After tearful prayers to the gods, he eventually leaves behind the Cypress Mountains and, as the narrative continues in *Lugalbanda and the Anzud Bird*, he ventures into the Zabu range where he encounters a monstrous bird which is half-lion and half-eagle—the guardian of this mountain region.[227] The narrator describes the Anzud: "When at daybreak the bird stretches himself, / when at sunrise Anzud cries out, / at his cry the ground quakes in the Lulubi mountains. / He has a shark's teeth and an eagle's claws. / In terror of him wild bulls run away into the foothills, / stags run away into their mountains."[228]

Just as the winged guardian of the uplands in the Lugalbanda narrative is no ordinary bird, the reptiles in v. 8 of the Joban poem are not ordinary snakes (see *serpents* in ch. 4.3). In the only other occurrence of the phrase in the OT, the *bĕnê-šaḥaṣ* are said to be the underlings of Leviathan (Job 41:26), clearly described as a fire-breathing dragon of the sea (41:4-26). This fact is reflected also in the translation of *bĕnê-šaḥaṣ* in 11Q10 with "sea-serpent" (*tnyn*). The beast thus evoked is of the same kind as the *bašmu* and the *mušḫuššu* in the Babylonian Map of the World who are said to live "inside the sea" (obv., line 5'). Both of these are serpents with leonine features.[229] The pairing of terms used both for

---

224 SB Gilg. IX. 42-45. Text and translation in *BGE*, 1:668-69.

225 See, however, Enkidu's nightmare about the Anzu-bird in SB Gilg. VII. 165-175 (*BGE*, 1:642-43) and in the OB Nippur school tablet (Antoine Cavigneaux and Johannes Renger, »Ein altbabylonischer Gilgameš-Text aus Nippur,« in *Wisdom, Gods and Literature: Studies in Assyriology in Honour of W. G. Lambert* [eds. A. R. George and I. L. Finkel; Winona Lake, Ind.: Eisenbrauns, 2000], 91-103).

226 *Lugalbanda in the Mountain Cave*, line 163. Translation in *LAS*, 15. Transliteration in Vanstiphout, *Epics of Sumerian Kings*, 112.

227 Sketch in *LAS*, 25; Dalley, *Myths from Mesopotamia*, 316; See glyptic representations in Collon, *First Impressions*, ## 885, 887-89 (p. 185).

228 *Lugalbanda and the Anzud Bird*, lines 44-49. Translation in *LAS*, 23. Transliteration in Vanstiphout, *Epics of Sumerian Kings*, 138.

229 See Horowitz, *MCG*, 22-23, 34-35; "The Lion-Serpent" in Foster, *BTM*, 581-82; Theodore J. Lewis, "*CT* 13.33-34 and Ezekiel 32: Lion-Dragon Myths," *JAOS* 116 (1996): 28-47; and discussion under *lion* in ch. 4.3.

serpents and lions in Job 28:8 (*šaḥaṣ* and *šaḥal*) evokes a similar composite lion-serpent creature of the ilk of the "twisting one," Leviathan.[230]

The mythic fauna conjured by juxtaposing birds, lions, and serpents in the two couplets in vv. 7-8 match their magical mountainous environs. But even as powerful and perceptive protectors of this highland temple, they know little of what lies in the watery depths beneath the mountains.

The hero returns to prominence in the three couplets in vv. 9-11, which are dominated by a vocabulary of violence (see *He assaults* in ch. 4.3). The evident display of frenzied force in these lines qualifies the search trope initiated in v. 3 as a *violent* search. And it is the mountains, explicitly named as the environs for the expedition in vv. 9-10 ("hard rock" // "summits" // "mountains"), which are brutalized by this violence.

This violent search trope also dominates the SB Gilg. epic, in which the common Mesopotamian *topos* of shattering mountains[231] takes on still more cosmic significance. Though during his journey to the Cedar Forest Gilgamesh dreams of being cast beneath the mountain,[232] he and Enkidu split the Cedar Mountain in two during their battle with Humbaba, the guardian of this divine dwelling.[233]

Though somewhat different in force, the uprooting of mountains in Job 28:9 also symbolizes an assault on the cosmic mountain, and its diction is loaded with divine overtones.[234] The language of the second line recalls Job's anti-hymn about God's overturning mountains in a display of raw power (9:5).[235] In effecting a similar act, the explorer has aban-

---

230 Heb. *liwyātān* is ultimately derived from LWY, meaning "to turn, twist," etc. It is also related to *labbu*, the typical Akk. term for "lion." See cognate evidence cited under LWH I in *HALOT* 2:522; and especially J. A. Emerton, "Leviathan and *LTN*: The Vocalization of the Ugaritic Word for the Dragon," *VT* 32 (1982): 327-31; as well as John Day, *God's Conflict with the Dragon and the Sea: Echoes of a Canaanite Myth in the Old Testament* (Cambridge: Cambridge University Press, 1985).

231 This theme is prominent at least from the OA period. See George, *BGE*, 1:466-67, and the pseudo-autobiography of Sargon the Great cited there.

232 MB fragment from Boghazköy obv. i 15'-17' (*BGE*, 1:318-21).

233 SB Gilg. V. 131-34 (*BGE*, 1:608-609); cf. OB Isčali rev. 30-31' (*BGE*, 1:262-63). Discussion in *BGE*, 1:467.

234 Müllner notes that the key words *ʾereṣ*, *šāmayim*, *hārîm*, *māqôm*, and *hāpak* connect Job 9:2-13 with Job 28 (»Der Ort des Verstehens,« 79).

235 See Whybray, *Job*, 122, and especially Newsom, "The Book of Job," 410. Though the convulsing of nature is commonly used in a positive fashion in theophany texts (as a side-effect of God's victory over chaos), it is in Job's mouth (in Job 9:5-6) a declaration as to why he could never receive a fair trial in court: he would simply be crushed by God's infinite and unrestrained power without ever knowing why it was levied against him. I am grateful to Brennan Breed for a helpful discussion of that passage.

doned the actions of world-ordering which characterized his journey's beginning (v. 3a) and now uproots cosmic foundations, as if trying to obtain the treasures of paradise by destroying it with violence. This play on the motif of the convulsion of nature in Iron Age theophany texts (see *overturns summits at the roots* in ch. 4.3) suggests not the defeat of chaos but the creation of it. The hero is thus exposed as an anti-hero, the very opposite of "a divine warrior who defeats the forces of chaos and creates an empire of order and peace."[236]

Though Gilgamesh was famous for achieving his ends through violence,[237] the standard version of the epic emphasizes the ultimate failure of this *modus operandi*. As he learns, force (*emūqān*) is not wisdom (*nēmequ*).[238] In fact, as Utnapishtim reminds him, his toil propels him toward death, which no amount of force can overcome: "You strive ceaselessly, what do you gain? / When you wear out your strength in ceaseless striving, / When you torture your limbs with pain, / You hasten the distant end of your days."[239]

In similar fashion, this mountain-toppling show of strength in Job 28:9 is a "prodigious excavation"[240] into Sheol, in which the base of the mountains is rooted (see Jon 2:6-7). Indeed, in Ugaritic literature, the god Mot enters the Netherworld by lifting the mountains with the backs of his hands. He receives this message from El: "Lift the mountain (*ǵr*) on your hands (*ʿl ydm*), / the hill (*ḫlb*) on top of your palms. / And descend to Hell (*ʾarṣ*), the House of 'Freedom,' / Be counted among the descendants to Hell (*ʾarṣ*); / And you will know, O God, that you are dead."[241] Considered in this light, the search in Job 28 has become much more than simply a frenetic search for wisdom. It is an exhibition of violence in which the poem's explorer undermines cosmic foundations and thereby opens wide the gates of hell.

The description of actions against the mountains continues in the couplet in v. 10, where the water motif that dominates the end of Section One begins its rise to prominence. These waters are the journey's final boundary. Against the preoccupation with dark and deserted re-

236 This is Favaro's description of a hero in *Voyages et voyageurs*, 108 (my translation).

237 This is the emphasis of the introduction to the OB version (see SB Gilg. I. 29ff), and violence runs as a thread throughout the whole epic, escalating at the sea-shore against Shiduri, Ur-Shanabi, and the "Stone Ones."

238 For the play between *emūqu* and *emēqu* in the SB epic, see Moran, "The Gilgamesh Epic," in *CANE* 4:2330-31.

239 SB Gilg. X. 297-300. Translation of Foster, *Epic of Gilgamesh*, 82.

240 The phrase is Pope's, commenting on *CTU* 1.5 v 11-16 (*El in the Ugaritic Texts*, 66).

241 *CTU* 1.5 v 13-17. Translation slightly altered from Smith, "The Baal Cycle," 148. Cf. Niccacci, "Giobbe 28," 44, and discussion of Pope, *El in the Ugaritic Texts*, 65-66.

gions up to this point in the poem, all four lines in vv. 10-11 either name or pun on water and light (*yĕʾōrîm, ʿênô, nĕhārôt, ʾôr*).

The language of the first line is again strongly suggestive of divine action, recalling God's splitting streams in the earth throughout the OT (Hab 3:9; Ps 74:15; Ps 104:10). Yet the objects of splitting in the Joban poem are more specifically the mountains (*ṣûrôt*). Despite being the very symbols of strength and permanence, they are miraculously liquefied by this superhuman breach. The parallelism of "mountains" (*ṣûrôt*) and "hard rock" (*ḥallāmîš*) across the couplets in vv. 9a and 10a undoubtedly tie these lines to the Israelite Water from the Rock tradition (Deut 8:15b; Deut 32:13b; Ps 114:8; cf. Exod 17:5-6; Num 20:10-11; Ps 78:16; 81:17; 105:41), thereby importing into the Joban poem the divine overtones of God's fructifying a barren land with life-giving waters.[242] In this *imitatio Dei*, the human creates edenic life in a dangerous wilderness (cf. Deut 8:15).

These fertile waters forced from the mountains flow from the highland garden of God. The cosmic significance of the symbolism in this line finds resonance with the Ezekielian imagery of the mountain of God, where waters flow from the base of the Temple on Zion (Ezek 47:1-12; cf. Joel 4:18; Zech 14:8) and where wisdom and riches reside (Ezek 28:12-13). The second line of v. 10 highlights the wealth that adorns this magical place. The explorer is depicted as gazing upon the place of lapis and gold dust figured in v. 6, having successfully trod the path of which its terrifying guardians remain ignorant. He has reached that mountain remembered in Israelite traditions as being adorned with sard, topaz, moonstone, beryl, carnelian, jasper, lapis-lazuli, turquoise, emerald, and gold (Ezek 28:13; cf. Gen 2:11-12; see *His eye sees every precious thing* in ch. 4.3)—an analogue, perhaps, to Baal's resplendent mountain, Ṣapān,[243] to Ea's "mountain," Eengura,[244] or to Mt. Mashu

---

242 Cf. Baldauf, »Menschliches Können und göttliche Weisheit,« 60-61; and Stephen A. Geller "The Language and Imagery in Psalm 114," in *Lingering Over Words: Studies in Ancient Near Eastern Literature in Honor of William L. Moran* (eds. Tzvi Abusch, John Huehnergard, and Piotr Steinkeller; HSS 37; Atlanta, Ga.: Scholars, 1990), 187 n. 24.

On the Water from the Rock tradition in general, see William Henry Propp, *Water in the Wilderness: A Biblical Motif and its Mythological Background* (HSM 40; ed. Frank Moore Cross; Atlanta, Ga.: Scholars Press, 1987), 1-3. Propp, however, does not interpret Job 28 as participating in the Water from the Rock tradition beyond the level of "verbal artifice" (ibid., 37).

Though far more prosaic in description, note also the breach (*hnqbh*) of a fissure (*zdh*) in the rock (*ṣr*) from which a fount (*mwṣʾ*) of water flowed in the Siloam Tunnel inscription (*Silm* 1 in *HI*, 500). For a discussion of the much disputed *zdh*, see *HI*, 503.

243 *CTU* 1.4 v 15-19; 1.4 vi 22-38. There is no conflict in drawing on imagery both from El's mountain and from Baal's mountain as analogues to the Israelite imagery here. As J. J. M. Roberts points out regarding Mt. Zion in biblical literature, "[T]he mytho-

and its grove in the Gilg. epic.[245] Yet to obtain the "dark stone," the explorer must enter the base of the mountain[246] and plumb its fresh waters at their very source.

The phrase "sources of the rivers" in v. 11 marks the distant residence of a wise creator god. The Joban diction most naturally parallels Ugaritic descriptions of El's mountain "at the sources of the two rivers, amidst the streams of the double-deep" (see *the sources of the rivers* in ch. 4.3). Yet Ea's watery abode "at the mouth of the rivers"[247] is also within the poem's metaphorical orbit.[248] As with the Apsu and El's fount, the

---

logical topography of Mt. Zion is a composite picture of two completely distinct holy places" ("The Davidic Origin of the Zion Tradition," *JBL* 92 [1973]: 336).

244 Enki's temple at Eridu is called a kur ("mountain land") in line 6 of the Sumerian temple hymns in ETCSL 4.80.1, and it is interchangeable with the Apsu (on which, see the sources cited in W. F. Albright, "The Mouth of the Rivers," *AJSL* 35 [1919]: 165-66). The *Hymn to the Enki Temple Eengura* speaks of its being built of silver, adorned with lapis-lazuli, and covered with gold (Falkenstein and von Soden, *Sumerische und akkadische Hymnen und Gebete*, 133 and 133-137).

In Ee. V 119, the Apsu is called "the abode of the *ḫašmānu*-stone" (*šubat ḫašmāni*), a blue-green colored stone, identified with the *saggilmud* (*CAD* Ḫ, 142, s.v.; *AHw* 1:334, s.v.). See Philippe Talon, *The Standard Babylonian Creation Myth Enūma Eliš: Introduction, Cuneiform Text, Transliteration, and Sign List with a Translation and Glossary in French* (SAACT 4; Helsinki: The Neo-Assyrian Text Corpus Project, 2005), 60, 97.

245 SB Gilg. IX. 171-176.

246 Compare the Ugaritic description of "revealing" or "uncovering" (*gly*) the *ḏd* of El in *CTU* 1.2 iii 5 [corrected]; 1.3 v 7; 1.4 iv 24; 1.6 i 34. Each of these immediately follows the standard epithet for El's abode, "at the sources of the two rivers, amidst the streams of the double-deep." Clifford's argument that *ḏd* means "tent" or the like is sensible (Clifford, *Cosmic Mountain*, 51-54), but other possibilities are not ruled out. Mark Smith, for example, renders *ḏd* as "mountain" in each of these instances and in *CTU* 1.1 iii 23, where *ḏd* // *ḫrš[n]* ("The Baal Cycle"). *DUL* 1:285, s.v. *ḏd* (II), glosses: "grotto, cave?" It seems to me cogent that the *ḏd* is the *inner chamber* of El's tent/temple/mountain, that is, a cella.

247 Drawing especially on the incantation text *CT* 16 46, Albright suggested that the "mouth of the rivers" (*pî nārāti*) was essentially a by-name for the Apsu ("The Mouth of the Rivers," 161-195, esp. 163-165). See also George, *BGE*, 1:520 and n. 268.

248 In the Syrian and Canaanite pantheon lists, Ea is not explicitly identified with El but with Kothar wa-Hasis. However, both El and Ea are wise creator gods who dwell in watery environs. W. G. Lambert proposes that Ea's apparent absence in the "Pantheon" tablet from Mari is explained by the fact that he is "disguised" as El ("The Pantheon of Mari," *MARI* 4 [1985]: 537-38). Edward Lipiński also points to the bilingual Karatepe inscription (*KAI* 26), where the Phoenician *ʾl qn ʾrṣ* ("El, creator of the earth") in A iii 18 corresponds to the Luwian ᵈ*I-ia-śa* (Ea) in §73 ("Éa, Kothar et El," *UF* 20 [1988]:143; cf. *COS* 2.31 [Phoenician] and *COS* 2.21 [Luwian]).

The geographical distance between the historical localizations of El's abode in the Lebanon (so Pope, *El in the Ugaritic Texts*, 72-81) and Ea's abode at the head of the Persian Gulf (see George, *BGE*, 1:519-21; Horowitz, *MCG*, 104-105) is unproblematic, as these are moveable cosmic spaces which ultimately transcend realistic topography. Cf. George's discussion of the *pî nārāti* in *BGE*, 1:520-21.

"sources of the rivers" in Job 28:11 are of mythical, non-geographical character and thus lie beyond space and time.[249] The undaunted explorer breaks into this divine dimension intent on exposing the hidden treasure in its distant deep.

For just such an act, Gilgamesh has found a place in the perpetuity of cultural memory for more than three millennia. At the tail-end of his journey, he seeks out Utnapishtim, from whom he plans to wrest immortality (SB XI. 5-7). To reach him, Gilgamesh must travel to the distant mouth of the rivers (*ina rūqi ina pî nārāti* (ÍD.MEŠ)) to "a place far removed from the world of mortal men."[250] Eventually disarmed by Utnapishtim's appearance and defeated by the mini-death that is sleep, Gilgamesh is forced to reckon with his own mortality and readied to return to Uruk a transformed king (SB XI. 1-6, 209-270). Yet as he leaves, Utnapishtim offers him counsel regarding a secret undisclosed since before the flood: "I will disclose, Gilgamesh, a secret matter (*amāt niṣirti*), / and [I will] tell you a mystery of [the gods] (*pirišta* (AD.ḪAL) *š[a ilī*-MEŠ). / It is a plant, its [*appearance*] is like box-thorn, / its thorn is like the dog-rose's, it will [prick your hands.] / If you can gain possession of that plant, …"[251] Acting quickly, Gilgamesh opens a water channel to gain access to the freshwater fount and its youth-restoring coral (SB XI. 287-288, 295-296, 300).[252] Diving down into the Apsu, Gilgamesh successfully retrieves the specimen and brings to the seashore a plant nourished by Ea's fresh water—a small piece of the "house of wisdom"[253] itself (XI. 289-293).

Like Gilgamesh, the explorer in Job 28:11 has reached the end of his journey, now finding himself in a place of mountains, jewels, and fountains of wisdom. To gain access to the "dark stone" that lies within the sources of the rivers, he engages in yet another divine act of harnessing the formless by binding the waters, just as he has done with the darkness in v. 3a. The damming of these fertilizing streams, however, threatens to transform this amply irrigated garden of God into a dusty Netherworld (cf. Ezek 31:3-17). Since these waters are themselves a *form*

249 Cf. Clifford's comments on El's abode (*Cosmic Mountain*, 50).

250 George, *BGE*, 1:519. The Akkadian phrase is from SB Gilg. XI. 205-206.

251 SB Gilg. XI. 281-85. Translation and text in *BGE*, 1:720-721. See also SB Gilg. XI. 9-10; I. 7-8.

252 For the plant as a type of coral, see George, *BGE*, 1:524.

253 The phrase *bīt* (É) *nēmeqi* is used with reference to the Apsu in the incantation ritual series *Šurpu*, II 149. See Rykle Borger, »*Šurpu* II, III, IV und VIII in ›Partitur,‹ « in *Wisdom, Gods and Literature: Studies in Assyriology in Honour of W. G. Lambert* (eds. A. R. George and I. L. Finkel; Winona Lake, Ind.: Eisenbrauns, 2000), 30; and Erica Reiner, *Šurpu: A Collection of Sumerian and Akkadian Incantations* (AfOB 11; Graz: E. Weidner, 1958).

of wisdom,[254] their restraint may ironically bind up the very insight that the explorer hopes to grasp. The cognitive parallel between the damming of waters and the loss of wisdom is operative in the epilogue to CH, where Hammurabi pronounces curses on any who would deface his stele or slight his judgments:

> May the god Ea, the great prince, whose destinies take precedence, the sage among the gods, all-knowing, who lengthens the days of my life, deprive him of all understanding and wisdom (*uznam u nēmeqam līṭeršū-ma*), and may he lead him into confusion; may he dam up his rivers at the source (*nārātīšu ina nagbim liskir*); may he not allow any life-sustaining grain in his land.[255]

Thus while the human's achievement of restraining the sources of the rivers is divine in scope, it may ironically undermine access to the very wisdom which he seeks.

Still, the imagery in the final line of the couplet is overwhelmingly positive. The root play between *yōṣīʾ* in v. 11b and *môṣāʾ* in v. 1a suggests the completion of the expedition to the "source" highlighted in the poem's incipit. By binding and entering this fount, the explorer has effected a marvelous reversal of the darkness that has shrouded his journey thus far. The "dark thing," figured in v. 3 as the "stone of deepest gloom,"[256] is brought into the rays of the sun, and the final note of Section One is "light" (*ʾôr*, v. 11b). Like Sargon the Great and Gilgamesh, his dark journey ends in brilliance.[257] This glowing image of illuminating the dark depths is a hallmark of divine wisdom in the OT.

254 Compare the Namburbi text K. 2577, in which the river (ÍD) is a form of Ea, endowed by Ea with wisdom (*nēmequ*, line 9'). For text and translation, see Richard Caplice, "Namburbi Texts in the British Musem. I," *Or* 34 (1965): 130-131. See also brief discussion in Richard Clifford, *Creation Accounts in the Ancient Near East and in the Bible* (CBQMS 26; ed. Michael Barré; Washington, D.C.: The Catholic Biblical Association of America, 1994), 58-59.

255 CH xlix 98 – l 13. Text and translation in Martha T. Roth, *Law Collections from Mesopotamia and Asia Minor* (2d ed.; ed. Piotr Michalowski; SBLWAW 6; ed. Simon B. Parker et al.; Atlanta, Ga.: Scholars, 1997), 137. As Van Leeuwen points out, the *nagbu* in this text "is not only the 'watery depths,' but also the 'source' of wisdom where Ea dwells in the Abzu" ("Cosmos, Temple, House," 73).

256 The metaphorical connection between the "stone of deepest gloom" in v. 3b and the "dark thing" in v. 11b is clear. For the possibility of an etymological connection, see *brings dark things to light* in ch. 4.3.

257 For Sargon the Great, see OB omen apodosis cited in Horowitz, *MCG*, 33; also Glassner, "Sargon 'roi du combat' " 124. For Gilgamesh, see SB Gilg. IX. 171. George argues that the brilliance (*namirtu*) there, however, refers to the glowing stones in the grove beyond Mt. Mashu (*BGE* 2:867).

Two hymnic fragments about God's confounding the sages offer remarkable metaphorical and verbal parallels to Job 28:11:[258]

Job 12:22: He reveals deep things from darkness (*ḥōšek*)
and brings deep darkness to light (*yōṣēʾ lāʾôr ṣalmāwet*).

Dan 2:22: He reveals things deep and hidden,
knows what is in the darkness (*baḥăšôkāʾ*),
and illumination (*nĕhîrāʾ*)[259] dwells with him.

By somehow achieving the divine prerogative of revealing secrets from the deep,[260] the explorer has perhaps attained not only to light, but to enlightenment—a feat that would undoubtedly set him among the ranks of kings and sages of old, immortalized in encomium as wisdom's "first discoverer."

3.7 Section Two (vv. 12-14, 20-22)

The opening line of the couplet in v. 12 marks the limits of human accomplishment.[261] The incredible feats of the expedition in vv. 3-11 are set within a proverbial frame which qualifies the reader's perceptions of epic success. The epigram begun in v. 1a is continued in v. 12a, where the reality of wisdom's elusiveness is underscored. The juxtaposition of these two lines communicates that even while the explorer discovered some sort of treasure in a far-distant fount (*môṣāʾ*), wisdom was not found (*timmāṣēʾ*) in it:

1a There is indeed a *fount* for silver …
12a but wisdom—where is it *found*?

The figurative association between wisdom and precious objects which was essential to the symbolic reading of Section One is dissolved by one rhetorical question.[262]

258 Cf. Niccacci, "Giobbe 28," 42; Geller, " 'Where is Wisdom?' " 164, 184 n. 64. *The Shamash Hymn* is also important in this respect, even though wisdom is not a prominent concept therein (see *BWL*, 126-38, esp. lines 4, 37, 57, 149-153, 176-177).

259 *Nĕhîrāʾ* is *Ketib*; *Qere* is *nĕhôrāʾ*.

260 Cf. SB Gilg. I. 1-8.

261 Müllner, »Der Ort des Verstehens,« 59.

262 Hoffman calls this tactic "the unexpected turnabout," in which "the reader is led to one conclusion, but then is suddenly shown an error, and is redirected to the opposite conclusion" (*A Blemished Perfection*, 280).

Thus, despite all appearances, the human's technical skill in that condensed heroic narrative is finally *not* a demonstration of "crafty wisdom."[263] The human has neither wisdom (*ḥokmâ*) nor the understanding (*bînâ*) that makes wisdom possible (see *understanding* in ch. 4.3). As van Hecke states, "The rhetorical question of v. 12 makes clear that however thorough man's exploration of the earth's extent and content may be, he is unable to find... wisdom. Wisdom is, thus, implicitly conceptualized as the (unattainable) object of a search."[264]

Section Two re-casts the quest to world's end in Section One as a *failed* quest, like Gilgamesh's expedition to the mouth of the rivers.[265] With immortality beyond human reach, Gilgamesh's characteristic recklessness jeopardizes his grasp on the secret "plant of heartbeat." Though he brings it up from the Apsu, he loses it to a serpent, which is physically transformed by the plant's rejuvenating power. Gilgamesh reacts in despair:

> Thereupon Gilgamesh sat down weeping,
> His tears flowed down his face,
> He said to Ur-Shanabi the boatman:
> For whom, Ur-Shanabi, have my hands been toiling?
> For whom has my heart's blood been poured out?
> For myself I have obtained no benefit,
> I have done a good deed for the 'Lion of the Earth.'
> Now, floodwaters rise against me for twenty double leagues,
> When I opened the shaft, I flung away the tools.
> How shall I find my bearings?
> I have come much too far to go back, and I abandoned the boat on the shore.[266]

It is not the magical powers of the plant of rejuvenation which change Gilgamesh. Rather, he is transformed by failure and weakness, return-

---

263 One important aspect of *ḥokmâ* in the OT and the ancient Near East is skill in craftsmanship (e.g., Exod 35:31; 36:4; Isa 40:20, etc.). See especially Van Leeuwen, "Cosmos, Temple, House," 67-90.

264 van Hecke, "Searching for and Exploring Wisdom," 158.

265 The failed human quest for divine wisdom is a *topos* found elsewhere in the OT, particularly in Gen 3; Ezek 28:2-10, 12-19; and Isa 14. In each case, the human desire to be "like God" (*wihyîtem*, Gen 3:5; *ʾeddammeh lĕʿelyôn*, Isa 14:14b) is made explicit. The king of Tyre is even portrayed as declaring divinity outright in Ezek 28:2 (*ʾēl ʾānî*). Each of these cases ends in judgment for the human breach of divinely ordained boundaries.

266 SB Gilg. XI 308-317. Translation of Foster, *Epic of Gilgamesh*, 95, with line 314 modified in light of George, *BGE*, 1:722-23, who retains the expression "lion of the earth."

ing to Uruk with an acute recognition of his limits and the desire to refocus his drive for accomplishment within the walls of his divinely ordained kingdom.

The explorer in Job 28, like Gilgamesh, has sought out wisdom through personal effort and individual skill. However, he has yet to complete a similar "inner adventure" that ends in humility.[267] In the course of the poem, his journey is exposed as a string of violent acts which not only mimic, but also mock, the creator.[268] But if he, like Gilgamesh, is to be remembered as wisdom's "first discoverer," it will have to be a wisdom rooted in recognition of human limits.

The structure of the poem in Job 28 leaves open the possibility for such a transformation. Though aphorisms typically effect maximal poetic closure,[269] the second line of the proverb begun in v. 1a delays closure by posing a pair of questions rather than axioms (vv. 12 and 20). This interrogative tone beckons the reader to answer the probing queries in Section Two about wisdom's elusive place.

In the couplet in v. 13 (and v. 21) the poet injects his voice, offering his own answers to those questions. But rather than stating where wisdom *is*, he states where wisdom is *not*: "A human has no knowledge of its abode / It is not found in the land of the living." When at last the subject of Section One is introduced in the first line of this couplet (*ʾĕnôš*; see *he* in ch. 4.3), it is in the context of ignorance, not of insight. The repeated negatives coloring the couplets in vv. 7-8 (*lōʾ* 4x and aural pun with *lô* in v. 6b) are again prominent in vv. 13-14 (*lōʾ* 3x; *ʾên* 1x). The bird of prey's lack of knowledge about the path to wisdom in v. 7a (*lōʾ-yĕdāʿô*) is matched by human ignorance of its abode in v. 13a (*lōʾ yādaʿ*; see *its abode* in ch. 4.3).

But as the second line makes clear, wisdom's elusiveness is not merely due to a lack of knowledge. It is not even to be found (*timmāṣēʾ*) in the land of the living (v. 13b). Wisdom is resident in an entirely different plane of the cosmos. Still, the phrasing in this line suggests another possibility: if wisdom is not to be found in the "land of the living" (*bĕʾereṣ haḥayyim*), perhaps it could be located in the realm of the dead. Having offered his own voice in v. 13, the poet animates the mythological forces of chaos and death in vv. 14 and 22 so that they may address the issue.

In a work so preoccupied with founts, riverbeds, and streams, it is fitting that the first reported speech in the poem should be granted to

267 These concepts are based on Buccellati's discussion of the polarity of dispositions toward the acquisition of knowledge in the SB Gilg. epic ("Wisdom and Not," 37-38).

268 For this phrasing, see Geller, " 'Where is Wisdom?' " 164.

269 On epigrams and poetic closure, see Smith, *Poetic Closure*, 196-210.

water. Ironically, however, the waters "beyond the periphery"[270] know nothing of the wisdom thought to reside in their springs: "Deep says, 'It is not in me.' / Sea says, 'It is not with me.' " The unparalleled personification of Deep and Sea in this poem is striking in light of the typical personification of Wisdom in the Wisdom Literature (see *wisdom* and *Deep says, "It is not in me"* in ch. 4.3). It is not Wisdom who speaks, as she does in Prov 8:17, stating that "Those who seek after me will find me;" rather, the Deep and Sea state that wisdom will *not* be found in their midst.

The pairing of Deep and Sea exhausts the possibilities for locating wisdom anywhere within the bounds of creation by creating a merism of depth and breadth. The Deep in v. 14 represents both the lowest part of the world of the living and the "springs of the double-deep" thought to lie at the base of El's mountain (see *Deep says, "It is not in me"* in ch. 4.3). With their confession, the very depths probed for wisdom in Section One belie the explorer's supposition that wisdom is a matter of depth.

"Sea" in the second line of the couplet represents breadth that cannot be traversed (see *Deep says, "It is not in me"* in ch. 4.3). Such pairing of vertical and horizontal dimensions in ancient Near Eastern literature commonly serves to underscore human limits. As a Sumerian proverb puts it: "The tallest (man) cannot reach heaven, / The widest man cannot cover the mountains."[271] The imagery and meaning in Job 11:7-9 are still closer to the force of Job 28:12-14:

> Would you find out the depth of Eloah?
> Would you attain to the boundary of Shaddai?
> Higher than the heavens—what can you do?
> Deeper than Sheol—what can you know?
> Its measure is longer than the earth
> and broader than the sea (*yām*).

Both the ocean (*tâmtu*) and the Waters of Death (*mû mūti*) are vast boundaries in the Gilgamesh epic. At the edge of the sea, Shiduri warns Gilgamesh:

> "There never was, O Gilgamesh, a way across,
> and since the days of old none who can cross the ocean.

270 See the brief discussion of water and spatialization in the Ugaritic texts in Mark Smith, *Origins of Biblical Monotheism*, 29.

271 Text and translation in Frederick E. Greenspahn, "A Mesopotamian Proverb and its Biblical Reverberations," *JAOS* 114 (1994): 33.

> The one who can cross the ocean is the hero Shamash:
>
> apart from Shamash, who is there who can cross the ocean?
>
> The crossing is perilous, its way full of hazard,
>
> and in between are the Waters of Death, that lie across the passage forward..."[272]

Still, as the remainder of the epic illustrates, a superhuman hero *can* break these boundaries and achieve impossible feats. Aspiring to prove that he was such a hero, the explorer in Section One set out to plumb impossible depths and traverse infinite expanses. But Job 28:14 holds out no possibility for attaining wisdom even if one were of the ilk of Gilgamesh. Crossing the length of the world and probing the watery depths would be futile, because wisdom is not to be found there.[273]

The nearly identical repetition of the poem's central question in v. 20 intensifies the problem: "But wisdom—from where does it come? / Where is the place of understanding?"[274] In the following couplets this question is addressed again by the poet (v. 21) and the cosmic forces of chaos (v. 22), all proclaiming ignorance about wisdom's place in both the world of the living and the world of the dead.

The language of darkness that overshadowed Section One surfaces again in v. 21 with the employ of ᶜLM. Though in the closing couplet of Section One, the human was said to have brought "the dark thing" (*taᶜălūmâ* [MT *taᶜălūmāh*]) to light (v. 11b), wisdom remains obscured (*neᶜelmâ*) from the eyes of all beasts (v. 21a). The "dark thing" that was illuminated in the course of the expedition is, apparently, *not ḥokmâ*.

The merismatic pair birds // beasts in vv. 7-8 is picked up once again with the pair beasts // birds in v. 21. While the couplet's distant

---

272 SB Gilg. X. 79-84 in *BGE*, 1:682-83.

273 Compare Deut 30:11-13: "This instruction (*hammiṣwâ*)... is not in the heavens (that one should) say, 'Who will go up to the heavens for us and get it for us and announce it to us, so that we might observe it?' Nor is it across the sea (*yām*) (that one should) say, 'Who can cross over for us, beyond the sea (*mēᶜēber layyām*), and get it for us and announce it to us, so that we might observe it?' "

The identification of wisdom with Torah informs early Jewish exegesis on Job 28:14. Tur-Sinai (*The Book of Job*, 403) notes a homily in the 3d. century by Rabbi Yehoshua ben Levi: "When Moses had stepped down from before the Lord, the Satan came and spoke to Him: Master of the World, where is the Torah? He said to him: I have given it to the Earth. He went to the Earth... He went to the Sea and it said to him: It is not with me. He went to the Depth; it said to him: It is not with me" (*b. Šab.* 89a; also cited in Fohrer, *Das Buch Hiob*, 398 n. 33; Lévêque, *Job et son Dieu*, 2:602). Fohrer (ibid.) and Lévêque (*Job et son Dieu*, 2:601) also point to Augustine's use of Job 28:12 in *Confessions* X. vi.

274 See ch. 5 for a treatment of vv. 15-19.

parallels in vv. 7-8 and vv. 13-14 frame statements with four negative particles (*lōʾ* and *ʾên*), the assertions in vv. 21-22 regarding the ignorance of beasts, birds, Destruction, and Death are not so emphatically negative. Rather than employing negative particles, these lines are governed by passive verbs emphasizing the inadequacy of sight (*neʿelmâ; nistārâ*, v. 21). Though the birds of prey suffered from nearsightedness in v. 7, it is here the beasts which are said to have eyes that fail them.

The "birds of the heavens" in v. 21b provide a heavenly counterpart to the Deep in v. 14a. They represent the ancient Near Eastern model of height in acquiring wisdom, now matching the model of depth already prominent in the poem.[275] In the *Etana* legend, for example, an eagle is portrayed as being able to pass through the three gates of heaven to obtain treasures of the gods.[276] Presumably, high-flying birds in Job 28:21 are similarly capable, but wisdom remains hidden even from them.

In v. 22, the forces of death that whispered from the symbolic plane of Section One rise to the surface of the poem. Like Deep and Sea in v. 14, Destruction and Death are personified so that they may address the question of wisdom's place. They respond with one voice that emphasizes second-hand knowledge at best, implicitly pitting their aural perception against firsthand visual experience: "We have heard its rumor with our ears." The emphasis on the ophthalmic deficiency of animals both above and on the earth's surface in v. 21 is thus matched by the declaration of aural hearsay by the forces of death in the lowest part of the cosmos in v. 22. But even while wisdom remains only a rumor, it would seem now that it is not far off.

3.8 Section Three (vv. 23-28)

The interrogative and negative moods which dominated Section Two are reversed in v. 23 with an answer to the poem's pressing question about wisdom: "*God* perceives its path. / *He* knows its place." [277] The syntax of the couplet emphatically introduces the poem's new subject by topicalizing "God" in its first line.[278] The personal pronoun "he"

---

275 Again see Greenstein, "The Poem on Wisdom in Job 28," 254-63. Note especially the ancient Near Eastern legends of *Adapa* and *Etana* as representatives of the heavenly model. See Foster, *BTM*, 525-554.

276 NA version, III. 102, 139. Translation in *BTM*, 551-52. Compare text and translation in Horowitz, *MCG*, 50-51, and discussion in ibid., 43-66.

277 Müllner, »Der Ort des Verstehens,« 72.

278 See also Fedrizzi, *Giobbe*, 200; Müllner, »Der Ort des Verstehens,« 60.

(*hûʾ*) in the second line strengthens the emphasis while also setting the divine subject in Section Three against the human explorer in Section One ("he," v. 3aβ).[279] This shift in the poem is so pronounced that Geller likens its effect to that of the divine theophany in Job 38-41.[280]

Consonant with the spatial metaphors which dominate Sections One and Two, the couplet in v. 23 reprises the imagery of "path" and "place" (see vv. 1, 6, 7, 12, 20; cf. vv. 8 [DRK], 13 ["abode"]). The "path" // "place" pair harks back to the pair "place" // "path" in vv. 6-7, suggesting God's intimate knowledge of the way of which birds and beasts were ignorant. Indeed, the question of knowledge is brought to the fore. While the bird of prey and the human in Section One were not privy to wisdom's path (v. 7a) and place (v. 13a), they are not beyond discovery—at least for God (v. 23b).

The language and imagery of vv. 23-27 suggest a contrast between God's technical skill in creation in Section Three and human technical skill cast in pseudo-creative language in Section One. The couplet in v. 23 emphasizes that God, unlike the human, both "knows" (*yādaʿ*) wisdom's path and "perceives" (*hēbîn*) wisdom's place. In attaining to wisdom, God employs the very understanding (*bînâ*) that produces wisdom itself.[281] To use the symbolic equation of the proverb in vv. 1a + 12a (GOLD IS UNDERSTANDING), God 'thinks' in gold.

The couplet in v. 24 portrays God as the "master of sight."[282] He can discern wisdom's place "Because *he* gazes at the edges of the earth, / sees beneath all the heavens." Limitless in extent, his vision outstrips that of the falcon (v. 7b; cf. v. 21b), the explorer (v. 10b), and the beasts (v. 21a). The same "edges of the earth" (*qĕṣôt hāʾāreṣ*) which the human circumscribed and probed in Section One (see *qēṣ* and *taklît* in v. 3a) are here the objects of God's gaze (v. 24a). The horizontal dimension in the first line is matched by a vertical dimension in the second: "[God] sees beneath all the heavens." The spatial merism created by this pairing underscores God's ability to see everything, everywhere (see *sees beneath all the heavens* in ch. 4.3). Rising above the treacherous obstacles of the landscape below, God peers out transcendently upon the breadth and depth of the world which he created—his cosmic temple.[283]

---

279 See also Newsom, "The Book of Job," 532.

280 Geller, " 'Where is Wisdom?' " 165.

281 Fox notes that wisdom (*ḥokmâ*) may both inform and be produced by understanding (*bînâ*) ("Words for Wisdom," 158). See discussion of *understanding* in ch. 4.3.

282 Alter, *Art of Biblical Poetry*, 94.

283 As Niccacci has noted, Ps 33:13-14 also connects divine knowledge with the fact that God's place in the heavens allows him to see and fathom all ("Giobbe 28," 32). Note the verbal parallels between Job 28:24 ("gazes" // "sees") and Ps 33:13-14 ("gazes" //

However, God's success in locating wisdom within the scope of the universe is more than simply about superior vision or understanding. As vv. 25-27 illustrate, wisdom is sighted by God during a world-creating act. The two couplets in vv. 25-26 offer a sort of "primordial parenthesis" which shifts the focus of Section Three back to a time when all existence was in its nascent stage, before returning to the subject of "sight" in v. 27a. Ubiquitous in ancient Near Eastern creation accounts,[284] a double protasis introduces God's creative acts: "When he made a weight for the wind, / apportioned the waters by measure, / when he made a groove for the rain, and a track for the thundershower..." The spatial dimension which has dominated the poem to this point is now coupled with a prominent temporal dimension.[285]

In distant days, God weighed the weightless (v. 25a; cf. Isa 40:12), measured the immeasurable (v. 25b; cf. Isa 40:12; Ee. IV. 143), and channeled the formless (v. 26; cf. Job 38:25). He manipulated the wind, water, rain, and thundershower as easily as Solomon's conscripts handled the wood beams, copper, bronze, silver, and gold with which they built the temple in Jerusalem (see 1 Kgs 5-7) or as skillfully as Bezalel and Oholiab constructed the tabernacle and its furnishings (see Exod 31:1-6). The metaphors of weights, measures, grooves, and tracks in vv. 25-26 (cf. Job 38:8-11, 17, 19-20, 22, 25, 27) connote the rigor of divine control, a motif embodied also in the formal parallelism of the first line of each couplet (note the matched syntax of v. 25a and v. 26a).

The imagery in the three couplets in vv. 25-27 portrays God as a skilled artisan[286] who surveys the world for the ancient pattern of its foundations, just as scholars were commissioned by Assyrian and Babylonian kings to probe building sites for the old ground plan of the temples they re-built.[287] To discover the outline, the site was surveyed

---

"sees" // "looks out"): "From the heavens Yhwh gazes (*hibbîṭ*) / He sees (*rāʾâ*) all humanity / From the site of his dwelling he looks out (*hišgîaḥ*) / over all those who dwell in the earth." On the temple-world homology, see Jon D. Levenson, "The Temple and the World," *JR* 64 (1984): 275-298, and idem, *Creation and the Persistence of Evil*, 78-99.

284 See, e.g., the opening lines of the *Hymn to Eengura*, KAR 4; *Gilgamesh, Enkidu, and the Netherworld*; Ee. I. 1, 7, 9; the temple dedication *When Anu Created the Heavens*; the disputation *Palm and Tamarisk* (Emar version); Prov 8:24a, b, 27a, b, 28a, 29a, b, 30a.

285 As pointed out by Newsom, "The Book of Job," 532; Geller, " 'Where is Wisdom?' " 166.

286 See also Van Leeuwen, "Cosmos, Temple, House," 76-77. Cf. similar imagery in other OT creation accounts: Job 38:4-7; Isa 40:12-14; Prov 8:22-31.

287 Victor (Avigdor) Hurowitz, *I Have Build You an Exalted House: Temple Building in the Bible in Light of Mesopotamian and Northwest Semitic Writings* (JSOTSup 115; ASOR Monograph Series 5; ed. David J. A. Clines et al.; Sheffield: Sheffield Academic Press,

with rope and measuring rods, both symbols of divine revelation of the temple plan.[288] Nabopolassar recounts the process in constructing the famous ziggurat Etemenanki in Babylon:

> At the commission of Ea, in accordance with the knowledge of Marduk, at the instruction of Nebo and Nisaba, with the spacious heart which the god, my Creator, provided me, I contemplated my great appointment. I dispatched expert craftsmen (*ummânī emqūtim*); I had the surveyor take the measurements (*umandida mindiātu*) with a standard measuring rod. The foremen pulled the ropes taut (*ištaṭṭū eblī*) and established the outline (*ukinnū kisurrîm*).[289]

Similar imagery is also evident in the OB hymns to Pap-due-garra: "Let him draw the border lines (*lišdud miṣrī*); let him make the path (*giridê līpuš*). / Let him lay out the temple correctly (*lištēšir bīt ili*); let him place the pegs (*sikkātim liškun*)."[290]

As Victor Hurowitz has noted, this survey motif informs both biblical and extra-biblical creation texts (see also Job 38:4-7).[291] Enki, the Mesopotamian god who incarnated technical wisdom,[292] uses these very techniques as he builds a model house in *Enki and the World Order*: "He tied down the strings and coordinated them with the foundations, and with the power of the assembly he planned a house and performed the purification rituals. The great prince put down the foundations, and

---

1992), 326-27 (Appendix 3). On the building rites for rebuilding former temples, see Ellis, *Foundation Deposits*, 12-17.

288 Hurowitz, *I Have Built You an Exalted House*, 326. For an iconographic representation of these symbols, note the Ur-Nammu stele from Ur (no. 306 in *ANEP*, 98, 285). On the right side of the second register, a deity bestows upon the king the rod, ring, and line.

289 VAB 4 62 ii 14-30 (*Nabopolassar* No. 1). My translation after *CAD* A/1, 51, s.v. *abi ašli*; *CAD* E, 14, s.v. *eblu*; *CAD* K, 434, s.v. *kisurrû*; and Langdon, *Die Neubabylonischen Königsinschriften* (trans. Rudolf Zehnpfund; VAB 4; Leipzig: Hinrichs, 1912), 63. On *ummânu* as a wisdom term in Akkadian literature, see Ronald Sweet, "The Sage in Akkadian Literature," 48, 57-58.

290 Plate IX rev. vi 18-19 in T. G. Pinches, "Hymns to Pap-due-garra," in *Journal of the Royal Asiatic Society Centenary Supplement, 1924* (London: Royal Asiatic Society of Great Britain and Ireland, 1924) (transcription on p. 73). Translation after Hurowitz, *I Have Built You an Exalted House*, 326; *CAD* Š/1, 28 s.v. *šadādu* 4d; and *CAD* E, 359 s.v. *ešēru* 12. See also Ellis, *Foundation Deposits*, 82 and n. 227

291 Hurowitz, *I Have Built You an Exalted House*, 327.

292 See Jean Bottéro, "Intelligence and the Technical Function of Power: Enki/Ea," *Mesopotamia: Writing, Reasoning, and the Gods* (trans. Zainab Bahrani and Marc Van De Mieroop; Chicago and London: University of Chicago, 1992), 323-50. Bottéro's essay was originally published as "L'intelligence et la function technique du pouvior: Enki/Éa—pour donner une idée de la systémique du pantheon," *Dictionnaire des Mythologies* (2 vols.; ed. Yves Bonnefoy; Paris: Flammarion, 1981), 2:102-111

laid the bricks."[293] In Ee. IV. 141-144, Ea's son, Marduk, the "sage of the gods,"[294] is depicted as architect and builder as he constructs three cosmic regions for Anu, Enlil, and Ea: "He crossed the Heavens and inspected (*iḫītam*) Ašrata. / He made a counterpart (*uštamḫir meḫrīt*) to Apsu, the dwelling of Nudimmud. / The Lord measured (*imšuḫ*) the construction (*binûtūšu*) of Apsu. / He established (*ukīn*) Ešarra, the duplicate of Ešgalla.[295]

The combination of creation and storm motifs in vv. 25-26 may be seen as a conflation of the functions of the Canaanite god El, the wise Creator of the earth, and Baal, the god of the squall who triumphs over Sea and Death. Though he is, like El, the Creator, God's artistic masterpiece is not the whole world, but a *thunderstorm*[296]—the very mode of revelation of Baal.[297] But unlike Baal in the Ugaritic texts, the theophany in Job 28:25-28 is not the storm itself. Rather, the elements of the storm are set in place in preparation for a revelation *from* the storm in the poem's closing triplet (v. 28). The ethical connotations of both *ḥōq* ("prescription") and *derek* ("[moral] path") in v. 26 anticipate that verbal decree—the characteristic mode of revelation of El (see *when he made a groove for the rain* in ch. 4.3). In fact, all the actions of weighing and channeling in vv. 25-26 are *regulations*. Thus, just as Yhwh will eventually address Job "from the storm" in Job 38:1, so also in vv. 25-26 God prepares to issue his decree about the content of wisdom from a well-crafted thunderstorm.

"Then" at the head of the first line in v. 27 marks the apodosis that hinges on the temporal structure in the previous two couplets. As Newsom has pointed out, vv. 25-27 exist in "a relationship of simulta-

---

293 Lines 341-344 of ETCSL 1.1.3. Translation in *LAS*, 222. Cf. Kramer and Maier, *Myths of Enki*, 51.

294 Ee. I. 80 (*apkal* (ABGAL) *ilī* (DINGIR.MEŠ)). Text in Talon, *The Standard Babylonian Creation Myth*, 36.

295 Translation of Horowitz, *MCG*, 112, modified slightly in light of Foster, *BTM*, 462. Text in Talon, *The Standard Babylonian Creation Myth*, 56. See discussion of the passage in Horowitz, *MCG*, 112-114.

296 Andersen, *Job*, 229. See also Job 36:27-33.

297 In Job 28:25-28, then, the typological distinctions between these two modes of revelation and their content (i.e., verbal decree and thunderstorm) are merged. This is true also in the description of the revelation at Sinai, on which Frank Moore Cross comments: "In the Epic descriptions of the revelation at Sinai this typological distinction does not hold up. The language of the storm theophany obviously is present. However, the legal decrees and judgments from the mount and from the Tent of Meeting are, so to speak, the business of ʾĒl" (*Canaanite Myth and Hebrew Epic* [Cambridge, Mass., and London, U.K.: Harvard University Press, 1973], 185). See also ibid., 164: "At Sinai he showed himself in stormy and fiery cloud as ruler and lawgiver."

neity."[298] The motif of "sight" which receded during the shift to divine creation in vv. 25-26 (cf. v. 24b) resurfaces in the first line of the couplet in v. 27: "Then he saw it and numbered it, / established it and even probed it." Wisdom is seen (*rāʾāh*, v. 27a) during a controlled act of world-ordering, not in a hubristic toppling of cosmic foundations (cf. *rāʾătâ*, v. 10b).

The diction of the couplet—seeing, numbering,[299] establishing, and probing—contributes to the building motif begun in v. 25.[300] Having surveyed his cosmic building site with weights, measures, and lines (vv. 25-26), God now looks at and probes wisdom, fixed like an ancient peg deposit in the depths of the earth. A Hittite ritual for the erection of a house suggests that these deposits are symbolic of the firm foundation of a building:

> When they rebuild a temple that had been destroyed or (build) a new house in a different place and they lay the foundations, they deposit under the foundations as follows: 1 mina of *refined* copper, 4 bronze pegs, 1 small iron hammer. In the center, at the place of the *kurakki* he digs up the ground. He deposits the copper therein, nails it down on all sides with the pegs and afterward hits it with the hammer. While doing so he speaks as follows: "Just as this copper is secured, (as) moreover it is firm, even so let this temple be secure! Let it be firm upon the dark earth!"[301]

Likewise, the wisdom that God sights, sets, and searches in v. 27 is the foundation of the world, the ancient plan of the universe to which all construction—divine or human—must conform.

There is a remarkable semantic overlap between the cluster of verbs in Job 28:27 and those used in Akkadian literature of finding and in-

---

298 Newsom, "The Book of Job," 532. This suggests that a necessary condition for the actions in v. 27 is that they are undertaken during the process of creation (see also van Hecke, "Searching for and Exploring Wisdom," 158-59 and n. 44; Janzen, *Job*, 197).

299 SPR-Piel, which I have translated as "numbering," may be understood in the sense of "measuring" (see NJPS at Job 28:27a: "gauged it").

300 Cf. Luis Alonso Schökel and J. L. Sícre Díaz, who suggest that the verbs in v. 27 portray the work of an artisan or engineer (*Job: Comentario Teológico y Literario* [Nueva Biblia Española; Madrid: Ediciones Cristiandad, 1983], 403). See also Aitken, "Lexical Semantics," 122 and n. 18. In commenting on *hĕkînāh* in this verse, Norbert Peters rightly notes »הֱכִינָהּ = *er stellte sie auf*, als Norm seiner Schöpfungstätigkeit nämlich, wie das der Künstler mit seinem Modell macht« (*Das Buch Job, übersetzt und erklärt* [EHAT 21; ed. Alfons Schulz-Breslau; Münster in Westfalia: Verlag der Aschendorffschen Verlagsbuchhandlung, 1928], 307 [italics original]).

301 "Ritual for the Erection of a House," obv. 1-10. Translated by Albrecht Goetze in *ANET*, 356. See also Ellis, *Foundation Deposits*, 79. Ellis concludes his study with the observation that "In the earlier periods the use of building deposits was apparently intended to insure and increase the 'effectiveness' of the building" (ibid., 168).

specting the old foundations of a building and its foundation deposits. The Akkadian texts speak of "looking at/for" (*amāru*, *palāsu*, *ṣubbû*, *buʾʾû*), "searching for" (*ḫâṭu*, *šeʾû*), and "establishing" (*kânu*) foundations.[302] In his reconstruction of Ebabarra at Sippar, Nabonidus recounts gathering "...wise mathematicians (*ṭupšar minâti enqūtu*), the residents of the temple workshop, who guard the secret knowledge of the great gods..."[303] to give him advice in the matter. Having commanded them to "search for (*šiteʾʾâ*) the ancient foundations," the scholars "saw (*ippalsū*) the ancient foundations" and "traced (*iḫītū*) the cella and the platform."[304] Then Nabonidus declared, "I saw (*appalis*) the ancient foundations of Naram-Sin, the distant king, the shrine of Šamaš, the legitimate, the residence of his divinity!"[305]

The SB Gilg. epic invests this royal motif with cosmic significance. In the prologue, Gilgamesh is said to have seen the Deep (*ša naqba īmuru*), the "foundation of the country" (*išdī māti*), which was the source of his unsurpassed wisdom.[306] As George comments, this refers to "the foundation stone on which Babylonian civilization was built."[307] The epilogue reprises the motif with Gilgamesh's invitation to Ur-Shanabi and, by extension, to the audience, to "survey (*ḫīti*) the foundation platform" and to "inspect (*ṣubbi*) the brickwork,"[308] all of which offers evidence of the revival of civilization that Gilgamesh brought forth in Uruk.[309]

Yet while the language of "seeing" (*rāʾāh*), "numbering" (*waysappĕrāh*), and "establishing" (*hĕkînāh*) in Job 28:27 contributes to the material metaphors of creation in Section Three, the same terms may also be understood in the mental senses of "assessing" wisdom, "fathoming"[310]

302 See especially *CAD* T, 338-339 s.v. *temmennu* 2a-c. Also *CAD* P, 57-58 s.v. *palāsu* 6.d.2'; *CAD* Ḫ, 161 s.v. *ḫâṭu* 3; *CAD* Š, 358-59 s.v. *šeʾû* 4a; *CAD* B, 362 s.v. *buʾû* 1d; *CAD* Ṣ, 226-227 s.v. *ṣubbû*; *CAD* A, 11 s.v. *amāru* A 1.d.e'; *CAD* K, 164-165 s.v. *kânu* A 3c-d.

303 VAB 4 256 i 32-33 (*Nabonidus* no. 6). My translation after Sweet, "The Sage in Akkadian Literature," 62 and n. 89. Cf. *CAD* P, 400 s.v. *pirištu* 2a.

304 VAB 4 256 i 34-37. My translation. Compare Paul-Alain Beaulieu, *The Reign of Nabonidus, King of Babylon, 556-539 B.C.* (YNER 10; eds. W. W. Hallo et al.; New Haven and London: Yale University Press, 1989), 7 (inscription 5). See also discussion of the inscription in ibid., 132-137.

305 VAB 4 256 i 38. My translation with an eye to Langdon, *Neubabylonischen Königsinschriften*, 257.

306 SB Gilg. I. 1, 3 in George, *BGE*, 1:538-539.

307 George, *BGE*, 1:445.

308 SB Gilg. XI. 324 in George, *BGE*, 1:724-725. See also SB Gilg. I. 19.

309 For a discussion, see George, *BGE*, 1:526-528.

310 Since it anticipates a verb of speaking in v. 28 (*wayyōʾmer*), it is also possible that the narrative aspect of Piel-SPR is in the background here. In fact, all the ancient versions understand *waysappĕrāh* in v. 27a as "and he explained it."

it, and "determining [its] qualities." Interpreted in this way, v. 27 turns the poem's dominant trope of objectifying wisdom inside-out, with wisdom now figured as a space which God explores from the inside, as subject (see *then he saw it... probed it* in ch. 4.3).

The remarkable achievement of this divine survey is underscored with an emphasizing particle, throwing the focus fully onto God's exploration of wisdom at the end of the second line: "...and even probed it."[311] Like a king who has gazed upon foundations obscured for millennia, God uncovers the ancient outline upon which the cosmos was established.[312] This act of "probing" forms an *inclusio* around vv. 3-27, again setting God's crafty wisdom against that of the explorer in Section One. However, the action depicted at the end of the poem represents a wholly different conceptual model of the search for wisdom than that found in Section One.[313] While the human explorer had probed "every limit" (*lĕkol-taklît hûʾ ḥôqēr*) for the dark stone which symbolized wisdom (v. 3), at the close of the poem God is portrayed as probing the limits of wisdom itself (*ḥăqārāh*, v. 27). Wisdom is not an object to be grasped, but a plan that must be known from within.

The poem closes with a divine revelation of wisdom's content in v. 28. While the cosmic forces of Deep, Sea, Destruction, and Death have all spoken only to reveal their ignorance about wisdom's place (vv. 14, 22),[314] God now answers the poem's persistent query with an ancient utterance from a thunderstorm: "...and he said to the human, / 'Behold, awe of the Lord, *that* is wisdom. / To turn from evil, understanding.' " The impact of the statement within the poem's rhetoric is nothing short of theophanic.[315]

Still, v. 28 is one of the most maligned verses in the Book of Job (see *and he said... understanding* in ch. 4.3). James Crenshaw's comments are

---

311 On *gām*, see *IBHS* §39.3.4d.

312 In this respect, compare the VAB 4 224 ii 55-65 (*Nabonidus* no. 1): "I removed (the debris) of that temple, looked for its old foundation deposit, dug to a depth of eighteen cubits into the ground and (then) Shamash, the great lord, revealed to me (the original foundations of) Ebabbar, the temple (which is) his favorite dwelling, (by disclosing) the foundation deposit of Narām-Sîn, son of Sargon, which no king among my predecessors had found in three thousand and two hundred years" (Paul-Alain Beaulieu, "The Sippar Cylinder of Nabonidus," in *COS* 2.123A). In lines 59-60, Nabonidus attributes the discovery of the temple's ancient plan to divine revelation (*kullumu*). See also *CAD* K, 523 s.v. *kullumu* 3b; and Hurowitz, *I Have Built You an Exalted House*, 326.

313 See van Hecke, "Searching for and Exploring Wisdom," 158-60, and *then he saw it... probed it* in ch. 4.3.

314 See also Müllner, »Der Ort des Verstehens,« 58.

315 Fedrizzi has also noted the revelatory nature of v. 28, even though he considers it suspect (*Giobbe*, 200).

representative: "The conclusion of this majestic poem is something of a let-down. One expects a profound statement; instead, a cliché brings readers back to earth."[316] By most it is thought to be "a simple answer to complex issues," a premature resolution.[317] Furthermore, many scholars believe that wisdom as the "awe of the Lord" in v. 28 is of a wholly different kind than that presented in vv. 1-27.[318]

The verse's apparent lack of profundity is undoubtedly tied to its proverbial and didactic flavor, which most commentators find acerbic. In his book, *How to Read a Poem*, Terry Eagleton speaks of a neurotic suspicion of the didactic in the modern age, "with its curious assumption that to be taught must be invariably unpleasant."[319] Because of this assumption, states Eagleton, "it tends to imagine that poems which seek to do this must be inferior modes of writing."[320] So Geller finds the line to be a "bold and bland... statement of traditional piety."[321] Newsom likewise characterizes it as "a cliché" much like one of "the shop-worn phrases of conventional instruction."[322]

Yet this epigrammatic assertion, often mistaken for an aesthetic flaw, is actually an indicator of poetic closure[323] which is strengthened by the formal deviation of a triplet in a work dominated by couplets.[324] In this final triplet, the proverbial frame of the whole poem is completed: "There is indeed a source for silver... / But wisdom—where is it found? / ...awe of the Lord, *that* is wisdom..." (vv. 1a, 12a, 28aβ).

This commendation of the "fear of God" is hardly simplistic moralism. As Samuel Terrien states,

> It would be a grave error... to soften the meaning of the expression and to ignore its central element of *mysterium tremendum*. Although many commentators and historians have fallen into this error during the past hun-

---

316 Crenshaw, "Job," in *The Oxford Bible Commentary* (eds. John Barton and John Muddiman; Oxford and New York: Oxford University Press, 2001), 345.

317 Ibid., 346.

318 E.g., van Oorschot, »Hiob 28,« 183-201, esp. 187; Whybray, *Job*, 124; Pope, *Job*, 206; Driver and Gray, *Job* 1:244-45; Max Löhr, »Job c. 28,« in *Oriental Studies Published in Commemoration of the Fortieth Anniversary (1883-1923) of Paul Haupt as Director of the Oriental Seminary of the Johns Hopkins University, Baltimore, MD* (Baltimore, Md.: The Johns Hopkins University Press, 1926), 68.

319 Eagleton, *How to Read a Poem*, 89.

320 Ibid.

321 Geller, " 'Where is Wisdom?' " 174.

322 Newsom, "The Book of Job," 533.

323 Smith, *Poetic Closure*, 171, 196-210.

324 David Wolfers correctly understands this final triplet to be a "conventional conclusion" in formal terms, and he draws an analogy with rhymed couplets at the end of scenes in the early plays of William Shakespeare ("The Volcano in Job 28," 237). On closure in BH poetry in general, see Watson, *Classical Hebrew Poetry*, 62-65.

> dred years, the fear of the Lord is not merely to be equated with reverence, piety, or religion...[325]

While rational and moral aspects are undoubtedly emphasized in the third line of v. 28, the "*yir'at* of the Lord" certainly includes the emotive responses of dread and love, and the core sense of YR' is best glossed as "awe" (see "*Behold, awe of the Lord... to turn from evil...*" in ch. 4.3)."[326] "Awe of the Lord" is perfectly fitting in the context of divine revelation from a thunderstorm.

The "fear of the gods" was an ideal for the Mesopotamian king, who was "the wise man *par excellence*."[327] As Ronald Sweet states, "The wisdom of kings was therefore not a bookish or intellectual affair. It was largely a matter of recognizing the supremacy of the gods and performing deeds pleasing to them. Reverence for the gods was the beginning of wisdom."[328] The attitude toward the "fear of the gods" in a letter from the exorcist Adad-šumu-uṣur to Assurbanipal seems to belie the typical characterization of the concept in Job 28:28 as platitudinous. Adad-šumu-uṣur describes the ideal conditions during the reign of his king:

> The reign is good, the days (of it) are truthful (and) the years mere justice; there are copious rains, abundant floods (and) a fine rate of exchange; the gods are appeased, there is much fear of god (*palāḫ ilī*), (and) the temples abound in riches; the great gods of heaven and earth have become revered again in the time of the king, my lord.[329]

For the poem in Job 28, true wisdom is not gained through brash ventures to the edges of the world, but by taking one's place within an ancient plan. Even while heroic exploration ultimately fails to reveal wis-

---

325 Terrien, "Fear," *IDB* 2:258.

326 See Clines, " 'The Fear of the Lord' " 64, 69-70; and Bruce K. Waltke, "The Fear of the Lord: The Foundation for a Relationship with God," in *Alive to God: Studies in Spirituality Presented to James Houston* (eds. J. I. Packer and Loren Wilkinson; Downer's Grove, Ill.: Intervarsity, 1992), 30. Gordis translates Job 28:28 as "To be in awe of the Lord – that is wisdom, / and to avoid evil – that is understanding" (*The Book of Job*, 539). Compare also the Akk. words *palāḫu, puluḫtu,* and *pulḫu* A, in connection with "god," "gods," or a divine name. See *CAD* P, 37-49, 505-509, 503-504.

327 Sweet, "The Sage in Akkadian Literature," 65.

328 Ibid. Note also the claim of the sufferer in *Ludlul bel nemeqi* II 25: "The day for reverencing the gods (*ūmu palāḫ ilī*-MEŠ) was a joy to my heart" (II. 25). Text and translation in Lambert, *BWL*, 38-39.

329 K. 183 (= ABL 2), obv. 9-15. Text and translation in Simo Parpola, *Letters from Assyrian Scholars to the Kings Esarhaddon and Assurbanipal* (2 vols.; Winona Lake, Ind.: Eisenbrauns, 2007), 1:88-91 (letter #121). Originally published under the same title as AOAT 5/1-2 (Kevelaer: Butzon & Bercker; Neukirchen-Vluyn: Neukirchener, 1970 and 1983). See discussion of this letter in ibid., 2:103-107.

dom, wisdom may nonetheless be born from that failure by recognizing, creating, and maintaining limits. Like the divine artisan who fixes the elements of the cosmos with measurements, outlines, and boundaries (vv. 25-26), humans may perceive wisdom while putting things in their place, separating one thing from another, and upholding those distinctions.[330] Wisdom is found in a moral universe that is fundamentally rooted in the awe of the God who ordered the world (v. 28).[331]

This wisdom is closely analogous to that implicitly commended by the SB Gilg. epic. Thorkild Jacobsen has characterized the standard version of epic as "a story about growing up."[332] After "a long history of heroic misdemeanours,"[333] Gilgamesh eventually faces the reality that immortality is off-limits to humans. The secrets of the gods remain secrets. As George states, "Gilgamesh's 'growing up' is, in fact, the story of a hero who grows wise in the sense of learning his place in the divinely ordained scheme of things."[334]

Despite Gilgamesh's failure to obtain immortality and grasp secret wisdom through expedition, he eventually embodies wisdom through his *just rule*. But the acquisition of this practical and personal knowledge is predicated in the SB epic on his ability to recognize his own weakness and to admit fear.[335] Prior to his journey, Gilgamesh was portrayed as a boisterous and fierce tyrant-king (SB Gilg. I. 56-91), but by the end of his journey, he is "tired and calm" (SB Gilg. I. 9). Now "reconciled to his mortal destiny,"[336] he finally leaves behind the celebration of his own heroic deeds and takes up his role as shepherd of Uruk-the-Sheepfold. He invests in building the foundations and walls of Uruk, as well as the Temple of Ishtar (I. 11-22; XI. 323-28)—both symbols of a well-ordered society.

---

330 As H. H. Schmid and others have argued, "righteousness" in the OT is essentially a concept of world order. See H. H. Schmid, *Gerechtigkeit als Weltordnung* (BHT 40; Tübingen: Mohr Siebeck, 1968); idem, "Creation, Righteousness, and Salvation: 'Creation Theology' as the Broad Horizon of Biblical Theology," *Creation in the Old Testament* (trans. B. Anderson and Dan G. Johnson; IRT 6; ed. B. Anderson; Philadelphia: Fortress, 1984), 102-17 (orig. pub. in *ZTK* 70 [1973]: 1-19); Hermann Spieckermann, »Schöpfung, Gerechtigkeit und Heil als Horizont alttestamentlicher Theologie,« *ZTK* 100 (2003): 399-419, and Leo G. Perdue, "Cosmology and the Social Order in the Wisdom Tradition," in *The Sage in Israel and the Ancient Near East* (ed. John G. Gammie and Leo G. Perdue; Winona Lake, Ind.: Eisenbrauns, 1990), 458-59.

331 See especially Newsom, "The Book of Job," 533; and Janzen, *Job*, 197.

332 Jacobsen, *The Treasures of Darkness*, 219; see also idem, "Romantic and Tragic Vision," 249; and Abusch, "The Development and Meaning of the Epic of Gilgamesh," 614-22.

333 George, *The Epic of Gilgamesh*, xlvii.

334 Ibid.

335 Buccellati, "Wisdom and Not," 38.

336 George, *BGE*, 1:446.

The themes of wisdom and justice are no less central to the pursuits of Job and his friends. In its canonical context, the poem in Job 28 is an important contribution to that larger debate. With Job as its implied author, Job 28:1-11 may be understood as Job's implicit critique of his friends' clambering after wisdom by searching out the tradition (see ḤQR in 5:27; 8:8; cf. also 32:11).[337] In Section One of the poem, he parabolizes their "wisdom expedition" and its shortcomings. In verse 28, Job addresses them in another communiqué of indirection by taking on the role of the "first man" which was rhetorically imputed to him elsewhere by Eliphaz (15:7; see *and he said to the human* in ch. 4.3). Thus, the words spoken in divine theophany in v. 28 are both spoken *by* Job, as their implied author, and are addressed *to* Job—the primal human. In this way, he slyly writes the content of God's revelation of wisdom in v. 28 to match his own persistent claims to righteousness and his unabated and unrestrained terror of God throughout the dialogues—his "fear of God." With this charade, Job appeals to his friends' means of legitimating authority through antiquity,[338] but as the "first man," he now is much older than they or their fathers. By extension, he is wise even by their standards. Now Job's life is, despite their protests, the ideal of "pious wisdom."[339]

The phrasing "fear of the Lord" and "turn[ing] from evil" in v. 28 also puts the line into conversation with the prose prologue, where identical language is used to describe Job's integrity by the narrator (1:1) and by Yhwh in the celestial council (1:8; 2:3).[340] Other descriptions throughout the Book of Job, where Job is terrified of a raging and seemingly capricious God, also play into the non-rational aspect of the "awe of the Lord" in v. 28b. Numinous dread has typically characterized his response to God throughout the dialogues, and Job naturally seeks reprieve from this abuse. Hoping for someone to turn God's wrath away from him, he proclaims, "then I would speak, and I would not fear him..." (9:35).

---

337 Cf. Müllner, »Der Ort des Verstehens,« 78.

338 See Edward L. Greenstein, " 'On My Skin and in My Flesh': Personal Experience as a Source of Knowledge in the Book of Job," in *Bringing the Hidden to Light: The Process of Interpretation. Studies in Honor of Stephen A. Geller* (eds. Kathryn F. Kravitz and Diane M. Sharon; Winona, Lake, Ind.: The Jewish Theological Seminary and Eisenbrauns, 2007), 63-77; and Norman C. Habel, "Appeal to Ancient Tradition as a Literary Form," *ZAW* 88 (1976): 253-272.

339 For this characterization of the friends' wisdom, see Rainer Albertz, "The Sage and Pious Wisdom in the Book of Job: The Friends' Perspective," in *The Sage in Israel and the Ancient Near East* (trans. Leo G. Perdue; eds. John G. Gammie and Leo G. Perdue; Winona Lake, Ind.: Eisenbrauns, 1990), 252.

340 See especially Newsom, "Dialogue and Allegorical Hermeneutics," 299-304.

David Clines objects to ascribing Job 28 to Job because of the connection between the phrasing of 28:28 and 1:1, 8; 2:3. He states, "And as for chap[ter] 28, it can hardly be Job who urges the acquisition of wisdom, still less who recommends the fear of the Lord and turning aside from evil, since it was precisely that that was his specialty as the book opened."[341] This objection, however, is insufficient grounds for rejecting these words as Job's, since Job in the narrative is completely ignorant of both Yhwh's and the narrator's assessment of him in the prologue.

As words *to* Job as the primal man, v. 28 reflects Yhwh's own evaluation of Job in the prose tale and thus serve to re-affirm Job's status throughout the dialogues as a righteous man. As words *by* Job but reported as the speech of God, Job is able to associate himself with wisdom without ever actually claiming that he is wise. Once the equation between "the awe of the Lord" and "wisdom" is made in v. 28, both the moral uprightness that Job has trumpeted and the numinous dread he has displayed are the equivalent of wisdom and understanding. Since he is both a "God-fearer" and one who "turns from evil," now Job is also truly wise.

---

341 Clines, " 'The Fear of the Lord' " 79. He also states, "[I]t is almost universally agreed that by no means could this poem be set in the mouth of Job" (ibid). See also idem, *Job 21-37*, 908.

Chapter Four: A Philological and Textual Study of Job 28

Poetry is the art of using words charged with their utmost meaning.[1]

The language of this book is more vigorous and splendid than that of any other book in all the Scriptures.[2]

4.1 Introduction

Determining the original text of ancient literary documents and the meaning of their words has been an emphasis of biblical interpretation for centuries. In poetry—and especially in Joban poetry—the task can be extremely complex. Both words and text are often in dispute. Matters are made even more challenging since these are embedded in contexts in which meaning is heavily dependent upon an accretion of effects such as metaphor, parallelism, and phonological play—many of which are often quite foreign to modern readers standing now thousands of years away from ancient Israelite culture. As Robert Alter notes, "In Job, one encounters an astonishing inventiveness in the use of figurative language."[3]

The textual and philological study in this chapter builds upon the comparative philological and text-critical analyses of some of the most adept minds in ancient Near Eastern studies in the last century. The primary aim is to employ these methods while at the same time taking seriously the aesthetic rationale for restoring the text of the poem as a work of art.[4] The basic conviction underlying this chapter, as well as the

---

1 Dana Gioia, "Can Poetry Matter?" *Atlantic* 267/5 (May 1991): 105.

2 Martin Luther, "Preface to the Book of Job," in *Luther's Works, Volume 35: Word and Sacrament I* (ed. E. Theodore Bachmann; Phildelphia, Pa.: Fortress, 1960), 252.

3 Robert Alter, *The Book of Psalms: A Translation with Commentary* (New York and London: W. W. Norton & Co., 2007), xxiv. Note also the comments of F. W. Dobbs-Allsopp: "[I]n some poets, like Job, one is never in doubt of the verbal artistry on display, the inventiveness of the poetic idiom" ("Poetry, Hebrew," *NIDB* 4:552).

4 On this, see G. Thomas Tanselle, *A Rationale of Textual Criticism* (Philadelphia, Pa.: University of Pennsylvania Press, 1989).

remainder of the study, is that the nature of ancient texts is intimately tied up with their composition and afterlife as poetic works. As a result, interpretation cannot move simply from philology to literary analysis; nor can one begin with literary analysis without taking philological and textual considerations into account. The philological and literary modes—if one can even refer to them as separate things—are interrelated and reciprocal.

A particular challenge in the linguistic study of Job 28 is that many scholars have proposed that the poet employs rather common words in unparalleled technical senses. While such presumptions about the language the poem are not entirely misplaced, semantic arguments must be made both by appeal to comparative Semitic philology and in consideration of the cognitive domains in which the poem participates. These conceptual domains are now the focus of cognitive grammar, in which "the meaning of a word can only be understood against the background of a complete set of knowledge, beliefs, intuitions, and the like."[5] While I make no claims to have set out such a "complete set of knowledge" in the discussion of philology and text in Job 28, I believe that philological and textual criticism are best carried out against one's perception of the artistic rationale of the whole, illuminated by every piece of knowledge available about its symbolic and cultural contexts. Thus the poem as an aesthetic work both motivates and arises from the language that comprises it.

While English glosses from the translation are given as headings for the following commentary, the comments are organized according to the syntax of the Hebrew.

4.2 Texts and Versions Consulted in this Study

4.2.1 Witnesses to the Masoretic Text

For the Hebrew text of Job 28, I have consulted both the Aleppo Codex[6] (ca. 925 C.E.) and the Leningrad Codex (1009 C.E.; siglum: $B19^{A}$). The

5 Ronald Langacker, *Foundations of Cognitive Grammar, Volume 1: Theoretical Prerequisites* (Stanford: Stanford University Press, 1987), 147, as summarized by Pierre van Hecke, "Shepherds and Linguists: A Cognitive-Linguistic Approach to the Metaphor 'God is Shepherd' in Gen 48,15 and Context," in *Studies in the Book of Genesis: Literature, Redaction, and History* (ed. A. Wénin; BETL 155; Leuven: Leuven University Press, 2001), 480.

6 A facsimile of the Aleppo Codex may be found in the edition of Moshe H. Goshen-Gottstein, *The Aleppo Codex. Provided with massoretic notes and pointed by Aaron ben Asher. The Codex Considered authoritative by Maimonides. Part One: Plates* (Jerusalem:

latter is the base text for the now standard diplomatic critical edition edited by K. Elliger and W. Rudolph, *Biblia Hebraica Stuttgartensia*.[7]

Of these two codices, Aleppo is undoubtedly superior. As Moshe H. Goshen-Gottstein states:

> [C]omparison showed the two codices for what they are: the Aleppo Codex—the perfect original masterpiece which authenticates itself by internal criteria; the Leningrad Codex—a none-too-successful effort to adapt a manuscript of a different Tiberian subgroup to a Ben Asher Codex. The very attempt of the 'harmonizing' massorete of the Leningrad Codex is the most telling proof one can imagine that Aaron ben Asher's text was used as a model a few decades after his death. No scribe in his right mind would go to the trouble to adapt an existing manuscript to another model unless he recognized its superiority.[8]

In Job 28, Aleppo and Leningrad are identical, except in the spelling of one word in v. 8a. While Aleppo reads *hidrîkûhû*, the orthography of the Leningrad codex is more conservative with *hidrîkūhû*. This is striking, since where Leningrad and Aleppo elsewhere disagree in matters of orthography, it is typically Aleppo that is more orthographically conservative.[9] However, in Job 28:6, the spelling of Leningrad is most likely original. Generally speaking, fuller spellings were the tendency of later traditions, not earlier ones.[10] Given the fact that the two witnesses agree at every other point in Job 28, I do not distinguish between Masoretic MSS when citing the Hebrew text. The siglum MT throughout is simply shorthand for both the Aleppo and Leningrad codices.

I have also consulted the readings of other Hebrew MSS collected by Benjamin Kennicott in *Vetus Testamentum Hebraicum cum Variis Lectionibus*[11] and by Johannes B. de Rossi in *Variae Lectiones Veteris Testa-*

Magnes, 1976). One should also note the magnificent resource on the Aleppo Codex online: http://www.aleppocodex.org/. The entire codex is uploaded in digitized form and can be read at various levels of magnification.

7 *Biblia Hebraica Stuttgartensia* (5th, corrected edition; Stuttgart: Deutsche Bibelgesellschaft, 1997).

8 "The Aleppo Codex and the Rise of the Massoretic Bible Text," *BA* 42/3 (Summer 1979): 150.

9 Moshe Goshen-Gottstein, "The Authenticity of the Aleppo Codex," *Text* 1 (1960): 28 and n. 31.

10 That the autograph(a) of Job was orthographically conservative is also suggested by the unusually large number of archaistic forms in the book as well as the archaizing spellings of 4QpaleoJob. See discussion at ch. 4.2.6.

11 *Vetus Testamentum Hebraicum cum Variis Lectionibus* (2 vols.; Oxford: Clarendon, 1776-80).

menti ex Immensa MSS.[12] I cite these MSS by number. However, these variants do not stem from ancient traditions.[13]

In the late 18th century, Kennicott set out to collate Masoretic variants from about 694 MSS and countless editions in hopes of recovering the original text. Inspired by Kennicott, de Rossi's work was intended as a supplement, and he found and collated the variants of 732 MSS and 310 editions.[14] Yet the value of these 18th century collations is questionable. Though Kennicott himself thought he had discovered many important variants, the fact of the matter is, as Paul Kahle states, that "The MSS. used by Kennicott and his collaborators were written centuries later, in a time when all the real various readings of the consonantal text had been for a long time eliminated."[15] Yet these variants may still be useful in both illuminating the types of scribal confusions that may occur in the Masoretic tradition[16] as well as providing examples of orthographic variation in that tradition.

4.2.2 Witnesses to the Greek Text

Citations of the Septuagint are from Joseph Ziegler's eclectic critical edition in the Göttingen Septuagint series.[17] The Greek text of Job 28 which is printed there is precisely the same as that in the manual eclectic edition of Alfred Rahlfs,[18] excepting a few minor orthographic variations (σαπφίρου vs. σαπφείρου [v. 6a] and σαπφίρῳ vs. σαπθείρῳ [v. 16b]). I cite the Old Greek text as OG. Otherwise, I mark the additions to OG with an asterisk (⁎) and refer to these additions plus the OG to-

12 *Variae Lectiones Veteris Testamenti ex Immensa MSS* (Parmae: Regio, 1784).

13 Compare the comments of Bruce K. Zuckerman, "The Process of Translation in 11QtgJob: A Preliminary Study" (Ph.D. diss., Yale University, 1980), 20-21.

14 See Ira Maurice Price, "The Hebrew Text of the Old Testament," *The Biblical World* 37/4 (April 1911): 252.

15 Paul E. Kahle, *The Cairo Geniza* (The Schweich Lectures of the British Academy for 1941; London: Oxford University Press, 1947), 54. Also cited in William McKane, "Benjamin Kennicott: An Eighteenth-Century Researcher," *JTS* 28 (1977): 455 n. 4. Compare also the comments of Ernst Würthwein, *The Text of the Old Testament: An Introduction to the Biblica Hebraica* (trans. Erroll F. Rhodes; 2d ed., revised and enlarged; Grand Rapids, Mich.: Eerdmans, 1995), 40-41.

16 See Zuckerman, "The Process of Translation in 11QtgJob," 21.

17 *Iob* (Septuaginta: Vetus Testamentum Graecum; Auctoritate Academiea Scientiarum Gottingensis editum; XI/4; Göttingen: Vandenhoeck & Ruprecht, 1982).

18 *Septuaginta, Id est Vetus Testamentum graece iuxta LXX interpres* (Stuttgart: Deutsche Bibelgesellschaft, 1935).

gether as LXX.[19] I have also had occasion to check the three great uncials (LXX^B, LXX^S, LXX^A) in matters of orthography.[20]

For the revisions to the Septuagint preserved in the Greek tradition, I have used the edition of Frederick Field,[21] with an eye to Ziegler's apparatus that includes them. I cite the revisions by name. In cases in which the readings given by Field and Ziegler are in disagreement, I follow Ziegler (e.g., the reading of Symmachus in v. 26b).

Roughly four hundred years after the production of the Old Greek in ca. 150 B.C.E.,[22] Origen attempted to bring this translation into alignment with the Hebrew by adding lines from subsequent Greek tradition. Later church tradition, not Origen, suggests that these additions were from Theodotion.[23] Nevertheless, Theodotion seemed to have been Origen's primary source for this task, as the study of Peter Gentry has confirmed.

The Old Latin text is from C. P. Caspari, *Das Buch Hiob (1,1–38,16) in Hieronymous's Übersetzung aus der alexandrinischen Version*,[24] which is based on MS Sangallensis 11 from the monastery of St. Gallen. I cite this as OL. Manuscript Sangallensis is the earliest extant MS of Jerome's Old Latin translation, dating to the 8th century. However, it does not preserve hexaplaric signs.[25]

---

19 On the nature of the asterisked materials in Job, see Peter John Gentry, *The Asterisked Materials in the Greek Job* (SBLSCS 38; Atlanta, Ga.: Scholars, 1995); idem, "The Place of Theodotion-Job in the Textual History of the Septuagint," in *Origen's Hexapla and Fragments: Papers presented at the Rich Seminar on the Hexapla, Oxford Centre for Hebrew and Jewish Studies, 25th July – 3rd August 1994* (ed. Alison Salvesen; TSAJ 58; eds. Martin Hengel and Peter Schäfer; Tübingen: Mohr Siebeck, 1998), 199-230.

20 For Codex Vaticanus of the Book of Job, see *Bibliorum Sacrorum Graecorum Codex Vaticanus B. Bibliothecae Apostolicae Vaticanae Codex Vaticanus Graecus 1209* (Roma: Istituto Poligrafico e Zecca Della Stato, 1999). For Codex Sinaiticus of Job, see *Codex Sinaiticus Petropolitanus et Friderico-Augustanus Lipsiensis. The Old Testament Reproduced in Facsimile from Photographs by Helen and Kirsopp Lake* (Oxford: Clarendon, 1922). For Codex Alexandrinus of Job, see volume 3 of *Facsimile of the Codex Alexandrinus. Old Testament* (4 vols.; London: The British Museum, 1879-1883).

21 *Origenis Hexaplorum quae supersunt: sive, Veterum interpretum graecorum in totum Vetus Testamentum fragmenta: post Flaminium, Nobilium, Drusium, et Montefalconium, adhibita etiam versione syro-hexaplari* (2 vols.; Hildesheim: G. Olms, 1964). Originally published by Oxford University Press, 1875.

22 See Witte, "The Greek Book of Job," 53, for this date of the OG.

23 Gentry, *The Asterisked Materials in the Greek Job*, 5, 7.

24 *Das Buch Hiob (1,1–38,16) in Hieronymous's Übersetzung aus der alexandrinischen Version* (Christiania: A. W. Brøggers Bogtrykkeri, 1893).

25 See James Herbert Gailey, "Jerome's Latin Version of Job from the Greek, Chapters 1-26: Its Text, Character, and Provenance" (Th.D. diss., Princeton Theological Seminary, 1945), 42.

Jerome undertook this Latin translation beginning in 387 from a hexaplaric Greek text prior to his new Vulgate translation from the "*hebraica veritas*" in 390.[26] "In general... Jerome's earlier Latin version of the Book of Job is witness to a somewhat modified form of the Fifth Column of Origen's *Hexapla*."[27]

The Syro-hexaplaric readings are from the facsimile edition of Antonio Maria Ceriani: *Codex Syro-Hexaplaris Ambrosianus, photolithographice editus*.[28] I cite this as Syh. This witness to the Greek text of Job was made in 616-17 C.E. in Alexandria, Egypt, by Paul, Bishop of Tella, and it is a translation of the fifth column of Origen's *Hexapla* into Syriac. It it is particularly useful in reconstructing the Theodotionic additions to the OG in LXX, since it marks these additions more consistently with Aristarchian signs.[29]

The value of the Septuagint in restoring the Hebrew text of Job has been doubted in the last century.[30] Not only are the MSS of LXX hexaplaric; many scholars have argued that the Greek version of Job is paraphrastic, exemplifying intentional changes by the translator based, for example, on theological bias or stylistic preference.[31]

In an important series of articles, Harry Orlinsky defended the usefulness of the Greek version of Job for reconstructing its *Vorlage* both by calling into question the assumption that the translator(s) of the OG

---

26 Dhorme, *Book of Job*, ccvi-ccvii, ccxii, ccxiv-ccxv.

27 Gailey, *Jerome's Latin Version of Job from the Greek, Chapters 1-26: Its Text, Character, and Provenance. An Abstract of a Dissertation Submitted in Partial Fulfillment of the Requirements for the Degree of Doctor of Theology, Princeton Theological Seminary, Princeton, New Jersey* (Princeton Seminary Pamphlet Series; Princeton, NJ: Committee on Publications, 1948), 11.

28 *Codex Syro-Hexaplaris Ambrosianus, photolithographice editus* (Monumenta Sacra et Profana 7; Florence and London: Mediolani, Impensis Bibliothecae Ambrosianae, 1874).

29 Dhorme, *Book of Job*, ccvii.

30 See the brief survey of positions in Witte, "The Greek Book of Job," 36-37.

31 See, e.g., ibid., 37; Dhorme, *Book of Job*, cxcvi; Driver and Gray, *The Book of Job*, 1:lxxi; Pope, *Job*, xliv; Henry S. Gehman, "The Theological Approach of the Greek Translator of Job 1-15," *JBL* 68 (1949): 231-40; Donald H. Gard, "The Concept of Job's Character According to the Greek Translator of the Hebrew Text," *JBL* 72 (1953): 182-86; idem, "The Concept of the Future Life According to the Greek Translator of the Book of Job," *JBL* 73 (1954): 137-143; Zerafa, *Wisdom of God*, 134-56; Fernández Marcos, "The Septuagint Reading of the Book of Job," 256; Kenneth Numfor Ngwa, *The Hermeneutics of the 'Happy' Ending in Job 42:7-17* (BZAW 354; ed. John Barton et al.; Berlin and New York: Walter de Gruyter, 2005), 34-35; Karl V. Kutz, "The Old Greek of Job: A Study in Early Biblical Exegesis" (Ph.D. diss., University of Wisconsin-Madison, 1997); idem, "Characterization in the Old Greek of Job," in *Seeking Out the Wisdom of the Ancients: Essays Offered to Honor Michael V. Fox on the Occasion of His Sixty-Fifth Birthday* (eds. Ronald L. Troxel, Kelvin G. Friebel, and Dennis R. Magary; Winona Lake, Ind.: Eisenbrauns, 2005), 346; cf. 354-55.

would have been so free as to shorten an original Hebrew *Vorlage* by 1/6 (about 390 "lines"[32]) and by providing specific examples of various theological and literary tendencies of the translator(s).[33] Once these tendencies are recognized, the Hebrew *Vorlage* may still be recovered. The question then becomes not whether LXX-Job is useful for restoring the Hebrew *Vorlage*, but how to understand the character of LXX-Job so as to be able to determine its *Vorlage* more accurately. The Greek translation of Job 28 offers very few challenges to discerning an underlying Hebrew *Vorlage*. The translator's obvious struggles with the Hebrew text at points are, in fact, a great help to this enterprise.

However, Orlinsky's argument that there are no theological biases at work in the shortening of the OG of Job has not received unanimous support.[34] Other scholars are much more willing to concede a great deal of freedom in the technique of the Greek translator(s). As a representative of this view, Natalio Fernández Marcos believes that the Greek translator had before him a Hebrew *Vorlage* "not too different from the preserved Masoretic text."[35] In this vein, Claude Cox states, "[I]t is the translator himself who abbreviated the text..."[36] Johann Cook, however, argues for a mediating position which moves back toward Orlinsky's

---

32 The count of 390 lines given by Fernández Marcos ("The Septuagint Reading of the Book of Job," 251). However, these are "lines" in the three great Greek uncials (LXX^B, LXX^S, LXX^A), not poetic lines, as I define "line" in this study (see ch. 1.5). As Fernández Marcos states, "The complete Greek text with asterisks has a total of 2200 lines in the extant Greek codices, while the non asterised [sic!; read: asterisked] text amounts to ca. 1800 lines only" (ibid., 252 n. 3). The distribution of the asterisked material throughout the Book of Job is uneven. For figures, see Driver and Gray, *The Book of Job*, 1:lxxv; and Dhorme, *Book of Job*, ccii-cciii.

33 Harry Orlinsky, "Studies in the Septuagint of the Book of Job," *HUCA* 29 (1957): 53-74; *HUCA* 29 (1958): 229-71; *HUCA* 30 (1959): 153-67; *HUCA* 32 (1961): 239-68; *HUCA* 33 (1962): 119-51; *HUCA* 35 (1964): 57-78; *HUCA* 36 (1966): 37-47.

34 Note Orlinsky's comments: "There is nothing theological or tendencious in the Greek; there is nothing but the usual factors involved in turning the Hebrew into Greek: the honest attempt on the part of the translator to interpret and translate the Hebrew correctly; the possibility of different Hebrew readings in his *Vorlage*; and the temper of the translator in the matter of style" ("Studies in the Septuagint of Job. Chapter III.B: Anthropopathisms," *HUCA* 32 [1961]: 250). He states elsewhere, "[I]t is simply incredible that with the overall philosophy of translation practiced by the Septuagint translators and from the internal evidence readily available in the Greek and Hebrew texts of Job to anyone who cared to study them directly and objectively, anyone could seriously charge the translator with deleting words and phrases and sections" ("The Septuagint as Holy Writ and the Philosophy of the Translators," *HUCA* 46 [1975]: 112).

35 Fernández Marcos, "The Septuagint Reading of the Book of Job," 263 and 254-55.

36 Claude E. Cox, "Methodological Issues in the Exegesis of LXX Job," in *VI Congress of the International Organization for Septuagint and Cognate Studies, Jerusalem 1986* (ed. Claude E. Cox; SBLSCS 23; Atlanta, Ga.: Scholars, 1987), 80.

more conservative view, suggesting that the length of the Greek text of Job may be due both to shorter Hebrew *Vorlagen* and to techniques of the Greek translators.[37] Cook's approach has much to commend it. But whatever the reasons for the shorter text, the Septuagint of Job reads differently than the MT as poetry and theology.[38]

4.2.3 The Peshitta

For the Peshitta, I have used the critical edition prepared by L. G. Rignell for the Leiden Peshitta project,[39] which I cite as Syr. The Leiden edition is diplomatic, based on MS B.21 *Inferiore* of the Ambrosian Library in Milan. The MS dates to the 6th century C.E., and it is the oldest complete MS of the OT in Syriac. Rignell has collated 44 MSS for variants, but they are most often of little consequence.[40]

It is typically believed that the translator(s) of the Peshitta consulted a Hebrew *Vorlage* very close to the MT.[41] The question remains, however, as to how reliable the Peshitta translation is for reconstructing that *Vorlage*. One important consideration is the extent to which the Peshitta has been influenced by other versions. While influence of the LXX seems reasonable in certain cases,[42] it should not be assumed that the Peshitta relies heavily on the Greek translation.[43] In fact, it is evident in the most difficult lines in Job 28 that the Peshitta did not rely on the LXX tradition (cf. LXX and Syr. in v. 4).[44] Heidi Szpek has also shown that significant influence by the rabbinic Targum on the Peshitta is unlikely.[45] On the whole, the Peshitta should be considered an inde-

---

37 Johann Cook, "Aspects of Wisdom in the Texts of Job (Chapter 28)—*Vorlage(n)* and/or translator(s)?" *OTE* 5 (1992): 26-27, 29-31, 34.

38 See the observations of Witte, "The Greek Book of Job," 38-52.

39 *The Old Testament in Syriac According to the Peshiṭta Version, II/1a* (edited on behalf of the International Orgainzation for the Study of the Old Testament by The Peshiṭta Institute; Leiden: E. J. Brill, 1982).

40 For the information contained in the above paragraph, see Heidi M. Szpek, "On the Influence of the Septuagint on the Peshitta," *CBQ* 60 (1998): 252-255. On the nature of the MS tradition of the Peshitta of Job, see L. G. Rignell, "Notes on the Peshiṭta of the Book of Job," *ASTI* 9 (1973): 103.

41 See, e.g., Szpek, "On the Influence of the Septuagint on the Peshitta," 255.

42 Heidi M. Szpek, "An Observation on the *Peshiṭta*'s Translation of *ŠDY* in Job," *VT* 47 (1997): 550-53.

43 Szpek, "On the Influence of the Septuagint on the Peshitta," 256-65.

44 Ibid., 259-60.

45 "On the Influence of the Targum on the Peshitta to Job," in *Targum Studies, Volume Two: Targum and Peshitta* (ed. Paul V. M. Flesher; SFSHJ 165; ed. J. Neusner; Atlanta, Ga.: Scholars and University of South Florida, 1998), 142-158.

pendent translation of the Hebrew. Once the character of the Peshitta is understood, it remains a reliable and important window to a Hebrew *Vorlage* very close to MT.[46]

4.2.4 The Vulgate

Citations from the Vulgate are based on the manual diplomatic edition of R. Weber, *Biblia Sacra Iuxta Vulgatam Versionem*,[47] which I cite as Vg. After an initial attempt to correct Old Latin translations of the LXX with recourse to Origen's *Hexapla* (especially the fifth column), Jerome became suspicious that both OL and LXX had been corrupted. Thus, in 390 he began his Vulgate translation from the "*hebraica veritas*," which was meant to replace Origen's *Hexapla* in the West. Though Jerome never completely freed himself from the revisions of "the three" in Origen's *Hexapla*, the Vulgate remains an important witness to the Hebrew text of Job.[48]

4.2.5 The Rabbinic Targum

Citations of the rabbinic Targum are primarily from David M. Stec's edition, *The Text of the Targum of Job*,[49] which I cite as Tg. There has also been occasion to refer to specific MSS as well—particularly MS Madrid, Biblioteca de la Universidad Complutense 116-Z-40, which is transcribed in Luis Díez Merino, *Targum de Job: Edición Principe del Ms. Villa-Amil n. 5 de Alfonso de Zamora*.[50] I cite this MS as Tg^{M}. Unfortunately,

---

46 On the character of the Peshitta of Job as a translation, see Heidi M. Szpek, *Translation Technique in the Peshitta to Job: A Model for Evaluating a Text with Documentation from the Peshitta to Job* (SBLDS 137; ed. David L. Petersen; Atlanta, Ga.: Scholars, 1992).

47 *Biblia Sacra Iuxta Vulgatam Versionem, Tomus I: Genesis-Psalmi* (3d, corrected edition; 2 vols.; Stuttgart: Deutsche Bibelgesellschaft, 1985).

48 Eva Schulz-Flügel, "The Latin Old Testament Tradition," in *Hebrew Bible/Old Testament: Its History of Interpretation* (ed. Magne Saebø; 2 vols.; Göttingen: Vandenhoeck and Ruprecht, 1996), I.1:642-62; Dhorme, *Book of Job*, xxxiv-ccxcvi. Dhorme states, "[W]e are compelled to admit the inestimable superiority of the genius of St. Jerome, whose concern to safeguard the *hebraica veritas* was reconciled with the demands of his taste in Latin" (ccxvi).

49 *The Text of the Targum of Job: An Introduction and Critical Edition* (AGJU 20; Leiden, New York, and Köln: E. J. Brill, 1994).

50 *Targum de Job: Edición Principe del Ms. Villa-Amil n. 5 de Alfonso de Zamora* (Bibliotheca Hispana Biblica 8; Madrid: Consejo Superior de Investigaciones Cientificas, Instituto "Francisco Suarez," 1984).

Díez Merino's transcription is rife with errors. Stec, however, provides a helpful appendix in his edition cataloguing the errors in this transcription of MS Madrid.[51] I have also consulted the old "critical edition" of the rabbinic Targum in Paul de Lagarde's *Hagiographa Chaldaice*,[52] which I cite as Tg^L. The English translation of Céline Mangan[53] in *The Aramaic Bible* is based on the critical edition prepared as a doctoral thesis by F. J. Fernández Vallina[54] under the supervision of A. Díez-Macho, which used MS Or. Ee. 5.9 of the Cambridge University Library as its base text. Unfortunately, I did not have access to this edition. However, I have made it a point to consult Stec's apparatus for the readings of MS Or. Ee. 5.9, since it is among the most important MSS of the rabbinic Targum of Job.[55] I cite this as Tg^C.

As a translation, "the Targum of Job displays a remarkable fidelity to the Hebrew source text and is quite scrupulous in its preservation of the form and order of MT Job."[56] A comparison of the translation of the rabbinic Targum with the Peshitta and with 11Q10 bears out this generalization in many cases.[57] This quite literal tendency of the rabbinic Targum enhances its usefulness in restoring the MT-like *Vorlage* used by the translator.[58] It contains some expansions, but the nature of these is rather predictable (see, e.g., Job 28:6 [Garden of Eden and Gehenna], v. 7 [Sammael], v. 22a [angel of death], v. 22b [wisdom = Torah], v. 27a [angels]).[59]

---

51 Stec, *The Text of the Targum of Job*, 331*-339* (Appendix 2).

52 *Hagiographa Chaldaice* (Leipzig: B. G. Teubneri, 1873), 105-106.

53 Mangan, "The Targum of Job. Translated with a Critical Introduction Apparatus, and Notes," in *The Aramaic Bible: The Targums of Job, Proverbs, and Qohelet* (ArBib 15; eds. Kevin Cathcart, Michael Maher, and Martin MacNamara; Collegeville, Minn.: Liturgical Press, 1991).

54 Fernández Vallina, "El Targum de Job" (Ph.D diss., Universidad Complutense de Madrid, 1982).

55 Of about 14 MSS of the rabbinic Targum of Job, MS Or. Ee. 5.9 may be the best (see Philip S. Alexander, "Targum, Targumim," *ABD* 6:325). See also the evaluation of most of the manuscripts of the rabbinic targums in Luis Díez Merino, "Manuscritos del Targum de Job," *Hen* 4 (1982): 41-64.

56 David Shepherd, *Targum and Translation: A Reconsideration of the Qumran Aramaic Version of Job* (SSN 45; ed. W.J. van Bekkum et al.; Assen, The Netherlands: Koninlijke Van Gorcum, 2004), 280.

57 Ibid. See also idem, "Will the Real Targum Please Stand Up?: Translation and Coordination in the Ancient Aramaic Versions of Job," *JJS* 51 (2000): 88-116.

58 Mangan, "The Targum of Job," 14.

59 Ibid., 15-16, and idem, "The Interpretation of Job in the Targums," 267-280.

4.2.6 Job at Qumran

For the text of the Qumran "targum"[60] to Job found in cave 11 (11Q10), I have consulted three studies: The first is the most recent edition prepared by Florentino García Martínez, Eibert J. C. Tigchelaar, and Adam S. van der Woude in the *Discoveries in the Judean Desert* series,[61] which incorporates the principal edition by J. P. M. van der Ploeg and A. S. van der Woude;[62] second is the 1974 edition of Michael Sokoloff, *The Targum to Job from Qumran Cave XI*;[63] finally, I have consulted the unpublished study of the first 15 columns of the scroll by Bruce Zuckerman.[64] I cite the Qumran text by item number (11Q10) or composition (11QtgJob).

Though 11Q10 is occasionally paraphrastic or expansive, it is fair to say, with Fitzmyer, that "By and large the targum is a rather literal translation of the Hebrew."[65] As Heidi Szpek notes, "[I]t is more cautious with explicit exegesis like Tg-Job, but lacking doublets and midrashic expansions like P-Job."[66] While it is not impossible that the translator(s) of 11Q10 had access to different *Vorlagen*, it seems that its Hebrew source text was quite close to MT.[67] If this is the case, the discrepancies between MT and 11Q10 may be seen as largely the result of the technique of the Aramaic translator(s).[68] Though 11Q10 is fragmen-

---

60 The possible infelicity of the term "targum" for 11Q10 has been brought into focus most recently by David Shepherd in his monograph, *Targum and Translation* (see also idem, "Will the Real Targum Please Stand Up," 113-116). Shepherd has reservations about calling 11Q10 a "targum," since 11Q10 is not nearly as "literal" in rendering every element of the Hebrew source text into Aramaic as is the rabbinic Targum. However, I have retained this nomenclature and still believe it to be viable. Shepherd himself recognizes that "The question is… at base a definitional one" ("Will the Real Targum Please Stand Up," 115), but his definition may not be inclusive enough (see Sally L. Gold, review of David Shepherd, *Targum and Translation: A Reconsideration of the Qumran Aramaic Version of Job*, *HS* 46 [2005]: 430-33).

61 *Qumran Cave 11/2 (11Q2-18, 11Q20-31)* (DJD 23; Oxford: Clarendon, 1998).

62 J. P. M. van der Ploeg and A. S. van der Woude (with the collaboration of B. Jongeling), *Le Targum de Job de la Grotte XI de Qumrân* (Leiden: E. J. Brill, 1971).

63 Sokoloff, *The Targum to Job from Qumran Cave XI* (Ramat-Gan: Bar-Ilan University, 1974).

64 Zuckerman, "The Process of Translation in 11QtgJob."

65 Joseph Fitzmyer, "Some Observations on the Targum of Job from Qumran Cave 11," *CBQ* 36 (1974): 509. Compare the comments of Bruce Zuckerman in "Job, Targums of," *ABD* 3:868-69, and idem, "Two Examples of Editorial Modification in 11QtgJob," in *Biblical and Near Eastern Studies: Essays in Honor of William Sanford LaSor* (ed. Gary Tuttle; Grand Rapids, Mich.: Eerdmans, 1978), 269.

66 Szpek, "On the Influence of the Targum," 158.

67 Sokoloff, *The Targum of Job from Qumran Cave XI*, 6.

68 Shepherd, *Targum and Translation*, 7.

tary for Job 28, what is preserved reflects a *Vorlage* very close to the received text.

Also significant for the study of the text of Job are the paleo-Hebrew fragments of Job 13-14 found in cave four at Qumran (4QpaleoJob^c = 4Q101).[69] While they contain no fragments of Job 28, the script and orthography of these MSS must be taken into account when considering the nature of the autograph(a) of the biblical Book of Job and its early copies.

David Noel Freedman has noted the conservative orthographic tendencies in the Book of Job, and from its orthography he draws the conclusions that Job is both northern and early.[70] However, the nature of 4QpaleoJob^c may suggest quite a different explanation.

The Qumran orthography and script are clearly archaizing rather than archaic—not only in accord with the early rabbinic tradition that the Book of Job was written by Moses,[71] but also possibly as an attempt to match the script and orthography of the autograph.[72] Though in a fragmentary context, the apparently fuller spelling of *ym*[*wt*] (instead of *ymt*) in 4Q101 of Job 14:14 may be evidence of the Qumran scribe's inconsistency in the task of orthographic archaizing.[73] In a similar fashion, the conservative spelling in the Book of Job is more likely to have been an intentional literary device of the Joban poet, who wrote as much for the eye as for the ear, than a clue to the text's date and provenance.[74] If this is the case, it gives the text critic of Job further evidence suggesting the originality of conservative orthography in weighing Masoretic vari-

69 See Patrick W. Skehan, Eugene Ulrich, and Judith E. Sanderson, eds., *Qumran Cave 4/IV: Palaeo-Hebrew and Greek Biblical Manuscripts* (DJD 9; Oxford: Clarendon, 1992), 155-57 and plate 101.

70 Freedman, "Orthographic Peculiarities in the Book of Job," *ErIsr* 9 (1969): 43*. James Barr has offered important criticisms of Freedman's presentation in his essay, "Hebrew Orthography and the Book of Job," *JSS* 30 (1985): 1-33. He states, "*The spellings of the MT of Job, and even of this group among them, may well have nothing to do with the origins and provenance of the book, and give no evidence about them*" ("Hebrew Orthography," 32 [emphasis original]). However, Barr also states, "I do not dispute that the incidence of defective spellings, as noticed by Freedman, may be rather higher in Job than in many other books" (ibid.).

71 See *b. Baba Batra* 14b, 15a.

72 C. L. Seow, "The Orthography of Job and its Poetic Effects" (paper presented at the annual meeting of the SBL, Boston, Mass., 24 November 2008).

73 For this reading, see Skehan, Ulrich, and Sanderson, *Qumran Cave 4/IV*, 156-57, but compare plate 101, in which the reading of a *wāw* on the right edge of the fragment is no longer clear. Another datum that is more clearly attested is the spelling of *ydyk* in 14:15b (see plate 101), though this could simply be an historical spelling of the diphthong (*yadayk*) rather than an internal *mater lectionis*, as the editors note (ibid, 155).

74 Seow, "The Orthography of Job."

ants or explaining the readings of the versions that arose from such spellings in their *Vorlagen*.

4.3 Commentary on Job 28:1-14, 20-28

1a. ***Indeed*** [*kî*]: This small word at the beginning of the poem is a *crux interpretum*. The translation of this particle and one's assumptions about the function of the chapter are integrally related. Since the poem begins with this particle without introduction, it is often supposed that something has been left out in the current text.[75] The judgment that commonly follows is that the poem appears to be disjoined from what immediately precedes it in ch. 27.[76] Thus the interpretation of *kî* in Job 28:1 often weighs heavily in treatments of the chapter as independent poem, whether composed by the poet of the Poem of Job or a later editor. Arnold Ehrlich's statement is representative: »Tatsächlich passt dieses ganze Kapitel nicht als Rede Hiobs und dasselbe kann hier nicht ursprünglich sein.«[77] This is the virtual interpretive consensus on Job 28. Despite this consensus, it is noteworthy that ch. 28 is not set off in any way from the end of ch. 27 in the Leningrad Codex.[78] D. C. Caspari, the editor of an edition of Jerome's Old Latin translation, remarked about ch. 28 in the 8th century codex on which his edition is based (MS Sangallensis 11): »Im Cod[ex] weder eine neue Zeile, noch ein Interpunktionszeichen.«[79]

The word *kî* poses no problems in the textual traditions. It is attested in all Heb. MSS. While Jerome's Vg. does not reflect it, this seems to have been more a matter of his taste in translation and is not evi-

75 This, of course, is a result of what these scholars believe to be the most probable function of *kî*. Note, for example, Bernhard Duhm, *Das Buch Hiob erklärt*, 134, who supposes that the current introduction was preceded by the refrain now found in 28:12, 20; Duhm is followed by Gordis, *The Book of Job*, 304; Fohrer, *Das Buch Hiob*, 389-90; *BHK*, and others. Compare also Driver and Gray, *The Book of Job*, 1:235. Claus Westermann, following Lindblom, König, and Lefèvre, raises the possibility that 27:11-12 was originally the introduction to ch. 28 (*Aufbau*, 130 and n. 1).

76 Morris Jastrow, however, argues in the opposite direction, suggesting that *kî* was added by a later editor in order to *connect* ch. 28 with ch. 27 (*The Book of Job: Its Origin, Growth, and Interpretation* [Philadelphia and London: J. B. Lippincott Company, 1920], 310 n. 31).

77 Arnold B. Ehrlich, *Randglossen zur Hebräischen Bibel. Textkritisches, Sprachliches, und Sachliches* (7 vols.; Leipzig: J. C. Hinrichs, 1908-14), 6:290.

78 In the Aleppo Codex, 28:1 begins on the following line, but there is no space which suggests a break between 27:13 and the beginning of ch. 28.

79 Caspari, *Hiob in Hieronymous's Übersetzung*, 89 n. 1.

dence of a textual variant. It is likewise unrepresented by many modern translations (NIV; JB; NJB; NEB; NJPS).[80]

The most common rendering of *kî* in 28:1 is the asseverative "surely," "indeed," or the like.[81] However, a few commentators prefer the more ambiguous "for," which often suggests causal or logical relation to what precedes it.[82] The translations of the ancient versions are of little help. Many of the semantic difficulties of Heb. *kî* are found in these terms as well (OG γάρ [Syh *gyr* and OL *enim*]; Syr. *mṭl d*; Tg. *ʾrwm*).

Recent studies of *kî* suggest a basic connective and causal function.[83] The logical or causal relation between the end of ch. 27 and the beginning of ch. 28, however, is not readily apparent.[84] It may be that a formula introducing direct speech once preceded *kî*, which could then be interpreted according to its "recitative" function.[85] If there has been an elision of a speech formula before 28:1, it may have been identical to those found in 27:1 and 29:1: *wayyōsep ʾiyyôb śĕʾēt mĕšālô wayyōʾmar*. Job 28, in fact, may be interpreted as a *māšāl* (see discussion in chs. 6.6-6.7).[86]

---

80 See also Pope, *Job*, 197; and Hartley, *The Book of Job*, 373.

81 E.g., RSV, NRSV, KJV, NKJV, NAS, NAB; Driver and Gray, *The Book of Job*, 1:236; Dhorme, *Book of Job*, 399; Rowley, *The Book of Job*, 179; Fohrer, *Das Buch Hiob*, 389; Hans Strauß, *Hiob 19,1-42,7* (BKAT 16/2; Neukirchen-Vluyn: Neukirchener Verlag, 2000), 130; Gordis, *The Book of Job*, 300, 304; Michel, "The Ugaritic Texts," 203; Habel, *The Book of Job*, 388-89; Samuel Terrien, *Job* (Commentaire de l'ancien Testament XIII; Neuchâtel: Delachaux & Niestlé, 1963), 190; Weiser, *Das Buch Hiob*, 195; Hesse, *Hiob*, 156; Geller, " 'Where is Wisdom?' " 177 n. 4. Compare Elwolde, "Non-Contiguous Parallelism," 111.

82 Tur-Sinai, *The Book of Job*, 394; Franz Delitzsch, *A Biblical Commentary on the Book of Job* (2 vols.; trans. Francis Bolton; Edinburgh: T & T Clark, 1966), 2:91. Edward J. Kissane, however, translates *kî* temporally ("when") suggesting that this marks the protasis with the apodosis following in v. 3a (*The Book of Job Translated from a Critically Revised Hebrew Text with Commentary* [Dublin: Browne and Nolan Limited / The Richview Press, 1939], 173, 176).

83 E.g., Anneli Aejmelaeus, "Function and Interpretation of כי in Biblical Hebrew," *JBL* 105 (1986): 193-209, esp. 203.

84 Edward Greenstein has relocated the chapter to the end of Elihu's speeches in 37:24. He thus treats *kî* in 28:1 as causal and connective, following the statement in 37:24, where *hûʾ* and *śām* in 28:3 would find an antecedent in *šadday* of 37:23 ("The Poem on Wisdom in Job 28," 271-72). He conjectures that ch. 28 suffered mis-location due to a mis-collation of manuscripts (ibid., 269).

85 R. J. Williams, *Hebrew Syntax: An Outline* (Toronto: University of Toronto Press, 1967), §452.

86 In raising the possibility that Job 28 may be interpreted as a *māšāl*, I do not intend to denote a formal genre but to emphasize its function within the dialogues. But even if stressing more of a functional approach to *mĕšālîm*, there is still a wide range of functions that a *māšāl* can serve in the OT. Generally speaking, it seems that a *māšāl* func-

The problems with this view are two-fold: First, none of the other speech formulae in the Book of Job use *kî* in this fashion. Second, positing an original speech formula before ch. 28 would seem to be proof of the poem's secondary nature. In other words, it would be easy to suppose that, if a section of the book is introduced by a speech formula, the named speaker cannot have been the speaker of the previous section. This is how the formulae work in the first and second cycles of the dialogues. However, in the third cycle of Job, some of these formulae are repeated between sections attributed to the same speaker (e.g., 26:1; 27:1; 29:1). Similar repetition is found in the speeches of Elihu (32:6; 34:1; 35:1; 36:1) and of Yhwh (38:1; 40:1).

The particle might also be considered concessive, being translated "although" or "even though." Several of the examples adduced by Joüon in which *kî* precedes the main clause serve this function indisputably (Jer 51:53; Zech 8:6; Ps 37:24; Prov 6:35).[87] In this case, a concessive statement in Job 28:1: "Though there is…" would be continued by *wĕhaḥokmâ mēʾayin timmāṣēʾ* in v. 12 and *wĕhaḥokmâ mēʾayin tābôʾ* in v. 20.[88] The concessive construction *kî... wĕ...* is attested also in Isa 54:10.

Edward Greenstein has recently expressed caution about the asseverative *kî* in BH: "The instances of asseverative כי in Biblical Hebrew are, contrary to popular belief, extremely rare."[89] Anneli Aejmelaeus and W. T. Claassen have also objected to the frequency with which scholars employ the emphatic interpretation.[90]

---

tions much like a metaphor (or simile) in that the mechanism is basically comparison; yet, the more specific use of the *māšāl* in context depends upon what aspects are highlighted. It may in some cases be more intentionally didactic, more allegorizing, or even serve to ridicule. It may include aspects of all of these. Following Timothy Polk's helpful study, I want to highlight here the nature of a *māšāl* as a *parable*, or *extended metaphor*, that draws the audience in to its world ultimately to force them to reflect on their experience in relation to the truth or integrity of that created world (see Timothy Polk, "Paradigms, Parables, and *Mĕšālîm*: On Reading the *Māšāl* in Scripture," *CBQ* 45 [1983]: 572-73).

87 Joüon §171b.

88 Hartley also suggests that "Possibly the *kî* works in conjunction with the *waw* of v. 12" (*The Book of Job*, 373 n. 1).

89 Greenstein, "The Poem on Wisdom in Job 28," 265. He points to the comments of Driver and Gray, who state, " 'Surely' (v.[1]) is a doubtful rendering of כי : if the particle has its usual meaning, *for* or *because*, something obviously must have preceded it…" (*Job*, 1:235). It is interesting that this is nonetheless exactly how they render it in their translation of the passage: "surely" (ibid., 1:236). See also ibid., 2:190.

90 Aejmelaeus, "Function and Interpretation of כי," 208. She admits an emphatic or asseverative function, though she believes that there is less and less room for this interpretation (ibid., 208). She also states, "I regard it as more appropriate... to remain with the causal interpretation of כי, that is, causal in the broadest sense of the word...

The emphatic interpretation of *kî* is based largely on two data. First, it rests heavily on the scholarly consensus of the particle's etymology. As Aejmelaeus states, "It is generally agreed that the origin of כי is to be found in a non-connective deictic or demonstrative particle."[91] Takamitsu Muraoka concurs: "It seems to me that there can hardly be any legitimate doubt about this etymological identification."[92] The arguments of James Muilenburg and Anton Schoors, which emphasize the emphatic function of the particle, rest heavily, though not solely, on this etymological connection.[93] Even though she grants the validity of this etymology, Aejmelaeus rightly points out that *kî* would not necessarily carry its etymology into its numerous other functions now attested in BH.[94] This is the case, even if its originally demonstrative function is likely the source for its use as an asseverative or emphatic particle.[95]

Second, the emphatic interpretation rests on cognate evidence in Semitic, particularly Ugaritic. It is commonplace to affirm that Ug. /k/ may be understood in some cases as emphatic, likely vocalized [kī].[96] Many scholars believe that, in addition to its uses as a preposition (=/km/), Ug. /k/ may function as a conjunction to mark a conditional clause, as a causal conjunction, or as an "emphasizing particle before [a]

---

and to regard כי as connective rather than an emphatic or asseverative particle" (ibid., 205).

W. T. Claassen ("Speaker-Oriented Functions of *Kî* in Biblical Hebrew," *JNSL* 11 [1983]: 29-46) argues that "emphasis" is often a default mode for when interpreters are uncertain about classifying the particle's function in any other, more commonly accepted, way. He believes that this interpretation has been abused and that commentators have most often neglected to consider the context *preceding* the particle for their intense occupation with the context that *follows* it. Claassen sets forth what he calls the "evidential" function of *kî* in addition to what has traditionally been understood as its causal function. His new category, which encompasses both evidence and motivation of various sorts, is then a subset of Aejmelaeus' "causal function," as she points out ("Function and Interpretation of כי," 203).

91 Aejmelaeus, "Function and Interpretation of כי," 195.

92 Takamitsu Muraoka, *Emphatic Words and Structures in Biblical Hebrew* (Jerusalem: The Magnes Press; Leiden: E. J. Brill, 1985), 159.

93 Muilenburg states, "For from an original exclamatory interjection or cry it has developed into a vast variety of nuances and meanings, yet always preserving in one fashion or another its original emphatic connotations…" ("The Linguistic and Rhetorical Usages of the Particle כי in the Old Testament," 160). Anton Schoors, "The Particle כי," in *Remembering all the way…: A collection of Old Testament studies published on the occasion of the fortieth anniversary of the Oudtestamentisch Werkgezelschap in Nederland* (*OtSt* 11; ed. A. S. van der Woude, et al.; Leiden: Brill, 1981), 240-76.

94 Aejmelaeus, "Function and Interpretation of כי," 203.

95 Muraoka, *Emphatic Words and Structures*, 164.

96 See Robert Gordis, "The Asseverative Kaph in Ugaritic and Hebrew," *JAOS* 63 (1943): 176-78.

verb at [the] end of [a] clause."[97] This emphatic interpretation of Ug. /k/ also finds support in the grammars of Daniel Sivan and Josef Tropper.[98] Tropper glosses it »ja!, gewiß, fürwahr,« but he admits, »Die Abgrenzung von *k* mit affirmativer (›emphatischer‹) Bedeutung von der kausal-koordinierenden Konj[unktion] *k* ist – insbesondere in satzeinleitender Position – schwierig.«[99] Thus emphatic/asseverative /k/ in Ugaritic is not beyond dispute.[100] Dennis Pardee has raised the possibility that, given the verb-final syntax of the clauses in which the so-called "emphatic *k*" is said to occur, it is the *word order* of the clause, not the particle itself, which creates emphasis. Thus /k/ could be understood as a coordinating conjunction placed in an emphatic *position*.[101] While this may provide a helpful analogy for *kî* in BH, the syntax and meaning of Ug. /k/ is not necessarily determinative for the syntax and meaning of Heb. *kî*.

In addition to its attestation in BH almost 4500 times, *ky* is attested in nine different Heb. inscriptions from the Iron II period, though in none of these cases is it asseverative or emphatic.[102] Cognate terms are attested in Phoen., Punic, Moabite, Old and Off. Aram., Akk., the Deir

---

97 Cyrus Gordon, *Ugaritic Textbook: Glossary, Indices* (ANOr 38; Rome: Pontificio Istituto Biblico, 1965; rev. reprint 1998), #1184; Note also the particle *ky*, the orthography of which may reflect the use of a *mater lectionis* in prose texts (*UT* glossary #1220). On the orthography of *ky*, see Daniel Sivan, *A Grammar of the Ugaritic Language* (HO 28; Leiden, New York, Köln: E. J. Brill, 1997), 13.

98 Daniel Sivan, *Grammar of the Ugaritic Language*, 190; Josef Tropper, *Ugaritische Grammatik* (AOAT 273; Münster: Ugarit-Verlag, 2000), 809.

99 Tropper, *Ugaritische Grammatik*, 809.

100 See Muraoka, *Emphatic Words and Structures*, 159-60, 164.

101 Dennis Pardee, review of Josef Tropper, *Ugaritische Grammatik*, *AfO* 50 (2003/2004) online version, 383. Barry Bandstra has suggested the same for both Heb. and Ug. ("The Syntax of the Particle *ky* in Biblical Hebrew and Ugaritic," [Ph.D. diss., Yale University, 1982]). He argues that emphasis in texts employing *kî* is tied more to syntactical topicalizing (i.e., word order) than to the lexical semantics of the particle itself (see especially pp. 25-61). Bandstra's point that "emphasis" with *kî* may be more syntactical than semantic may be correct for Hebrew prose. However, the case may be different in poetry (Bandstra's study does include a sampling of Hebrew poetry, but it is only from the Psalter). The wide variety of word order in BH poetry may well have pushed *kî* in such contexts toward encompassing "emphasis" as a *semantic* feature and not simply a syntactic one.

102 For the purposes of this work, Heb. inscriptions are cited using the system found in F. W. Dobbs-Allsopp, J. J. M. Roberts, C. L. Seow, and R. E. Whitaker, *Hebrew Inscriptions: Texts from the Biblical Period of the Monarchy, with Concordance* (New Haven: Yale University Press, 2004). By their count, Heb. *kî* occurs once at Arad (*Arad* 40.13); 10 times at Lachish in five different ostraca (*Lach* 2.4; 3.obv.6; 3.obv.8; 4.obv.4; 4.rev.1; 4.rev.2; 4.rev.4; 5.4; 6.3; 6.13); once in the Silwan tomb inscription (*Silw* 1.2); once in the Siloam Tunnel inscription (*Silm*.3); and once in the Ketef Hinnom silver amulets (*KHin* 1.11).

'Alla plaster texts, and possibly in Palmyrene Aram.[103] The editors of *The Dictionary of the North-West Semitic Languages* cite the sarcophagus inscription of Eshmunazor II (*KAI* 14:13) and the Aramaic *Proverbs of Ahiqar* (line 122) in support of their first entry for *ky*, "used as introduction of principal clause, verily, surely."[104] Yet neither of these examples reflects the emphatic function beyond doubt.[105]

Greenstein, Claassen, Aejmelaeus, and others are correct to voice caution about a pervasive tendency to translate *kî* as asseverative or emphatic when interpreters are uncertain about classifying the particle's function in any other, more commonly accepted, way. But despite its relative rarity, there is no doubt that emphatic *kî* is productive in BH. It functions most clearly in this fashion in oath formulae, where the emphatic meaning may have originated.[106]

Yet it also has this function outside of oath formulae. Greenstein himself points to Isa 15:1, the only other place in BH in which *kî* begins a poem (besides 28:1).[107] It opens with a double exclamation: *kî bĕlêl šuddad ʿār môʾāb nidmâ / kî bĕlêl šuddad qîr-môʾāb nidmâ*. He acknowledges that the emphatic interpretation of the double *kî* construction seems likely, though he points out that both the RSV and NRSV choose to interpret *kî* in these lines as introducing a circumstantial clause ("because").[108] He states, "At most we can conclude that the hypothesis that כי in Job 28:1 begins a new poem is improbable."[109]

Also germane to the discussion are instances in which *kî* begins a new poetic *stanza*. Quite striking is the instance in Job 14:7a (*kî yēš lāʿēṣ tiqwâ*) which provides an exact syntactic parallel to Job 28:1a (*kî yēš lakkesep môṣāʾ*). Given their identical syntax, it is very likely that the *kî* in

103 For citations of the relevant Northwest Semitic inscriptions (excluding Ugaritic), see J. Hoftijzer and K. Jongeling, *Dictionary of the North-West Semitic Inscriptions. Part One:ʾ-L* (HO 1/21; Leiden, New York, Köln: E. J. Brill, 1995), 1:497-98.

104 *DNWSI* 1:497. The lineation of the Ahiqar passage is that of James Lindenberger in *The Aramaic Proverbs of Ahiqar* (Baltimore and London: The Johns Hopkins University Press, 1983).

105 Compare the translations of /k/ in Eshmunazor by P. Kyle McCarter in *COS* 2:183 ("for") and of *ky* in Ahiqar by Lindenberger in *The Aramaic Proverbs of Ahiqar*, 110 ("for").

106 Williams, *Hebrew Syntax*, §449. The most commonly cited passage in support of this interpretation outside of the context of oaths is Gen 18:20, in which *kî* immediately precedes the predicate (see Schoors, "The Particle כי," 243; and William L. Moran, "The Hebrew Language in its Northwest Semitic Background," in *The Bible and the Ancient Near East: Essays in Honor of William Foxwell Albright* [ed. G. E. Wright; Garden City, NY: Doubleday, 1961], 61; also GKC §148d; and Joüon §164b).

107 Greenstein, "The Poem on Wisdom in Job 28," 265.

108 Ibid.

109 Ibid.

each of these passages serves the same function. The emphatic function in both texts is, in my estimation, very likely.[110]

In conclusion, though recent scholarship has cast doubt on the pervasiveness of non-connective, emphatic *kî*, it is productive in BH. It seems to me very likely that in the one other instance in which the particle begins a poem—Isa 15:1—it does function in an exclamatory fashion. In the case of Job 14:7a, where it begins a stanza that is an exact syntactic parallel to Job 28:1a, it also seems to function this way. The speeches immediately preceding Job 28, which are attributed to Job, also begin with emphatic constructions (*meh-ʿāzartā*, 26:2; *ḥay-ʾēl*, 27:2; possibly also *kî* in 27:3).

1a. *source* [*môṣāʾ*]: *Môṣāʾ* is most commonly related to mining (see NJPS, JB, NJB, NEB, RSV, NRSV, NAS, NAB, NIV, NKJV).[111] Marvin Pope points out, "The meaning 'mine' is regularly assumed in the present passage, although this sense is not attested elsewhere."[112]

Pope renders "smelter," based on Dahood's understanding of Heb. YṢʾ and its supposed semantic relation to Arab. WḌʾ, "to be clean, shine."[113] However, in its 27 occurrences in BH, *môṣāʾ* never means "mine" or "smelter" in any other passage.[114]

It is regularly used of a spring of water (2 Kgs 2:21; Isa 41:18, 58:11; Ps 107:33, 35; 2 Chr 32:30), what comes out of the mouth (Deut 8:3, 23:24; Dan 9:25; Num 30:13; Jer 17:16; Ps 89:35), an architectural exit (Ezek 42:11, 43:11), a starting point (Num 33:2a, b), a point of appearance (Hos 6:3; Ps 65:9), and the place in which the sun rises (Ps 19:7, 75:7).[115] In its only other occurrence in Job, it is used of the sprouting of

110 See, e.g., Georg Fohrer's translation of Job 14:7 in *Das Buch Hiob*, 235.

111 Also numerous commentators: Delitzsch, *Book of Job*, 2:91-92; Gordis, *The Book of Job*, 300, 304; Driver and Gray, *Job*, 1:236, 2:190; Terrien, *Job*, 190; Hartley, *The Book of Job*, 373.

112 Pope, *Job*, 199.

113 Ibid., 197, 199; Mitchell J. Dahood, "Northwest Semitic Philology and Job," in *The Bible in Current Catholic Thought* (ed. J. L. McKenzie; New York: Herder and Herder, 1962), 67. So also Walter Michel, "The Ugaritic Texts," 203.

114 Raymond Van Leeuwen, however, has argued for a technical metallurgical use of the root of YṢʾ in Prov 24:4 and elsewhere ("A Technical Metallurgical Usage of יצא," *ZAW* 98 [1986]: 112-13). For attestation of words in BH, I have used Lisowski's concordance throughout this study. Gerhard Lisowski, *Konkordanz zum Hebräischen Alten Testament: nach dem von Paul Kahle in der Biblia Hebraica edidit Rudolf Kittel besorgten Masoretischen Text: unter verantwortlicher Mitwirkung von Leonard Rost* (3d ed.; ed. Hans Peter Rüger; Stuttgart: Deutsche Bibelgesellschaft, 1958).

115 On the latter, note also EA 288:6, from ʿAbdi-Heba of Jerusalem, which mentions »der Aufgang der Sonne« (*mu-ṣi* ^{ilu}*šamši*^{ši}). See J. A. Knudtzon, *Die El-Amarna-Tafeln* (2 vols.; Leipzig: J. C. Hinrichs, 1915), 1:868-69.

the grass (38:27; there spelled *mōṣāʾ*). The feminine nominal form *môṣāʾâ*, means "origin" in Mic 5:1. The term *mwṣʾ* is also attested in the Siloam Tunnel inscription from ca. 700 B.C.E., in which it refers to a spring of water (*Silm*.5; cf. 2 Chr 32:30).

Akk. *mūṣû* A shows a similar semantic range to BH *môṣāʾ*, being used of an exit or road, an outflow of water, the rising place of the sun, openings in various objects, and produce springing from the earth.[116] Cognate terms in Phoen., Punic, Samalian, and Off. Aram. confirm that *mwṣʾ* essentially denotes a point of origin.[117]

Tur-Sinai suggests the possibility of reading from MṢʾ in Job 28:1 instead of YṢʾ and pointing it as the infc. *mĕṣôʾ*, assuming metathesis of *wāw* and *ṣādê*.[118] Joüon likewise reads from MṢʾ in order to match MṢʾ // *māqôm* in v. 12. He proposes a *miqṭāl* pattern noun *mimṣāʾ*, glossing it as "a place where one finds (silver)."[119] However, these emendations minimize the wordplay throughout the poem between YṢʾ and MṢʾ (*yāṣāʾ* [vv. 5a, 11b] and *māṣāʾ* [vv. 12a, 13b]), and they destroy one of the poem's fundamental metaphors represented by *môṣāʾ*—the "source."

Môṣāʾ in v. 1a is best interpreted as "issue," "source," or "origin," as in most other contexts in BH and in various dialects of Phoen., Aram., and Akk. Rather than being a technical term, the sense of *môṣāʾ* in Job 28:1 is so general that the reader is left wondering exactly how to understand the image of the line. To be sure, a "source for silver" (*lakkesep môṣāʾ*) might be construed as a "mine," but translating it as such cuts off other possibilities for meaning which present themselves throughout the course of the poem.

The typical connection of *môṣāʾ* with water is activated in the symbolic plane of Section One, which climaxes at "the sources of the rivers" (*mabbĕkê nĕhārôt* [MT *mibbĕkî*]). Though archaic, the translation "fount" for *môṣāʾ* would mimick the phonological play in the Hebrew between *môṣāʾ* (v. 1) and *māṣāʾ* (vv. 12a, 13b) by a similar play in English: "fount"—"found."

1b. ***a place for gold which is refined*** [*māqôm lazzāhāb yāzōqqû*]: The asyndeton in this line lends to ambiguity in interpretation. Does *yāzōqqû* modify *lazzāhāb* or *māqôm*? The translation of Dhorme, for example, reflects the latter: "And for gold a place where it is refined."[120] But as

116 *CAD* M/2, 247-49 s.v. *mūṣû* A; *AHw* 2:679-80 s.v. *mūṣû(m)*.

117 *DNWSI* 2:604-605 s.v. *mwṣʾ*.

118 Tur-Sinai, *The Book of Job*, 395-96.

119 Joüon, "Notes philologiques sur le texte hébreu de Job 1, 5; 9, 35; 12, 21; 28, 1; 28, 27; 29, 14," *Bib* 11 (1930): 323.

120 Dhorme, *Book of Job*, 399.

Habel states, "In line with the logic of v. 1a, *māqōm*, 'place,' is not the *locus* of the refining process, but of the gold which is subsequently refined."[121] The chiastic structure in the core of the couplet in v. 2 (*lakkesep* : *môṣāʾ* :: *māqôm* : *lazzāhāb*) also supports this interpretation.[122] And as Delitzsch points out, the disjunctive *rĕbîaʿ mūgrāš* in the Masoretic tradition separates *māqôm* from the following *lazzāhāb yāzōqqû*, which are connected by the conjunctive *mêrĕkāʾ*.[123]

The meaning of *yāzōqqû* is fairly clear. Gold and silver are said to be refined or purified in Mic 3:3. Refined gold is mentioned in 1 Chr 28:18 and refined silver in 1 Chr 29:4. The root occurs elsewhere in Job in the G-stem, where it refers to the distillation of water (36:27). But the versions provide different renderings. Some are singular, and others are plural; some are active, and others are passive.

OG renders with the passive singular διηθεῖται ("it is refined"), though MT's *yāzōqqû* is plural. Aq, Sym, and Th follow this interpretation, translating with the passive singular χωνευθῇ ("it is smelted").[124] Vg. likewise translates with *conflatur* ("it is melted"). By contrast, Syr. renders with an active plural participle, *mšḥlyn* ("they refine"). Tg. follows with *msnnyn*. The variation in voice and number in the versions is likely due to different interpretations of the masculine plural *yāzoqqû* (preserved in MT), either as an impersonal passive (which may be rendered as a singular, as in OG, the revisions, and Vg.) or as an active plural (in Syr. and Tg.).

However, Syr. begins v. 2 with a *wāw*, raising the possibility that MT's *yāzōqqû barzel* is the result of incorrect word division or haplography, and thus should be **yāzōq ûbarzel* or **yāzōqqû ûbarzel*. OG begins the verse with μὲν γάρ ("for indeed"), which could support Syr. if OG is reading an emphatic *wāw* (cf. also Syh.). But the addition of a *wāw* conjunction is, in fact, quite common in the Peshitta to Job, and it may thus be understood as a translational tendency rather than reflective of a *wāw* in the Hebrew *Vorlage*.[125] OG's μὲν γάρ also may reflect no textual datum, as seems to be the case in the Greek translation of Job 41:19.

---

121 Habel, *The Book of Job*, 389 n. 1b, citing Samuel Terrien.

122 See also Geller, " 'Where is Wisdom?' " 177 n. 6.

123 Delitzsch, *Book of Job*, 2:92.

124 Though Field attributes this reading to Aquila, Ziegler objects that Aquila cannot have translated with χωνεύειν, since he elsewhere translates Heb. ZQQ with διυλίζειν (*Beiträge zum griecheschen Iob* [Göttingen: Vandenhoeck & Ruprecht, 1985], 60). See also Joseph Reider, *An Index to Aquila* (completed and revised by Nigel Turner; VTSup 12; eds. G. W. Anderson et al.; Leiden: E. J. Brill, 1966), 59, s.v. διυλίζειν.

125 David Shepherd states, "While the Qumran translator is more likely to omit the waw conjunction in his rendering, his Syriac counterpart shows more willingness to sup-

2b. *hard* [*yāṣûq*]: The form as pointed in MT may be understood as a masculine singular Qal passive particle of YṢQ or as a finite verb (Qal impf. 3ms) from ṢWQ, both roots meaning "to pour out." ṢWQ is likely a byform of YṢQ.[126] However, several emendations have been proposed. Budde, followed by Fohrer, proposes reading the Hophal/Qal passive impf. 3ms of YṢQ (*yûṣaq*, originally *yūṣaq*) as a parallel to *yuqqaḥ* in v. 2a, thus translating "copper is poured out" (see also *BHK*, *BHS*).[127] Duhm suggests a Qal impf. 3ms from YṢQ (*yiṣṣôq*), which could be translated impersonally: "one smelts."[128] Torczyner originally proposed understanding the verb as a Qal impf. 3 mp from YṢQ (*yīṣĕqû*), in parallel with his emended *yiqqĕḥû* in v. 2a.[129] Blommerde reads an infc. from YṢQ, pointed *yĕṣôq*.[130] The infc. of this root occurs elsewhere in Job as *ṣeqet* (38:38), though byforms of the infc. of some I-*yôd* verbs are attested with the *yôd*. Niccacci, following Dahood, proposes *yāṣûqā* (Qal passive participle feminine singular), modifying the feminine noun *ʾeben*. Pointing to the occurrence of the form *yāṣûq* used adjectivally three times in Job 41:15-16, he translates: "Iron from the clay is extracted / and from the solid rock, copper."[131] Both Dhorme and Geller translate similarly, though they are willing to understand *ʾeben* as masculine in Job 28:2 (cf. 1 Sam 17:40; Eccl 10:9) to retain the pointing of MT.[132] The form *yāṣûq* occurs four other times in the Book of Job, functioning both adjectivally ("hard," 41:15; "hard like stone," 41:16a; "hard like a lower millstone," 41:16b) and verbally ("rocks poured out channels of oil," 29:6).[133]

None of the versions interpret *yṣq* (or *yṣwq* or *ywṣq*) in their *Vorlagen* as an adjective modifying *ʾeben*. Rather, the translations of Syr., Vg., and Tg. interpret the text as a verbal description of smelting or pouring. While Syr.'s *mtnsk* ("is smelted") and Vg.'s *solutus calore* ("melted by heat") could be understood as reflecting a participle in the *Vorlage*, such as that preserved in MT (i.e., *yāṣûq*), Tg.'s *ytyk* suggests, rather, a pas-

---

ply or add this conjunction…" (*Targum and Translation*, 244-25). See also idem, "Will the Real Targum Please Stand Up," 97-99.

126 *HALOT* 2:1014 s.v. ṢWQ II.

127 Budde, *Das Buch Hiob*, 157; Fohrer, *Das Buch Hiob*, 390.

128 Duhm, *Das Buch Hiob erklärt*, 134 (»…Gestein schmelzt man zu Kupfer um«). The form is identical to a Niphal impf. 3ms from ṢWQ, which Hartley incorrectly attributes to Duhm (*The Book of Job*, 374 n. 6)

129 Torczyner, *Das Buch Hiob*, 195. He offers no emendation of either word in his later commentary (Tur-Sinai, *The Book of Job*, 396).

130 Blommerde, *Northwest Semitic Grammar and Job*, 106.

131 Niccacci, "Giobbe 28," 29-30; Dahood, "Chiasmus in Job," 125.

132 Dhorme, *Book of Job*, 400; Geller, " 'Where is Wisdom?' " 177-78 n. 7.

133 See *HALOT* 1:428 s.v. YṢQ, in which the editors suggest a metaphorical meaning ("firm") for the Qal passive participle form *yāṣûq* in Job 41:15, 16a, b.

sive finite verb form which is parallel to another passive finite verb in the first line (Tg. *ytnsb*; cf. MT *yuqqaḥ* in v. 2a). OG (followed by Syh. and OL) reads χαλκὸς δὲ ἴσα λίθῳ λατομεῖται ("and copper is hewn out as stone").[134] This is somewhat strange, since λατομέω generally reflects Heb. ḤṢB. It seems that OG has been influenced by Deut 8:9, in which the root ḤṢB occurs.[135] Houtsma, however, would follow OG unquestioningly, suggesting the emendations *kĕʾeben* and *ḥāṣûb*.[136]

Despite the evidence of the ancient versions, the reading of MT is to be preferred. In line with the proposals of Dhorme and Geller, one should retain the Qal passive participle *yāṣûq* (from the root YṢQ) translating adjectivally as "hard, solid," or the like (cf. Job 41:15, 16a, b). Against the proposal of Dahood and Niccacci to re-point as a feminine participle (*yāṣûqā*), it is easier to assume that *yāṣûq* modifies *ʾeben* according to sense (*constructio ad sensum*), as Heb. prefers the masculine gender (*IBHS* §6.5.3a).

The translations of the versions are conditioned by technical imagery in these lines (e.g., *yāzōqqû* in v. 1b) and perhaps even from other biblical contexts (e.g., Deut 8:9). The readings of Syr., Tg., and Vg. related to smelting or pouring were also likely facilitated by conservative orthography (*yṣq*) in their *Vorlagen*, which could give rise to a number of interpretations.[137] Thus the assumption of metathesis of *wāw* and *ṣādê* in the MT based on the versional renderings would be unfounded (see *BHK*, *BHS*, Budde, Fohrer et al.).

Against the interpretations of the versions, *yuqqaḥ* has no verbal parallel in the second line of the couplet. Rather, it is gapped in v. 2b, as is the preposition *min* (on the gapping of *min*, cf. Syr. and Tg^{M,S}). The passive participle *yāṣûq* basically functions as a "ballast variant" which compensates for the gapping of the verb and preposition in the second line of the couplet: Iron : from dirt : is taken / [from] hard rock : [is taken] : copper.[138]

---

134 Cf. also "The Hebrew translator" referenced in the Hexapla (ὁ Ἑβραῖος), who rendered similarly with χωνεύω. In the first line, Tg^{M} and Tg^{S} read *ytntk*.

135 Aquila renders ḤṢB with λατομέω at Deut 8:9; Prov 9:1; Hos 6:5; Isa 10:15. See Reider, *An Index to Aquila*, 146, s.v. λατομεῖν.

136 Houtsma, *Textkritische Studien*, 63.

137 The more orthographically conservative *yṣq* is, in fact, attested in Ken. MS 223. See Kennicott, *Vetus Testamentum Hebraicum*, 2:505.

138 The term "ballast variant" originated with Cyrus Gordon in the study of Ugaritic verse. On the concept in BH poetry, see Edward L. Greenstein, "Aspects of Biblical Poetry," *JBA* 44 (1986-1987): 37-38; W. G. E. Watson, *Classical Hebrew Poetry: A Guide to Its Techniques* (Edinburgh: T&T Clark, 2005), 343-48 (Originally published as JSOTSup 26; Sheffield: JSOT Press, 1984); and Stephen A. Geller, *Parallelism in Early*

3a-4b. ***Setting a bound... {they wander}*** [*qēṣ śām... {nāʿû}*; MT *qēṣ śām... nāʿû*]: Textual, philological, and syntactical problems in these verses are numerous. In addition to important variant readings by the ancient translations, vv. 3aβ-4aα (*ûlĕkol-taklît... mēʿim-gār*) are lacking in the OG (⋇καὶ... κονίας·/), though Origen filled in the gaps with Th and marked them with an asterisk.

3aβ. ***he*** [*hûʾ*]: The independent pronoun *hûʾ* without a determined subject raises some grammatical difficulties. The first of these is the grammatical gender of *hûʾ*. In the last two decades, some scholars have sought to revive the old view that *hûʾ* is an epicene pronoun, that is, it was originally used for both the masculine and the feminine third person singular.[139] John Emerton, however, has argued convincingly that there was no epicene *hūʾ* in early Hebrew and that the rise of the perpetual *Qere hīwʾ* in the Pentateuch may plausibly be explained as the result of scribal activity.[140] On this view, the pronoun *hūʾ* was used only for the masculine third person singular pronoun "he."

Arnold Ehrlich and Georg Beer have raised still more challenging questions regarding the indeterminate subject of both *śām* and *hûʾ* in this line. Ehrlich states, »Das Subjekt zu שם kann wohl unbestimmt sein, aber das folgende הוא muss eine bestimmte Beziehung haben, denn dieses Fürwort kann nicht im Sinne von ›man‹ gebraucht werden.«[141] In light of this fact and others, some scholars such as Edward Greenstein have proposed relocating the entirety of ch. 28 after Job 37:24, assuming that it was originally part of the Elihu speeches.[142] As a result, *kî* in 28:1 is understood in a causal and connective sense, and both *śām* and *hûʾ* in 28:3 would also find an antecedent in *šadday* of 37:23.

Biblical Poetry (HSM 20; ed. Frank Moore Cross; Missoula, Mont.: Scholars, 1979), 299-313.

139 See, e.g., Gary A. Rendsburg, "A New Look at Penteteuchal *HWʾ*," *Bib* 63 (1982): 351-69; and, more recently, Richard S. Hess, "Adam, Father, He: Gender Issues in Bible Translation," *BT* 56 (2005): 144-53, especially 150-53.

140 J. A. Emerton, "Was There an Epicene Pronoun *hūʾ* in Early Hebrew?" *JSS* 45 (2000): 267-76.

141 Ehrlich, *Randglossen*, 6:290. Note also Georg Beer: »Da הוא ein Beziehungswort verlangt…« (*Der Text des Buches Hiob*, 177); and Karl Budde: »Das הוא in b kann nur auf ein genanntes Subjekt zurückgehen, niemals auf das in שָׂם enthaltene ungenannte« (*Das Buch Hiob*, 157-58).

142 Greenstein, "The Poem on Wisdom in Job 28," 271-272. David Clines came to an almost identical conclusion independently, though he re-locates the Elihu speeches between Job 27 and 28 ("Putting Elihu in his Place," 243-53; idem, *Job 21-37*, 905-909, 925-26).

Other scholars have assumed that a subject has fallen out after *śām*. Budde proposes *ʾādām*, while Bickell suggests *ʾĕnôš*.[143] Geller also raises the possibility of *ʾĕnôš* being omitted by vertical haplography, as *ʾĕnôš* is also attested in v. 4b (and v. 13a).[144]

It is instructive to note that the subject of Job's speech in the preceding poem is definitely humanity (*ʾādām*, 27:13). If an antecedent is to be found in the current context, it is there. Yet it is very likely that the referent of *hûʾ* in v. 3a is only named in the verses that follow. This is an example of what Anthony Ceresko calls the poetic technique of "delayed identification," which creates the effect of drama and anticipation.[145] A clear example in the Book of Job is found in 23:6, where *hûʾ* is disambiguated by *ʾēl* // *šadday* in 23:16. Job 13:28 may also offer a parallel, since the independent pronoun *hûʾ* (there *wĕhûʾ kĕrāqāʿ yibleh*) begins a new section without an antecedent. Finally, *hûʾ* in 8:16 may refer to what follows rather than what precedes, as pointed out by Gordis and Greenstein.[146]

If one considers *hûʾ* in Job 28:3 along these lines, it is very likely that the subject of Section One is not disambiguated until ten verses later in 28:13a, which states that a human (*ʾĕnôš*) does not know wisdom's abode (*ʿerkāh*; see commentary on *its abode*).[147] This view is also supported by the larger structure of the poem, where emphatic constructions in vv. 23b (*wĕhûʾ yādaʿ*) and 24a (*hûʾ*) introduce *ʾĕlōhîm*. This correspondence between v. 3a and vv. 23-24 trongly suggests that the subject

---

143 Budde, *Das Buch Hiob*, 157-58; Bickell as cited in Beer, *Der Text des Buches Hiob*, 177.

144 Geller, " 'Where is Wisdom?' " 178 n. 8. Possible reconstruction: *qēṣ śām ʾĕnôš laḥōšek*.

145 Ceresko, *Job 29-31 in the Light of Northwest Semitic*, 200, 203-204. See also Watson, *Classical Hebrew Poetry*, 336, and Alviero Niccacci, "Analysing Biblical Hebrew Poetry," *JSOT* 74 (1997): 81-82 and n. 18.

For examples outside of Job, note the delay in introducing God as the agent of the sufferings of "everyman" in Lam 3:1-18, where Yhwh is not explicitly named until v. 18b, despite the fact that the verbs and suffixes in the preceding seventeen verses are consistently third person masculine singular. Adele Berlin states, "The literary strategy here is to name God just at the turning point, when, on the one hand, God seems most remote and, on the other hand, just as he is about to become the main topic of the discourse" (*Lamentations* [OTL; Louisville and London: Westminster John Knox, 2002], 92). See also F. W. Dobbs-Allsopp, *Lamentations* (IBC; Louisville, Ky.: John Knox, 2002), 114. The Book of Nahum also provides an excellent example in 1:9-2:2, where Nineveh, the object of the oracles of judgment (see 1:1), is not explicitly named. It is referenced only with second person feminine pronouns. As Tremper Longman notes, "This delay of precise identification causes the reader to be more attentive and also produces a dramatic sense of suspense" ("Nahum," in *The Minor Prophets: An Exegetical and Expository Commentary* [ed. Thomas McComiskey; 3 vols.; Grand Rapids, Mich.: Baker Academic, 1993], 2:769).

146 Greenstein, "The Poem on Wisdom in Job 28," 266 n. 30; Gordis, *The Book of Job*, 305.

147 Cf. Müllner, »Der Ort des Verstehens,« 69.

in Section Three (vv. 23-27) is different from that in Section One (vv. 3-11).

3aβ. *probes* [*ḥôqēr*]: Despite the fact that ḤQR is found 27 times in the OT (including Job 28:3, 27), 9 in Ben Sira, and 9 at Qumran, there is still some dispute over core meaning of the verb.[148] In a recent essay, Pierre van Hecke has convincingly argued that its core meaning includes "to search (within an area)" and "to explore (the inner content of an object or area)" but not merely "to search for (an object)."[149] On similar grounds, James Aitken has argued that ḤQR in Job 28:3 "must denote the examining of an unknown place and not the searching for a known but not yet found object, namely, the precious stone (אבן)."[150] Yet, as van Hecke points out, the search may be conducted in an area or domain for the purpose of locating a particular item in that domain that is the object of the search.[151] "In some cases, the verb indeed means 'to search (an area) for (an object).' "[152] The verb is used elsewhere in the OT of searching the land (*ʾereṣ*) for habitation (Judg 18:2) and for corpses (Ezek 39:14). In addition, one text from Qumran seems to use the verb in the sense of searching for an object ("the path toward life") even without specifying a domain (*ḥqrw lkm drk lḥyym*; 4Q185 1-2 ii 1-2).

Though the syntax of Job 28:3 is difficult, it is clear that ḤQR is used of searching an area for an object. This area is, in fact, circumscribed by the explorer, who establishes a boundary in which the search will take place (*qēṣ śām*), and then searches out every limit (*lĕkol-taklît hûʾ ḥôqēr*) for the the stone (*ʾeben*).[153] The metaphors of place (vv. 1b, 6a, 12b, 20b, 23b) and source (vv. 1a, 12a, 20a) are so dominant in the poem that it seems impossible to see the "search" in Job 28 as lacking an object. Carol Newsom has rightly emphasized that the objectification of wisdom is a fundamental trope in the poem.[154] While ḤQR recurs again in v. 27b, the meaning is quite different, as it operates out of a different

---

148 For references, see Aitken, "Lexical Semantics," 126 and nn. 36, 37, 38.

149 van Hecke, "Searching for and Exploring Wisdom," 154 and 146-53.

150 Aitken, "Lexical Semantics," 131. See also ibid., 132.

151 van Hecke, "Searching for and Exploring Wisdom," 140, 153.

152 Ibid., 140-41.

153 This is a double accusative construction (*IBHS* §10.2.3), where *lāmed* marks the first element (*IBHS* §10.4a).

154 Newsom, *Moral Imaginations*, 179. Van Oorschot has also drawn attention to the material and objectified quality of wisdom in the poem, and he notes a possible parallel to Eg. *mꜣʿt*, which may also be presented in material form (»Hiob 28,« 187 and n. 31, 189 n. 40).

conceptual model of the quest for insight, with the meaning "to explore (the inner content of an object or area)."[155]

The root ḤQR in the Book of Job often has to do with searching out the wisdom tradition (5:27; 8:8; 32:11). Yet it is also tied up with a model of depth that cannot be fathomed by humans, which is often symbolic of God's wisdom (11:7; 36:26; 38:16). ḤQR is clearly connected with wisdom in 28:27. While the use of ḤQR in v. 3 may be understood in the poem's realistic plane of meaning as a physical object ("the stone of deepest gloom"), it may be understood in the poem's symbolic plane as a symbol for wisdom itself.

3b. ***stone of deepest gloom*** [*ʾeben ʾōpel wĕṣalmôt*; MT *ṣalmāwet*]: LXX (and Syh. and OL) reads v. 3b with MT v. 4a. Of its 9 occurrences in the OT, *ʾōpel* occurs 6 times in the Book of Job (3:6; 10:22a, b; 23:17; 28:3; 30:26). Cognate nouns are attested elsewhere in the OT. It is often used in context with *ḥōšek* or *ṣalmāwet*, with reference to death and a cessation of existence (3:6; 10:22a, b), and being cut off from God and light (23:17; 30:26).

In view of Job 10:22, in which Job suggests his departure to land of deep darkness (*ṣalmāwet*) in which light "shines" as un-light (*ʾōpel*), one might suggest emending *ʾeben* here to *ʾereṣ*, as Houtsma does.[156] In this case, it would be explicitly stated that the human in v. 3 searches in a land of gloom and deep darkness. The nature of this land (*ʾereṣ*) would be expounded upon further in v. 5. Yet this emendation is without textual support, and it is also inadvisable on literary grounds. On this reading, the setting of the search would be clear, but the object of that search would not. Other imagery of the poem resonates with *ʾōpel* and *ṣalmāwet* in v. 3b to communicate that the search for the "stone" (*ʾeben*) is, in fact, taken out in such a place.[157] As the poem later states directly, wisdom is not found in the land of the living (v. 13b; cf. 21a).[158]

Though *ʾeben* elsewhere in Job is used to connote hardness or durability (5:23; 6:12; 8:17; 14:19; 38:6; 38:20; 41:16; 41:20), the term should be understood as a mineral deposit (cf. Deut 8:9) or a precious stone in this verse. While its density is underscored in 28:2b, *ʾeben* in v. 5a clearly refers to precious stones, namely, lapis-lazuli (*sappîr*). The term is used

155 van Hecke, "Searching for and Exploring Wisdom," 153, 158-60.

156 Houtsma, *Textkritische Studien*, 63.

157 Note terms which are used in connection with death and the Netherworld elsewhere in the OT and in cognate literature: *ʿāpār*, v. 2a; *naḥal*, v. 4a; *ʾereṣ*, v. 5a; *taḥtît*, v. 5b. On these terms, see Tromp, *Primitive Conceptions*. This is also underscored by references to personified *tĕhôm*, v. 14a; *yām*, v. 14b; *ʾăbaddôn*, v. 22a; and *māwet*, v. 14a.

158 Neither should one follow Ehrlich in reading *yābîn* for *ʾeben* (*Randglossen*, 6:290).

of precious stones elsewhere in the OT—as descriptive of Eden and its surroundings (Gen 2:12; Ezek 28:14, 16), in priestly vestments (Exod 28:9, 10, 11, 12, 13, 14, 16, 17 et al.), as a jewel in a crown (Zech 9:16), as settings in a throne (Ezek 1:26; 10:1), sacred gems (Lam 4:1), and in the foundations, walls, and gates of Zion (Isa 28:16; 54:11-12!). Cognate terms in Semitic, such as Akk. *abnu*, may also be used of precious stones of various kinds.[159] In fact, the adjective *yāqār* is used in the majority of its attestations in the OT to modify *ʾeben* (2 Sam 12:30; 1 Kgs 5:31; 7:9, 10, 11; 10:2, 10, 11; Ezek 27:22; 28:13; Dan 11:38; 1 Chr 20:2; 29:2; 2 Chr 3:6; 9:1, 9, 10; 32:27; cf. Akk. *abnu aqartu*).

Many commentators read the phrase *ʾeben ʾōpel wĕṣalmāwet* as "the stone of darkness and shadow of death" (see KJV).[160] This basic sense is correct. While the terms *ʾōpel* and *ṣalmāwet* in the Book of Job most often describe places or states (3:5, 6; 10:21-22; 23:17; 24:17; 30:26; 34:22), they may also symbolize dark things or objects (esp. Job 12:22, where *ʿămūqôt* // *ṣalmāwet*). In Job 28:3b, these terms function primarily to describe the object of the search, *ʾeben*. In this case, *ʾōpel* and *ṣalmāwet* are best translated as a hendiadys, and they are linked to *ʾeben* in an attributive genitive construction (*IBHS* §9.5.3b).[161] This connection is supported by the Masoretic accentuation (*ṭarḥāʾ*).

David Wolfers would understand *ʾeben ʾōpel wĕṣalmāwet* as "the stone of darkness and the shadow of death," where the phrase *ʾōpel wĕṣalmāwet* signifies the Underworld. He further reasons that the "stone of the Underworld" is lava and that the verses detail a volcanic eruption.[162] Robert Gordis suggests a similar reading in his commentary, though on his understanding, *ʾeben* alone means "lava," and *ʾōpel wĕṣalmāwet* describes its color.[163] While creative, neither the view of Gordis or of Wolfers is persuasive. It is difficult to see how a volcanic eruption is germane here.

The "stone" (*ʾeben*) is referred to as that "of deepest darkeness" precisely because it is found in places characterized by *ʾōpel* and *ṣalmāwet*. This stone, which in this poem evokes both precious stones and, eventually, wisdom itself, is the deep thing that the human seeks to draw

159 *CAD* A/1, 54-61, s.v.

160 E.g., Driver and Gray, *Job*, 1:238; Terrien, *Job*, 190; Geller, " 'Where is Wisdom?' " 161.

161 Others understand *ʾōpel wĕṣalmāwet* to be used as an adverbial accusative of place. See the translations of Dhorme, *Book of Job*, 400; Hartley, *The Book of Job*, 374; Habel, *The Book of Job*, 388; NKJV, NIV, NJB, RSV, NRSV, NAS).

162 Wolfers, "The Stone of Deepest Darkness: A Mineralogical Mystery (Job XXVIII)," *VT* 44 (1994): 274-276; idem, "The Volcano in Job 28," 236-37; idem, *Deep Things Out of Darkness. The Book of Job: Essays and a New English Translation* (Grand Rapids, Mich.: Eerdmans, 1995), 495-96.

163 Gordis, *The Book of Job*, 305.

out from the darkness, the dark thing which he hopes to bring to light (cf. Job 12:22).

The morphology of *ṣalmāwet* (occurring 18 times in BH and 10 times in the Book of Job: 3:5; 10:21; 10:22a, b; 16:16; 24:17a, b; 28:3; 34:22; 38:17) has engendered a good deal of scholarly discussion. In the Masoretic tradition, the word is vocalized as a compound noun, *ṣal* (a construct form of *ṣēl*) + *māwet*, interpreted by the ancient traditions and by some modern scholars as "shadow of death," in many, if not in all, of its occurrences.[164] This is evidenced in Job 28:3b by the translations of LXX and the revisions (*σκιὰ θανάτου; so also Syh. and OL), Vg. (*umbram mortis*), Syr. (*ṭllh dmwtʾ*) and Tg. (*ṭwly mwtʾ*). This modern view arose partially out of skepticism that the root ṢLM, "to be dark, black," existed in BH.

However, the most common analysis of the word is as an abstract noun (thus the *-ût* suffix) from the root ṢLM, "to be dark, black." This position is not difficult to argue, since it is supported by cognates in Akk. (*ṣalāmu*), Arab. (ẒLM), and Eth. (*ṣalma*). But an aural wordplay in Job 38:17 (*šaʿărê-māwet // šaʿărê-ṣalmāwet*) is rendered nugatory if one accepts *ṣalmût* as the original vocalization.

The traditional vocalization, *ṣalmāwet*, allows this pun. Yet this vocalization as a compound noun from *ṣēl* and *māwet*, is most likely a secondary folk etymology that does not reflect the word's original pronunciation, even if it correctly describes in many cases the use of the imagery of darkness.

The best solution in light of Job 38:17 is to vocalize *ṣalmôt / ṣalmōt*, which, despite being an alternate abstract pattern (*-ōt*) from the root ṢLM (thus meaning "darkness"), still preserves the wordplay between *māwet* and *môt / mōt* in Job 38:17 and equally connotes the realm of the dead, or the "shelter of Mot."[165] If this abstract suffix is indeed Phoeni-

164 See, e.g., Walter Michel, "ṢLMWT, 'Deep Darkness' or 'Shadow of Death'?" *BR* 29 (1984): 5-20; and James Barr, "Philology and Exegesis: Some General Remarks, with Illustrations from Job," in *Questions disputes d'Ancien Testament: Méthode et théologie. XXIIIe session des Journées Bibliques de Louvain* (ed. C. Brekelmans; BETL 33; Leuven: Leuven University Press, 1974), 39-61. This view had previously been defended by Theodor Nöldeke, Karl Budde, Karl Marti, *BDB*, and others. D. Winton Thomas ("צַלְמָוֶת in the Old Testament," *JSS* 7 [1962]: 191-200), defends this vocalization, but he believes it means "deepest shadow, thick darkness," with *-māwet* functioning as a superlative (as in English "bored to death" = "really bored").

165 This is the view of Chaim Cohen, "The Meaning of צלמות 'Darkness': A Study in Philological Method," in *Texts, Temples, and Traditions: A Tribute to Menahem Haran* (ed. M. V. Fox et al.; Winona Lake, Ind.: Eisenbrauns, 1996), 307; and C. L. Seow, "The Poetics of Job's Malediction" (unpublished essay), 4-5 and nn. 13-22. Gary Rendsburg ("Hebrew Philological Notes (II)," *HS* 42 [2001]: 189) cites Eg. evidence from the *Book of the Dead* ("dark valley" [*ỉnt kkt*]) paralleling the expression *gê*

cian in origin, it also comports very well with the conservative orthographic peculiarities evident in the Book of Job.[166] It also provides a sufficient starting point for the secondary vocalization as *ṣalmāwet* throughout the OT.

The term *ṣalmôt* / *ṣalmāwet* is used as an epithet for the Netherworld in Job 10:21-22 and 38:17, and, given the number of other words in the first section of the poem that may also serve as names for the Netherworld (*ʿāpār*, v. 2a; *naḥal*, v. 4a; *ʾereṣ*, v. 5a; *taḥtît*, v. 5b; *ʾăbaddôn*, v. 22a; and *māwet*, v. 14a), such a connotation is undoubtedly operative here.[167]

Whether interpreted according to its most likely scientific etymology (*ṣalmôt*) or its folk etymology (*ṣēl* + *māwet*), the visual pun between "deep darkness" and "shadow of death" would be patently obvious in an un-pointed text.

4aα. ***He breaches course<s> far from dwellers*** [*pāraṣ nĕḥāl<îm> mēʿim-gār*; MT *naḥal*]: This verse is a notorious *crux interpretum*. The versions are in utter disagreement on how to render the consonantal Hebrew text. Some scholars, despairing of its difficulty, even refuse to translate it.[168] For convenience in discussion, I include the renderings of v. 4aα in the ancient versions here:

LXX: ※διακοπὴ χειμάρρου ἀπὸ κονίας ·/

Aq: ...χειμάρρους ὅπου κονία (Syh. marg. *ʾrgltʾ ʾykʾ dʿprʾ*)

Sym: διακοπὴ φάραγγος ὅπου κονία

Syh.: *twrʿtʾ dʾrgltʾ mn ʿprʾ*

OL: *discissio torrentis a cinere*

Vg.: *Dividit torrens a populo peregrinante*

Syr.: *twrʿtʾ yrtw mn ʿmʾ gywrʾ*

Tg.: *tqp nḥlʾ mn ʾtr dmzlḥ mrzybʾ*

Several things should be pointed out: (1) LXX, Syh., OL, Sym, and Syr. read PRṢ (MT *pāraṣ*) as a noun (*pereṣ*, "breech"). (2) Syr. reads NḤL (MT *naḥal*) as a verb (*nāḥal*, "he inherited"). (3) LXX, Syh., OL, Aq, and Sym read GR (MT *gār*) as *gīr* ("lime[stone]"). (4) Vg. and Syr. render MʿM-GR (MT *mēʿim-gār*) as *mēʿam gēr* ("from a foreign people"). (5) Tg. (*mzlḥ mrzybʾ*) understands GR (MT *gār*) or even MʿM-GR (MT *mēʿim-gār*) as

---

ṣalmāwet in Ps 23:4a that also supports the meaning "darkness" for *ṣalmāwet* in that text and others.

166 See Freedman, "Orthographic Peculiarities in the Book of Job," 35*-44*.

167 On these terms as epithets for the Netherworld, see Tromp, *Primitive Conceptions*.

168 E.g., Geller, " 'Where is Wisdom?' " 155, though he offers a few tentative solutions at 178 n. 9. Cf. also NAB, which omits it altogether.

being derived from Heb. NGR ("to flow"), possibly reading a Hophal participle *muggārîm* (see Mic 1:4).[169]

MT's *pāraṣ naḥal* is basically correct (perhaps *pāraṣ nĕḥālīm*). This reading is supported by the larger context of the poem. In 28:10, the subject "splits streams in the mountains" (*baṣṣûrôt yĕʾōrîm biqqēaʿ*), using similar terms BQʿ (// *pāraṣ*) and YʾR (// *naḥal*). Still another term for a river, stream, or canal is used in 28:11—*nĕhārôt*—which sometimes parallels *naḥal* in the OT (Isa 66:16).

Yet many would understand the actions in this verse in a much more technical sense. There has been a longstanding trend, reaching even into the ancient period,[170] to read the first section of the poem as referring to ancient mining techniques, despite the fact that there is not a single word in the poem that is typically used of excavating or mining elsewhere in the OT.[171] Modern scholars simply assume that "[T]he writer of Job 28 apparently knew more about the process of mining than any other writer..."[172] and that "The difficulties of interpretation in the first section (vv. 1-11) are due in largest measure to our lack of knowledge of the technical vocabulary of ancient mining operations."[173]

This technical interpretation has also become engrained in the standard English lexica of BH. *HALOT*, *BDB*, and *DCH* all suggest a meaning such as "mine shaft" for *naḥal* in this verse.[174] This trend has continued to hold sway in modern scholarship in relation to this term and others, despite a few sober comments issued by previous scholars that "There is no evidence that *naḥal* can mean a mining *shaft*, although this is widely favoured by modern scholars."[175]

---

169 As suggested by Houtsma, *Textkritische Studien*, 64. See also Dhorme, *Book of Job*, 401; and Beer, *Der Text des Buches Hiob*, 177.

170 This interpretation is reflected in Olympiodorus of Alexandria's commentary on Job (6th c. C.E.), in which he refers to mining (see his "Commentarium in Beatum Job," PG 93:287). This is cited in a marginal note in Syh., which speaks of stones which are cut off from the mine (*hlyn kʾpʾ dmtpsqn mn mʾṭlʾ*). But such an interpretation may be evident even in the OG translation in the second century B.C.E., which renders MT's *yāṣûq* in v. 2b with λατομέω (for a discussion of the date of LXX-Job, see Dhorme, *Book of Job*, cxcvi). This Gk. word typically reflects Heb. ḤṢB, and this rendering in Job 28:2b is likely under the influence of ḤṢB in Deut 8:9.

171 The words to which I refer are those such as KRH, ḤṢB, ḤPR, ḤTR, KWR, etc. (see Greenstein, "The Poem on Wisdom in Job 28," 267). One should also mention NQB (in addition to the biblical passages, see also *Silm*.2).

172 Waterman, "Note on Job 28 4," 167.

173 Gordis, *The Book of Job*, 538.

174 *HALOT* 2:687, s.v.; *DCH* 5:659, s.v.; *BDB*, 636, s.v.

175 Andersen, *Job*, 225 (emphasis his). Compare also the comments by Driver and Gray decades earlier in *Job*, 2:192: "Nowhere else does נחל mean *a shaft*, the meaning adopted by most recent scholars, nor a *gallery* of a mine" (italics original).

In the OT, *naḥal* is used of a ravine, river valley, wadi, or stream in realistic or cosmic senses (for the latter, see 2 Sam 22:5 // Ps 18:5; Isa 30:33; Mic 6:7; Ps 36:9; Job 20:17). It is used of the grave or of shaft-tombs in Job 21:33. In its realistic senses, it may or may not (see Neh 2:15 et al.) be filled with water. Given the fact that *naḥal* very often denotes a dry channel that may be used as a passageway, it is not unreasonable to suppose that *naḥal* could be used in Job 28:4 of an expedition that consists of breaking open a tunnel in the earth. In fact, the Sumerian glosses on Akk. *naḫallu*, which mean "cave" or "hole in the ground" may provide an analogy in Semitic. Sum. aruba consistently means "pitfall" or the like in that literature.[176] The term sidug means "hollow" (*Enki and the World Order*, line 14)[177] and "pit, deep hole" (*Lugalbanda in the Mountain Cave*, ll. 108, 358, 368, 374).[178] In light of these meanings for its Sum. equivalents, it is likely that Akk. *naḫallu* carries similar senses when it is not connected with water.[179] Thus it is not unreasonable to suggest the same for BH *naḥal*. *Naḥal* in v. 4 most likely has nothing at all to do with mining technology *per se*.

Yet some slight restoration of the Heb. text may be necessitated by the fact that MT reads the singular *naḥal*, when the plural participle (*hanniškāḥîm*) and plural verbs (*dallû, nāʿû*) later in the verse suggest a plural antecedent (though these could also modify a collective singular noun). In this case, one could posit that the final *mêm* of an originally plural *nĕḥālîm* was omitted by haplography before *mēʿim-gār*.

Numerous other suggestions have been put forth. Michael Dick, in what is perhaps the most creative reading of the verse as a whole, suggests reading *pereṣ nāḥal mēʿam gēr* ("an excavation is carved out by the foreign work-force"), with *nāḥal* being a Niphal of ḤLL II ("to pierce, hollow out").[180] The emendations *mēʿam-gēr* or *mēʿam-gār* are quite common, following the renderings of Syr. (*ʿmʾ gywrʾ*) or of Vg. (*populo peregrinante*), though G. R. Driver is wrong to assert that these readings

176 Gloss from the Pennsylvania Sumerian Dictionary online: http://psd.museum.upenn.edu/epsd/index.html). See text and translations from the Electronic Text Corpus of Sumerian Literature: http://etcsl.orinst.ox.ac.uk. Sum. aruba occurs in *Ninurta's Exploits* (ETCSL 1.6.2), *Death of Ur-Namma* (ETCSL 2.4.1.1), the *Praise Poem of Shulgi* (ETCSL 2.4.4.02), and *He is a Good Seed of a Dog* (ETCSL 5.4.12).

177 ETCSL 1.1.3.

178 ETCSL 1.8.2.1.

179 See the comments of the editors of *CAD* N/1, 125, s.v. *naḫallu*. The Sum. glosses are also briefly mentioned in Geller, " 'Where is Wisdom?' " 178 n. 9; and van Wolde, "Wisdom, Who Can Find It?" 7 n. 23.

180 Dick, "Job xxviii 4," 217. At the end of the 19th century, Delitzsch had already suggested a nominal form from the root ḤLL ("to pierce, hollow out"), here signifying "an excavation made in the earth" (*Book of Job*, 2:95)

"show that [MT's] עִם *must be* vocalized as עַם..."[181] The ancient versions simply provide their interpretation of the consonantal Hebrew text. Driver himself would understand Heb. PRṢ as related to Arab. PRḌ ("notched, incised") and NḤL as related to an uncertain Akk. term *niḫlu*, which he glossed as "excavation."[182] Leroy Waterman proposed reading *pāraṣ nĕḥālîm ʿam nēr* ("The people of the lamp break open passageways"), assuming orthographic confusion between *gîmel* and *nûn* in the Aramaic square script.[183] Still more conjectural is the suggestion of Max Löhr to read *pāraṣ nĕḥālîm bĕmagzērâ* ("he breaks open tunnels with an ax").[184] Tur-Sinai suggested restoring *ûmaʿyān* after *naḥal*, assuming that the graphic similarity between MʿM and MʿYN resulted in the loss of the latter by haplography. He thus reads *pāraṣ naḥal* <*ûmaʿyān*> ("he broke open rivers <and fountains>"), drawing attention to a similar phrase in Ps 74:15, in which the psalmist says of God: *ʾattâ bāqaʿtā maʿyān wānāḥal*.[185] Tur-Sinai correctly understands the symbolic weight of v. 4a, and he perceptively notes the thematic link with v. 10a.[186] Nevertheless, his conjectural emendation is problematic from a paleographic standpoint. While there are graphic similarities between MʿM and MʿYN, particularly in later Aramaic scripts, I believe that they are too distant to assume haplography on that basis.

The larger literary context may support reading *mēʿim-gīr* ("from the lime[stone]") with LXX (*ἀπὸ κονίας) and the revisions (Aq and Sym: ὅπου κονία).[187] Note particularly v. 10, where rivers are split *in the rocks* (*baṣṣûrôt*). If one follows LXX, v. 4a would provide a parallel, where courses are breached from limestone.

One of the greatest difficulties with many of the proposed emendations is that they necessitate an odd change in subject from v. 3 to v. 4, whether the new subject be "a foreign people" (Ehrlich et al.) "people of the lamp" (Ley, followed by Peake, Waterman et al.)[188] or "a strange

---

181 G. R. Driver, "Problems in Job," *AJSL* 52/3 (1936): 162 (emphasis mine).

182 Ibid. See, however, *CAD* N/2, 219 s.v., and the comment of Clines, *Job 21-37*, 897 n. 4d.

183 Waterman, "Note on Job 28 4,"168.

184 Löhr, »Job c. 28,« 70 n. 1.

185 N. H. Tur-Sinai, *The Book of Job*, 396, 398.

186 Ibid., 397-98.

187 Joseph Reider proposed a similar reading ("chalk valleys") in 1953 without comment about the Gk. versions ("Contributions to the Scriptural Text," *HUCA* 24 [1952/53]: 105-106). A. Guillaume reads *mēʿām gīr*, translating "from the covering of chalk," relating the re-pointed *ʿām* to Arab. *ġamma*, "chalk" (*Studies in the Book of Job with a New Translation* [ALUOS Supplement 2; ed. John MacDonald; Leiden: Brill, 1968], 110).

188 Julius Ley, *Das Buch Hiob nach seinem Inhalt, seiner Kunstgestaltung und religiösen Bedeutung* (Halle: Verlag der Buchhandlung des Waisenhauses, 1903), 78; Arthur Sam-

people" (Grätz, followed by Dick et al.).[189] Others would read v. 3b with 4a, making *ʾeben ʾōpel wĕṣalmāwet* the subject of *pāraṣ*, supposing that these verses speak of a volcanic eruption.[190] Yet later in the poem, the human explorer splits rivers in the rocks (v. 10) and stretches out his arm against the hard rock (v. 9). In light of this prevalent theme in Section One, it seems likely that a similar act is depicted in v. 4a.

Considering the difficulties presented by the line, it is tempting to emend *mēʿim-gār* to *mēʾim-gēw*, assuming graphic confusion between *wāw* and *rêš* in the Persian period Aramaic and proto-Jewish scripts, translating "from society" or "from civilization."[191] *Gw* is used in this sense four times in a Phoenician inscription from Greece (Piraeus) dated to around 96 B.C.E., where it is glossed with τὸ κοινόν.[192] This proposal would also fit the semantic parallelism noted previously (now: "civilization" // "passers-by" // "humans"), and it could find support in Job 30:5, where Job angrily and colorfully describes his mockers as those who are driven out from society (*min-gēw*) as if they were thieves, to roam and scavenge the desolate lands that are the habitation of wild beasts and the disgruntled dead.[193] Both Joban passages (30:1-8 and 28:4) detail dry wastelands far away from human existence.

But despite the difficulties of the text, all the ancient versions are interpreting a consonantal text GR. This fact alone does not guarantee the correctness of MT; however, one gains little from the conjectural emendation to *gēw*, ("civilization"), since the meaning of MT's *gār* is hardly different.

The syntactic and semantic parallelism between *mēʾim-gār*, *minnî-rāgel*, and *mēʾĕnôš* suggests that MT's *gār* be read as a substantive Qal

---

uel Peake, *Job: Introduction, Revised Version with Notes and Index* (Century Bible; Edinburgh: T & T Clark and E. C. Jack, 1905), 248.

189 H. H. Grätz, *Emendationes in plerosque Sacrae Scripturae Veteris Testamenti Libros* (3 fascicles; Breslau: Schlesische Buchdruckerei, 1892).

190 See Gordis, *The Book of Job*, 305; Wolfers, "The Stone of Deepest Darkness," 274-276; idem, "The Volcano in Job 28," 236-37; and idem, *Deep Things Out of Darkness*, 495-96.

191 See *HALOT* 1:182 s.v. *gēw* II. Compare, for example, *wāw* and *rêš* in the Saqqara papyrus, the Elephantine papyri, and the Daliyeh papyri. For script charts, see Frank Moore Cross, "The Development of the Jewish Scripts," in *The Bible and the Ancient Near East: Essays in Honor of William Foxwell Albright* (ed. G. Ernest Wright; Garden City, NY: Doubleday, 1961), 170-264; and idem, "The Papyri and their Historical Implications," in *Discoveries in the Wâdī ʾed-Dâliyeh* (eds. P. W. Lapp and N. L. Lapp; AASOR 41; ed. Delbert R. Hillers; Cambridge, Mass.: American Schools of Oriental Research, 1974), 17-29, and plate 59.

192 *KAI* 60:2, 5, 7, 8. Donner and Röllig render it »[die] Gemeinde« in each case. Gibson translates in a similar fashion (*TSSI* 3:148-51). See also *DNWSI* 1:215 s.v. *gw*1.

193 For a good discussion of this passage, see Newsom, "The Book of Job," 544-45. This imagery also obtains to ancient descriptions of the Babylonian Netherworld.

active participle (though in form, it could also be a Qal pft. 3ms), meaning "wanderers" or "dwellers" in a collective sense. On this view, *gār* would then parallel the other collective nouns *regel* in v. 4aβ ("passers-by" by synecdoche) and *ʾĕnôš* ("humans") in v. 4b.[194]

GWR I is commonly used in BH of those who dwell in a land that is not their home—a sense highlighted in the two other occurrences of the root in Job (19:15 [*gārê bêtî*]; 31:32 [*gēr*]).[195] In this vein, the rendering of GR in the Vg. of Job 28:4 emphasizes transience (*populo peregrinante*). While this sense is fitting (// *regel* in v. 4b), it may also simply highlight residence, as elsewhere in BH (// YŠB in Jer 49:18, 33; Jer 50:40).[196]

The compound preposition *mēʿim* occurs a total of 70 times in BH and 2 other times in the Book of Job (Job 1:12; 34:33).[197] The use of the preposition here is ablative, specifying movement "away from" (see *IBHS* §11.2.11b).

4aβ. *ones forgotten by passers-by* [*hanniškāḥîm minnî-rāgel*]: I again provide the translations of the versions for v. 4aβ:

OG: οἱ δὲ ἐπιλανθανόμενοι ὁδὸν δικαίαν

Syh.: *hnwn dyn rṭnyn ʾwrḥʾ zdyqtʾ*

OL: *qui vero obliviscuntur viam iustitiae*

Vg.: *eos quos oblitus est pes egentis hominis et invios* (MT v. 4aβ + 4b)

Syr.: *ʾtṭʿyw mn rgltʾ*

Tg.: *dmtnšyyn lmʿbr brglʾ*

11Q10: *rgl*

OG, Syh., and OL provide a theological interpretation of MT's *hanniškāḥîm minnî-rāgel*, where *regel* functions as a synecdoche for "path." Against this interpretation, *regel* in MT more likely serves as a synecdoche for those traveling on foot. This sense is aptly captured by Tg^{C}'s *mʿbr brglʾ* ("the one who passes by on foot").

Dick's rendering of this line describes the "foreign work force" of v. 4aα as being "stooped over by disease/Nergal" (*hanniškāḥîm minnēr-*

194 Alviero Niccacci also notes this parallelism ("Giobbe 28," 30).

195 See *HALOT* 1:184 s.v. GWR I. Cf. Syr. *gywrʾ* (J. Payne Smith, ed., *A Compendious Syriac Dictionary* [Oxford: Clarendon, 1903], 68) and Moabite [*g*]*rn and* [*gr*]*t* (Mesha, lines 16-17; *DNWSI* 1:232 s.v. *gr*2).

196 See also the Aram. substantive *gēr* with the general meaning "dweller" (Jastrow, *Dictionary*, 1:263), Arab. *jār* with the sense "neighbor" (Edward William Lane, *An Arabic-English Lexicon* [8 vols.; London and Edinburgh: Williams and Norgate, 1863-93], 2:483), and the phrase *gr yšb* ("resident foreigner") in a scribal exercise tablet from Ugarit (*CTU* 5.22:28; see *DUL* 1:306 s.v. *gr* (I)).

197 Count given in *HALOT* 2:840, s.v. *ʿim*.

gal).[198] The first part of this translation is based upon a hypothetical Hebrew root *ŠKḤ II, a possible cognate of Ug. ṮKḤ.[199] After an examination of the Ug. evidence for √ṮKḤ, J. J. M. Roberts states, "In summary, 'bend down, droop' and its semantic extensions will fit all the passages involved."[200] Dick accepts Heb. √*ŠKḤ II and the meaning suggested for its supposed cognate ṮKḤ.[201] While reading √*ŠKḤ II in Job 28:4 is not impossible, it makes perfectly good sense to read √ŠKḤ I.[202] As Dhorme correctly points out, the phrase *hanniškāḥîm minnî-rāgel* conforms to the biblical idiom found also in Deut 31:21 (*haššîrâ hazzōʾt... lōʾ tiššākaḥ mippî zarʿô*; cf. also Ps 31:13).[203] In Job 28:4aβ, to be "forgotten by foot" suggests a place in which human travellers no longer roam.

4b. *They are bereft of humanity* [*dallû mēʾĕnôš* {*nāʿû*}; MT *dallû mēʾĕnôš nāʿû*]: The translations of the versions for v. 4b are as follows:

OG: ἠσθένησαν ἐκ βροτῶν.
Sym: ... ἐσείσθησαν (Syh. marg. *ʾttwlw*)
Th: ... ἐσαλεύθησαν
Syh: *ʾtmḥlw mn bnynšʾ*
OL: *infirmati sunt ab hominibus et commoti sunt*
Vg.: *eos quos oblitus est pes egentis hominis et invios* (MT v. 4aβ + 4b)
Syr.: *wʾtdllw mn ʾnšʾ*
Tg.: *ʾzdqpw mn bny nšʾ ʾṭlṭlw*

Three observations are relevant here: (1) OG, Syh., and OL understand DLL (MT *dallû*) as relating to human illness rather than scarcity or poverty.[204] (2) There is no equivalent to MT's *nāʿû* in OG or Syh., though it is attested in OL, Sym, and Th. (3) Syr. reads MT's *nāʿû* with with the following line (MT's v. 5a).

As for *dallû*, it has become quite common in modern scholarship to understand the root DLL in this line to mean "to dangle" or "to swing to and fro" (RSV, NRSV, NIV, NAS, NKJV, NJB). This meaning is based on Arab. *dalla* II ("to suspend"), Arab. *tadaldala* ("to dangle"), and Eth.

198 Dick, "Job xxviii 4: A New Translation," 219.

199 For discussion, see *HALOT* 4:1490-91, s.v.

200 Roberts, "*NIŠKAḤTÎ... MILLĒB*, Ps. xxxi 13," *VT* 25 (1975): 800-801 n. 13.

201 Dick, "Job xxviii 4: A New Translation," 218, 219 n 17.

202 Guillaume offers yet another proposal, assuming metathesis in MT's *hanniškāḥîm* from the hypothetical root KŠḤ, relating it to the Arab. *kasaḥa*, "swept away" (*Studies in the Book of Job*, 110). Compare Eitan's proposal for Ps 137:5, based on the Arab. *kasiḥa*, as catalogued in *HALOT* 2:502, s.v. cj. KŠḤ).

203 Dhorme, *Book of Job*, 402.

204 See *HALOT* 1:223, s.v. DLL I.

dĕlūl ("dangling curls").[205] This is another case in which the supposition that the first section of the poem details ancient mining technology has unnecessarily influenced interpretations of the poem's lexicon.[206] Dhorme's comment is representative: "The two verbs דלל and נוע depict the miner hanging down to the rope which holds him suspended in the void."[207] David Clines likewise follows this line of thought, though he is reticent about it.[208]

None of the ancient versions understand DLL as "to dangle" or "to swing." Tg.'s *ʾṭlṭlw* should not be interpreted in this sense.[209] Tg's reading is derived from Aram. ṬLṬL, "to move from place to place," descriptive not of a dangling rope or a miner on a dangling rope, but of the passers-by of v. 4aβ (see Tg^{C}'s *mʿbr brglʾ*). Syr. reads "they become rare" or "they are cut off" (*ʾtdllw*). Vg. understands DLL to be related to sickness or poverty (*egentis*). The Gk. traditions also understand DLL to be related to human illness. Geller summarizes well: "Evidence for 'hang down, suspend' is weak—a supposed Arabic cognate *daldala*, 'to dangle, vacillate;' and several dubious Hebrew words, of which the best may be *dalyû*, of Prov 26:7."[210] Byington suggests that the meaning "dangle" is only secondary even in the supposed Arab. cognate.[211]

The verb DLL I occurs only 8 times outside of our passage in the OT. In every case, it may be seen to indicate a low state. This can be of physical health or spiritual humility (Ps 79:8; 116:6; 142:7; Isa 38:14), of general population or military might (Judg 6:6; 2 Sam 3:1; Isa 17:4!), or of water in tributaries (*yĕʾōrîm*, Isa 19:6).

205 See *HALOT* 1:223, s.v. DLL II. See also *HALOT* 1:222 s.v. *dallâ* I, and Isa 38:12; Song 7:6.

206 *HALOT* 1:223, s.v., glosses DLL in Job 28:4b as "dangle (of miners on a rope)."

207 Dhorme, *Book of Job*, 402.

208 Commenting on MT's *nāʿû*, Clines states, "[T]hough the *Translation* above adopts the view that the miners are suspended by ropes, it must be admitted that neither this verb nor the last explicitly refers to hanging from ropes…" (*Job 21-37*, 898 n. 4j; italics original).

209 *Contra* Mangan, "The Targum of Job," 64, who translates, "they swing to and fro." It seems that this translation has been overly influenced by common interpretations of the Hebrew. Contrast the Latin translation by Luis Díez Merino: "translati sunt" ("they were moved"; *Targum de Job*, 207). See also Michael Sokoloff, *A Dictionary of Jewish Palestinian Aramaic of the Byzantine Period* (2d ed.; Ramat-Gan, Israel: Bar Ilan University Press; Baltimore and London: Johns Hopkins University Press, 2002), 225 s.v. ṬLṬL.

210 Geller, " 'Where is Wisdom?' " 178 n. 9. Ehrlich also argues against the meaning "to dangle" (*Randglossen*, 6:290-91). Nevertheless, Clines opts for this interpretation (*Job 21-37*, 898 n. 4*i*).

211 Byington, "Hebrew Marginalia II," 205.

The uses attested in Isa 17:4 and 19:6 again raise the problem of the ambiguous antecedent in our passage, since DLL I is there predicated both of water sources (Isa 19:6) and of human population (Isa 17:4).[212] These two options are also available in Job 28:4. The emphasis in our passage on the lack of human population is evident in the preceding *hanniškāḥîm minnî-rāgel* (v. 4aβ) and *mēʿim-gār* (v. 4a). Given the parallelism between the three lines of v. 4, such a "low state" of human population is likely the upshot in v. 4b as well. Thus Geller's proposal to understand the line as "poor in men" or the like is cogent.[213] The supposition that DLL II ("to hang, dangle") is employed in Job 28:4 should be abandoned.

Heb. *nāʿû* in v. 4b is particularly difficult. It is one of two verbs in the short asyndetic clause of v. 4b, and it is textually problematic. Though attested in Syr. and Vg., it seems to have been lacking in the *Vorlage* of OG. It is untranslated in the three great uncials, LXX^{B} (4th cent.), LXX^{S} (5th cent.), and LXX^{A} (5th cent.). The daughter versions provide mixed evidence. It is omitted in Syh., but is attested in OL (*et commoti sunt*), possibly restored following Th (ἐσαλεύθησαν). Syh. records a reading of Sym in the margin as well (ἐσείσθησαν = *ʾttzyʿw*).

It is very likely that MT's *nāʿû* is the result of partial dittography from the preceding *ʾĕnôš*, originally written with conservative orthography (*ʾĕnōš*).[214] The final *nûn* and *šîn* of ʾNŠ were copied twice, and the dittograph in those Heb. MSS (נש) was subsequently interpreted as NʿW (נעו).[215] As D. N. Freedman has argued, a conservative orthographic *Tendenz* in the Book of Job is purposeful, original, and pervasive.[216] Such a spelling of *ʾĕnōš* is attested in one Heb. MS (Ken. 283) in both vv. 4b and 13a, while 11Q10 also attests conservative orthography in its translation of Heb. *ʾĕnôš* in v. 13a ([*ʾn*]*š*).[217] This spelling should be understood as original.

That MT's *nāʿû* arose from a partial dittograph of the preceding *ʾĕnôš* (that is, NŠ) may find support in the Tg., which translates what is

212 KJV would understand a lack of water in Job 28:4. See also Greenstein, "The Poem on Wisdom in Job 28," 267 n. 32.

213 He is now followed by Newsom, "The Book of Job," 530.

214 Houtsma comes to a similar conclusion: »נעו fehlt in G. und konnte aus den letzten Buchstaben von אנוש entstanden sein; viellecht steckt darin eine abgeleitete Form von נשה vergessen.« (*Textkritische Studien*, 64). Contrast Beer, who thinks that *nāʿû* could simply be a gloss on *dallû* (*Der Text des Buches Hiob*, 178).

215 Note the formation of *ʿayin*, *wāw*, and *šîn* in both formal and semicursive proto-Jewish and Jewish scripts. For charts, see Frank Moore Cross, "The Development of the Jewish Scripts," 176-77, 189-90.

216 Freedman, "Orthographic Peculiarities in the Book of Job," 35*.

217 Kennicott, *Vetus Testamentum Hebraicum*, 2:505.

now preserved in MT as Heb. *nāʿû* with *ʾzdqpw*, from ZQP, meaning "to lift, raise up," which is a synonym of Heb. NŚʾ.[218] This suggests the possibility that the *Vorlage* for the Targumim read DL(W) MʾNŠ NŠ, or possibly DL(W) MʾNŠ NŚʾ, where the dittograph ʾNŠ was metathesized to NŚʾ.[219]

5a-9a: The OG for vv. 5a-9a is missing (⁎γῆ ... αὐτοῦ /), again filled in with Th.

5a. ***A land from which food springs forth*** [*ʾereṣ mimmennāh yēṣēʾ-lāḥem;* MT *mimmennâ*]: This line offers no serious textual difficulties, besides the fact that the expected *mappîq* in the 3d feminine singular object suffix on the preposition *min* is lacking in both the Leningrad and the Aleppo codices (normally written *mimmennāh*). However, *mappîq* is often lost in the 3fs pronominal suffix (GKC §91e, 58g, 23k). See, for example the exact same form, *mimmenā(h),* in Gen 17:16 (x 2) and Ps 132:11.

While *ʾereṣ* is used here to denote a fecund terrestrial paradise, it may also connote the Netherworld. It is clearly used in the latter sense several times in the Book of Job (10:21-22; 3:14; possibly 18:17 and others), and numerous other examples in BH could be cited (see e.g., Jon 2:7).[220] Cognates in Ug. and Akk. are often used of the Netherworld as well (see e.g., *CTU* 1.5 v 13-17 et al; and Gilgamesh XII. 4, 5, 8, 9, 11, 17, 20, 22, 27, 31, etc.).[221]

Heb. *leḥem* has troubled some interpreters, and several alternate readings have been proposed. Francis Andersen has suggested reading *luḥ-m* (with enclitic *mêm*), translating as "stone," despite the fact that the term *lûaḥ* is used for a tablet made of stone and not the stone itself.[222] On this reading, v. 5 would emphasize the contrasting quality and color of the stones above and below the earth's surface, while v. 6 would be epexegetical, detailing the appearance of this subterranean paradise. Tur-Sinai reads *yēʾāṣēl ḥōm,* "heat emanates," assuming me-

218 Sokoloff, *Dictionary of Jewish Palestinian Aramaic,* 181, s.v.; Jastrow, *Dictionary,* 1:410, s.v.

219 It is possible, however, that the Ithpaal of ZQP in the Targums is to be understood as "to be suspended" or the like, which many suggest is the meaning of Heb. *nûaʿ* in Job 28:4b (see Jastrow, *Dictionary,* 1:410, s.v. *zĕqap, zĕqôp*). In this case, the Targums and MT show enough semantic overlap to rule out the possibility of a different consonantal *Vorlage* for the Targums. In short, the Targums could be reading a text much like MT's *nāʿû.*

220 See *HALOT* 1: 90-91, s.v. *ʾereṣ;* and Tromp, *Primitive Conceptions,* 23-46.

221 See also Horowitz, *MCG,* 273-74, and *passim* on the Mesopotamian literature.

222 Andersen, *Job,* 226. Hartley follows this proposal (*The Book of Job,* 375 n. 13).

tathesis of *ṣādê* and *ʾālep*, along with incorrect word division in the MT.[223] Gordis accepts MT's pointing, but interprets the term to mean "heat" in this context.[224] Houtsma even goes so far as to propose the meaning »Sturmwind« here.[225] But the language here is unproblematic and requires no emendation.

5b. ***beneath transformed as fire*** [*wĕtaḥtêhā nehpak kĕmô-ʾēš*]: The only significant text-critical issue presented by v. 5b revolves around MT's *kĕmô-ʾēš* ("like fire"). Though the preposition *kĕmô* is supported by LXX (*ὡσεί; Syh. *ʾyk*; OL *quasi*), Syr. (*ʾyk*), and Tg. (*kmt*), Vg.'s *igni* ("by fire") suggests *bĕmô* instead. If the Vg. is correct, it raises the possibility that MT and the *Vorlagen* of the other ancient versions have suffered corruption due to the similarity of *bêt* and *kāp* in the Aramaic square script. Yet the corruption could just as easily have been in the *Vorlage* of Vg. or a misreading of it.[226] While the reading *bĕmô* also seems to be attested in Ken. MS 118, this could also preserve a corrupt tradition.[227] The phrase *bĕmô-ʾēš* does occur elsewhere in the OT (Ps 44:16, 19), though outside of Job 28:5, the phrase *kĕmô-ʾēš* is just as frequent (Ps 79:5; 89:47). The shorter forms of both prepositions with *ʾēš* are amply attested.

The text-critical support for the reading of MT is superior, but it is equally important to consider what sense the reading makes. The crucial question is whether fire in v. 5b is meant to evoke destruction or brilliance. Descriptions of destruction by fire or compared to fire are quite common in the OT. The verb *hāpak* in the Niphal clearly signifies destruction in Jon 3:4 and Job 41:20. Geller also points out that the verb *hāpak* is used almost as a technical term for the overthrow of Sodom by fire (see particularly HPK in Gen 19:25, 29, and *hahăpēkā* in 19:29).[228] The verb in the G-stem is undoubtedly used of destruction later in the poem in v. 9b.[229] The description of a region of destruction in v. 5 would mesh well with imagery of darkness and desolation in vv. 3-4, often applied to desert regions and to the Netherworld. In Mesopotamian incantation

223 Tur-Sinai, *The Book of Job*, 398-99.

224 Gordis, *The Book of Job*, 306. See also his discussion of *bilḥûmô* in Job 20:23 (ibid, 219).

225 Houtsma, *Textkritische Studien*, 63.

226 Delitzsch believes that Jerome arbitrarily altered the text (*Book of Job*, 2:98).

227 Kennicott, *Vetus Testamentum Hebraicum*, 2:505 ("118 videtur").

228 Stephen Geller, " 'Where is Wisdom?' " 162 and references there. Thomas Aquinas also draws upon the overturning of Sodom in Gen 19:24 to explain v. 5 (*The Literal Exposition on Job*, 333).

229 For more references, see *HALOT* 1:253 s.v. HPK.

texts, demons, which were thought to roam in the desert, are described as "scorching the country like fire" (*māta kīma išāti iqammû*).[230]

However, *ʾēš* is also used elsewhere in metaphors or similes to describe various objects: the appearance of the glory of Yhwh (Exod 24:17), a chariot of fire pulled by a team of fiery horses (2 Kgs 2:11), eyes like fiery torches (Dan 10:6), the fiery appearance of a heavenly messenger (Ezek 8:2), and "stones of fire" (Ezek 28:14, 16). In each of these images, fire suggests brilliance. What, however, would be described with such imagery in Job 28:5?

In the OT *taḥat* is used both of what is beneath the surface of the soil and to what lies beneath some higher point on the surface of the earth, such as at the foot of the mountain (*taḥat hāhār*, Exod 24:4; Deut 4:11).[231] If interpreted in the latter sense, v. 5b may well describe stones on the surface of the earth whose brilliant appearance is compared to fire.[232] In this case, the verb HPK may be interpreted not as a term for destruction but as indicative of changing appearance.[233] HPK in the G-stem has to do with a change of color in Lev 13:55 (cloth) and Jer 13:23 (skin). In Lev 13:25 HPK is in the Niphal of a hair changing coloration due to a burn (*mikwat-ʾēš*). Akkadian texts mention stones set aflame in glass production[234] as well as stones which look like sulphur fire (*abnu šikinšu kīma išāti* (IZI) *kibrīt*).[235] Such may have been the motivation for the description of "fire stones" (*ʾabnê-ʾēš*) in Ezek 28:14, 16.

It may be that the language of the poem is intentionally ambiguous so as to encompass both senses. The larger context of the poem is of little help in untangling these images. The dark, deserted region figured in vv. 3-4 may be either the desert or the mountains, and precious stones are also in the near context in v. 6a. However, given the unambiguously positive description in v. 5a, it would seem odd by any account that v. 5b should paint such an intensely negative picture. In Deuteronomic terms, Job 28:5a would depict a land of bread, there descriptive of the Promised Land (Deut 8:9), while v. 5b depicts a land of no bread,

---

230 See citations in *CAD* I/J, 229 s.v. *išātu*, b.2'. This is from the demonological series *"Evil Demon."* See the brief citation of this passage in JoAnn Scurlock, "Death and the Afterlife in Ancient Mesopotamian Thought," in *CANE* 3:1892-1893.

231 *HALOT* 4:1721-23 s.v. *taḥat* I.

232 See Pope, *Job*, 201; Janzen, *Job*, 193, 199-200; Habel, *The Book of Job*, 396; and cf. Rowley, *The Book of Job*, 181.

233 *HALOT* 1:253 s.v. HPK.

234 *CAD* I/J, 232 s.v. *išātu*, 3', and citation there.

235 *CAD* I/J, 232 s.v. *išātu*, 5', and citation there. Such also may be the rationale behind describing the flashing red gold alloy *ṣāriru* as the product of the Netherworld in K. 2801 of Esarhaddon (*ARAB* 2, §673; text in *CAD* E, 189 s.v. *eperu*, 5.b). See also *CAD* Ṣ, 111-112 s.v. *ṣāriru* A.

descriptive in Deuteronomy of the wilderness (Deut 29:6). Thus while the desert and demonic imagery connoted especially in v. 5b remains an important subtext, the primary sense of the description in this line is positive—most likely having to do with the fiery appearance of the lower regions of the earth's surface.

6a. ***A place of lapis is its stones*** [*mĕqôm-sappîr ʾăbānêhā*] The term *sappîr* has traditionally been rendered as "sapphire" in English, following LXX's *σαπφίρου (or *σαπφείρου) in Job 28:6a, 16b, and elsewhere.[236] OL reads *sapiri*; Syr. *spylʾ*; Vg. *sapphiri*; and 11Q10 *spyrʾ*. Syh. translates *sppyrʾ*, with a marginal notation of its Gk. equivalent, CAΠΦIPA. Yet this is an anachronism, since the "sapphire" with which moderns are familiar was not known until Roman times.[237] Given Pliny's description in *Historia Naturalis*, it is more likely to be identified with the rich azure-blue lapis-lazuli.[238] Though the etymology of *sappîr* is sometimes traced to Sanskrit *śanipriya-*, this identification is questionable.[239]

Outside of Job 28 (vv. 6a, 16b), *sappîr* occurs 9 other times in the OT, where, aside from idealized descriptions of people or their body parts (Song 5:14; Lam 4:7), it always describes cosmic realities and their reflections in sacred icons, such as the pavement under the feet of God (Exod 24:10), priestly vestments (Exod 28:18; 39:11), the throne of God (Ezek 1:26; 10:1), stones in Eden, the Garden of God (Ezek 28:13), and the foundations of the New Jerusalem (Isa 54:11).

Similar uses are attested of its semantic equivalents in Akk. (Sum. ^{na4}ZA.GÌN = Akk. *uqnû*) and Ug. (*iqnu*). Particularly noteworthy is its appearance in the magical grove of stones in SB Gilg. IX. 172-94 and its use in the building of Baal's palace in *CTU* 1.4 v 18-19. All of these are tied together as metaphoric representations of sacred space.

---

236 For this translation in Job 28:6, see NJPS, JB, NJB, KJV, NKJV, NAS, NAB, RSV (but see text note), NRSV (but see text note), NIV (but see text note); Dhorme, *Book of Job*, 403; Delitzsch, *Book of Job*, 2:97; Pope, *Job*, 197; Tur-Sinai, *The Book of Job*, 398; Habel, *The Book of Job*, 388; Terrien, *Job*, 190; Hesse, *Hiob*, 156; Weiser, *Das Buch Hiob*, 195; Driver and Gray, *Job*, 1:238 (but see their discussion in *Job*, 2:194); Gordis, *The Book of Job*, 300 (but see discussion in ibid, 306);

237 See especially P. L. Garber and R. W. Funk, "Jewels and Precious Stones," *IDB* 2:898-905, with discussion on lapis-lazuli and sapphire at 901; Rowley, *The Book of Job*, 181; and Newsom, "The Book of Job," 530 n. 418.

238 See Pliny, *Natural History* 37.38, where he describes *sappirus* as being *caeruleus* ("blue"). So NEB; Hartley, *The Book of Job*, 375; Fohrer, *Das Buch Hiob*, 389; Strauß, *Hiob 19,1-42,17*, 130; De Wilde, *Das Buch Hiob*, 272; and text notes of NIV, RSV, NRSV. On Heb. *sappîr*, see *HALOT* 2:764 s.v.

239 Sylvia Powels, »Indische Lehnwörter in der Bibel,« *ZAH* 5 (1992): 198.

6b. ***which has dust of gold*** [*ʿaprōt zāhāb lô*]: For the first word of this line, MT reads a plural construct of *ʿāpār*. Aq and Sym, however, read *ʿōperet* ("lead"), as reflected in their translation: μόλιβος (Syh. marg. *ʾbrʾ*).[240] Syr. paraphrases in 28:6 with *šḥlʾ* ("deposit [of gold]"), also interpreting MT's *nātîb* in v. 7a with this line.[241] LXX's ⁎χῶμα can be understood as "dust" or as "mound, lump, heap" (Syh. *mdrʾ*; OL *aggeres*), as can Heb. *ʿāpār* and *ʿaprōt* (see Vg. *glebae*).

ʿaprot here most transparently means "soil, clods" as *ʿāpār* in v. 2a. The pair *ʾeben* // *ʿaprōt* in v. 7 undoubtedly picks up on the pair *ʿāpār* // *ʾeben* in v. 2. In addition to its more common meaning ("dust"), *ʿaprōt* is also pregnant with negative connotation connected with *ʿāpār*, profiled in Job (7:21; 14:5; 17:16; 20:11; 21:26) and elsewhere in the OT in descriptions of the Netherworld or the tomb.[242] In Ug., *ʿpr* often forms a formulaic pair with *ʾrṣ*, where both designate the Underworld (see *CTU* 1.161:21-22). Both *ʾereṣ* and *ʿaprōt* also occur in Job 28:5-6 in distant parallel.

The antecedent of *lô* in the line is ambiguous. Gordis suggests that *lô* refers to *māqôm* in the first line. On Gordis' view, *māqôm* is feminine in v. 6a, modified by the 3fs suffixed pronoun on *ʾăbānêhā*, but masculine in v. 6b, where it is modified by the 3ms suffixed pronoun in the prepositional construction *lô*.[243] Numerous other scholars, including Budde, Duhm, Driver and Gray, Waterman, and Niccacci, would understand *lô* to refer to *sappîr* in v. 6a.[244]

However, it is more likely that *lô* in v. 6b refers to the whole construct phrase *mĕqôm-sappîr* in v. 6a. The 3fs suffix of *ʾăbānêhā* in v. 6a refers to the feminine *ʾereṣ* of v. 5a, for which *mĕqôm-sappîr* in v. 6a is a paradigmatic substitute.[245] While adding to some of the syntactical con-

---

240 See also *ʿōperet* in the MT of Job 19:24 (// *barzel*).

241 Since Syriac *šḥlʾ* by itself often means "distillation" or "purgation," Eberhard Baumann questions whether Syr. might be reading a form of ʿRP (»Die Verwendbarkeit der Pešita zum Buche Ijob für die Textkritik,« *ZAW* 20 [1900]: 188). On the other hand, Gösta Rignell attributes the translation of Syr. here to an inner-Syriac error (*The Peshitta to the Book of Job, Critically Investigated with Introduction, Translation, Commentary, and Summary* [ed. Karl-Erik Rignell; Kristianstad: Monitor, 1994], 219). More likely is that Syr. translates with *šḥlʾ* as an abbreviation for the fuller phrase *šḥlʾ ddhbʾ*, "deposit, veins of gold" (see Payne Smith, *Compendious Syriac Dictionary*, 571, s.v. *šḥlʾ*).

242 Tromp, *Primitive Conceptions*, 85-90; *HALOT* 2:862 s.v.

243 Gordis, *The Book of Job*, 306.

244 Budde, *Das Buch Hiob*, 158-59; Duhm, *Das Buch Hiob erklärt*, 135; Driver and Gray, *Job* 2:194; Waterman, "Note on Job 28 4," 168; Niccacci, "Giobbe 28," 31.

245 Geller draws the same conclusion (" 'Where is Wisdom?' " 179 n. 11). Ehrlich offers a very similar analysis, interpreting the lines as asyndetic relative clauses: »ספיר אבניה, worin das Suff[ix] auf ארץ im vorherg[ehend] Verse geht, bildet einen auf

fusion of the couplet, the poet may have favored the use of *lô* in v. 6b not only for its terseness in relation to the longer phrase *ʿaprōt zāhāb* in the line, but especially for its phonetic similarity to the negative particle *lōʾ*, which occurs in every line of the two couplets in vv. 7-8.

7a. *path* [*nātîb*]: Syr. reads this word with v. 6b.[246] The Masoretic accentuation suggests that *nātîb* is a nominative absolute, paralleling the same construction with *ʾereṣ* in v. 5a. The Heb. *casus pendens* here stands as the head of an asyndetic relative clause.

Nātîb / *nĕtîbâ* occurs 26 times in the OT, and 7 of those are in the Book of Job, where the term is parallel to *ʾereṣ* (Job 18:10), *ʾōraḥ* (19:8; 30:13), and *derek* (24:13). Most striking is its occurrence in the Yhwh speeches at Job 38:19-20, where it parallels both *māqôm* and *derek*: "Where is the path (*derek*) where light dwells? / And darkness—where is its place (*mĕqômô*) / that you may take it to its territory / and that you may discern the ways (*nĕtîbôt*) to its home?" All three of these terms are fundamental metaphors of the poem in Job 28. In Job 28:5-7, we have parallel terms *ʾereṣ* // *māqôm* // *nātîb*, and these are picked up with *derek* in v. 23a.

7a. *bird of prey* [*ʿayiṭ*]: The exact identification of this bird is uncertain. LXX translates with ⁎πετεινός, the same term used to render Heb. *ʿôp haššāmayim* in Job 28:21b. Syh. follows this non-specific rendering with *prḥtʾ* and OL with *avis* (also later Vg.). The translation of Syr. is more on the mark with *ṭyrʾ*, "bird of prey." The Tg. contains several traditions. Tg. 2b is closest to the Hebrew text, and it translates Heb. *ʿayiṭ* in v. 7a with *ʿwpʾ* ("bird, winged creature"), reserving "bird of prey" (*ṭrpytʾ*) for the interpretation of v. 7b, where *ʿyn ṭrpytʾ* translates Heb. *ʿên ʾayyâ*. However, Tg. 1 uses the imagery of the *ʿayiṭ* in v. 7a as a trigger for expounding upon the seducer of Eve in the garden, Sammael (*smʾl*). In Jewish tradition, Sammael is not only identified with the serpent, but also with Satan.[247] According to Tg. 1 in Job 28:7, he is one

מקום bezüglichen Relativsatz, mit dem sich letzteres in der dem Hebräischen eigentümlichen Weise im st[atus] constr[uctus] verbindet. Das Ganze aber ist Apposition zu ארץ« (*Randglossen*, 6:291). Alternately, one might argue that *lô* also has its antecedent in *ʾereṣ* in v. 5a, being a *constructio ad sensum*, given that gender concord is less constrained the farther away a pronoun is from its antecedent (see *IBHS* §6.6b) and that Heb. prefers the masculine gender (*IBHS* §6.5.3a).

246 Baumann reconstructs the *Vorlage* as *ʿal nĕtîbōtāyw* (»Die Verwendbarkeit der Pešita,« [1900], 188).

247 Louis Ginzberg, *The Legends of the Jews* (7 vols.; Philadelphia, Pa.: Jewish Publication Society, 1928), 5:120-121 (n. 116).

"who flies like the bird" (*dprḥ hyk ʿwpʾ*),[248] and this flying serpent is described in traditions about Moses' ascension as a massive angel who is full of glaring eyes.[249] The path of which he is ignorant in Job 28:7 is the "path of the tree of life" (Tg. 1; cf. Tg. 2a). Though Heb. *ʾayyâ* in v. 7b is translated with "falcon" in the Rabbinic Bible,[250] other targumic MSS continue the serpent imagery in the second half of the verse as well with *ḥwyʾ* ("snake"; Tg[S, M]). All this follows from Tg.'s Edenic interpretation in v. 6, and is perhaps also triggered by the serpent-like creatures of the next couplet in MT v. 8.

ʿayiṭ is clearly used of some kind of bird of prey in the OT. This is most clear in Gen 15:11, where the *ʿayiṭ* is said to swoop down to feed on the carcasses of Abram's sacrificial animals. It is used in the same fashion in every other occurrence in the OT (Isa 18:6 [x 2]; Jer 12:9 [x 2]; Ezek 39:4), except in Isa 46:11, where it is used as a metaphor for Cyrus who comes from the east as a conqueror. The *ʿayiṭ* is an unclean carrion and scavenger.

7b. ***gazed*** [*šĕzāpattû*]: This word occurs only 3 times in the OT—one other in Job (20:9), and once in the Song of Songs (1:6). In Job 20:9, it is used with reference to the eye (*ʿayin šĕzāpattû*), just as in Job 28:7b, and it is in parallel with the verb ŠWR.[251] In Song 1:6, ŠZP occurs in parallel with RʾH, playing on the "looking (down)" (RʾH) of the addressees and the "looking" (ŠZP) of the sun. It seems clear that *šāzap*, used of the eye literally in Job 20:9a and 28:7b and metaphorically in Song 1:6, means something like "to look, gaze." All the ancient versions understand the term to function generally in this sense. LXX reads ⁎παρέβλεψεν (OL *vidit*); [252] Syr. *ḥzt*; Vg. *intuitus est*; and Tg. with the root SQR ("to look, gaze," etc.).

Nevertheless, Tur-Sinai suggests "to obtain, attain," citing Arab. *šaḏafa*. He understands *lōʾ šezāpattû* in v. 7b to be semantically parallel to *lōʾ-hidrîkūhû* in v. 8a and translates "they have not attained it."[253] This is unlikely in light of the biblical and versional evidence.

248 Ibid., 5:85 (n. 35).

249 Ibid., 2:308-309.

250 See Mangan, "The Targum of Job," 64 and n. e.

251 The meaning of ŠWR is disputed. See *HALOT* 4:1449-51, s.v. However, ŠWR occurs in parallel with RʾH in Num 23:9, where "to gaze" is a fitting translation (so NJPS).

252 The Syh. diverges from the other LXX traditions here with the verb *ṭwr* ("to fly"), a cognate of Syriac *ṭyrʾ*, "bird of prey."

253 Tur-Sinai, *The Book of Job*, 312; see also his translation in ibid., 400.

7b. ***falcon*** [*ʾayyâ*]: The origin of this word is likely onomatopoeic. It occurs only 2 other times in the OT (Lev 11:14; Deut 14:13), both in lists of unclean scavenger birds. *ʾayyâ* is used of either a black kite or a falcon.[254] LXX translates "vulture" (⁎γυπός [also Syh. *kwdrʾ*; OL *vulturis*]). Syr. translates similarly with *dytʾ*, and Vg. with *vulturis*. In some traditions, Tg. is very close: *ṭrpytʾ* (see Tg. 2a, b). In others, it renders Heb. *ʾayyâ* as "snake" (*ḥwyʾ* in Tg^{S,M})[255] based on Edenic imagery seen here by the translators (Tg. 1). Along with the *ʿayiṭ* in v. 7a, the *ʾayyâ* also represents a class of unclean predators and scavengers[256] proper to a place lying far outside the bounds of social order.[257] It is possible that the *ʾayyâ* is a hyponymn of the more general class designated by *ʿayiṭ*.

8a. ***thrashed*** [*hidrîkūhû*]: This presents no problems in the versions, though the translator of 11Q10 turned the verb into a singular with [*hd*]*r^{k}h*.[258] It should be noted, however, that the Aleppo Codex of the MT shows its only divergence from Leningrad in Job 28 with a fuller spelling of the word as *hidrîkûhû* (with the internal *wāw mater lectionis*).[259] Based on the supposition that the autograph(a) of Job was orthographically conservative,[260] Leningrad most likely preserves the original spelling. This spelling has been updated (perhaps unintentionally) in v. 8 by the copyist of the Aleppo Codex.

The verb DRK may be used in the Hiphil with the meanings "to tread upon," "tread down (= thrash)," or perhaps "to reach." The latter meaning may be operative in Judg 20:34, though *hidrîkūhû* is there parallel to *hidrîpūhû*.[261] As Stephen Geller points out, the causative stem of the root in Syriac means "to find, apprehend, understand."[262] Tur-Sinai would translate "to attain" here in parallel to *šĕzāpattû* in v. 7b, which

254 All of the above in *HALOT* 1:39, s.v. *ʾayyâ* I. Also Driver, "Birds in Law," 11.

255 However, the majority of MSS in Tg. 1 read "Eve" (*ḥwh*), which is phonetically quite close to "snake" (*ḥwyʾ*).

256 See the dispute about the *ʾayyâ* in *b. Ḥul.* 63b.

257 This is also true of similar creatures in Job 39:26-30. For a helpful discussion of that passage, see Newsom, "The Moral Sense of Nature," 22.

258 Zuckerman, "The Process of Translation in 11QtgJob," 431.

259 Zuckerman also notes the more conservative spelling in eight Ginsburg editions, but he wrongly attributes the fuller spelling to Leningrad rather than to Aleppo (ibid.). The more conservative *hidrîkūhû* is also found in Codex Leningrad in Judg 20:43.

260 Seow, "The Orthography of Job."

261 *HALOT* 1:231, s.v.

262 Geller, " 'Where is Wisdom?' " 179 n. 13. See Payne Smith, *Compendious Syriac Dictionary*, 97, s.v. DRK: "to follow closely, overtake, come upon, seize; to find, attain, obtain." In Syr., the root DRK in the C-stem shows significant semantic overlap with DRŠ in the G-stem. Syr. actually renders Heb. *hidrîkūhû* in this verse with DRŠ.

he translates "to reach, attain."[263] While one might plausibly understand Hiphil-DRK as "to find, attain," or the like in v. 7b, it is not on account of the word's parallel to *šĕzāpattû*, but is due to a play between the possible meanings "tread down/upon, thrash" and "to attain, reach" within the verb's semantic range.

8a. ***serpents*** [*bĕnê-šaḥaṣ*]: The phrase *bĕnê-šaḥaṣ* occurs only here and in Yhwh's speech in Job 41:26, where the *bĕnê-šaḥaṣ* are said to be the underlings of Leviathan, who is their "king" (*hûʾ melek ʿal-kol-bĕnê-šāḥaṣ*). Cognate terms in Mishnaic Heb. (*šaḥaṣ*, "pride, conceit"), Jewish Aram. (*šaḥṣāʾ*, "pride" > "proud lion"), and Eth. (*šĕḥṣat*, "fierceness, presumptuousness"; *šĕḥĕṣa*, "to be impudent, daring"; *šĕḥūṣ*, "bold") suggest the meaning "pride, conceit," or the like for BH *šaḥaṣ*.[264] The translation "proud beasts" or the like is almost unanimously attested in the commentaries and in the English versions (contrast, however, KJV with "lion's whelps").

The translations of the other ancient versions show more variation. LXX reads *υἱοὶ ἀλαζόνων ("sons of braggarts"; see Syh. *bnyʾ dšbhrnʾ*; OL *filii arrogantium* or *filii adrocantum*). Sym's reading, τέκνα σκανδάλου ("sons of offense") is similar to the LXX traditions. But Aq's (υἱοὶ) βαναυσίας ("[sons of] vulgarity") is outstanding. This seems to be the source of Vg.'s otherwise strange *filii institorum* ("sons of peddlers / merchants"). Classical Gk. βαναυσία, meaning "vulgarity, bad taste," is descriptive of the habits of an artisan, and thus possibly also a merchant.[265] One Tg. tradition reads *bnyyʾ dʾrywwn* ("sons of lions"; Tg. 2). Another reads *bnyʾ dʾdm* ("the son of Adam"; Tg. 1).[266] Syr. generalizes to *ḥywtʾ* ("living creatures"). The translation of 11Q10 is the most striking with *tnyn* ("serpent").[267] In Aram., this word always denotes a sea-monster, crocodile, or large snake, but never a lion.[268] Heb. *tannîn* may also be used of a serpent (e.g., Exod 7:9, 10, 12), but throughout the OT and in the Book of Job, it is used of the mythological sea-dragon (Job 7:12).[269] It may be that the translator(s) of 11Q10 are operating in a

---

263 Tur-Sinai, *The Book of Job*, 400.

264 For all the above cognates and their glosses, see *HALOT* 4:1463, s.v. **šaḥaṣ* and *ŠḤṢ.

265 Henry George Liddell and Robert Scott, *A Greek-English Lexicon* (Oxford: Clarendon, 1996), 305, s.v. Note also Aquinas, who follows the Latin tradition with "sons of peddlers" (*The Literal Exposition on Job*, 323).

266 Mangan, "The Targum of Job," 65 n. 7.

267 Sokoloff's reading is the same, but he treats the final *nûn* as a reconstruction: *tny*]*n* (*The Targum of Job from Qumran Cave XI*, 50).

268 See Jastrow, *Dictionary*, 2:1682 s.v.

269 On the *tannîn* in the OT and cognate literature, see G. C. Heider, "Tannin," in *DDD*, 834-36.

similar hermeneutical framework as the rabbinic Targums, which interpret v. 7 as a reference to the primeval serpent in Eden (see note on *bird of prey* in v. 7a). Yet, given the relatively conservative nature of 11Q10, this is unlikely.[270] 11Q10 translates the same phrase in Job 41:26 with *rḥš* ("reptile, creeping thing").[271] In the Talmud, the word *šaḥaṣ* continues to carry the meanings "arrogant, vainglorious" and "abomination, disgrace," though it is also used along with *šaḥal* as one of six names for "lion."[272]

Georg Fohrer translates *bĕnê-šaḥaṣ* in Job 28:8 as »stolze Tiere,« suggesting that it is a poetic phrase for a large game animal, probably chosen because of its alliteration with the following *šaḥal*.[273] The interpretation of *bĕnê-šaḥaṣ* as an embellished epithet for a large predatory beast was already presented by Duhm in 1897,[274] and this view was thought to be "probably correct" by A. S. Yahuda in his 1903 essay on *hapax legomena* in the Old Testament.[275]

Etymologically, Yahuda believes that the Heb. phrase *bĕnê-šaḥaṣ* is more properly related to Arab. *šaḫṣ* ("something that is obviously visible") than to Arab. *šaḫaṣa* ("rise up, stand out"), which he thinks was a later semantic development. Arab. *šaḫṣ* highlights something that is bulky or corpulent. Mishnaic Heb. *šaḥaṣ* ("superior, smug, and showy behavior") could also be seen as a semantic derivative from this more basic meaning.[276] He concludes that BH *bĕnê-šaḥaṣ* was used to describe the massiveness of large predatorial beasts.[277]

Based on cognates in Arab. and Eth., two meanings of BH *šaḥaṣ* emerge. One highlights the physical size of a person or thing, and the

---

270 See Carol A. Newsom, "Job, Book of," and Adam S. van der Woude, "Job, Targum of," in *Encyclopedia of the Dead Sea Scrolls* (2 vols.; eds. Lawrence H. Schiffmann and James A. Vanderkam; Oxford: Oxford University Press, 2000), 1:412-14. In fact, David Shepherd has argued against calling 11Q10 a "targum," partially due to the fact that it shows remarkable fidelity to its Hebrew *Vorlage* in contrast to the rabbinic Targums (*Targum and Translation*, 280-86).

271 As pointed out by Grabbe, *Comparative Philology*, 92.

272 See *b. San.* 95a.

273 Fohrer, *Das Buch Hiob*, 389, 391 n. 8.

274 Duhm, *Das Buch Hiob erklärt*, 135.

275 A. S. Yahuda, »Hapax Legomena im Alten Testament,« *JQR* 15 (Oct.-Jul., 1902-1903): 707 (»wohl richtig«).

276 Ibid., 708.

277 Ibid., 707-708. *HALOT* glosses Arab. *šaḫṣ* as "someone or something high and conspicuous, or having height and appearance," following E. W. Lane in his Arabic-English lexicon, and *šaḫaṣa* as "rise up, tower above," (*HALOT* 4:1463, s.v. *šaḥaṣ and ibid., s.v. *ŠḤṢ; Lane, *An Arabic-English Lexicon*, 4:1517).

other highlights an arrogant attitude. Both are preserved in the gloss *HALOT* gives for Heb. *šaḥaṣ*: "size, pride."[278]

It is clear from the parallelism in Job 41:26 that "pride" is at issue there, as *bĕnê-šaḥaṣ* parallels *kol-gābōah*. As Carol Newsom has pointed out, "pride" is essential to the speech's rhetoric.[279] Nevertheless, Leviathan's pride is rooted in his corporeal size and strength. This is clear throughout his description in Job 40:25-41:25, and, if the text is correct, it is stated outright in the MT of 41:7: "the channels of (his) armor are arrogance" (*gaʾăwâ ʾăpîqê māginnîm*).[280] This connection may also be presumed for his underlings, the *bĕnê-šaḥaṣ*. In fact, the semantic range of *šaḥaṣ* itself facilitates this pun on two possible aspects of meaning: both physical size and mental egoism.

In his now-famous essay on *šaḥal* in the OT, Sigmund Mowinckel comments on Job 41:26: "The context... seems to indicate that the בני שחץ whose king is Leviathan, are beings of the same kind as himself, i.e. serpent-like and dragon-like beings, primarily conceived of as living in the sea."[281] Mowinckel's emphasis on the literary context in which the phrase *bĕnê-šaḥaṣ* occurs in the Book of Job is helpful, and these contextual considerations commend the translations of 11Q10 in Job 41:26 with *rḥš*, and in 28:8 with *tnyn*. The *bĕnê-šaḥaṣ* in Job 28:8 are best understood as creatures characterized by their massive size and by their massive ego, cut from the same cloth as their king, Leviathan. Their reptilian nature is underscored by the hissing consonance of the names of both creatures in the couplet: *bĕnê-šaḥaṣ* // *šaḥal*.

In light of the relationship of the *bĕnê-šaḥaṣ* to Leviathan and the cosmic overtones that emerge throughout Section One, there remains the distinct possibility of a composite creature figured in Job 28:8, which is described as a "serpent" in the first line (v. 8a) and as a "lion" in the second (v. 8b; see note on *lion* below). Though Mowinckel's opinion that "The *bĕnē šaḥaṣ* do not so much belong to zoology as to mythology"[282] is probably an overstatement, his intuition that the creatures figured in Job 28:8 may well challenge modern conceptions of zoology is correct.

---

278 *HALOT* 4:1463, s.v.

279 See Newsom, "The Moral Sense of Nature," 23-25.

280 MT reads *gaʾăwâ* ("arrogance, pride"), but LXX's τὰ ἔγκατα αὐτοῦ, Aq's σῶμα αὐτοῦ, and Vg's *corpus illius* reflect Heb. *gēwōh* ("his back").

281 Sigmund Mowinckel, "שׁחל," in *Hebrew and Semitic Studies Presented to Godfrey Rolles Driver* (eds. D. Winton Thomas and W. D. McHardy; Oxford: Clarendon, 1963), 97.

282 Ibid.

8b. *moved over* [*ʿādâ*]: This verb is used only here in the Qal, though it occurs in the Hiphil in Prov 25:20. It is often considered to be an Aramaism, based on its frequent use in that language.[283] The verb *ʿădāʾ* is common in Targumic Aram., meaning "to pass by" in the G-stem.[284] The verb also occurs with this meaning in Off. Aram. on a stele from Daskyleion.[285] In the targums it commonly translates Heb. ʿBR (e.g., Gen 15:17 [Onqelos]; Jer 9:9). As such, Driver and Gray consider Heb. *ʿādâ* to be poetic for ʿBR.[286] Similar meanings are found for cognates in Mand., Syr., and Eth.[287] The sense "to remove" (< *"to move") is found for the Ug. verb *ʿdy* in the D-stem, occurring about fifteen times in administrative texts.[288] The meaning "to pass by, to pass over" is fitting in Job 28:8 in parallel to the Hiphil of DRK, "to tread upon, thrash." If *ʿādâ* is an Aramaism, as many suggest, Tg. doesn't recognize it as such. Tg. 2 translates with *zʾr* ("it passed around"), and Tg. 1 translates with *sṭʾ* ("it deviated"), rather than with Aram. ʿDʾ, ʿDY.

8b. *lion* [*šaḥal*]: The meaning of this word is perhaps the single most vexing philological issue in the poem. From an etymological perspective, there is evidence of possible cognates meaning either "lion" or "lizard," which basically represent the two main options for BH *šaḥal*. Arab. *saḥlal* ("the offspring of a lion") supports the former, and Eg. Arab. *siḥlīya* ("lizard") supports the latter.[289] The meaning "lion" persists in post-biblical Hebrew with Talmudic *šaḥal* and *šaḥălāʾ* (see *b. San.* 95a). Heb. *šaḥal* should not be related to the Arab. verb *saḥala* ("to bray" [of a donkey]) or the Akk. verb *šaḫālu*, as formerly supposed.[290]

---

283 On the poetic use of supposed Aramaic words in the Book of Job, see Avi Hurvitz, "The Chronological Significance of 'Aramaisms' in Biblical Hebrew," *IEJ* 18 (1968): 234-40; idem, "Hebrew and Aramaic in the Biblical Period: The Problem of 'Aramaisms' in Linguistic Research on the Hebrew Bible," in *Biblical Hebrew: Studies in Chronology and Typology* (ed. Ian Young; JSOTSup 369; ed. D. J. A. Clines et al.; London and New York: T & T Clark, 2003), 32-33; and Greenstein, "The Language of Job and Its Poetic Function," 653, 657-59.

284 Jastrow, *Dictionary*, 2:1043, s.v. *ʿădāʾ*, *ʿădê*.

285 Gibson, *TSSI*, 2:157-58 (text 37, line 4). Also *DNWSI* 2: 829, s.v. *ʿdy*ı.

286 Driver and Gray, *Job*, 2:194.

287 *HALOT* 2:789, s.v. and cognates cited there.

288 *DUL* 1:152 s.v. *ʿ-d-y*.

289 For the Arab. *saḥlal*, see *HALOT* 4:1461, s.v. *šaḥal*. The Eg. Arab. gloss is from Geller, " 'Where is Wisdom?' " 179 n. 14.

290 See Brent A. Strawn, *What is Stronger than a Lion?: Leonine Image and Metaphor in the Hebrew Bible and the Ancient Near East* (OBO 212; Fribourg: Academic Press; Göttingen: Vandenhoeck and Ruprecht, 2005), 322. Marcus Jastrow, for example, cites Akk. *šaḫālu*, which he glosses "to cry" as a basis for Talmudic *šaḥal* and *šaḥălāʾ*, supposing a development from "roaring" to "a roaring beast." Yet Akk. *šaḫālu* is now under-

Stephen Geller has drawn attention to the later Heb. verb *šāḥal* ("to perforate," or, in the Hiphil, "to pass through a hollow space, or groove; to slide").[291] As he notes, this seems to be related to Akk. *saḫālu* ("to pierce"), with the verbal adjective *saḫlu* ("pierced"), and it "sounds most serpentine."[292] While the semantic overlap is clear, one would have expected ŠḪL in Akkadian. The Akk. verb *šaḫālu,* however, does not mean "to pierce," but "to filter."[293]

Ug. *šḫlmmt,* attested 4 times in the Baal cycle (*CTU* 1.5 v 19; 1.5 vi 7; 1.5 vi 30; 1.6 ii 20), has been understood as "mythical place of the divine dead, antechamber to the Underworld" and "lions of death," among other interpretations.[294] Mark Smith follows the first suggestion and renders "Death's Realm" in each instance,[295] and I believe this translation to be correct.[296] Ug. *šḫlmmt* cannot contribute to the etymological discussion of Heb. *šḥl,* though a play between the two could be operative in poetic connotation.[297]

Heb. *šaḥal* occurs only 7 times in BH, 3 of which are in the Book of Job (Job 4:10; 10:16; 28:8; Ps 91:13; Prov 26:13; Hos 5:14; 13:7). The term is clearly used of a lion in Job 4:10 (// *ʾaryēh* and *kĕpîr*), Job 10:16 (where God hunts Job like a *šaḥal* during his royal lion hunt), Prov 26:13 (// *ʾărî*), Hos 5:14 (// *kĕpîr*), and Hos 13:7 (// *nāmēr, dôb,* and *lābîʾ*). While the meaning of parallel terms alone may not be entirely foolproof, the imagery of these passages fully supports the meaning "lion." The evidence from Job suggests that the primary sense of *šaḥal* is "lion."

However, this gloss hardly seems to encompass all that *šaḥal* evokes in the context of Job 28:5-8. Other biblical texts illustrate the complexity of identifying or classifying the *šaḥal,* at least in modern zoological terms. In Ps 91:13, for example, *šaḥal* parallels both *peten* and *kĕpîr*. Even if one translates *šaḥal* in this context as "lion," as seems most likely to

---

stood to mean "to filter" or the like (*CAD* Š/1, 77-78, s.v. *šaḫālu*; Jastrow, *Dictionary*, 2:1548 s.v. *šāḥal*).

291 Geller, " 'Where is Wisdom?' " 179 n. 14. See also Jastrow, *Dictionary*, 2:1548, s.v. *šāḥal*.

292 Geller, " 'Where is Wisdom?' " 179 n. 14. See *CAD* S, 28-29, s.v. *saḫālu* and *CAD* S, 61, s.v. *saḫlu*.

293 *CAD* Š/1, 77-78, s.v.

294 *DUL* 2:812; For the translation "lions of death," see Clifford, *The Cosmic Mountain*, 84 n. 57.

295 Smith, "The Baal Cycle," 148-50, 156.

296 Supposing *šḥl* + *mmt*, "Mortality Shore," as suggested by *DUL* 2:812. See also the Arab. evidence cited there.

297 The possible relation between Heb. *šaḥal* and Ug. *šḫlmmt* is also problematized by the fact that one would expect ŠḪL in Ug. rather than ŠḤL, as attested.

me, one is compelled to ask how a "viper" (*peten*) is a fitting semantic parallel to a "lion" (*kěpîr*) and to a "*šaḥal*."

The ambiguity inherent in terms for "lion" and "serpent" is evidenced numerous other terms in Semitic and in their translations in antiquity. The same polysemy suggested by the varying translations of *běnê-šaḥaṣ* in the ancient versions in Job 28:8a and 41:26b is suggested by conflicting evidence for the interpretation of *šaḥal* in the versions as well. In Job 28:8, LXX (*λέων [Syh. *ʾryʾ*; OL *leo*]), Syr. (*ʾryʾ*), Vg. (*leaena*), and some Targumic traditions render "lion" or "lioness" (*lywnʾ*; see Tg. 2). However, other Targumic traditions translate as "serpents" (*ḥywyʾ*; see Tg. 1). In the six occurrences of *šaḥal* in BH outside of our passage, the translations of the versions are also mixed. LXX translates *šaḥal* with four different terms: πανθήρ ("panther," Hos 5:14; 13:7), λέων ("lion," Job 10:16 [and 28:8b]), λέαινα ("lioness," Job 4:10), and ἀσπίς ("asp," Ps 91:13 [LXX 90:13]). A fifth at Prov 26:13, ἀποστελλόμενος, reflects the verb *šālaḥ* by metathesis. The Targumic traditions again provide two different kinds of translations with *lytʾ* ("lion," Hos 5:14; 13:7), *šḥlʾ* ("lion," Prov 26:13; Job 4:10), *ʾryʾ* ("lion," Job 10:16), and *br ʾrywn* ("son of serpents," Ps 91:13). Vg. translates with two terms, *leaena* ("lioness") and *aspis* ("asp," only at Ps 91:13).[298]

Though he admitted the translation "lion" in other contexts, Mowinckel championed the view that *šaḥal* in Job 28:8 is a mythological serpent-dragon, and that this was the original meaning of the term. According to him, *šaḥal* came to mean "lion" only later, based on composite lion-serpent creatures known in mythology of the ancient Near East.[299] Despite nods in his direction, virtually all commentators have chosen to render "lion" in Job 28:8, though Tur-Sinai translates "large beast" and Terrien and Dhorme translate "leopard."[300] Marvin Pope, however, tentatively follows Mowinckel and translates "serpent."[301] The English translations also prefer "lion," though NEB translates "serpent."

While Mowinckel's philological methods are sometimes questionable,[302] the genius of his argument was the supposition that the

298 For the versional evidence outside of Job 28:8, see Strawn, *What is Stronger than a Lion*, 323.

299 Mowinckel, "שַׁחַל," 95-103, esp. 102-103.

300 Tur-Sinai, *The Book of Job*, 400, 80; Terrien, *Job*, 190; Dhorme, *Book of Job*, 404.

301 Pope, *Job*, 197, 202.

302 One aspect of Mowinckel's method deserves brief mention here. Stephen Geller and others have criticized Mowinckel's attempts to relate all possible roots having to do with lions or serpents (such as *šaḥal*, *nāḥāš*, *lāḥaš*, etc.; see Geller, " 'Where is Wisdom?' " 179 n. 14). However, it should be noted that there are numerous instances in any language in which there is a denial of the arbitrariness of the sign and in which

polysemy of *šaḥal* and other terms for "lion" or "serpent" in Semitic owes to the combination of lions and serpents in composite creatures in ancient Near Eastern mythology. This is clearly illustrated in the Akk. Lion-Serpent myth (*CT* 13 33-34) in which Tishpak, the chief god of Eshnunna, battles an enormous lion-serpent creature.[303] The composite nature of the creature seems to have provided a realistic basis for the semantic overlap between terms for "lion" and "serpent." As Lewis points out, in lines 4-5 of *CT* 13 33-34 (obv.), the creature is called a *bašmu* which, by the preceding determinative (^{MUŠ}*bašmu*), clearly indicates a serpent.[304] This is a cognate of Heb. *peten* ("viper") and Ug. *bṯn* ("serpent, dragon").[305] Yet in lines 17, 20, 24 (obv.), and lines 4, 7, 9 (rev.), a common Akk. word for "lion" is used—*labbu*—though a serpent is obviously still meant here.[306] This is a cognate of Heb. *lābîʾ*

certain consonant clusters gain morphemic status (see Andrew Goatly, *The Language of Metaphors*, 78). This may well be one motivating factor for some semantic overlap between these phonetically similar words in BH: *šaḥal* ("lion" or "serpent"), *nāḥāš* ("serpent"), *lāḥaš* ("to whisper" [of a snake-charmer]), *zāḥal* ("to glide" [of snakes]). Note also Arab. *ḥanaš* ("snake") and Akk. *saḫālu* ("to pierce"), among numerous other examples in Semitic. Though it is etymologically a Sum. loanword derived from muš ("snake") and laḫ$_4$ ("to bring"), Akk. *mušlaḫḫu* ("snake charmer") might also be included in this list from a phenomenological perspective (cf. Ug. *mlḫš* ["exorcist"]).

303 See Benjamin Foster's translation, "The Lion-Serpent," in *BTM*, 581-82.

304 Lewis, "Lion-Dragon Myths," 33. See pp. 30-32 for text and his translation.

305 Heb. *peten* is likely an Aram. loanword, since one would expect PŠN or BŠN in BH. See Syr. *ptnʾ* ("asp"; Payne Smith, *Compendious Syriac Dictionary*, 471, s.v.). See also *HALOT* 3:990-91, s.v. *peten* and cognate evidence cited there. On the basis of the attested evidence, the "Proto-Semitic" base form may be assumed to be √*BṮN, which is precisely what occurs in Ug., with the meaning "serpent, dragon" (*DUL*, 1:252, s.v. *bṯn*). Heb. √BŠN does occur in the OT, often as a place-name ("Bashan;" see *HALOT* 1:165, s.v. *bāšān* I). But it is very likely that BH also had a homonymous root (**bāšān* II) meaning "snake" (see *HALOT* 1:165, s.v. *bāšān* II). This meaning is most probable in Deut 33:22 (where *bāšān* is parallel with *ʾaryēh*), and in Ps 68:23 as well (on *bāšān* in the last passage, see James H. Charlesworth, "Bashan, Symbology, Haplography, and Theology in Psalm 68," in *David and Zion: Biblical Studies in Honor of J. J. M. Roberts* [ed. Bernhard F. Batto and Kathryn L. Roberts; Winona Lake, Ind.: Eisenbrauns, 2004], 351-72, here 354-61). Note also BṮN in the Proto-Sinaitic inscriptions, which W. F. Albright translates "Serpent lady" (*The Proto-Sinaitic Inscriptions and Their Decipherment* [HTS 22; Cambridge, Mass.: Harvard University Press; London: Oxford University Press, 1969], 19-22 [texts 351 and 353]).

306 *CAD* L, 24-25, s.v. *labbu*. As Lewis notes, F. A. M. Wiggermann proposed that *labbu* is an epithet of the dragon meaning "the raging one" (Lewis, "*CT* 13.33-34 and Ezekiel 32," 34; Wiggermann, "Tišpak, His Seal, and the Dragon *mušḫuššu*," in *To the Euphrates and Beyond: Archaeological Studies in Honour of Maurits N. van Loon* [ed. O. Haex et al.; Rotterdam: Balkema, 1989], 118; cf. also *CAD* L, 24, s.v. *labbu* B). A saying in the Aram. *Proverbs of Ahiqar* may also attribute the name *labbu* to a sea-snake: *ʾryh lʾ [ʾy]ty bymʾ / ʿl kn yqrʾwn lqpʾ lbʾ*. Lindenberger translates, "There is no lion in the sea, therefore the *sea-snake* is called *labbu*" (*The Aramaic Proverbs of Ahiqar*, 105-107, saying

("lion").[307] As Lewis states, "The choice of the word *labbu* with its leonine connotations is not accidental. I suggest returning to Heidel's notion of a 'composite monster or dragon with leonine and serpentine attributes.' "[308] Lewis goes on to point out iconographic representations of creatures with leonine bodies and serpentine heads as well as serpentine bodies with leonine heads.[309] He states, "The common denominator for associating these two creatures seems to be that they could both inspire paralyzing, heart-stopping fear when encountered."[310] Such a rationale seems to be the basis for the pairing of *kĕpîr* and *tannîn* in Ps 91:13, *lābîʾ* and *ʾepʿeh* in Isa 30:6, and *ʾărî* and *nāḥāš* in Amos 5:19. Ps 58 also evidences some connections between terms for "serpent" and "lion," as the suppliant compares his enemies to serpents (*nāḥāš*) and vipers (*peten*) in v. 5, but then pleads with Yhwh in v. 7 to break the teeth of the young lion (*kĕpîr*). But in Ezek 32:2, the significance seems even greater: the parallel terms "lion" (*kĕpîr*) and "serpent/dragon" (*tannîm*) work together, perhaps both being two epithets for a single horrific creature.

Other terms in Semitic may be used either of a lion or a serpent. One of the most obvious is *nēšu* in SB Gilg. XI. In line 305, the creature is called a "snake" (*ṣēru* (MUŠ)), but in line 314, it is referred to as a "Lion of the Earth" (*nēši* (UR.MAḪ) *ša qaq-qa-ri*).[311] Akk. *nēšu* is a cognate to Heb. *nāḥāš* ("serpent"). Mowinckel has also pointed to Eth. *ʾarwē*, meaning "serpent," a cognate of Heb. *ʾaryēh* / *ʾărî* ("lion").[312]

Thus several Semitic terms whose cognates are used for "lion" in the OT are used both for "lion" and "serpent" in other ancient Near Eastern literature. This is true for Heb. *ʾărî* / *ʾaryēh* and Eth. *ʾarwē*, as

---

34 = saying 165 in Bezalel Porten and Ada Yardeni, *Textbook of Aramaic Documents from Ancient Egypt* [3 vols.; Jerusalem: Hebrew University, Department of the History of the Jewish People; Winona Lake, Ind.: Eisenbrauns, 1993], 3:47). Lindenberger believes that this proverb reflects a false etymologizing "abetted by the fact that in the Semitic languages… many aquatic creatures are called by the names of more familiar land animals which they resemble in some way" (*The Aramaic Proverbs of Ahiqar*, 105).

307 See *HALOT* 2:517 s.v., and cognate evidence cited there.

308 Lewis, "*CT* 13.33-34 and Ezekiel 32," 34, citing A. Heidel, *The Babylonian Genesis* (2d ed.; Chicago: University of Chicago Press, 1951), 141.

309 See discussion in Lewis, "*CT* 13.33-34 and Ezekiel 32," 35-36 and plates there (esp. figs. 5, 6, 8, 9, 10).

310 Ibid., 35.

311 Text and translation in George, *BGE*, 1:722-23. See also discussion in ibid., 2:896-97.

312 Mowinckel, "שׁחל," 98. Lewis, however, cites personal communication from Stephen Kaufman who points out that the Eth. expression for a serpent is actually *ʾarwe mĕdr*, "animal of the ground," rather than *ʾarwē* alone (Lewis, "*CT* 13.33-34 and Ezekiel 32," 41 n. 101).

well as Heb. *lābîʾ* and Akk. *labbu*. A similar phenomenon is evident in cognates for Heb. words for "snake," such as *nāḥaš* (cf. Akk. *nēšu*) and *peten* (cf. Akk. *bašmu*) that can be used for "snake" or "lion" in the cognate literature.

In sum, the comparative Semitic semantic evidence suggests that the various renderings of *šaḥal* in the ancient translations of the OT owe to the polysemic nature of the word itself. Such semantic polysemy is clearly evident in other Semitic words for "serpent" and "lion." Particularly striking are those used for "lion" in the OT that are used both for "lion" and "serpent" in other ancient Near Eastern literature.

The flexibility of the term *šaḥal* and the other Semitic terms which may mean "lion" in some contexts and "serpent" in others may well be rooted in a composite lion-serpent that may be described either as a lion or a serpent (or perhaps as each in parallel poetic lines). It seems that, generally speaking, *šaḥal* simply became a flexible term in BH, applicable to either "lion" or "serpent," as are several other terms in Semitic. It is not possible or relevant for our purposes to suggest the primacy of the meaning "serpent" over "lion," as Mowinckel attempts to do.[313] When relevant to the context, authors could play on either aspect of the term, and, in some cases, on both, when they wished to conjure up a mythological composite lion-serpent figure.

But how is *šaḥal* to be understood in Job 28:8? The parallel phrase, *bĕnê-šaḥaṣ*, suggests that *šaḥal* may be some kind of reptile rather than a lion, unless we are to understand v. 8 as a description of a composite figure which extends across the couplet, with "serpents" in the first line and "lion" in the next.[314] To keep this latter possibility open, and respecting the leonine denotation of *šaḥal* elsewhere in Job (4:10; 10:16), "lion" should be considered primary in Job 28:8. Nonetheless, this gloss does not encompass all the possible uses of the term, and modern scholars must recognize the degree to which their interpretations of *šaḥal* often impose contemporary (and typically reductive) zoological conceptions on ancient terminology. Mowinckel is justified in keeping current the idea of a mythological lion-serpent creature in connection with *šaḥal*, even if he sometimes overstates his case.

9a. *hard rock* [*ḥallāmîš*]: This term occurs only 4 times outside our passage in the OT (Deut 8:15; 32:13; Isa 50:7; Ps 114:8). In 3 of these 4 passages, it is used in connection with streams from the rock. These are

---

313 Mowinckel, "שׁחל," 103.

314 One might compare the division of divine epithets for one god over two poetic lines, which is common enough in Semitic poetry. See the example of Kothar wa-Ḫasis as Kothar // Ḫasis in *CTU* 1.17 v 10-11, among others.

cosmic streams of water in Deut 8:15 and Ps 114:8, but oil in Deut 32:13. The salvific acts of God in making water and oil flow from the *ḥallāmîš* are bound up with the imagery of cosmic streams of life-giving water flowing from the base of the mountain of God. In these passages and in Job 28:9-10, *ḥallāmîš* is invariably collocated with or parallel to *ṣûr*.

The translations of the versions are fairly uniform. LXX renders with ⁎ἀκρότομος ("sharp [rock];" also at Ps 114:8 [LXX 113:8]), which is translated as "flint stone, hard rock" by Syh. (*ṭrnʾ*) and "very hard rock" by OL (*durissimo lapide*). Syr. translates similarly with *ṭrn* ("flint stone, hard rock"), as also Vg. with *silicem* ("flintstone") and Tg. with *šmyr* ("very hard stone"). Elsewhere LXX translates with στερεά πετρά ("hard rock," Deut 32:13; Isa 50:7) and πετρά ἀκρότομος ("sharp rock," Deut 8:15).

The term *ḥallāmîš* is commonly derived from Akk. *elmešu*. Of *elmešu* *CAD* states: "Since no econ[omic] text ever mentions the *e*[*lmešu*]-stone and even the personal name Elmešu becomes very rare after the OB period, the word must be taken as referring to a quasi-mythical precious stone of great brilliancy and with a color which one tried to imitate with dyes."[315] This meaning is eminently clear in the Sumerian disputation *Tree and Reed*, for example.[316] Yet *CAD* would relate Akk. *elmešu* to Heb. *ḥašmal* rather than to Heb. *ḥallāmîš*. As they state, "In this peculiar quality, *elmešu* may well be connected with Heb. *ḫašmal* [*sic*!; read: *ḥašmal*] which likewise appears only in similes referring to the extraordinary sheen of a quasi-mythical stone."[317] Heb. *ḥašmal* occurs in Ezek 1:4, 27; 8:2, where it describes an appearance of radiance. But von Soden dissociates Akk. *elmešu* and Heb. *ḥallāmîš* from Akk. *ešmarû* (a silver alloy) and Heb. *ḥašmal*.[318] He suggests, rather, that Heb. *ḥallāmîš* and Akk. *elmešu* are to be derived from an original root *ḤMŠ, "to be hard," formed with an *l*-infix.[319] Thus Heb. *ḥallāmîš* and Akk. *elmešu* are

315 *CAD* E, 108 s.v. *elmešu*. Note the description of Stephanie Dalley: "*elmešu-stone*: a lustrous, precious, semi-mythical stone, possibly amber, often used with rock crystal" (*Myths from Mesopotamia*, 129 n. 52).

316 See line 3: "She adorned herself with diorite, chalcedony, carnelian (and) elmeshu" (as cited in Clifford, *Creation Accounts*, 26).

317 *CAD* E, 108 s.v.

318 Wolfram von Soden, »Kleine Beiträge zum Ugaritischen und Hebräischen,« in *Hebräische Wortforschung. Festschrift zum 80. Geburtstag von Walter Baumgartner* (VTSup 16; ed. G. W. Anderson et al.; Leiden: E. J. Brill, 1967), 298: »Mit akkad. *ešmarû*, Heb. *ḥašmal* (s. *AHw* 257a) haben *elmēšum* und *ḥallāmîš* weder der Bedeutung noch der Herkunft nach das Geringste zu tun.«

319 Ibid., 298-300. Walter Michel also accepts this view ("The Ugaritic Texts," 410 n. 552). However, he translates "boulder," treating it as an epithet for Zaphon (ibid., 203). While I believe that he is correct in seeing cosmic mountain imagery here, it is not so explicit in the word *ḥallāmîš* but is a picture resulting from the whole poem.

cognates, while Heb. *ḥašmal* should be related to Akk. *ešmarû*. This view is the most cogent etymologically, though the apparent semantic overlap between Akk. *elmešu* and Heb. *ḥašmal* is undeniable.

The contexts in which Heb. *ḥallāmîš* is attested in the OT support this derivation, as they each emphasize hardness. Further, in Deut 8:15 and 32:13, *ḥallāmîš* is used together with *ṣûr* (*miṣṣûr haḥallāmîš* [Deut 8:15]; *mēḥalmîš ṣûr* [Deut 32:13]). In Ps 114:8, *ḥallāmîš* and *ṣûr* are parallel. In the couplet in Job 28:9-10, *ḥallāmîš* is in parallel both to *hārîm* (v. 9b) and *ṣûrôt* (v. 10a). Yet if Heb. *ḥallāmîš* is indeed a cognate of Akk. *elmešu*, perhaps even an Akk. loan word, then it may also evoke quasi-mythical overtones that seem to be attached to *elmešu*.

Considering the immediately preceding context in v. 8, which mentions the *bĕnê-šaḥaṣ* and the *šaḥal*, *ḥallāmîš* in v. 9 could also evoke Akk. *ḫulamēsu* / *ḫulamīšu* ("chameleon"), as Geller notes.[320] This is apparently a reptile with a short head, and it is listed together in one text with the *iškarissu*-rat, the *kurusisu*-rat, and the *iškippu*-worm. It is also associated with the "lion of the earth" (UR.MAḪ *qaq-qa-ri*), an epithet for the serpent in SB Gilg. XI. 314.[321] The question, however, is whether an Israelite audience would recognize such an allusion.

9a. *He assaults* [*šālaḥ yādô bĕ…*]: The idiom *šālaḥ yād* + OBJECT is most often used in contexts of violence. It may be used in general of theft (Exod 22:7, 10) or of plunder (Dan 11:42). But when directed against persons, it has to do with seizing someone in order to kill them. In the latter case, the object is most often marked with *bĕ-*, though sometimes it is marked with *ʾel-*.[322] The idiom is particularly well-attested in the relatively short book of Esther (Est 2:21; 3:6; 6:2; 8:7; 9:2), and it occurs in other portions of the OT as well (e.g., Gen 37:22). The attestations of this idiom in the Book of Job also function within contexts of violence. In the prologue, the Adversary asks God to stretch out his arm and strike all that belongs to Job (*šĕlaḥ-nāʾ yādĕkā wĕgaʿ bĕkol-ʾăšer-lô*, 1:11). When God responds to the Adversary, he uses similar phrasing, only this time the object is marked with the preposition *ʾel-* (*raq ʾēlāyw ʾal-tišlaḥ yādĕkā*, 1:12). In 2:5, the Adversary again addresses God, this time with *ʾel-* marking the object (*šĕlaḥ-nāʾ yādĕkā wĕgaʿ ʾel-ʿaṣmô wĕʾel-bĕśārô*). The requested object of God's wrath is now not Job's possessions, but his person. This theme crops up again in 30:24, where *bêt* marks the object (*ʾak lōʾ-bĕʿî yišlaḥ-yād*). The idiom *šlḥ yd* is also

320 Geller, " 'Where is Wisdom?' " 184 n. 61.

321 All of the above in *CAD* Ḫ, 227-28, s.v.

322 On all of the above, see *HALOT* 4:1512, s.v. ŠLḤ I.

found in the context of war, as the Old Phoen. inscription of Kilamuwa attests.[323] In short, the phrase is always used within an aggressive context, including Prov 31:19.[324]

9b. ***overturns summits at the roots*** [*hāpak miššōreš hārîm*]: This line is textually unproblematic. Though 11Q10 uses the verb *ʿāqar* to translate the phrase *hāpak miššōreš*, all the versions seem to be reading HPK MŠRŠ HRM in their *Vorlagen*, and their translations accord with the sense of the Masoretic vocalization. Yet Blommerde, following Hummel, re-divides the consonants: *hāpak-m šōreš hārîm*, supposing enclitic *mêm*.[325]

This is the second time the verb HPK has occurred in the first section of the poem, and this time, even more clearly than the first (v. 5b in the Niphal), it is used in a context of destruction. The verb HPK is attested in the Qal elsewhere in the Book of Job only in Job 9:5; 12:15; and 34:25. In Job 9:5, it is used with reference to God's destruction of the foundations of creation by overturning mountains: "The one who displaces mountains, though they are unaware / who overturns them (*hăpākām*) in his rage." Similar images of shattering, crushing, or melting mountains occur in theophany texts throughout the OT (e.g., Hab 3:6; Nah 1:5) and in epigraphic Hebrew. Particularly intriguing is the theophany text from Kuntillet 'Ajrud, in which God shines forth, melting mountains (*wymsn hrm*, line 2) and crushing peaks (*wydkn gbnm*, line 3). Though fragmentary, it seems that mountains are uprooted as well (*wšrš*, line 4).[326]

Fohrer has rightly commented that the phrase *miššōreš* is not to be equated with the foot of the mountains, but to the foundations upon which the mountains are supposedly set.[327] He correctly understands this phrase as approximating *môsĕdê hārîm* in Deut 32:22b and in 1QH[a] iv 13 (*mwsdy hrym*). As both of these texts also make clear, however, the base of the mountains is associated with Sheol. This association is found in other biblical texts as well, such as Jon 2:6-7, where the bottom of the mountains lie in the watery netherworld: "Water enveloped me

323 Gibson, *TSSI*, 3:30-39 (text 13, line 6); *KAI* 23:6.

324 See Paul Humbert, "Entendre la main," *VT* 12 (1962): 387.

325 Blommerde, *Northwest Semitic Grammar and Job*, 106; see H. D. Hummel, "Enclitic Mem in Northwest Semitic, Especially Hebrew," *JBL* 76 (1957): 103.

326 *HI*, 286-89 (*KAjr* 15.2-4). An *editio princeps* for this inscription is still lacking. But note the literature cited in ibid. On the reading *wšrš* in line 4, see the discussion in ibid., 288.

327 Fohrer, *Das Buch Hiob*, 391 n 9a: »nicht mit dem Fuß des Berges gleichzusetzen, sondern ähnlich den Grundfesten, auf denen die Berge ruhend gedacht sind.«

to my throat / the deep surrounded me / Seaweed was wrapped around my head / To the bases of the mountains (*liqṣĕbê hārîm*) I descended / The underworld's bars were shut behind me forever."[328] In Ug. literature, one enters the dwelling place of Mot through the base of a mountain (*CTU* 1.4 viii 5-9; 1.5 v 13-17).

The translation "summits" for *hārîm* in this case reflects a resort to synechdoche, given the relative paucity of terms for "mountain" in American English.

10a. ***He splits streams in the mountains*** [*baṣṣûrôt yĕʾōrîm biqqēaʿ*]: The Gk. traditions and Syr. present significant interpretive differences from MT, particularly with regard to *baṣṣûrôt*. On the other hand, Vg. (*in petris rivos excidit*) and Tg. (*bṭynryn nhryn bzʿ*) support MT.[329] The OG as preserved in LXX^B reads δίνας ("whirlpool"), the same term used to render *sûpâ* ("whirl wind") in Job 37:9. Syh. follows this tradition with *ṣmrtʾ* ("whirlpool"). LXX^S and LXX^A reflect a different orthography with δεινάς. Syh. also records the marginal readings of Aq, Sym, and Th. Aq reads "in closed up places they divided streams" (*bṭmymʾ rdyʾ sdqw*; Gk. ῥεῖθρα ["streams"] is preserved). Sym translates similarly with "they divided constrained streams of rivers" (*rdyʾ mtʾlṣnʾ dnhrwtʾ sdqw*; Gk. τὰ ῥεῖθρα is preserved). The translation of OG relating to "whirlpools of rivers" (δίνας δὲ ποταμῶν) and that of Sym suggesting "streams (of rivers)" (in Syh. marg.: *rdyʾ... dnhrwtʾ*) are difficult to explain. Dhorme suggests that Sym may be reading from Heb. BṢR, "to cut, tear," whence "torrents," etc.[330] This might also explain OG's δίνας.[331] However, it is possible that OG and Sym reflect a conflation or a graphic mistake influenced by *mabbĕkê nĕhārôt* [MT *mibbĕkî*] in v. 11a. These two phrases in the most conservative orthography would have been written BṢRT (v. 10a) and BKNHRT (v. 11a).

Syr. reads *bḥwsnh* ("with his strength"), from the root ḤSN, "to be difficult" in the G-stem, but "to strengthen, fortify, secure" in the D-stem.[332] The Heb. root BṢR III shows a similar semantic range, meaning "to be inaccessible, impossible" in the Niphal, and "to make inaccessi-

328 Translation of Douglas Stuart, *Hosea-Jonah* (WBC 31; Dallas, Tex.: Word, 1987), 468.

329 Geller incorrectly states that Tg. reads *nṭryn*, and he uses this evidence to suggest that Tg. may have understood *nĕṣûrôt* for MT's *baṣṣûrôt* (" 'Where is Wisdom?' " 180 n. 16).

330 Dhorme, *Book of Job*, 405. See *HALOT* 1:148, s.v. BṢR I and cognate evidence cited there.

331 Cook, "Aspects of Wisdom in the Texts of Job," 35.

332 Payne Smith, *Compendious Syriac Dictionary*, 152, s.v.

ble" (> "fortify") in the Piel.[333] Rignell is probably correct that Syr. read ṢWR in its *Vorlage* but wanted to stress the quality of the rock as being strong.[334] The 3ms possessive pronoun suffix in Syr. seems to be interpretive. Th also understands "strongholds" (Syh. marg. *ḥsnʾ* = τὰ ὀχυρώματα). This is likewise the origin of Aq's translation as "closed up places" (Syh. marg.: *ṭmymʾ*) and Sym's translation as "constrained"; Syh. marg.: *mtʾlṣnʾ*).

Yet the 5th century palimpsest Codex Ephraem (LXX^C) reads θῖνας ("heap, bank"), which seems to be the basis for Jerome's *ripas fluminum* ("banks of the rivers") in OL. Elsewhere in the LXX, θίς always translates Heb. *gibʿâ*, with the meaning "dune, mound, hill" (Gen 49:26; Deut 12:2; Job 15:7; Bar 5:7).[335] Alternatively, these readings might also be explained by Heb. BṢR III, meaning "to fortify" (of a wall) in the Piel.[336]

The orthography preserved in nine Ken. MSS—BṢWRT—could have easily given rise to these versional readings from √BṢR.[337] Consonantal Heb. BṢWRT could have been interpreted as a feminine plural noun from *bāṣûr*, thus *bĕṣûrōt*, or a feminine singular construct form of that noun, *bĕṣûrat*. Tur-Sinai reads from *beṣer*, "gold ore," translating "he broke through to the treasures of the rivers," based on a parallel passage in Job 22:24, where he interprets *bĕṣûr* in v. 24b as a nominal form parallel to *beṣer* in v. 24a rather than as the prepositional phrase *bĕ* + *ṣûr*.[338]

Yet reading from *ṣûr* in v. 10 evokes imagery consistent with the language and imagery of the first section of the poem that is evocative of divine action in both ordering and destroying creation. The language of "splitting rivers in the mountains" in Job 28:10a fits well with the Water from the Rock tradition found in Exod 17:6; Deut 8:15; Ps 78:20; Ps 114:8; and elsewhere.

William Propp has argued correctly that one should interpret *ṣûr* in most of its biblical attestations as American English "mountain."[339] This meaning for the term is most clearly evident in the ancient Balaam ora-

---

333 *HALOT* 1:148, s.v.

334 Rignell, *The Peshitta to the Book of Job*, 219.

335 Edwin Hatch and Henry A. Redpath, *A Concordance to the Septuagint and the Other Greek Versions of the Old Testament (Including the Apocryphal Books)* (2d ed.; Grand Rapids, Mich.: Baker, 1991), 652, s.v. Originally published by Oxford: Clarendon, 1897-1906.

336 *HALOT* 1:148, s.v.

337 Kennicott, *Vetus Testamentum Hebraicum*, 2:505 (18, 30, 33, 80, 82, 102, 118, 223, 283). Eleven other MSS attest BṢRWT (1, 48, 94, 111, 117, 137, 173, 192, 235, 240, 248).

338 Tur-Sinai, *The Book of Job*, 400, 347.

339 Propp, *Water in the Wilderness*, 21-22.

cle in Num 23:9: *kî-mērōʾš ṣūrîm ʾerʾennû / ûmiggĕbāʿôt ʾăšûrennû.*[340] It also occurs in parallel to *har* in Job 14:18.

In Ug., the cognate *ǵr* is the typical term for "mountain," used with reference to the mountains of the gods, such as *ǵr ll*, El's mountain of divine assembly, or *ǵr tlʾiyt*, Baal's mountain of victory (= Ṣapān).[341] The Aram. cognate *ṭûrāʾ* is also used with the meaning "mountain" in BA in Dan 2:35, 45; in Ahiqar 62; at Qumran; and in Targumic and Talmudic Aram.[342]

Heb. *yĕʾōrîm*, an Eg. loan word from *ỉtrw* ("Nile" > "river"), has been an object of abuse in modern interpretation of Job 28.[343] Many commentators suppose that it should be understood in Job 28:10 as a technical mining term for the horizontal (water-bearing) galleries of a mine, despite the fact that the term is elsewhere consistently used for the Nile River or for streams of water.[344] As with *naḥal* in v. 4, these suppositions have greatly influenced the interpretation of the term in the standard lexicons, many of which offer a new, technical meaning for *yĕʾōr*.[345]

All the ancient versions understand *yĕʾōrîm* as "rivers, rivulets, streams" (OG, Aq, Sym, Syr., Tg., Vg.) or "channels" (11Q10, [*ṭy*]*pyn*).[346] Moreover, *yĕʾōrîm* in v. 10a is clearly parallel to *nĕhārôt* ("rivers") in v. 11a. Ehrlich, however, proposes emending to *ʾôrîm*, pointing to Isa 58:8,

---

340 Ibid. See also Angel Sáenz-Badillos, *A History of the Hebrew Language* (trans. John Elwolde; Cambridge: Cambridge University Press, 1993), 61; and Kevin J. Cathcart, "The Comparative Philological Approach to the Text of the Old Testament," in *The Old Testament in Its World: Papers Read at the Winter Meeting, January 2003, The Society for Old Testament Study, and at the Joint Meeting, July 2003, The Society for Old Testament Study and Het Oudtestamentisch Werkgezelschap in Nederland en België* (eds. Robert P. Gordon and Johannes C. de Moor; *OtSt* 52; ed. J.C. de Moor et al.; Leiden and Boston: Brill, 2005), 9-10.

341 Clifford prefers to read *ǵr ʾil* rather than *ǵr ll* (*The Cosmic Mountain*, 42).

342 For distribution, see Heinz-Josef Fabry, "צוּר," in *TDOT* 12:311-321, and Jastrow, *Dictionary*, 1:526 s.v. *ṭûr* II.

343 On the development of this word in Eg. and its borrowing into Hebrew, see Thomas O. Lambdin, "Egyptian Loan Words in the Old Testament," *JAOS* 73 (1953): 151.

344 E.g., Fohrer, *Das Buch Hiob*, 391 n. 10b: »hier als term[inus] techn[us] der Bergmannssprache die wasserführenden Stollen eines Bergwerks« (See also idem, 397); Driver and Gray, *Job*, 2:194-195; Duhm, *Das Buch Hiob erklärt*, 135; Budde, *Das Buch Hiob*, 159; De Wilde, *Das Buch Hiob*, 273.

345 See, e.g., *HALOT* 2:382, s.v. *yĕʾōr*: "galleries of mines filled with water;" *DCH* 4:71, s.v. *yĕʾōr*: "channel, i.e., gallery, of mine (Jb 28:10);" *BDB*, 384, s.v. *yĕʾōr*: "shafts, made in mining Jb 28[10]."

346 This reading of 11Q10 is reconstructed in García Martínez, Tigchelaar, and van der Woude, *Qumran Cave 11.II*, 110-111. However, Sokoloff offers no reconstruction of this word, transcribing only]*yn* (*The Targum to Job from Qumran Cave XI*, 50).

where light is said to burst forth (BQʿ).[347] But rather than emending *yĕʾōr* to *ʾôr*, it is better to understand the poet's use of *yĕʾōr* as a visual, and also perhaps aural, pun on "light" (*ʾôr*), a key word that occurs in the next verse at the climax of the first section (v. 11b).[348] Presuming an originally conservative orthography, these would have been written YʾR and ʾR.

10b. ***His eye sees every precious thing*** [*wĕkol-yĕqār rāʾătâ ʿênô*]: Heb. *yĕqār* is often seen as an Aramaism,[349] due to the reduction of an originally short vowel (**yaqar*) in the pretonic syllable to *šĕwāʾ* (though in the first line of the couplet, *yĕʾōr*—undoubtedly an *Egyptian* loan word—also has a *šĕwāʾ* in the pretonic syllable). Heb. *yĕqār* is sometimes used for "treasure" or "wealth" as in Ezek 22:25; Jer 20:5; Ps 49:13, 21. It could function in this collective sense here. The more abstract meaning "honor" is closely associated with wealth, as is demonstrated by the parallelism of *ʿōšer kĕbôd* and *yĕqār tipʾeret gĕdûllātô* in Est 1:4 (it is used more abstractly of "honor" in Est 1:20; 6:6, 7, 11; 8:16).

Ehrlich believes that MT has suffered from haplography and that one should read *ûkĕlî yāqār* (»kostbare Sachen«).[350] A similar phrase occurs in Prov 20:15, where it is used of a precious object. Yet as Dhorme notes, *kĕlî* "implies an object that is manufactured rather than what is found in the earth."[351] Walter Michel translates "Nobel One," supposing that it may refer to proud creatures of the Underworld, in parallel to the typical rendering of *bĕnê-šaḥaṣ* in v. 8a as "proud beasts" or the like.[352] None of these proposals is convincing.

The adjective *yāqār* in the OT is predominantly used as a modifier of "stones" (*ʾeben* or *ʾăbānîm*; 2 Sam 12:30; 1 Kgs 5:31; 7:9, 10, 11; 10:2, 10, 11; Ezek 27:22; 28:13; Dan 11:38; 1 Chr 20:2; 29:2; 2 Chr 3:6; 9:1, 9, 10; 32:27; cf. *šōham yāqār* in Job 28:16b). In light of this fact, it is best to understand the nominal form *kol-yĕqār* in Job 28:10b as an abbreviation for the phrase *kol-ʾeben yĕqārâ*, attested in Ezek 28:13, which lists sard, to-

347 Ehrlich, *Randglossen*, 6:292.

348 See also Geller, " 'Where is Wisdom?' " 164, followed by Greenstein, "The Language of Job and its Poetic Function," 655 n. 21.

349 Strauß, *Hiob 19,1-42,7*, 132 n. 10a; Geller, " 'Where is Wisdom?' " 184 n. 63.

350 Ehrlich, *Randglossen*, 6:292.

351 Dhorme, *Book of Job*, 405.

352 Michel, "The Ugaritic Texts," 204, 411.

paz, moonstone, beryl, carnelian, jasper, lapis-lazuli, turquoise, emerald, and gold.[353]

The translation of OG in v. 10bβ (μου ὁ ὀφθαλμός) reflects *ʿênî* ("my eye") for MT's *ʿênô*, and this reading is reflected also in the daughter versions (OL *oculus meus*; Syh. *ʿynʾ dyly*). However, Syr., Vg., and Tg. support MT with the 3ms pronominal suffix. The reading of OG and the daughter versions may reflect confusion between *wāw* and *yôd*, which are particularly close in the later Aram. scripts (e.g., at Qumran).[354] Alternatively, their *Vorlage(n)* may have been emended under the influence of Job's statement in 42:5 ("Now my eye sees you!;" see also 13:1; 19:27), if the subject in 28:10 was understood to be Job.[355]

11a. ***the sources of the rivers*** [*mabbĕkê nĕhārôt*; MT *mibbĕkî*]: MT's *mibbĕkî* ("from weeping") is a mis-pointing of the consonantal text. Heb. MBKY NHRWT is undoubtedly a reflex of the first half of the standard Ug. epithet for El's abode: *mbk nhrm qrb ʾapq thmtm*, "at the sources of the two rivers, amidst the streams of the double-deep."[356] The Masoretic interpretation as *min* + *bĕkî*, however, suggests little knowledge of the expression in LB Ug. mythical texts.

A similar interpretation of the consonantal MBKY NHRWT is also found in Tg., which reads *mn zlḥy qlyly nhryʾ zryz* ("from the gurgling of swift [torrents] he ties up the river").[357] De Wilde, however, raises the interesting possibility that the tradents were well aware of the Canaanite connotations of the phrase and that the pointing of MT reflects an intentional act of demythologizing.[358]

Based on the stereotyped Ug. epithet noted above and the occurrence of the phrase *nibkê-yām* ("the sources of the sea") in Job 38:16, it is now commonly supposed that MT's *mibbĕkî nĕhārôt* in Job 28:11a should

353 The identification of most of these stones is disputed. See the helpful presentation by Daniel I. Block, *The Book of Ezekiel: Chapters 25-48* (NICOT; Grand Rapids, Mich., and Cambridge, U.K.: Eerdmans, 1998), 107-110.

354 See the charts comparing *wāw* and *yôd* at around 100 B.C.E. in Bruce K. Zuckerman, "The Date of 11Q Targum Job: A Paleographic Consideration of its *Vorlage*," *JSP* 1 (1987): 57-78.

355 Zerafa, *Wisdom of God*, 136. See also the discussion in Witte, "The Greek Book of Job," 47.

356 This occurs primarily in the Baal cycle (*CTU* 1.2 iii 4; 1.3 v 6-7; 1.4 iv 21-22; 1.6 i 33-34; it is restored by A. Herdner in *CTA* 5 vi 2*-1*, and this is accepted by Mark Smith in "The Baal Cycle," 148 [*CTU* makes no such restoration]). It also occurs in Aqhat (*CTU* 1.17 vi 47-48). This is only one of three types of descriptions of El's abode (for which, see Clifford, *Cosmic Mountain*, 35-57), and there is a variant form of this one in in *CTU* 1.100:3: *il mbk nhrm b ʿdt thmtm*. See also *HALOT* 2:542 s.v. *mabbāk*.

357 *qlyly* is omitted by Tg^{M} and Tg^{S}, though it is attested in twelve other MSS.

358 De Wilde, *Das Buch Hiob*, 273.

be re-pointed to *mabbĕkê nĕhārôt*, with the meaing "sources of the rivers." This pointing supposes the bound form of a *maqṭāl* noun from the verb *NBK,[359] with the meaning "source" or "spring." Job 38:16, however, attests the bound form of a hypothetical *qiṭl* noun **nēbek* with *nibkê*, having the same meaning. An alternate *miqṭāl* form *mibbĕkê*—remarkably close to the Masoretic pointing—is also possible via "*qatqat* > *qitqat*" dissimilation.[360] While forms with the prefix *ma-* predominate in the Hexaplaric and Babylonian traditions, the Tiberian tradition does preserve many of these nouns as *miqṭāl* forms.[361] Yet the Masoretic tradition preserved in MT (cf. Tg.) clearly reflects an interpretation of MBKY as the prepositional phrase *min* + *bĕkî*, not as a nominal form.

The translations of MBKY NHRWT in other ancient versions seem to throw the consonantal Heb. text into doubt. OG preserves βάθη δὲ ποταμῶν ("and the depths of the rivers;" OL *altitudines fluminum*; Syh. *wʿwmqʾ dnhrwtʾ*). Vg.'s *profunda quoque fluviorum* ("[also] the depths of the rivers") is also in line with this tradition. However, Syr. reads *wʿwšnʾ dnhrwtʾ* ("and the strength/swelling of the rivers"). While OG and Vg. could possibly be explained with recourse to an alternate pointing of the Masoretic consonantal text (MBKY or perhaps MBK), this is more difficult with Syr. As Beer points out, »Woran P *ʿwšnʾ* = מבכי denkt, ist unklar.«[362]

OG, Vg., and Syr. are all reading a form of ʿMQ.[363] Beer himself suggested as much for the OG in *BHK*.[364] Indeed, the LXX translators typically use βάθος to translate some form of the root ʿMQ (LXX Ps 68:3 [69:3 MT]; 68:15 [69:15 MT]; Eccl 7:25; Isa 7:11; 51:10; Ezek 27:34).[365] Yet in addition to ʿMQ meaning "to be deep" (see Heb. ʿMQ I; Akk.

359 See *HALOT* 2:663, s.v. *NBK and **nēbek*. The root also occurs in Qumran Heb. in 1QH^{a} xi:15: *nbwky mym*; in Syr. as NBG (Payne Smith, *Compendious Syriac Dictionary*, 325); and in Ug. as NBK or NPK (*DUL* 2:617 s.v. *nb/pk* (I); *UVST*, 151).

360 Dissimilation from /a/ > /i/ in the declension of nouns in closed, unaccented syllables (see Joüon §29g, §88L.d and note 1, §88L.e; Hans Bauer and Pontus Leander, *Hebräischen Sprache des alten Testaments* [Hildesheim: Georg Olms, 1962], §61 *xε* [pp. 489-90]; originally published: Tübingen: Max Niemeyer, 1922]).

361 Compare the Gk. and Latin transliterations with Tiberian pointing of numerous *m*-preformative nouns in Alexander Sperber, "Hebrew Based upon Greek and Latin Transliterations," *HUCA* 12 (1937-38): 234-40.

362 Beer, *Der Text des Buches Hiob*, 180.

363 Zerafa has also suggested this reading, though he is quite tentative about it (*Wisdom of God*, 143).

364 See his text note: βάθη = עִמְקֵי ?

365 Hatch and Redpath, *A Concordance to the Septuagint*, 189, s.v. See also the brief discussion of the translation of Aram. *ʿammîqātāʾ* in Dan 2:22 with βαθέα by both Th and OG in T. J. Meadowcroft, *Aramaic Daniel and Greek Daniel: A Literary Comparison* (JSOTSup 198; Sheffield, U.K.: Sheffield Academic, 1995), 170-71.

emēqu; etc.), a homograph in Semitic means "to be strong" (see Akk. *emūqu*). The first accounts for OG and Vg., and the last accounts for the translation of Syr.

Given this versional evidence, there may have originally been two consonantal traditions in the *Vorlagen* or a conflate tradition. While MT and Tg. read MBKY NHRWT, OG, Vg., and Syr. are probably reading ʿMQY NHRWT.[366] The fact that OG renders *nibkê* in Job 38:16 with πηγή, but reads βαθός in Job 28:11a, supports this conclusion.

11a. ***He binds up*** [*ḥibbēš*]: The translations of some of the Gk. and Latin versions seem to call into question the consonantal text in MT. Aq and Th's ἐξερεύνησεν ("he searched out") and Vg.'s *scrutatus est* ("he examined") suggest the Piel *ḥippēś* ("he explored, searched out") rather than MT's *ḥibbēš*.[367] The verb ḤPŚ is well attested in BH. Though most commentators also cite the reading of OG as evidence for ḤPŚ in its Hebrew *Vorlage*, ἀνεκάλυψεν ("he revealed") reflects Heb. ḤŚP instead.[368]

Yet the Aram. traditions support MT. Syr. reads *ḥbš*; 11Q10 translates with *k*]*l*ʾ;[369] and Tg. translates with *zryz* ("to tie around, gird, harness," etc.).[370]

The Gk. revisions and the Latin traditions probably do reflect *ḥippēś*. However, this may simply be a dialectical variant due to voiced-unvoiced /b/ > /p/ interchange in Semitic. Thus the consonantal חבש in their Heb. *Vorlagen* could be understood to mean "to explore, search out" (as BH ḤPŚ). Blommerde cites several examples of what he believes to be "free interchange" of /b/ and /p/ in Semitic, including several in Job (28:11; 31:39; 38:10; etc.).[371] Lester Grabbe is more cautious,

366 Compare the phrase *bĕʿimqê šĕʾōl* in Prov 9:18, from *ʿōmeq*, "depth."

367 Remarkably, a medieval MS from the Cairo Geniza contains a transliterated gloss in Aramaic characters—*ʾymwṭwśyn*—of Heb. [*ḥy*]*bš*, which probably reflects the Gk. ἐμότωσεν ("he bound up") (N. R. M. de Lange, "Some New Fragments of Aquila on Malachi and Job?" *VT* 30 [1980]: 292). If this fragment accurately reflects the tradition of Aq, as de Lange suggests, then Aq may have understood "to bind" (ḤBŠ) in Job 28:11, rendering with μοτοῦν just as in Job 5:18 (See Reider, *An Index to Aquila*, 160, s.v. μοτοῦν, and de Lange, "Some New Fragments," 294). The Gk. evidence for Aq (ἐξερεύνησεν) and this much later Heb. evidence (< ἐμότωσεν?) are thus in conflict.

368 See Takamitsu Muraoka, "Words of Cognition in Job 28: Hebrew and Greek," in *Job 28: Cognition in Context* (ed. Ellen van Wolde; BI 64; eds. Rolf Rendtorff and R. Alan Culpepper; Leiden and Boston: Brill, 2003), 98. Compare also Zerafa, *Wisdom of God*, 144.

369 Sokoloff offers no reconstruction of the *kāp* (*The Targum to Job from Qumran Cave XI*, 50).

370 Jastrow, *Dictionary*, 1:412, s.v. *zĕraz* I.

371 Blommerde, *Northwest Semitic Grammar and Job*, 5-6.

however, drawing attention to the fact that the phonetic environment must be considered. He believes that the normal change is /b/ > /p/ before *šîn* and not the reverse.[372] Yet what is striking is that the shift between these labials is evidenced in a similar environment (preceding the voiceless fricative *šîn*) in a late 7th century Heb. inscription from Arad (*Arad* 24.rev.7), where the shift is from unvoiced to voiced labial in *nbš* (< *npš*). This /p/ > /b/ voicing of *npš* is also attested in line 13 of the Kilamuwa inscription from Zinjirli, where this change seems to have been a feature of the Ya'udi dialect.[373] A similar interchange is found before *śîn* in some MSS of the Samaritan Pentateuch in Gen 31:35, which reads *wyḥbś* where the MT preserves *wayḥappēś* (see *BHS*).

If the consonantal text of MT may be understood either way, then OG, the revisions, and Vg. cannot be cited for textual support for reading *ḥippēś* since they do not reflect true variants. They would only provide evidence in the early history of interpretation of this phonetic variation (b/p) and orthographic ambiguity (ש as /š/ or /ś/).

The argument for meaning must ultimately be made on literary grounds. The theme of "exploring" (ḤPŚ) undoubtedly fits one of the governing metaphors of the poem. This is reinforced by the inclusion of ḤQR around the poem (vv. 3a, 27b), of which ḤPŚ is a synonym. Yet the structure of the first section itself suggests that the idea of "binding" (ḤBŠ) is correct. The first section presents themes of binding and splitting in vv. 3 and 4, mirrored with those same actions—splitting and binding—in vv. 10 and 11. While the explorer breaches courses in v. 4a, he splits streams in v. 10a. While he binds the darkness in v. 3a, he binds the sources of the rivers in v. 11a. While a visual pun between between ḤBŠ and ḤPŚ in the unpointed Heb. text is likely intended,[374] the dominance of themes of splitting and binding in the context of the first section suggests that the consonantal tradition חבש should primarily be understood to denote "binding" (*ḥibbēš*).

11b. ***brings the dark thing to light*** [*taʿălūmâ yōṣīʾ ʾôr*; MT *taʿălūmāh*]: The Gk. traditions understand MT's *taʿălūmāh* to be derived from ʿLM, but with the meaning "strength."[375] OG translates with δύναμιν (OL

372 Grabbe, *Comparative Philology*, 96-97.

373 *KAI* 24:13, and Gibson, *TSSI*, 3:34 and discussion at 38.

374 In addition, Geller notes the possibility of an *aural* play between *ḥibbēš* and *ḥippēś*, if the pronunciation of *šîn* and *śîn* was close enough to facilitate it (" 'Where is Wisdom?' " 181 n. 18).

375 Note also the comments of Muraoka which confirm my argument here. He suggests that OG read *taʿălūm* or *taʿălūmâ* in light of a common Semitic root, ʿLM, meaning "strength" ("Words of Cognition in Job 28," 98). By contrast, Johann Cook suggests *taʿălûlîm*, but this means "acts of mischief," "mischief-maker," or "ill treatment," not

virtutem; Syh. *ḥylʾ*). Sym's translation, ἀπὸ δὲ ὑπερορωμένου προῆλθε φῶς ("and from the despised man light goes forth"), suggests that he understood TʿLM as a substantive much like *ʿelem* in BH, which has to do with youthfulness and lack of experience, and thus a low social position.[376] Yet youthfulness also suggests virility, and this is the basis for the translations of OG and the daughter versions. This semantic relation is seen in the English cognate "virility," suggesting masculine strength, from Latin *vir* ("man"). Aram. *ʿălêm* / *ʿălēm*, in fact, means "to be strong."[377] Syr. and Vg. both understand the consonantal text in much the same way as MT (Syr. *tḥpytʾ*; Vg. *abscondita*). Tg.'s reading seems to have been derived from MT, though it may also reflect the name of one of the stations of the sun ("from the window of darkness" [*mn ḥrkʾ dtʿlwmʾh*]).[378]

HALOT distinguishes two verbal homonyms, ʿLM I ("to conceal, hide") and ʿLM II ("to be dark, black"), deriving the noun *taʿălūmâ* from ʿLM I and glossing it "what has been hidden."[379] Yet differentiating two verbal homonyms ʿLM I and ʿLM II in BH is unnecessary. It is easy enough to explain the semantic development from an original "to be dark, black" to "to conceal, hide" as a cause-effect metonymy.[380] The noun *taʿălūmâ*, then, may work off of either of these meanings: "to become dark" or "to hide, conceal," from one root ʿLM.

The primacy of the meaning "to be dark" is suggested by the cognates adduced by *HALOT* for ʿLM II. These are Ug. ĜLM, Akk. *ṣalāmu*, and Eth. *ṣalma* / *ṣalama*, all meaning "to be(come) dark."[381] However, these comparative data are at least superficially problematic, since each of these words would seem to have its phonemic equivalent in the Heb. root ṢLM, not ʿLM. But a confusion of related roots is also evidenced in Ug., with *ġlm* (see *CTU* 1.14 i 19; *CTU* 1.16 i 50),[382] *ġlmt* (vocalized *ġulmatu*; see syllabic *ḫu-ul-ma-tu*₄ [*Ugaritica* V 137 iii 15']), and *ẓlmt* (//

"power," as he suggests ("Aspects of Wisdom in the Texts of Job," 35; see *HALOT* 4:1768-69, s.v.).

376 See *HALOT* 2:835, s.v. and cognates cited there.

377 Jastrow, *Dictionary*, 2:1084, s.v.

378 Ibid., 2:1684, s.v. *taʿălûmâ*.

379 See *HALOT* 2:834-35, s.v. ʿLM I and ʿLM II; *HALOT* 4:1769, s.v. *taʿălūmâ*.

380 Goatly, *The Language of Metaphors*, 59; and Moisés Silva, *Biblical Words and Their Meaning: An Introduction to Lexical Semantics* (rev., expanded edition; Grand Rapids, Mich.: Zondervan, 1994), 84.

381 *DUL*, 1:320-21, s.v. *ġlmt* (I); *AHw* 3:1076, s.v. *ṣalāmu*; Eth. as cited in *HALOT* 3:835, s.v. ʿLM II.

382 But cf. Greenstein, who renders *ġlm* in *CTU* 1.14 i 19 as "lad" ("Kirta," 12 and 42 n. 5).

ǵlmt in *CTU* 1.4 vii 54-55; *CTU* 1.8 ii 7-8).[383] As Huehnergard states, "It is possible that part of the confusion of roots **ṯ-l-m*, Ugar. *ẓ-l-m* and *ǵ-l-m*, Hebrew *ᶜ-l-m* is the result of both archaism and interdialectical mixing."[384] By analogy, one may legitimately draw upon Ug. ǴLM, Akk. *ṣalāmu*, and Eth. *ṣalma* / *ṣalama*, as well as Arab. ẒLM[385] in a discussion of Heb. ᶜLM.

In its two other occurrences in the OT, *taᶜălūmâ* is collocated with the heart (*lēb*, Ps 44:22b) and with secret wisdom (*ḥokmâ*, Job 11:6). While in Ps 44:22, the context has to do with God searching out (ḤQR) and knowing the dark things of the heart, the context in Job 11:6 has to do with God's "telling [Job] the dark things of wisdom." The use in Job 28:11 undoubtedly plays off the "wisdom" context found in Job 11:6, as was recognized by the translator(s) of OG.[386] It likewise recalls the object being sought throughout the first section of Job 28: the "stone of deepest gloom" (*ʾeben ʾōpel wĕṣalmôt* [MT *ṣalmāwet*]). The possibility of dialectical variation in development suggests that the connection between *ṣalmôt* in v. 3b and *taᶜălūmâ* in v. 11b may be etymological as well as semantic.[387]

Most commentators have suggested that the *mappîq* in the final *hê* of MT's *taᶜălūmâ*, which is attested in both the Leningrad and Aleppo codices, should be deleted (see *BHK*, *BHS*). John Elwolde believes that a scribe added the *mappîq* to make explicit the implicit presence of wisdom in the verse.[388] In any case, the *hê* is certainly not consonantal.

HALOT understands *taᶜălūmâ* to be a *nomen unitatis* (see Joüon §134p), suggesting a "single hidden/dark thing."[389] It is questionable, however, whether an abstract word like "darkness" or "hiddenness" could be formed as a unit noun. Furthermore, the attestation of the plural *taᶜălūmôt* in Job 11:6 and Ps 44:22 argues against it. It is more likely that *taᶜălūmâ* is a pseudo-Aramaism, morphologically mimicking the determined noun in Aramaic for poetic effect.[390] This provides a fitting parallel to *yĕqār* in v. 10b, a substantitive adjective also vocalized according to a typical Aramaic noun pattern. Whether true Aramaisms or

---

383 See *UVST*, 98-99 and 164 s.v. ǴLM.

384 Ibid., 99 n. 67.

385 For the Arab. evidence, see Lane, *Arabic-English Lexicon*, 5:1924 # 4.

386 That the OG translator(s) recognized an intertextual link between Job 28:11b and Job 11:6 is evidenced by the use of δύναμις to translate *taᶜălūmâ* / *taᶜălūmôt* in both cases (Muraoka, "Words of Cognition in Job 28," 98).

387 See *HALOT* 2:835 s.v. ᶜLM II.

388 Elwolde, "Non-Contiguous Parallelism," 117.

389 *HALOT* 4:1769, s.v., also suggests that *taᶜălūmâ* is a unitary noun.

390 Compare the discussion in Greenstein, "The Language of Job and its Poetic Function," 662.

false, this noun pattern is productive in Job (e.g., *nĕhārâ* in Job 3:4, anticipating *rĕnānâ* in 3:7).[391]

Blommerde translates the entire second line, "and makes dark places shine with light," following Dahood's suggestion that YṢʾ may mean "to shine."[392] Michel attempts to preserve both "bring forth" and "make shine."[393] Yet these suggestions are misguided both philologically and literarily. That what is dark is being brought into the light is already clear in the larger context of the line. This meaning need not be semantically encoded in *yōṣīʾ* on the basis of a hypothetical Heb. homonym.

The question concerning the place where hidden wealth "comes forth" (YṢʾ) runs throughout the poem. The import of this question is suggested by the rhetoric of v. 1a, in which "the source" (*môṣāʾ*) is highlighted as governing metaphor. YṢʾ in v. 11b is an allusion to that rhetoric. This allusion provides a sense of completion in the first section that would be destroyed if one translates the root as "to shine" or the like. Further, it ignores the larger literary context of the book that is invoked by this phrasing. Verse 11b points to what seems for the moment to be the climax of human success. The human, like god, can "reveal deep things from darkness and bring deep darkness to light" (Job 12:22). The use of YṢʾ in the Hiphil in Job 12:22 also supports MT's *yōṣīʾ* (Hiphil) in Job 28:11b. The Hiphil of YṢʾ is spelled "defectively" as it is here in five of its six occurrences in Job.[394]

12a. *wisdom* [*haḥokmâ*]: Many scholars understand wisdom to be either personified or hypostasized in this poem.[395] Some point to the

---

391 Ibid.

392 Blommerde, *Northwest Semitic Grammar and Job*, 106-107. Dahood's discussion of this passage is found in his commentary on Ps 44:22 in *Psalms I* (AB 16; Garden City: Doubleday, 1966), 267, and his comments on YṢʾ in ibid., 93-94. See also idem, "Northwest Semitic Philology and Job," 67. Dahood adduces this argument related to YṢʾ in both Job 28:11b (*yōṣīʾ*) and 28:1a (*môṣāʾ*). See commentary on *source* above.

393 See his translation in "The Ugaritic Texts," 204.

394 See Freedman, "Orthographic Peculiarities in the Book of Job," 38*; Barr, "Hebrew Orthography," 10-12.

395 For personification, see, e.g., Leo Perdue, "Wisdom in the Book of Job," in *In Search of Wisdom: Essays in Memory of John G. Gammie* (eds. Leo G. Perdue, Bernard Brandon Scott, and William Johnston Wiseman; Louisville, Ky.: Westminster/John Knox, 1993), 96; Dhorme, *Book of Job*, 412; Habel, *The Book of Job*, 397; Martino Conti, *La Sapienza Personificata negli Elogi Veterotestamentari (Pr 8; Gb 28; Sir 24; Bar 3; Sap 7)* (Spicilegium Pontificii Athenaei 36; Rome: Pontificium Athenaeum Antonianum, 2001).

For hypostatization, see, e.g., Houtsma, *Textkritische Studien*, 65; Fohrer, *Das Buch Hiob*, 394-96; Driver and Gray, *Job*, 1:243; De Wilde, *Das Buch Hiob*, 277-278;

definite article on *ḥokmâ* in v. 12 in support. However, Geller rightly points out that no hypostatization is implied by the definite article.[396] The idea that wisdom is personified, hypostatized, or deified at any point in the poem should be rejected.[397] The very typical personification of Wisdom in wisdom texts (e.g., Prov 1, 8, 9; Sir 4, 6, 24, 51; and Wis 8) is *countered* here, not mimicked. It is the *forces of the deep* in v. 14 (*tĕhôm* and *yām*) that are personified so that they may declare their ignorance about wisdom. The definite article with *ḥokmâ* in Job 28:12, 20 is simply a generic use of the article found with abstract terms referring to attributes, qualities, or states (*IBHS* § 13.5.1g). The generic use of the article is found also in the opening lines of the poem in v. 1 with *lakkesep* and *lazzāhāb*, reinforcing the connection between silver, gold, and wisdom that is developed in the first section on a metaphorical level.

The connection between wisdom and silver and gold is found most clearly in the Book of Proverbs. There wisdom often said to supercede earthly wealth (e.g., Prov 3:14-15; 8:10-11, 19). Yet in the same passages, Woman Wisdom appeals to her wealth in order to make her insight desireable (e.g., Prov 8:18). In fact, she promises to provide those who love her with an inheritance and to fill their treasuries (Prov 8:21). A similar relationship between wisdom and wealth is found in Job 28.

McKane, "The Theology of the Book of Job," 716, 721; Martin Hengel, *Judaism and Hellenism: Studies in their Encounter in Palestine during the Early Hellenistic Period* (2 vols.; Philadelphia, Pa.: Fortress, 1974), 1:153-56; trans. of *Judentum und Hellenismus: Studien zu ihrer Begegnung unter besonderer Berücksichtigung Palästinas bis zur Mitte des 2 Jh.s v.Chr* (2d revised and enlarged edition; WUNT 10; ed. J. Jeremias and D. Otto Michel; Tübingen: J. C. B. Mohr [Paul Siebeck], 1973). Compare also Gustav Hölscher, *Das Buch Hiob* (2d ed.; HAT 17; ed. Otto Eissfeldt; Tübingen: J. C. B. Mohr [Paul Siebeck], 1952), 68-69; and Peters, *Das Buch Job*, 294-95.

Judith Hadley and Michael Coogan focus on the relation of wisdom and the goddess, and both assume that *haḥokmâ* in Job 28 is a reference to Lady Wisdom (see Hadley, "Wisdom and the Goddess," in *Wisdom in Ancient Israel: Essays in Honour of J. A. Emerton* [eds. John Day, Robert P. Gordon, and H. G. M. Williamson; Cambridge: Cambridge University Press, 1995], 234-43; Coogan, "The Goddess Wisdom," 203-209). While Hadley believes that Lady Wisdom is "a literary compensation for the eradication of the worship of [the goddess]" ("Wisdom and the Goddess," 236; cf. 243), Coogan goes further in saying that she is "an orthodox legitimation of the worship of the goddess…" ("The Goddess Wisdom," 208; cf. ibid., 204).

396 Geller, " 'Where is Wisdom?' " 181 n. 19, and 184 n. 69.

397 Van Oorschot rightly points out that wisdom as personified figure or as hypostasis of an attribute of God both fall short of capturing the essence of wisdom in the poem (»Hiob 28,« 188). Von Rad also rejects both these views: »Sicher ist sie keine verselbständigte göttliche Eigenschaft. Von einer Personifizierung zu reden, is auch kein Anlaß« (*Weisheit in Israel*, 193). Fiddes critiques both those who view wisdom as personified and von Rad's notion of wisdom as the " 'meaning' set into creation by God" and argues instead for the *objectification* of wisdom in Job 28 (" 'Where Shall Wisdom Be Found?' " 174-75).

They are not simply in a contrasting relation.[398] Wisdom and wealth are metonymically related, here by their connection to the "source" (*môṣāʾ*) in or near which both are ostensibly found. The metonymic connection between wisdom and riches is precisely why the rhetoric of the first section of the poem (vv. 1-11) works as a setup for the rhetorical questions concerning the locus of wisdom found in vv. 12, 20, and the statements that only the divine has discerned its place (v. 23b; see also vv. 13, 22, 27).

12a. *where is it found* [*mēʾayin timmāṣēʾ*]: MT reads a Niphal of MṢʾ, and all the ancient versions support this reading. Yet not all Heb. MSS are in accord. Ken. 150 reflects what seems to be a conflate reading of the majority at vv. 12a and 20a: *tābōʾ timmāṣēʾ* (see *BHK*). Ken. 157 simply reads *tēṣēʾ* in v. 13a instead of MT's *timmāṣēʾ*.[399]

Unhappy with the sense of the Masoretic pointing, some scholars have proposed alternate solutions. Niccacci re-points to *timṣāʾ*, following Dahood's proposals at Ps 116:3, Job 11:7 and elsewhere, to relate Heb. MṢʾ to cognates in Ug. (MṢAʾ, MǴY, MẒAʾ) meaning "to reach, come, arrive."[400] Tur-Sinai suggests a similar translation, supposing that the Heb. may be an incorrect translation of Aram. *tmṣʾ*, according to his theory that the book was originally written in Aramaic.[401] Given the use of *timṣāʾ* in the Book of Job already with the meaning "to reach, arrive" (11:7a, b), the proposals of Dahood and Niccacci bear some weight.

Dhorme, Zerafa, and Geller have argued for reading *tēṣēʾ* with Ken. 157, suggesting that v. 12a in the MT—and the majority of Heb. MSS—reflects a text altered under the influence of *timmāṣēʾ* in v. 13b.[402] Dhorme and Geller suggest that the reading of Ken. 157 also produces a better sense, as *mēʾayin* seems to require a verb of motion.[403]

This proposal is tempting, given the fact that this emendation to *tēṣēʾ* would create yet another root play with YṢʾ, picking up on the governing metaphor of "issue" or "outflow" found in *môṣāʾ* in v. 1a. Nevertheless, three factors argue against this reading: (1) the lateness of

---

398 *Contra* Geller, " 'Where is Wisdom?' " 181 n. 19.

399 Kennicott, *Vetus Testamentum Hebraicum*, 2:505.

400 Niccacci, "Giobbe 28," 31 and n. 13; Dahood, "Northwest Semitic Philology and Job," 57; idem, *Psalms I*, 195; idem, *Psalms III* (AB 17A; Garden City, NY: Doubleday, 1970), 146. Dahood suggests this reading for Job 28:12 at this latter citation.

401 Tur-Sinai, *The Book of Job*, 402.

402 Geller, " 'Where is Wisdom?' " 181 n. 19; Dhorme, *Book of Job*, 406; Zerafa, *Wisdom of God*, 145.

403 Geller, " 'Where is Wisdom?' " 181 n. 19; Dhorme, *Book of Job*, 406. Clines also suggests that *mēʾayin* "does not fit with the verb תמצא 'shall be found' " and thus emends to *ʾayin* (*Job 21-37*, 901 n. 12c).

Ken. 157 as a witness to the consonantal Hebrew, (2) a parallel construction with the Niphal of MṢʾ... *min* in Hos 14:9, and (3) the fact that *mēʾayin tēṣēʾ* is the *lectio facilior*.

An appeal to Ken. 157 as the original reading over against the majority of Heb. MSS is inadvisable. Though Ken. collated numerous MSS, these have negligible value as witnesses to the original text, since they post-date the time in which any significant variants still existed in the consonantal text.[404] The couplet in Hos 14:9 likens Yhwh to a tree on which fruit can be found. The final line reads: *mimmennî peryĕkā nimṣāʾ*. The preposition *min* in both Hos 14:9 and Job 28:12 (*mēʾayin*) may be understood as spatial and static, not dynamic (see *IBHS* §11.2.11b). By contrast, the parallel refrain in Job 28:20 is a dynamic construction, with a verb of motion (*mēʾayin tābôʾ*). Stuart's rendering of Hos 14:9 is apt: "...on me your fruit is found."[405] The sense in Job 28:12 is similar: "(In) where is it found?"

12b. ***understanding*** [*bînâ*]: This term occurs again in the poem at v. 20b, at the beginning of the third section of the poem in v. 23a, and in the poem's concluding line in v. 28b. As such, it is a *Leitwort* of the poem. As Michael Fox states, "*Binah* is the conceptual, interpretive activity of thought, operating in the field of meaning; it aims at perception and comprehension."[406] However, it is not related to visual perception.[407] It may be applied to faculties, like reason or intelligence, or to content, like teaching and understanding.[408] Considering its relation to the parallel term *ḥokmâ* in v. 12a, *bînâ* is related to specific objects in a way that *ḥokmâ* is not. While *ḥokmâ* makes understanding possible or is used of the knowledge produced by understanding, *bînâ is* that understanding.[409] As a more specific term than *ḥokmâ*, *bînâ* provides a fitting parallel in the second line of Job 28:12, the whole couplet sharpening from the broader term to the more specific.[410]

---

404 See the brief discussion of the Kennicott collations in ch. 4.2.1 of this study. Compare also the level-headed judgment of Driver and Gray on this reading in v. 12a (*Job*, 2:195).

405 Stuart, *Hosea-Jonah*, 211.

406 Fox, "Words for Wisdom," *ZAH* 6 (1993): 152.

407 Ibid., 151.

408 Ibid., 154-55.

409 Ibid., 158.

410 Also noted by Fox in ibid., 158. See Muraoka on the OG translations of *bînâ* with ἐπιστήμη in v. 12b (and v. 28b) and σύνεσις in v. 20b (and a verbal form in v. 23a) ("Words of Cognition in Job 28," 101).

13a. ***its abode*** [*ʿerkāh*]: The translation of OG, ὅδὸν αὐτῆς ("its way;" see also Syh. *ʾwrḥʾ dylh*; OL *viam eius*), suggests Heb. *darkāh*, which is widely assumed to be the correct reading (see *BHK*, *BHS*).[411] However, the revisions (Aq: τάξιν αὐτῆς; Sym: τίμημα αὐτῆς), Syr. (*gzh*), Vg. (*pretium eius*), and Tg. (*ʿlwyh*) support MT's *ʿerkāh*.[412] Th's σύνεσιν, which typically reflects BYN, is difficult to explain except by assuming an error related to *bînâ* in v. 12b.

Dahood believes that the consonants of MT can be retained by understanding ʿRK in this context as "place" or "home," citing its use in Phoen., Nab., and primarily Ugaritic.[413] Niccacci, Michel, Hartley, and eventually Pope accepted this proposal.[414] The attestation of *ʿrkm* in Ug. is difficult (*CTU* 1.105:17-18). Lete and Sanmartín cite this passage in their recent Ug. lexicon, but they suggest that it may refer to a type of offering.[415] Without recourse to Ug., Gordis argues that MT's *ʿerek* can mean "place."[416]

Despite the widespread assumption that OG reflects the original reading (i.e., *darkāh*), this view runs against the majority of textual evidence. Syr., Vg., and Tg. support MT. Only OG and the daughter versions suggest *darkāh*. The reading of OG, moreover, is the *lectio facilior*. Along these lines, Johann Cook has suggested that the OG translator may have interpreted *ʿerkāh* in the Heb. *Vorlage* of v. 13a as *darkāh* in anticipation of *derek* in v. 23a.[417] Alternately, Harry Orlinsky has noted the possibility that the *Vorlage* of the OG translator had been corrupted to DRKH due to a scribal error from ʿRKH.[418] The graphic similarity of

---

411 See, e.g., Clines, *Job 21-37*, 901 n. 13a.

412 Both Syr. and Tg. understand the verse as a whole to say that wisdom is not found anywhere except in heaven or in its cultic representations. Syr. understands MT's *ʿerkāh* in Job 28:13 to be related to *ʿerkô* in Exod 40:4, which refers to the presentation of the show-bread (see also Exod 40:23). Tg.'s *ʿlwyh* may be used of "height" or "heaven," which is put in contrast with its free rendering of v. 13b: "and it is not found in the land of the violent ones who sinned in their lives" (See Jastrow, *Dictionary*, 2:1069, s.v. *ʿēlāʾ* / *ʿêl*).

413 Mitchell J. Dahood, "Hebrew-Ugaritic Lexicography VII," *Bib* 50 (1969): 355.

414 Niccacci, "Giobbe 28," 31 and n. 14; Michel, "The Ugaritic Texts," 412 n. 556; Hartley, *The Book of Job*, 378 n. 2; Pope reads *darkāh* (following OG's ὁδὸν) in the first edition of his commentary, but he follows Dahood's suggestion in the third edition (*Job*, 203). On the Phoen. and Nab. evidence, see *DNWSI* 2:888, s.v. *ʿrkh*₁ and *ʿrkw*.

415 *DUL*, 1:183, s.v. *ʿrk* II.

416 Gordis, *The Book of Job*, 308.

417 Cook, "Aspects of Wisdom in the Texts of Job," 35.

418 Orlinsky, "Studies in the Septuagint of the Book of Job. Chapter V: The Hebrew *Vorlage* of the Septuagint of Job: A. The Text and the Script," *HUCA* 35 (1964): 76. See also Peters, *Das Buch Job*, 302.

dālet and *ʿayin* in the paleo-Hebrew script during several periods certainly could have facilitated such an error.[419]

While the exact meaning of Ug. *ʿrk* II in *CTU* 1.105:17-18 remains unclear, Dahood's proposal is most sensible. It is not too great a semantic development from a verb ʿRK ("to arrange, to set out, to place") to a nominal form meaning "place."[420] Given the parallel with *māqôm* in the preceding line in v. 12b, a meaning such as "abode," adopted by Pope, is fitting.[421]

The reading *ʿerkāh* also seems to be borne out literarily by vv. 15-19 in which the root ʿRK is a *Leitwort* (vv. 17a, 19a). These verses seem to be an addition to the original poem which was facilitated, in part, by a reading such as MT's *ʿerkāh* in v. 13a. See the brief comments on vv. 14a-19b below and the fuller discussion in ch. 5.3.

13b. ***Nor is it found in the land of the living*** [*wĕlōʾ timmāṣēʾ bĕʾereṣ haḥayyîm*]: The translations of the versions are quite free in this line. While OG flattens the Hebrew expression with "nor was it found among men" (οὐδὲ μὴ εὑρεθῇ ἐν ἀνθρώποις; Syh. *ʾp lʾ dyn tštkḥ bbnynšʾ*; OL *nec invenietur hominibus*), Syr. reverses the sense by adding *ʾlʾ ʾn*: "and it is not found *except in* the place of life" (*wlʾ mštkḥʾ ʾlʾ ʾn bʾtrʾ dḥyʾ*). Rignell suggests that Christian influence on Syr. is evident here, since the text focuses on the life to come.[422] Vg. reads "it is not found living sweetly on earth" (*nec invenitur in terra suaviter viventium*). Tg. theologizes like Syr., but in a different direction: "and it is not found in the land of the violent ones who sinned in their lives" (*wlʾ tštkḥ bʾrʾ zydnyn dmḥṭyyn bḥyyhwn*). Despite these theological interpretations in the early versions, the Heb. text is not in doubt.

14a-19b: These verses are lacking in OG and were filled in with Th (*ἄβυσσος ... συμβασταχθήσεται. /). They are likewise asterisked in Syh. and in two OL MSS. The general supposition that vv. 15-19 result from later expansion is often supported by appeals to the fact that they

---

419 Note particularly the 6th cent. paleo-Hebrew script, in which the tail of the *dālet* is very short, and the *ʿayin* is somewhat angular. See Johannes Renz and Wolfgang Röllig, *Handbuch der Althebräischen Epigraphik* (3 vols.; Darmstadt: Wissenschaftliche Buchgesellschaft, 1995-2003), 3:tables 32-33.

420 Compare *HALOT* 2:884-85, s.v. ʿRK, and *HALOT* 2:885, s.v. *ʿērek*, with *DUL* 1:182, s.v. *ʿrk*, and *DUL* 1:182-83, s.v. *ʿrk* (II).

421 Pope, *Job*, 197, 203.

422 See Rignell, "Notes on the Peshiṭta of the Book of Job," 100, 104; idem., *The Peshitta to the Book of Job*, 220. Compare Baumann, »Die Verwendbarkeit der Pešita zum Buche Ijob für Textkritik,« *ZAW* 19 (1899): 26.

are lacking in OG.[423] However, such a conclusion is precarious if it rests solely on the absence of vv. 14a-19b in the OG of Job. The OG of ch. 28 by itself (vv. 1-3aα, 4aβ, 9b-13, 20-21a, 22b-26a, 27b-28) is very difficult, and it does not make up a very coherent text, much less a coherent poem. Furthermore, if Fernández Marcos is correct in his supposition that the translator of OG was responsible for the shorter Gk. text, these might have been omitted at the whim of the translator.[424] However, the same gap in 11Q10 is not likely incidental.[425] These common textual lacunae over such a long stretch of the poem strongly suggest that vv. 15-19 (or perhaps vv. 14-19) are secondary. Textual considerations, however, must be supplemented with literary arguments, which I take up in ch. 5.3.

14a. ***Deep says, "It is not in me"*** [*tĕhôm ʾāmar lōʾ bî-hîʾ*]: Since *tĕhôm* is typically feminine in the OT, Duhm and Blommerde propose reading *ʾāmĕrā* in place of MT's *ʾāmar*.[426] Blommerde assumes conservative orthography and believes this emendation is necessary not only for gender concord between subject and verb, but also to produce an 8:8 syllable count in both lines of the verse.[427] Yet *tĕhôm* is masculine in Jon 2:6; Hab 3:10; and Ps 42:8, and the degree to which one can use syllable counting as a basis for textual emendation is very questionable.[428]

---

423 See, e.g., Elwolde, "Non-Contiguous Parallelism," 108 and n. 16.

424 Fernández Marcos, "The Septuagint Reading of the Book of Job," 251-66.

425 See also the comments of Witte, "The Greek Book of Job," 46-47.

426 Blommerde, *Northwest Semitic Grammar and Job*, 107; Duhm, *Das Buch Hiob erklärt*, 136: »[I]n v. 14a ist vielleicht אָמְרָה zu schreiben, da תְּהוֹם immer fem[inin] ist.« Duhm is wrong, however, about *tĕhôm* always being feminine (see Jon 2:6; Hab 3:10; and Ps 42:8).

427 Blommerde, *Northwest Semitic Grammar and Job*, 107.

428 As Dennis Pardee remarks in commenting on the now dated study of Douglas Stuart (*Studies in Early Hebrew Meter* [HSM 13; Missoula, Mont.: Scholars Press, 1976]), "[T]he regularity of syllabic count is attained in too many cases by an arbitrary and unverifiable variation in vocalization" ("Ugaritic and Hebrew Metrics," in *Ugarit in Retrospect: Fifty Years of Ugarit and Ugaritic* [ed. Gordon Young; Winona Lake, Ind.: Eisenbrauns, 1981], 120).

Apart from the question of syllable counting, the larger question is one of *rhythmic patterning*. Hebrew poetry may well have been composed according to some kind of rhythmic patterning, but this falls far short of metric regularity. As Patrick Miller states, "There is no *clear* system of meter in biblical poetry of the precision of classical meter that leads one to be able to predict how lines will follow in terms of stressed or unstressed syllables or patterns of the same" ("Meter, Parallelism, and Tropes," 102 [emphasis his]). It is common now for scholars to speak of a "free rhythm… confined within the limits of its poetics" (Benjamin Hrushovski, "Prosody, Hebrew," *EncJud* [16 vols.; Jerusalem: Keter, 1971], 13:1201; cf. Alter, *Art of Biblical Poetry*, 8-9; and Stephen A. Geller, "Hebrew Prosody and Poetics: I. Biblical," in *NPEPP*, 510-11; et al.). Such "free rhythm" can rarely serve as a reliable criterion for

Tĕhôm is not deified here as often in Mesopotamian texts (Tiamat) and apparently also at Ugarit.[429] Rather, it is personified as nowhere else in the OT. Though the Deep is said to speak in Hab 3:10 and Ps 42:8, no actual words are cited, as in Job 28:14.[430] The personification of Deep and Sea in a text about the source and place of wisdom is particularly striking in contrast to the very typical personification of Woman Wisdom in the Wisdom Literature (e.g., Prov 1, 8, 9; Sir 4, 6, 24, 51; Wis 8), which is not operative in Job 28.

Tĕhôm is used in the OT in both positive and negative contexts. Like *yām*, *tĕhôm* may signify both inexhaustible sources of life-giving water and the threatening powers of chaos.[431] Positively, the deeps fertilize the earth and thus give life (Ezek 31:4; Prov 31:20). In Prov 3:20, the bursting of the deeps is evidence of Yhwh's founding the earth "by wisdom." The deeps gain cosmic import in connection to God's provision for Israel by making water flow from the cosmic rock (Ps 78:15-16).

Mention of the Deep (*tĕhôm*) in v. 14, like the "sources of the rivers" (*mabbĕkê nĕhārôt* [MT *mibbĕkî*]) in v. 11, recalls a portion of the typical Ug. epithet for El's abode at the "at the sources of the rivers, amidst the springs of the double-deep" (*mbk nhrm qrb ʾapq thmtm*). Spatially, *tĕhôm* often represents the lowest point in the world of the living, in contrast to the heavens (Gen 49:25; Deut 33:13; Prov 8:27, 28; Ps 36:7; 107:26; 135:6; cf. also *CTU* 1.1 iii 4; 1.3 iii 25, iv 17). The Deep here represents the cosmic fount known in Mesopotamia as the Apsu.[432]

While in the OT and in other ancient Near Eastern literature the deeps are associated with both life and wisdom, they also swallow up life and are thus associated with death (Gen 7:11; 8:2; Exod 15:5; Ezek 26:19; 31:15; Jon 2:6). Elsewhere in the OT, *tĕhôm* is paired with sea monsters (*tannînîm*; Ps 148:7) and the wilderness (Isa 63:13). Yet nowhere is the chaotic aspect of the Deep profiled more clearly than when it is paired with *yām*, as in Exod 15:4-5, 8; Isa 51:10; Pss 33:7; 106:9. In

textual emendation. See especially the discussion in F. W. Dobbs-Allsopp, "Poetry, Hebrew," *NIDB* 4:553-54.

429 There is a name for a double deity "Mountains-and-the-Waters-of-the-Abyss" in the Ug. ritual texts. Typically, the pair seems to have been *ǵrm wʿmqt* or the like (see *CTU* 1.47:19; 1.118:18; 1.148:6; and Dennis Pardee, *Ritual and Cult at Ugarit* [SBLWAW 10; ed. Theodore J. Lewis; Atlanta, Ga.: Society of Biblical Literature, 2002], 14-15, 18-19, 44-49). However, see also *Ugaritica V*, 9:41, where the phrase is [*ǵr*]*m wthmt*. See discussion of this text in Bendt Alster, "Tiamat," *DDD*, 868-69.

430 Coogan, "The Goddess Wisdom," 207 and n. 15.

431 F. Stolz has made this point with regard to Yam ("Yam," *DDD*, 737).

432 Though *apsû* and *tâmtu* seem to be differentiated at points (i.e., freshwater vs. saltwater) in Mesopotamian sources, this is not uniformly the case. In Ee. I. 3-5, *apsû* and *tâmtu* are an undifferentiated mass of primeval water (see Clifford, *Creation Accounts*, 65, 83, 86-87; and Bendt Alster, "Tiamat," *DDD*, 867-68).

each of these texts, Yhwh defeats these powers of chaos. In addition to their pairing in Job 28:14, *tĕhôm* and *yām* are coupled twice elsewhere in the Book of Job (38:16; 41:23-24). *Ym* and *thm* are also paired once in the Ug. texts (*CTU* 1.23:30), but there they seem simply to signify bodies of water.

The cluster of related symbols in Job 38:16 is striking. There Yhwh queries: "Have you gone to the sources of the sea / or have you walked about in the depths of the deep? (*hăbāʾtā ʿad-nibkê-yām / ûbĕḥēqer tĕhôm hithallāktā*)." In addition to the pairing *yām // tĕhôm*, Yhwh's speech also employs the phrase *nibkê-yām*, recalling *mabbĕkê nĕhārôt* [MT *mibbĕkî*] in v. 11a as well as *ḥēqer*, which is a keyword in Job 28 (*ḥôqēr*, 28:3a; *ḥăqārāh*, 28:7b). It is reasonable to suppose that Job 38:16 plays off of Job 28:1-14 or vice-versa. This is also suggested by the language of the following verses in Job 38:17-21, especially v. 17, where Yhwh asks Job if he has seen (*tirʾeh*) the "gates of death" (*šaʿărê-māwet*) and "deep darkness" (*šaʿărê-ṣalmôt* [MT *ṣalmāwet*]). In this context, the Deep and the Sea signify the deepest cosmographical point, the locus of wisdom; yet at the same time they are associated with deep darkness and death.

Also striking in Job 28:14 is the unusual order of the pair *tĕhôm // yām*, being matched only by Exod 15:8b, where the depths (*tĕhōmōt*) are said to be "in the heart of the sea" (*bĕleb-yām*).[433] Elsewhere in the OT and in Ug. literature, the pair is always *yām // tĕhôm*. The Exodus passage suggests that *tĕhôm* signifies a depth within the breadth of the sea. *Yām* also signifies breadth in Deut 30:13 and Job 11:8-9.[434] This spatial relation may be recalled by the ordering of the word pair in Job 28:14 (*tĕhôm // yām*). The semantic relation of the two terms, signifying breadth and depth, corresponds well with the movement of the human explorer in the first section of the poem. In the opening verses, the explorer searches out every (horizontal) limit (v. 3), while in the closing verses he plunges into the depths of the rivers (v. 11) at the base of the mountains (v. 10).

14b. ***Sea says, "It is not with me"*** [*yām ʾāmar ʾên ʿimmādî*]: Though *yām* is clearly deified in the Ug. texts, it is merely personified here (cf. also *yām* in Job 26:12). While several OT texts clearly reflect Baal's defeat of Yam in the Ug. texts (e.g., Ps 74:12-17; 77:14-21; 89:10-11; 114), this is not one of them.

---

433 Contrast Marjorie O'Rourke Boyle, who denies that the phrase "heart of the sea" in Exod 15:8 is spatial. She emphasizes, rather, that it is the sea's *volition* that is expressed by that phrase (" 'In the Heart of the Sea': Fathoming the Exodus," *JNES* 63 [2004]: 17-27).

434 As noted by Geller, " 'Where is Wisdom?' " 184 n. 66.

20a. ***But wisdom—from where does it come?*** [*wĕhaḥokmâ mēʾayin tābôʾ*]: Both OG and 11Q10 resume at v. 20, though 11Q10 is only attested for the second line. On the definite article on *haḥokmâ*, see discussion above on *wisdom* in v. 12a. The Gk. traditions read *timmāṣēʾ*, as reflected in OG εὑρέθη and in the daughter versions (Syh. *ʾštkḥt*; OL *inventa est*), just as they did in v. 12a. This reading is also attested in Ken. MS 76.[435] But Syr. (*ʾtyʾ*), Vg. (*venit*), and Tg. (*tyty*) support MT's *tābôʾ*, which is the correct reading. OG's εὑρέθη is a harmonization to *timmāṣēʾ* in v. 12a.

20b. ***Where is the place of understanding?*** [*wĕʾê zeh mĕqôm bînâ*]: OG translates *bînâ* here with σύνεσις, though it translated with ἐπιστήμη in v. 12a. Muraoka suggests that this substitution "probably indicates that the translator understood the latter in its fientic sense."[436] 11Q10 translates with *ʿrymwtʾ* ("experience, wisdom"), a cognate to Heb. *ʿormâ* ("shrewdness, cleverness").[437]

21a. ***It is darkened from the eyes of all beasts*** [*wĕneʿelmâ mēʿênê kol-ḥayyā*; MT *kol-ḥāy*]: MT's initial *wāw* is called into question by the fact that it is not represented in OG, Syr., and Vg. As such, it is omitted by Driver and Gray, Fohrer, and others.[438] The *wāw* could be the result of vertical dittography from v. 20a, as Geller suggests, though this presumes stichometric division similar to that in MT.[439] However, the *wāw* is attested in the rabbinic Tg. (*wksyyʾ*), and possibly also in 11Q10, which may understand it as an emphatic *wāw* ([ʾ]*rw*; also in v. 23b).[440]

Blommerde, citing an essay by Pope on the "pleonastic" *wāw*, interprets it as emphatic.[441] On the other hand, Gordis believes that it "in-

435 Kennicott, *Vetus Testamentum Hebraicum*, 2:506.

436 I.e., describing a change of state. Muraoka, "Words of Cognition in Job 28," 101.

437 Zuckerman speculates that this was due to the fact that the translator already employed *ḥkmh* to translate its Heb. cognate in v. 20a, despite the fact that elsewhere in 11Q10, the translator uses *ḥkmh* for Heb. *bînâ* ("The Process of Translation in 11QtgJob," 445).

438 Driver and Gray, *Job*, 2:196; Fohrer, *Das Buch Hiob*, 392 n. 21a.

439 Geller, " 'Where is Wisdom?' " 182 n. 27. So already Fohrer, *Das Buch Hiob*, 392 n. 21a.

440 García Martínez, Tigchelaar, and van der Woude suggest this restoration and interpretation (*Qumran Cave 11.II*, 112-13). Sokoloff, however, states that "[*wmn*] should definitely be restored at the end of 1.1 on the basis of MT *wmʿwp*" (*The Targum to Job from Qumran Cave XI*, 120). I cannot discern traces of either an *ʾālep* (so DJD) or a *wāw* (so Sokoloff) from the plate included in the DJD volume. Zuckerman offers no restoration ("The Process of Translation in 11QtgJob," 446).

441 Blommerde, *Northwest Semitic Grammar and Job*, 107-108. See also Niccacci, "Giobbe 28," 32 n. 19. Blommerde refers to Marvin Pope's comments at the conclusion of his

troduces a subordinate clause of condition," thus translating it "for."[442] Hartley also retains it on the questionable basis of syllable counting.[443]

Given the fact that the versions are divided at this point, it is probably best to retain the *wāw* at the head of the line as preserved in MT. The fact that it is reflected in every MS of the rabbinic Tg. is significant, since "in its treatment of the *waw*, the Rabbinic targum is scrupulously *literal* in comparison with the other Aramaic versions."[444] The *wāw* in MT is best understood as "pleonastic," though this does not necessitate an emphatic interpretation. [445] It may simply be left untranslated.

OG omits MT's *mēʿênê*, though it is restored with an asterisk by Th (Syh. marg. *mn ʿynʾ* = ἐξ ὀφθαλμῶν ["from eyes"]). Though this revision is not incorporated into the translation of Syh., it is reflected in OL's *ab oculis*. MT is supported by Syr., Vg., and Tg[M, S] and others with *mʿyny*. Other Targumic MSS, however, read more abstractly with "from their sight" (*mmḥmyhwn*; see Tg[L]).

OG translates *kol-ḥāy* with "every man" (πάντα ἄνθρωπον; also OL and Syh.), while Syr. (*kl dḥy*), Vg. (*omnium viventium*), and Tg. (*kl dḥy*) follow MT more closely with "every living thing" or "all which lives."

However, Niccacci is correct that one should understand "every animal" or "all beasts" here, in parallel with *ʿôp haššāmayim* in v. 21b. He thus re-points to *kol-ḥayyā* (see also *BHK*), pointing out the parallelism between "birds of the sky" (*ʿôp haššāmayim*) and "beast of the field" (*ḥayyat haśśādeh*) in Ezek 31:6, 13; 38:20; and Hos 2:20; 4:3 (also *ḥayyat kol-hāʾāreṣ* in Ezek 32:4).[446] The phrase *kol-ḥay* is also found in Job 12:10 and 30:23, where it is used generally of living things. If it refers specifically to animals in 12:10, as Dhorme suggests, it may be unnecessary to re-point MT to *kol-ḥayyā* in 28:21.[447] But the parallelism *kol-ḥay // kol-bĕśar-ʾîš* in 12:10 runs against Dhorme's interpretation. Furthermore, the phrase *ḥayyat haśśādeh* is used to designate the beasts of the field in Job 5:23; 39:15 and 40:20, while *ḥayyâ* alone is used of a beast in Job 37:8. A synonym, *bĕhēmôt*, parallels *ʿôp haššāmayim* in Job 12:7. Niccacci notes a

---

essay, " 'Pleonastic' Wāw Before Nouns in Ugaritic and Hebrew," *JAOS* 73 (1953): 95-98. Pope thinks it may be used as "a stylistic device for emphasis and artistic variation" (ibid, 98).

442 Gordis, *The Book of Job*, 310, 300.

443 Hartley, *The Book of Job*, 381 n. 1.

444 Shepherd, *Targum and Translation*, 245.

445 Despite his earlier treatment of " 'Pleonastic' Wāw," Pope makes no comment about this initial *wāw* in his commentary; nor is it reflected in his translation (*Job*, 197, 204).

446 Niccacci, "Giobbe 28," 32. See also Driver and Gray, *Job*, 1:242.

447 Dhorme, *Book of Job*, 411.

possible sharpening from Job 28:13 to v. 21, based on the ancient idea that animals and birds may have possessed knowledge of the secrets of the universe superior to that of humans. This idea may be reflected in the rhetoric of Job 12:7-8 and 35:11.[448] Whether or not this latter assertion can be sustained, Niccacci's suggestion to read *ḥayyā* is correct.[449]

21b-22a: These verses are lacking in OG and were filled in by Origen with Th (⁎καὶ... εἶπαν /).

22a. ***Destruction and Death say*** [*ʾăbaddôn wāmāwet ʾāmĕrû*]: The forces of death are personified here, just as the forces of aquatic chaos were personified in v. 14. Heb. *ʾăbaddôn* occurs 5 times in the OT, 3 being in Job (Job 26:6; 28:22; 31:12; Ps 88:12; Prov 15:11). In each case, it is used in a locative sense, and it most often is parallel to or collocated with *šĕʾôl* (Prov 15:11; Job 26:6). A variant form occurs in Prov 27:20 together with *šĕʾôl* (*ʾăbaddô* [*Qere*]), where there is also a move toward personification, as both Sheol and Abaddon have insatiable appetites. It also occurs in parallel to *qeber* in Ps 88:12.

ʾăbaddôn is the place of destruction. However, the personification of Destruction in texts like Job 28:22 and Prov 27:20 is "the biblical starting point for speculations about *ʾăbaddôn* as a separate entity, as the realm of an angel of death and the netherworld."[450] This kind of speculation is the basis for the reading of Tg. in v. 22. Though Destruction is still understood to be a place (*byt ʾwbdnʾ*), it is also said to be the home of an angel of death (*mlʾk mwtʾ*).

Though Job 28:22 seems to be the only clear instance in which Destruction is personified in the OT (perhaps also Prov 27:20), Death is personified elsewhere in the OT (see Jer 9:20; Hos 13:14; Ps 49:15; Job 18:13) and is deified in Canaanite literature (Mot). Death does not seem to have been deified in the OT, presumably because of intentional demythologizing (but see, possibly, Isa 25:8).

While *ʾăbaddôn* and *māwet* are nowhere else paired in the OT, *māwet / môt* is often paired with *šĕʾôl*, the typical counterpart of *ʾăbaddôn* (Hab 2:5; Hos 13:14; Prov 7:27; Ps 49:15; etc.). The personification of Destruction and Death in Job 28:22 contributes to the poem's mythological overtones.

---

448 Niccacci, "Giobbe 28," 32. However, it is difficult to use Job 12:7 and 35:11 as evidence, as he does, since Job's assertion in 12:7-8 is subversive, and the exact sense of Elihu's response to that statement in 35:11 is difficult to ascertain.

449 Pointing to Bar 3:29, Peters suggests the rationale that wisdom was to be found in the heavens (*Das Buch Job*, 305; cf. also Deut 30:12; Prov 30:4).

450 Manfred Hutter, "Abaddon," *DDD*, 1.

Tromp compares the compound expressions "Sheol and Abaddon" and "Abaddon and Death" in Prov 15:11; Job 28:22; and Prov 27:20 to the Ug. expression *mt wšr*, where the WA is appositional.[451] Thus the expression *ʾăbaddôn wāmāwet* would refer to one personified figure rather than two. Yet the plural verb *ʾāmĕrû* in Job 28:22 suggests two personified figures.

22a. *"Our ears have heard its rumor"* [*bĕʾoznênû šāmaʿnû šimʿāh*]: The phrase *bĕʾoznênû šāmaʿnû* is also found in Ps 44:2, where Israel's forebears recount God's deeds of old (see also 2 Sam 7:22). The nature of this phrasing suggests a contrast between aural recollection and firsthand visual perception. The statement that God "gazes to the ends of the earth" (*liqṣôt-hāʾāreṣ*) in v. 24a underscores this contrast between seeing and hearing, and such a contrast is precisely the point in Job 42:5 as well, where Job confesses, "By the hearing of the ear I had heard of you, / but now my eye sees you!" In Job 28:22, wisdom remains hidden from view. Its fame is known, but all news is only hearsay.

OG abbreviates the phrase and translates for sense with Ἀκηκόαμεν δὲ αὐτῆς τὸ κλέος ("we have heard its rumor"). Tg. compounds cognate terms like MT with *bšmʿnʾ šmʿnʾ šmwʿtʾ* ("with our hearing we have heard rumor"), though the rumor is not of wisdom's place, but rather of its being given to Israel (*bmythbʾ lyśrʾl*).[452] 11Q10 preserves a text very similar to that found in MT with *bʾdnynʾ šmʿnʾ š*]*mʿh* ("with our ears we have heard its rumor").[453]

The various translations of *šēmaʿ* in the versions as "fame" (OG κλέος; Vg. *famam*) or "glory" (OL *gloriam*; Syh. *tšbwḥtʾ*) are more colorful than the prosaic "report" (Sym ἀκοήν; Syr. *šmʿʾ*), and they suggest wisdom's brilliant repute even in the abode of the dead. In this vein, the translation "rumor" for Heb. *šēmaʿ* suggests sensational speculation about the still-unseen wisdom.

---

451 Tromp, *Primitive Conceptions*, 80-81. He is followed by Michel in "The Ugaritic Texts," 413 n. 563.

452 As Mangan notes, "The idea of wisdom being given exclusively to Israel is already in the late Jewish scriptures and Apocrypha: see Bar 3:36; Sir 24:22ff" ("The Targum of Job," 67 n. 15). Mangan states that this targumic addition in v. 22 (*bmythbʾ lyśrʾl*) may suggest a critique of Job's deficiency in his relationship to the Torah, which is evidence of his acting outside of God's wisdom ("The Interpretation of Job in the Targums," in *The Book of Job* [ed. W. A. M. Beuken; BETL 114; Leuven: Leuven University Press, 1994], 275-76).

453 Sokoloff's edition (*The Targum of Job from Qumran Cave XI*) does not include *š*]*mʿh*. Zuckerman is equally cautious, presenting no restoration ("The Process of Translation in 11QtgJob," 450). Its attestation is not clear from the plates in DJD 23.

23a. ***God perceives its path*** [*ʾĕlōhîm hēbîn darkāh*]: OG and the daughter versions read *hēkîn* ("he established") for MT's *hēbîn* (OG συνέστησεν; OL *commendavit*; Syh. *qym*), as do several Heb. MSS.[454] Yet Sym (συνῆκεν), Syr. (*bynn*), Vg. (*intelligit*), and Tg. (*ʾtbyyn*) support the reading of MT. 11Q10 only preserves *bh* for this portion of the verse, which seems to render MT's *darkāh*, so it cannot contribute to a discussion of MT's *hēbîn*.

In addition to its attestation in Sym, Syr., Vg., and Tg., MT's *hēbîn* is preferable on literary grounds. The parallel term in v. 23b, *yādaʿ*, commonly parallels BYN in the Book of Job (Job 14:21; 15:9; 23:5; 38:18; 42:3) and elsewhere in the OT. Both verbs in v. 23, then, refer to intellectual faculties (see discussion of *understanding* in v. 12b). Tur-Sinai translates BYN in v. 23 as " 'he taught' (wisdom its way)," and he re-point the parallel *yādaʿ* in v. 23b to the Piel *yiddaʿ* ("he made known").[455] This proposal, however, is unnecessary.

Dhorme plausibly suggests that Syr.'s translation in v. 23a, *mṭl d*, anticipates *kî* in v. 24a.[456] Though unlikely, it is not impossible that *kî* was present in the *Vorlage* of Syr., resulting in a double emphatic construction in vv. 23a, b, such as that found in Isa 15:1 (see discussion of *indeed* in v. 1a). García Martínez, Tigchelaar, and van der Woude have, in fact, suggested reconstructing [*ʾrw*] at the beginning of v. 23a in 11Q10 as well.[457] The 3fs pronominal suffix on *darkāh* is datival (see Joüon §125ba).

23b. ***He knows its place*** [*wĕhûʾ yādaʿ ʾet-mĕqômāh*]: The reading *ʾrw* in 11Q10 may reflect an interpretation of the initial *wāw* in v. 23b as emphatic *wāw* (see also *It is darkened from the eyes of all beasts* in v. 21a). On the other hand, Zuckerman suggests that either 11Q10's *ʾrw* reflects the influence of Heb. *kî-hûʾ* in v. 24a or that it has arisen from an inner-Aramaic corruption.[458] If the restoration of *ʾrw* in v. 21a by García Martínez, Tigchelaar, and van der Woude is correct, 11Q10 most likely understands an emphatic *wāw* in vv. 21a and 23b. Whether or not one translates the *wāw* in MT as such, the syntax of this line is nonetheless emphatic.

---

454 Kennicott lists MSS 89 and 384 (*Vetus Testamentum Hebraicum*, 2:506), while de Rossi lists MSS 422, 379, 597, and other sources (*Variae Lectiones*, 4:123).

455 Tur-Sinai, *The Book of Job*, 407.

456 Dhorme, *Book of Job*, 411. Baumann suggests the same, though he believes it was a copying error rather than an anaphoric translation (»Die Verwendbarkeit der Pešita,« [1899], 24).

457 García Martínez, Tigchelaar, and van der Woude, *Qumran Cave 11.II*, 113.

458 Zuckerman, "The Process of Translation in 11QtgJob," 452-53.

24a-27b. ***Because... probed it*** [*kî... ḥăqārāh*]: There are some significant problems in the Gk. traditions in vv. 24-27. The problems in OG may either stem from a corrupt Heb. *Vorlage* in which the text was lineated differently or from anaphoric translations in OG.[459] Phrases are transposed in the two lines of v. 24 in OG, which has no equivalent for Heb. *liqṣôt*. OG also reads Heb. *laʿăśôt* with v. 24b instead of v. 25a as in MT. OG has no verbal equivalent for *tikkēn* in v. 25b, and there is no translation of *ḥôq* in v. 26a. Ken. 245 also provides evidence of a different order in vv. 24-26 with MT's v. 26, then v. 24, then v. 25.[460] Though the ordering in Ken. 245 does not explain the differences in the lineation of OG, it does show that these verses were arranged differently in different Hebrew MSS.

To make matters more complicated, the daughter versions also suggest differences in their Gk. *Vorlagen*. While some cursive MSS of OG read ὑετόν in v. 26a, reflecting MT's *māṭār*, the great uncials read the participle ἰδών (LXX^{B,A}), which is translated in OL with *videt*. Both Ziegler and Rahlfs suggest that ὑετόν is the original reading. Gk. ἰδών might possibly be the result of an inner-Greek error. The whole phrase in LXX^{B} and LXX^{S} in v. 26a, οὕτως ὑετὸν ἠρίθμησεν, seems to be equivalent to v. 27a in MT rather than MT's v. 26a.[461] OL's Gk. *Vorlage* seems to have lacked πάντα in v. 24b. Though Syh. reflects πάντα in v. 24b with *klh*, its *Vorlage* seems to have lacked the entire phrase οὕτως ὑετὸν ἠρίθμησεν in v. 26a. On the other hand, Vg., Syr., 11Q10, and Tg. reflect the same Heb. text in the same order as the text preserved in MT.

24a. ***Because he gazes at the edges of the earth*** [*kî-hûʾ liqṣôt-hāʾāreṣ yabbîṭ*]: Though there are some problems in the Gk. traditions, Syr., Vg., 11Q10, and Tg. support the text of MT.[462] The question of translating *kî* here revolves around the same kinds of issues that were posed by *kî* in v. 1a (see *indeed* in v. 1a). As in v. 1a, *kî* could be translated emphatically in v. 24a. The syntax of v. 24 is clearly emphatic. Yet this very fact suggests that an emphatic translation of the particle itself may be superfluous.

---

459 Homer Heater, Jr., defines "anaphoric translation" as iterpolating or adapting "words or phrases from other passages of Scripture where the underlying idea is the same or similar" (*A Septuagint Translation Technique in the Book of Job* [CBQMS 11; Washington, DC: The Catholic Biblical Association of America, 1982], 4). For his treatment of anaphoric translations in vv. 24-25, see ibid., 17, 113. Note also Zuckerman, "The Process of Translation in 11QtgJob," 456 n. 36.

460 Beer, *Der Text des Buches Hiob*, 183.

461 As noted in Heater, *Septuagint Translation Technique*, 17, 113.

462 The interpretation of Syr., however, is somewhat different, due to its attempt to clarify that God focuses on the "end of *all who are in* the earth" (*lswp kl dbʾrʿʾ*).

The form of other ancient Near Eastern creation texts bears upon the discussion of *kî* in v. 24a. These texts suggest a temporal function, which would create a triple protasis in vv. 24a, 25a, and 26a with *kî... laʿăśôt... baʿăśōtô,* the apodosis being marked by *ʾāz* in v. 27a.[463] The Babylonian creation story, *Enūma eliš*, contains a double protasis (I. 1, 7) before the verbal apodosis in Tablet I. 9: "when... when... then they were created" (*enūma... enūma... ibbanû-ma*).[464] The creation text in Prov 8:22-31 contains numerous protases introduced by the preposition *bêt* or *bêt* + infc. (vv. 24a, b, 27a, b, 28a, 29a, b) before the apodosis in v. 30a, which is marked by *wāw*. The preposition *bêt* (+ infc.) also marks the apodoses of this "cosmogonic formula" in Gen 2:4b-7a and in Ps 114:1.

Dhorme, Pope, Gordis, Andersen, Michel, Janzen, and others interpret *kî* in v. 24a as temporal.[465] While this is possible, I do not believe it is probable in this context. The emphatic constructions in vv. 23a, b, and v. 24a suggest, rather, that v. 24 enumerates the *reasons* that God has perceived the way to wisdom and knows its place (thus the translation "because"). Further, the typical use of the infc. in such formulae in the OT suggests that the "cosmogonic formula" in Job 28 does not begin until v. 25a with the infc. *laʿăśôt* and then continues with *baʿăśōtô* in v. 26a, creating a double protasis construction in these verses, followed by the apodosis in v. 27a: "when…when… then…"[466]

The temporal translation of *kî* in v. 24a would also require an interpretation of the verbs in the line (*yabbîṭ // yirʾeh*) as prefixed preterites,[467] perhaps functioning as past participles in English: "When he was gazing…"[468] Such a translation is unproblematic and has parallels else-

---

463 See discussion in Dhorme, *Book of Job*, 412; and Newsom, "The Book of Job," 532. Newsom points to the ancient Near Eastern creation accounts with similar constructions, but she does not think that the protases begin until v. 25a.

464 See Talon, *The Standard Babylonian Creation Myth*, 33, 79.

465 Dhorme, *Book of Job*, 411-412; Pope, *Job*, 198; Gordis, *The Book of Job*, 300; Andersen, *Job*, 228; Michel, "The Ugaritic Texts," 204-205; and Janzen, *Job*, 197; Clines, " 'The Fear of the Lord is Wisdom' " 78 and n. 47.

466 So Budde, *Das Buch Hiob*, 162 (»Als... Als... da«); Driver and Gray, *Job*, 1:243, 2:197; Newsom, "The Book of Job," 532.

467 Clines plausibly translates the verbs here as preterites despite interpreting *kî* according to its causal function (*Job 21-37*, 904 n. 24c).

468 The prefixed preterite (YQṬL) in Biblical Hebrew has been the subject of much discussion in the past two decades, especially in light of Amarna Canaanite. For one clear presentation of some of the semantic issues involved, see Edward L. Greenstein, "On the Prefixed Preterite in Biblical Hebrew," *HS* (1988): 7-17. However, Alviero Niccacci has recently argued against the existence of a YQṬL preterite in BH poetry ("The Biblical Hebrew Verbal System in Poetry," in *Biblical Hebrew in its Northwest Semitic Setting: Typological and Historical Perspectives* [eds. Steven E. Fassberg and Avi Hurvitz; Publication of the Institute for Advanced Studies 1; Jerusalem: Magnes; Winona Lake, Ind.: Eisenbrauns, 2006], 247-68).

where in the OT.[469] Yet, on this interpretation, one would still need to explain how the language of v. 24 relates to God's creative acts. Dhorme believes that "V. 24 indicates the time when God took knowledge of [the way which leads to wisdom]. It was when He was observing the ends of the earth with a view to organizing the elements (vv. 25-6). It was then that He saw and examined Wisdom (v. 27)."[470] But this temporal interpretation seems unlikely in light of the spatial language used in v. 24 (*qĕṣôt* and *taḥat*) and the parallel in Ps 33:13-14.[471]

The most common translations among English, German, and French commentators are "for," »denn,« and "car," all of which are ambiguous.[472] Presumably, however, a causal relationship is understood between God's ability to discern the path to wisdom in v. 23 and his ability to see everything under the heavens all the way to the edges of the earth.[473] "Because" is a better translation in this case, highlighting more clearly the causal function of the particle, as it is to be understood here.

Some commentators object that a "place" or "path" of wisdom is precisely what the poem has argued against.[474] But the two couplets in vv. 23-24 answer the poem's rhetoric up to this point which has underlined the failure of animals and humans to find wisdom's "place" (vv. 1b, 12a-b, 20b, 23b), its "path" (vv. 7a, 13a, 23a), or its point of issue (vv. 1a, 20a). The emphatic construction in v. 24a (*hûʾ... yabbîṭ*; see also vv. 23a, b) suggests that God's abilities in v. 24 are set over against creaturely shortcomings in the previous sections of the poem (cf. also *hûʾ* in v. 3aβ).

The phrase "ends of the earth" (*liqṣôt-hāʾāreṣ*) in v. 24a suggests the horizontal dimension of God's vision. It is used elsewhere in Isa 41:5a, 9a et al., of an ingathering of people from the edges of the world to its

---

469 See especially *kî ʾădabbēr...* in 1 Kgs 21:6, as pointed out by Greenstein ("On the Prefixed Preterite," 15-16). He translates: "When I was speaking..." (ibid., 16). By contrast, Zerafa sees the prefix conjugation in v. 24 as mitigating against a chronological reference to the time of creation (*Wisdom of God*, 151).

470 Dhorme, *Book of Job*, 412.

471 On which, see Niccacci, "Giobbe 28," 32. Tur-Sinai also asserts that this verse does not relate to God's creating the world. Instead, he suggests that the creation has already happened, and that God is pictured here as surveying it (*The Book of Job*, 408; cf. Gen 1:4).

472 This is also the translation of virtually all the English versions of the Bible (see RSV, NRSV, KJV, NKJV, JB, NJB, NEB, NIV, NAS, NAB, NJPS). See also OG and Vg.

473 See e.g., Newsom "The Book of Job," 532; Driver and Gray, *Job*, 2:197; Clines, *Job 21-37*, 903 n. 24b.

474 For this reason, Beer follows Budde (*Das Buch Hiob*, 162) in deleting v. 24 altogether (Beer, *Der Text des Buches Hiob*, 182-83).

cosmic center in Zion.[475] This and related constructions parallel the "coastlands" in Isa 41:5 and the "distant seas" in Ps 65:6, all of which would have surrounded the water-bound disc of land known to the Israelites as *hāʾāreṣ*.[476] This is matched by a vertical dimension in the second line with "beneath all the heavens."

24b. ***sees beneath all the heavens*** [*taḥat kol-haššāmayim yirʾeh*]: OG suggests *kol taḥat-haššāmayim* with ὑπ' οὐρανὸν πᾶσαν (Syh. *lhy dtḥyt šmyʾ klh*; OL *omne quod est sub caelo*) rather than MT's *taḥat kol-haššāmayim*. Vg. supports the syntax in OG with *omnia quae sub caelo sunt*. However, Syr. and Tg. support the word order found in MT. Some scholars suggest following the OG phrasing here (see *BHK*, *BHS*), but this is unnecessary. While the phrase preserved in MT suggests that God sees "under all the heavens," this naturally includes the fact that he sees "everything that is under the heavens" as well. The word order preserved in MT has exact parallels elsewhere in the Book of Job and in the OT (Job 37:3; 41:3; Gen 7:19; Deut 2:25; 4:19), and this phrasing seems to have been most productive.[477] Thus Niccacci and Geller are correct to argue for its originality.[478]

MT's *taḥat kol-haššāmayim yirʾeh* is a fitting circumlocution. As the use of the phrase in Gen 7:19 illustrates most clearly, *taḥat kol-haššāmayim* suggests totality and expanse—more specifically, all the terrain over which heaven is outstretched. By aiming the language at the expansive domain in which all creatures dwell, the line incorporates those creatures in its purview without making them the point of focus as they would have been in the phrase *kol taḥat-haššāmayim*.

By pairing the horizontal and vertical dimensions, the parallel phrases "edges of the earth" and "beneath all the heavens" in v. 24 create a spatial merism which is equivalent to "everywhere and everything."[479] Note also a similar parallel in the reverse order in Elihu's speech in Job 37:3: *taḥat-kol-haššāmayim // ʿal-kanpôt hāʾāreṣ*.

25a. ***When he made a weight for the wind*** [*laʿăśôt lārûaḥ mišqāl*]: Ehrlich complains that MT's *laʿăśôt* »ist hier syntaktisch unmöglich,« and

475 On Zion's status as the center of the world in cosmic geography, see Levenson, *Sinai and Zion*, 115-122.

476 Compare the Babylonian Map of the World discussed in Horowitz, *MCG*, 21, 26-42.

477 Niccacci also points to the variant phrases *kol ḥayyat haśśādeh* in Ezek 31:6, 13 and *ḥayyat kol-hāʾāreṣ* in Ezek 32:4 which may provide a helpful analogy ("Giobbe 28," 32 n. 20).

478 Geller, " 'Where is Wisdom?' " 182 n. 28.

479 Gordis, *The Book of Job*, 310; and Müllner, »Der Ort des Verstehens,« 72.

suggests reading *baʿăśôt*, based partially on the fact that the translations of OG, Vg., and Syr. seem to reflect a substantive participle of ʿŚH.[480] OG reads *laʿăśôt* with v. 24b and translates with a relative construction plus a finite verb (ἃ ἐποίησεν). The translations of Syr. (*dʿbd*) and Vg. (*qui fecit*) are similar. However, the translation of Tg. follows MT closely with *lmʿbd* ("making"). This form is attested in every Targumic MS with only minor orthographic variations. MT is correct, and suggestions to emend to *baʿăśôt* are superfluous, despite the translations of OG, Vg., and Syr.[481]

Though the infinitive construct with the prefixed preposition *lāmed* is most often used to signify purpose, such an understanding of the form is not necessary here. The *lāmed* in an infc. often seems to have little or no value and may be seen as an integral part of the infc., as it is in late Aramaic.[482] Thus MT's *laʿăśôt* may simply be translated "in doing" or "in making," with the temporal nuance being clarified by *baʿăśōtô* in v. 26a.[483] In fact, 11Q10 translates *laʿăśôt* in v. 25a as a temporal infinitive with *bmʿbdh*, which is precisely how it renders *baʿăśōtô* in v. 26a. Even if it is a harmonization to the Heb. of v. 26a, the exegesis of 11Q10 is correct.[484] The double-protasis construction before the apodosis in v. 27a begins here.[485]

The term *mišqāl* is only used here in connection with elements of creation.[486] Elsewhere in the OT and in Semitic inscriptions, it is used of

480 Ehrlich, *Randglossen*, 6:293. Compare also Duhm, *Das Buch Hiob erklärt*, 136-37; Fohrer, *Das Buch Hiob*, 392 n. 25b; Budde, *Das Buch Hiob*, 162; and De Wilde, *Das Buch Hiob*, 277.

481 The failure to represent *bêt* in the Heb. text is very likely an example of omission by Syr. See discussion in Shepherd, *Targum and Translation*, 81-82.

482 Joüon §49*f* n. 2 and §124*l* and n. 1.

483 Driver and Gray, *Job*, 2:197; cf. Gordis, *The Book of Job*, 310. Niccacci rightly states that "the clear *baʿăśōtô* makes explicit the syntactic value and the subject of the ambiguous *laʿăśôt*" ("Giobbe 28," 32 [my translation]).

484 See Zuckerman, "The Process of Translation in 11QtgJob," 461-62.

485 So also Budde, *Das Buch Hiob*, 162; Driver and Gray, *Job*, 1:243, 2:197; and Newsom, "The Book of Job," 532.

486 In Heb. MS A of Sir 16:23, the expression *ʾabbîaʿ rûḥî bĕmišqāl* is also used metaphorically, but there of the "spirit" (= "learning, teaching") rather than the "wind" ("I will show forth my spirit by weight"). The Gk. translates with the correct sense (LXX 16:25): ἐκφανῶ ἐν σταθμῷ παιδείαν ("I will impart learning by weight"). For the text of Ben Sira, I have consulted the edition of Francesco Vattioni, *Ecclesiastico: Testo ebraico con apparato critico e versioni greca, latina e siriaca* (Pubblicazioni del Seminario di Semitistica: Texts 1; ed. Giovanni Garbini; Naples: Istituto Orientale di Napoli, 1968), here 82-83.

weights made of stones or precious metals.[487] But with the language of "making a weight for the wind," the description participates in the widespread conceptualization of creation as house- or temple-building in the ancient Near East and the OT (e.g., Isa 40:12; Job 38:4-6, 8-11; Prov 3:19-20; 24:3-4; etc).[488]

The metaphor used here of weighing the wind simultaneously ties into the dominant metaphor of weighing and arranging in vv. 15-19, even if these verses are not original to the poem (see discussion in ch. 5.3). Thus v. 25 participates in two conceptual metaphors at once: house-building (= cosmos building) and market exchange. While humans trade in silver, gold, and copper, God's currency is the wind.

25b. ***apportioned the waters by measure*** [*ûmayim tikkēn bĕmiddâ*]: OG has no verbal equivalent for *tikkēn* in v. 25b. However, οὕτως may reflect *kēn* after *baʿăśōtô* in v. 26a (see also OL and Syh.). Alternatively the OG translator could have read TKN as *tōken* ("a measure;" see OG ὕδατος τε μέτρα). But LXX^B and LXX^A in v. 26a read οὕτως ἰδών ἠρίθμησεν (instead of οὕτως ὑετὸν ἠρίθμησεν as preserved in some cursives), which seems to be equivalent to v. 27a in MT rather than MT v. 26a. It is difficult to draw any conclusions about the Heb. *Vorlage(n)* from OG, since OG itself seems to have suffered from corruption. However, Aq (καὶ ὕδωρ ἐσταθμήσατο ["and water is measured in measure"]) and Sym (ὕδωρ δὲ ἐξίσωσε μέτρῳ ["and water he made equal in measure"]) do reflect the verb *tikkēn*. Syr. lacks MT's *mayim*, translating with "weight" (*mtqlʾ*) instead. This may reflect a double translation of the consonantal TKN as *tikkēn tōken*.[489] The ancient versions are in disagreement over the translation of TKN. Tg.^{M,S,C}, for example, reads *wmyʾ ʾtqyn bmšḥtʾ* ("and waters he *established* in measure"), while Vg. translates with *et aquas appendit in mensura* ("and waters he *weighed out* in measure").

The exact sense of TKN in the Piel is difficult. *HALOT* glosses the verb "to measure up, assess, calculate the size" for Job 28:25 and Isa 40:13, but their gloss "to make correct, meaning to keep steady…" for Ps 75:4 seems to presume that TKN in the Piel is related to the Niphal of

---

487 Both *mišqāl* and *middâ* are used together in the OT in Lev 19:35 in an exhortation for honest weights. For inscriptional evidence in Phoen., Punic, and Off. Aram., see *DNWSI*, 2:705, s.v. *mšql*.

488 See Van Leeuwen, "Cosmos, Temple, House," 67-92.

489 On double translations in Syr., see Rignell, "Notes on the Peshiṭta of the Book of Job," 101-102, 104; Szpek, *Translation Technique*, 153-60; and Baumann, »Die Verwendbarkeit der Pešita,« (1899): 15-22. Note also the the double translation of *piṭdatkuš* in v. 19a. See *Topaz stones of Cush cannot be estimated against it* in ch. 5.4.

KWN.[490] For all these instances, Driver recommends abandoning the meanings "measure, assess," etc., and translating "to bring into order, arrange," assuming that TKN is an expanded form of Niphal-KWN. He thus translates *ûmayim tikkēn bĕmiddâ* in Job 28:26 as "he *adjusted* (the limits of) the waters by measure."[491]

Driver's arguments are overdrawn. The sense of "measuring the waters" is upheld by the recurrence of this imagery in OT and ancient Near Eastern creation texts. In Isa 40:12aβ, God is said to have "gauged the heavens with a span (of the hand)" (Piel-TKN; *wĕšāmayim bazzeret tikkēn*). Similar metaphors occur in v. 12aα as well: "who measured the waters with the hollow of his hand?" (*mî-mādad bĕšoʿŏlô mayim*). The imagery of this text emphasizes God's ability to measure the water and the heavens with a cupped palm or widened hand, and similar metaphors are operative in Job 28:25, where, as in Isa 40:12, the language is architectural.[492] As De Vaux states, "Architects, masons, and craftsmen measured with their own arms, their extended hands, their palms, and their fingers."[493]

This imagery is also found in a ritual for the Babylonian New Year festival in which Marduk is called "one who measures the water of the sea" (*mādidi mê tāmtim*).[494] A similar description is given in Ee. IV. 142-43, where Marduk is said to have "measured the construction of Apsu" (*imšuḫ-ma... ša apsî binûtūšu*).[495] In Job 28:25, God is portrayed as measuring the immeasurable and counting the non-countable during the process of creation.

26a. ***when he made a groove for the rain*** [*baʿăśōtô lammāṭār ḥōq*]: As noted above (see *Because... probed it* in vv. 24a-27b), some cursive MSS of OG read ὅτε ἐποίησεν οὕτως ὑετὸν ἠρίθμησεν, reflecting at least part of MT v. 26a, though LXX[B] and LXX[A] translate with ὅτε ἐποίησεν οὕτως ἰδὼν ἠρίθμησεν, the latter part of which (οὕτως ἰδὼν ἠρίθμησεν) seems to be equivalent to v. 27a in MT (*ʾāz rāʾāh waysap-*

490 *HALOT* 4:1734 s.v.

491 G. R. Driver, "Hebrew Notes," *VT* 1 (1951): 243 (emphasis mine).

492 On this imagery in Isa 40:12, see Joseph Blenkinsopp, *Isaiah 40-55* (AB 19A; New York: Doubleday, 2002), 191. Driver would translate this passage: "(who) has adjusted the heavens with a span?" (Driver, "Hebrew Notes," 243).

493 Roland de Vaux, *Ancient Israel: Its Life and Institutions* (trans. John McHugh; London: Darton, Longman, and Todd, 1961), 197. Originally published as *Les institutions de l'Ancien Testament* (2 vols.; Paris: Cerf, 1958).

494 François Thureau-Dangin, "Le rituel des fêtes du nouvel an a Babylone" in idem, *Rituels accadiens* (Paris: E. Leroux, 1921), 134, line 241.

495 Translation of Foster in *BTM*, 462; for text, see Talon, *The Standard Babylonian Creation Myth*, 56.

pĕrāh) rather than MT v. 26a (note OL's *videt*, which also reflects ἰδών). However, Vg., Syr., and Tg. support MT. 11Q10 lacks most of the line, but it does preserve *bmᶜbd*]*h*, reflecting MT's *baᶜăśōtô* (precisely the same rendering it gave for *laᶜăśôt* in v. 25a).

There is a nice pun in the line by the use of *ḥōq*. *Ḥōq* is often used of a legal decree or prescription, and in such cases, it is a synonym of terms like *miṣwâ*, *mišpāṭ*, and *bĕrît*.[496] While this common sense of *ḥōq* is operative in Job 28:26, there is also a play on the word's etymology, from the root ḤQQ, meaning "to etch, engrave, inscribe" (see Isa 30:8; 49:16; Ezek 4:1; 23:14). This evokes the imagery of an artisan engraving in metal or the like.[497] The root is used in the Book of Job of inscribing Job's words in a scroll[498] (// ḤṢB, "to incise;" 19:23-24), as well as of God's setting a limit for humanity (14:5; 23:12-13), a boundary on the surface of the waters (26:10), a limit for the sea (33:10), and the laws of heaven (38:33).

The picture of God as a skilled craftsman participates in the metaphor of creation as artistic construction. The metaphorical relation between incising and world-ordering is also evident in the etymology of the Sum. phrase, ĝeš-ḫur ("wood-scratch"), which may be used of a "plan [of the universe]."[499] The two senses of etching out a "groove" through which the rain flows down to earth and setting a "legal decree" that cannot be transgressed are both activated in vv. 25-26, where God's magnificent artistic masterpiece is a thunderstorm.[500] Heb. *ḥōq* also occurs in other creation texts in the OT, such as Ps 148:6; Job 26:10; 38:10, 33; Prov 8:27, 29; Jer 5:22. In many cases, the same play may be active.[501]

That the sense of "groove" for *ḥōq* is primary in v. 26a is supported by the language of the parallel line in which thundershowers travel on

496 See *HALOT* 1:346, s.v., for numerous citations.

497 Artisans worked soft metals with tools made of bone or hardwood. See Ann C. Gunter, "Materials, Technology, and Techniques in Artistic Production," in *CANE* 2:1547.

498 Edward Greenstein has made the very plausible suggestion to interpret *bspr* (MT *bassōper*) in Job 19:23 as "in bronze," comparing Akk. *siparru*, "bronze" ("The Poetic Use of Akkadian in the Book of Job" [paper presented at the annual meeting of the SBL, Boston, Mass., 24 November 2008]).

499 See Clifford, *Creation Accounts*, 51. The Pennsylvania Sumerian Dictionary glosses "to draw." Online: http://psd.museum.upenn.edu/epsd/nepsd-frame.html. See also Akk. *eṣēru* with the same meaning (*AHw* 1:252-53 s.v.; *CAD* E, 346-49 s.v. *eṣēru* A) and cf. Heb. YṢR.

500 Andersen, *Job*, 229.

501 See Geller, " 'Where is Wisdom?' " 185 n. 71.

tracks (*wĕderek laḥăzîz qōlôt*).[502] This exact phrase is also found in Job 38:25b, where *derek* parallels *tĕʿālâ* ("channel, conduit"). Such a conception is also supported by ancient commentary on meteorological phenomena in the *Genesis Rabbah*: "The clouds gain strength from the earth and rise to the firmament and receive the water, as from the mouth of a water-skin... They distill it as from a sieve, so that one drop does not touch another."[503]

The double material and non-material (or "artistic" and "ethical") senses latent in the language of v. 26 with *ḥōq* and *derek* allow the poet to be consistent with the immediate context concerning the physical design of creation while also anticipating the non-material, ethical language of v. 28, which is an exhortation to *hāʾādām* about how to fit into that design.

26b-27a: These verses are lacking in the OG and were filled in by Origen with Th (※καὶ ... αὐτήν /).

26b. ***and a track for the thundershower*** [*wĕderek laḥăzîz qōlôt*]: 11Q10 preserves only *qlylyn*, but the second line may be restored on the basis of its rendering of the same phrase in Job 38:25: *dt wʾrḥ lʿnnyn*] *qlylyn*. Thus, the whole of v. 26 in 11QtgJob probably read *bmʿbd*[*h lmṭrʾ dt wʾrḥ lʿnnyn*] *qlylyn*. Apparently, 11Q10 understood a form much like MT's *qōlôt* as an adjective from *qal*, "light."[504] LXX's ※καὶ ὁδὸν ἐν τινάγματι φωνάς ("and a way for the quaking of thunder") supports the text of MT. Aq reads similarly with εἰς κτύπον φωνῶν ("into a crash of thunderings;" Syh. marg. *bnqšʾ dqlʾ*), as did Sym with ὄμβρον φωνῶν or ὄμβρων βροντάς ("rainstorm[s] of thunder;" Syh. marg. *mṭrʾ dqlʾ*).[505]

The phrase *wĕderek laḥăzîz qōlôt* also occurs in Job 38:25b (see also *qōlôt* in Heb. Sir 40:13 [LXX βροντὴ μεγάλη]), but the Gk. translator there renders *laḥăzîz qōlôt* somewhat differently than in Job 28:26 with

---

502 For this meaning of *ḥōq*, see Pope, *Job*, 229. Clines' objections to this meaning do not take into consideration the conceptual background of the images evoked in these verses (*Job 21-37*, 904 n. 26a).

503 Gen. Rab. XIII. 10. Translation of Jacob Neusner, *Genesis Rabbah: The Judaic Commentary to the Book of Genesis. A New American Translation. Volume I: Parashiyyot One through Thirty-Three on Genesis 1:1 to 8:14* (BJS 104; Atlanta, Ga.: Scholars Press, 1985), 142.

504 For all the above on the reading of 11Q10, see García Martínez, Tigchelaar, and van der Woude, *Qumran Cave 11.II*, 113; and Zuckerman, "The Process of Translation in 11QtgJob," 465-66. This understanding is also preserved in the Babylonian Talmud (*b. Taʿan.* 9b), as pointed out by Tur-Sinai (*The Book of Job*, 408) and Gordis (*The Book of Job*, 310).

505 Ziegler and Field record different Gk. readings for Sym. Those listed here are given in Ziegler's Göttingen edition of LXX-Job.

the phrase ὁδὸν δὲ κυδοιμῶν ("and a way of roarings"). Syr. translates *ḥāzîz* in Job 28:26 with *ḥzwnʾ* ("visions, spectacles"), indicating a confusion of *nûn* and *zayin* (perhaps also *wāw* and *yôd*) in the Aramaic square script.[506] Vg. and Tg. support MT.

The term *derek* may be used of a "path" in a material or an ethical sense. Both senses may be at work here in v. 26b, just as there seems to be a play in v. 26a between the ethical sense "decree" and the more material meaning of *ḥōq*, having to do limiting, etching, or engraving. The phrase *wĕderek laḥăzîz qōlôt* in Job 38:25 is embedded in a context in which most of the meteorological phenomena are conceptualized as materials that can be stored up in containers or channeled through grooves. The sea has doors and limits (Job 38:8-11), the deep has gates (v. 17), light and darkness both have homes (vv. 19-20), snow and wind are contained in vaults (v. 22), torrents and thunderstorms are guided through channels and paths (v. 25), and the heavens are bottles that can be tipped over, spilling out the contents (v. 27).[507] While both material and the ethical senses are at work in *derek* in Job 28:26, the metaphors of tracks and channels in the design of creation are primary.

The exact meaning of *ḥāzîz* is disputed. Aside from Job 28:26 and the aforementioned parallel in Job 38:25b, it occurs only in Zech 10:1, where it parallels both *malqôš* ("late rain") and *mĕṭar-gešem* ("downpour").[508] On this basis alone, one could safely assume "rainstorm" in our passage. This also has some precedent in the ancient versions of Job 28:26, as Sym translates with ὄμβρον ("rainstorm"). One might also appeal to Vg.'s *procellis* ("storms"). The Gk. translation of *ʿab ḥăzîzîm* in Sir 35:20 also connects *ḥāzîz* with rain (LXX 35:26 νεφέλαι ὑετοῦ).[509]

Several Semitic cognates for Heb. *ḥāzîz* have been cited by philologists. *HALOT* records Ug. *ḫḏḏ*, Aram. *ḥăzîzāʾ*, Arab. *ḫinḏīḏ*, and Arab. *ḥāzīz*.[510] Strictly speaking, Semitic phonemics would not allow Heb. *zayin* to correspond both to /ḏ/ (Arab. *ḏāl*; Ug. /ḏ /) *and* to /z/ (Arab. *zāy*; Ug. ZI). The guttural correspondences are difficult as well. Could Heb. *ḥêt* correspond to /ḫ/ (Arab. *ḫā*; Ug. ḪA) *and* to /h/ (Arab. *ḥā*; Ug. Ú)?

---

506 Note also Ken. MS 245, which reads *laḥăzîn* (*Vetus Testamentum Hebraicum*, 2:506).

507 See also E. F. Sutcliffe, "The Clouds as Water-Carriers in Hebrew Thought," *VT* 3 (1953): 99-103.

508 On terms for rain in the OT, see Mark D. Futato, "Sense Relation in the 'Rain' Domain of the Old Testament," in *Imagery and Imagination in Biblical Literature: Essays in Honor of Aloysius Fitzgerald, F.S.C.* (ed. Lawrence Boadt and Mark S. Smith; CBQMS 32; Washington, D.C.: The Catholic Biblical Association of America, 2001), 83-97.

509 Vattioni, *Ecclesiastico*, 185-86. Note, however, that Vattioni's edition incorrectly reads *ʿēt* instead of *ʿab*.

510 See *HALOT* 1:302, s.v. **ḥāzîz*.

To explain *ḥāzîz* in Job 28:26, Pope draws on a portion of the Kirta narrative (*CTU* 1.14 ii 39-40): *hlk . l alpm . ḫḏḏ / w l rbt . km . yr* (also *CTU* 1.14 iv 17-18). Here *ḫḏḏ* is parallel to *yr* ("early rain"). Pope translates the word in question as "showers."[511] On Pope's interpretation, the whole can be translated: "Let them march by the thousands as showers / and by myriads like early rain."[512] In the Kirta text, this translation evokes the image of Kirta's soldiers as being innumerable as raindrops (see also *CTU* 1.14 ii 35-38).[513] However, the meaning "showers" is not beyond dispute in *CTU* 1:14 ii 39-40. In fact, Lete and Sanmartín gloss *ḫḏḏ* here as "downpour, squall," and *yr* as "early rain."[514]

Köhler and Fohrer point to Arab. *ḫinḏīḏ*, which Köhler defines as "the cyclone (produced by the wind)."[515] Fohrer adopts this meaning for Heb. *ḥāzîz* in Job 28:26 and suggests that it naturally includes thunderclouds, translating as »die donnernde Gewitterwolke.«[516]

Both Dhorme and Hölscher cite Arab. *hāzīz* ("rumbling, roaring"), and they also understand it to be connected with thunder. Dhorme translates *ḥăzîz qōlôt* in Job 28:26 as "rumble (of thunder)."[517] Hölscher translates similarly with »Rollen des Donners.«[518] More easily connected to Heb. *ḥāzîz* from an etymological standpoint is Akk. *azāzu* (< **ḫazāzu*), which has to do with unnatural sounds of various sorts.[519]

Delitzsch, Driver, and Gray have proposed the meaning "lightning" for Heb. *ḥāzîz* in Job 28:26, assuming a verbal root ḤZZ ("to cut, notch") and citing Arab. *ḥazza* ("to cut").[520] From a semantic standpoint, this proposal is unconvincing. Tur-Sinai also translates in this fashion, but his suggestion is even more problematic. He argues that Heb. ḤZZ is a non-emphatic phonetic variant of the emphatic geminate ḤṢṢ ("to

511 *Pope*, Job, 206. Cf. *DUL*, which glosses *ḫḏḏ* as "downpour, squall," and *yr* as "early rain" (1:387 and 2:977).

512 My translation. The preposition *km* is gapped in the first line.

513 Compare the translation of Greenstein, who translates *ḫḏḏ* as "in rows" and *km . yr* as "by rank arrayed" without any explanation ("Kirta," in *Ugaritic Narrative Poetry* [SBLWAW 9; ed. Simon B. Parker; Atlanta: Scholars Press, 1997], 15, 19).

514 *DUL* 1:387 and 2:977.

515 See Köhler, »Hebräische Vokabeln II,« 173 (»der [durch den Wind erzeugte] Wirbelsturm«).

516 Fohrer, *Das Buch Hiob*, 392 n. 26a; translation at 390.

517 Dhorme, *Book of Job*, 413.

518 Hölscher, *Das Buch Hiob*, 70.

519 *CAD* A/2, 528-29 s.v. *azû*; *AHw* 1:92 s.v. *azāzu* (»sausen«).

520 Delitzsch, *Book of Job*, 2:112; Driver and Gray, *Job*, 2:197-98; and Rowley, *The Book of Job*, 184.

separate"), whence Heb. *ḥēṣ* ("arrow"). He points to Ps 77:18b, where God's "arrows" are lightning bolts.[521]

Appeal to comparative Semitics alone does not bring much clarity to the meaning of *ḥăzîz qōlôt* in Job 28. Furthermore, the connection between *ḥāzîz* and *all* the proposed cognates seems problematic on the surface. However, the semantic overlap between Ug. *ḫḏḏ* (probably "downpour"), Arab. *ḫinḏīḏ* ("cyclone"), and Arab. *hāzīz* ("rumbling") is remarkable. And despite apparent incongruities in phonemic correspondence between these terms, it surely must carry some weight that, in addition to semantic overlap, these are all geminate verbs (voiced affricatives: /ḏ/; or fricatives: /z/) with the initial guttural (all voiceless fricatives: /ḫ/; /ḥ/; /h/).[522] Nevertheless, the possible connections of Heb. *ḥāzîz* both to Ug. *ḫḏḏ* and Arab. *ḫinḏīḏ* are to my mind the most impressive.

The ancient interpretive traditions are of equal or greater value in clarifying the meaning of *ḥāzîz*. Some ancient traditions interpret *ḥāzîz* as "cloud." 11Q10 translates *ḥāzîz* in Job 38:25b with *ʾnnyn*. "Cloud" also seems to be the meaning of *ḥăzîzāʾ* in the rabbinic Tgs. of Song 2:9 and Job 28:26.[523]

The meaning "quaking" or "clap" is attested in 28:26 both the translation of Th in LXX (⁎τινάγματι ["quaking"]) and in the translation of Aq (κτύπου ["crash"]). This meaning is also evident in the Gk. translation of Sir 40:13 (βροντή ["thunder"]). Furthermore, the OG in Job 38:25 translates the entire phrase *ḥăzîz qōlôt* with κυδοιμῶν ("roarings").

However, given the clear use of *ḥāzîz* in Zech 10:1 as "rainstorm," the translations of Sym in Job 28:26 ("rainstorm"), LXX Sir 35:24 ("rain clouds"), and the use of *ḫḏḏ* in *CTU* 1.14 ii 39 (probably "downpour"), a meaning like "rainstorm" for *ḥāzîz* in the absolute state would seem quite fitting.[524] But collocated with *qōlôt* (Job 28:26b; 38:25b; Sir 40:13 [Heb.]), the whole phrase may very sensibly be translated as "thundershower" or the like.[525] Poetically speaking, heightening from "rain" (*māṭār*) to "thundershower" (*ḥăzîz qōlôt*) in the couplet in Job 28:26 is apt.

---

521 Tur-Sinai, *The Book of Job*, 408, 116; cf. also Gordis, *The Book of Job*, 310. Note also Jer 10:13; 51:16; and Ps 135:7b, where God makes lightning flashes for the rain.

522 Köhler finds the fact that Arab. *ḫinḏīḏ* is quadriliteral unproblematic. He suggests that the *nûn* is infixed, and he offers another example with Arab. *ḫinzīr* and Heb. *ḥăzîr* (»Hebräische Vokabeln II,« 173). See *HALOT* 1:302 s.v. *ḥăzîr*.

523 Jastrow, *Dictionary*, 1:443, s.v.

524 *HALOT* 1:302, s.v. **ḥāzîz* suggests "squall."

525 See Geller, " 'Where is Wisdom?' " 156; Pope, *Job*, 205; and Michel, "The Ugaritic Texts," 205. cf. NEB, NIV, Vg. (*procellis*; "storms").

27a-b. ***then he saw it... probed it*** [*ʾāz rāʾāh... ḥăqārāh*]: Aside from the fact that LXX^B and LXX^A may reflect a double translation of v. 27a with both οὕτως ἰδὼν ἠρίθμησεν in the OG of v. 26a and ⋇τότε εἶδεν αὐτὴν καὶ ἐξηγήσατο αὐτήν in the LXX of v. 27a (see discussion under *Because... probed it*), the versions present no textual problems in the first line, only different interpretations of the consonantal text preserved in MT.

In v. 27b, however, OG has no formal equivalent for the 3fs pronominal suffixes or for *gām* in MT. But Th does reflect the pronominal suffixes with διέταξεν αὐτὴν καὶ ἐξηρεύνησεν. The translation of Vg. does not reflect *gām*. However, Syr. and Tg. support MT on both of these points.

Though some scholars suggest reading *hēbîn* in v. 27b for MT's *hēkîn*, none of the ancient versions reflect this reading.[526] OG (ἑτοιμάσας), Th (διέταξεν), Vg. (*praeparavit*), and Tg. (*ʾtqnh*) all support MT. However, several Heb. MSS do read *hēbîn*.[527] Syr. reads *tqlh*, probably reflecting the Hiphil of KWL under the influence of the imagery in 28:25. Despite the fact that BYN would initially seem to be a more fitting parallel to RʾH in the first line, MT is to be preferred, due to the fact that the Hiphil of KWN is typical in ancient Near Eastern and biblical texts portraying creation as divine artisanship.

Each of the ancient translations understands the root SPR in v. 27a to suggest God's narration or report about wisdom ("he reported it"). Joüon also points to Sir 43:31 (Σ) (τίς ἑώρακεν αὐτὸν καὶ ἐκδιηγήσεται) which he believes to reflect the sense of *waysappĕrāh* in Job 28:27a.[528] The Tg. specifies God's conversation partners: "Then he saw it and discussed it with the angels of his service" (*hydyn ḥmyyh wʾštʿyh ʿm mlʾky šyrwtʾ*).[529]

However, Piel-SPR should be understood as "to count" or the like in Job 28:27. The meaning "to count" is most common in the Qal, but it

---

526 Pope, *Job*, 206; Dhorme, *Book of Job*, 413; Geller, " 'Where is Wisdom?' " 182 n. 33; Hölscher, *Das Buch Hiob*, 70; Michel, "The Ugaritic Texts," 205. Though Hartley claims that it is not necessary to read BYN, his translation nonetheless reflects it with "discerned" (*The Book of Job*, 381 and n. 4).

527 Kennicott lists MSS 260, 271A, 80 (*Vetus Testamentum Hebraicum*, 2:506), while de Rossi lists MSS 57, 610, 737, 801, and other sources (*Variae Lectiones*, 4:123).

528 "Notes philologiques sur le texte hébreu de Job," 323-24. This connection, however, does not seem strong.

529 This interpretation seems to stem from the idea that angels were involved in the creative task along with God. According to William Brownlee, this cosmic role of angels in seen in 11QtgJob Job 37:10, where he restores: "[Through the breath of His angels He puts ice] / on the surface of the water." These angels are thus "personal agents who listen to God's voice and go forth to their assigned tasks" ("The Cosmic Role of Angels in the 11Q Targum of Job," *JSJ* 8 [1977]: 83-84).

also occurs indisputably in the Piel in Ps 22:18 and in Job 38:37.[530] Thus it is not necessary to re-point to the Qal, as suggested by Gordis and Ehrlich (also Beer in *BHK*).[531] The connection between the two meanings which is evident in the semantics of SPR in BH can also be seen in the English "to give an ac*count* of (something)" or "to re*count* (a scenario)." In anticipation of the verb of speaking in v. 28 (*wayyōʾmer*), marking actions simultaneous to or directly following God's actions in v. 27, *waysappĕrāh* likely carries the secondary sense, "and he recounted it."

Alternatively, Reider has suggested interpreting SPR here as a phonetic variant of SBR due to /b/ > /p/ interchange (see also discussion of *He binds up* in v. 11a). SBR in Aram. and Arab. means "to probe."[532] Accepting this proposal would amount to acknowledging a byform of BH ŚBR, meaning "to test, investigate" in the Qal.[533] However, this interpretation of SPR in Job 28:27 does not commend itself from a literary point of view.

There is some question as to how to read the 3fs pronominal suffixes throughout the line (*rāʾāh... waysappĕrāh... hĕkînāh... ḥĕqārāh*). These have most commonly been interpreted to refer to "wisdom" (*ḥokmâ*), found in vv. 12a and 20a, just as the 3fs pronominal suffixes on *darkāh* and *mĕqômāh* in v. 23 do. Yet Scott Harris has argued that the 3fs suffixes instead refer to the content of vv. 23-26 as a whole, that is, creation (see GKC §135p). He attempts to demonstrate that the four verbs in v. 27 are used only with reference to creation, and not to wisdom, in the rest of the OT.[534]

It is true that the OT often speaks of God relating to elements of creation in terms of numbering (Piel-SPR) or establishing (Hiphil-

530 None of the other citations for the meanings "to count out, count over again" or "to count up" in the Piel listed in *HALOT* 2:766, s.v. SPR I, are beyond dispute, and most are unconvincing. Note also the use of SPR in *Arad* 3.obv.7, where it is used of measuring out what and bread (*spr . hḥṭm . whlḥm*). However, since the root with this meaning is most productive in the Qal, it is preferable to assume a Qal impv. in this inscription rather than a Piel. See *HI*, 16; *DNWSI* 2:798, s.v. *spr*₁.

531 Gordis, *The Book of Job*, 311. In addition to re-pointing as *wayyispĕrehā*, Ehrlich offers the strange suggestion that one should understand the verb here to mean that God conscripted wisdom into his service so that it would fight for him against foolishness, comparing Isa 22:10 (*Randglossen*, 6:293).

532 Reider, "Etymological Studies in Biblical Hebrew," *VT* 2 (1952): 127. A similar meaning was already proposed by Duhm without recourse to Aram. or Arab. (»studieren«; *Das Buch Hiob erklärt*, 137). Duhm understands the verb here to be a denominative from Heb. *sōpēr*. On the evidence cited by Reider, see Jastrow, *Dictionary*, s.v. *sĕbar* III. Both Aram. *sĕbar* III and Arab. *sĕbar* are used of examining an injury or piercing for the purpose of blood-letting.

533 *HALOT* 4:1304-1305, s.v.

534 Scott L. Harris, "Wisdom or Creation? A New Interpretation of Job xxxviii 27," *VT* 33 (1983): 419-27.

KWN) *by* wisdom rather than numbering or establishing *wisdom itself*. Two examples are particularly noteworthy. In Jer 10:12 (= 51:15), it is said that God established the world by his wisdom (*mēkîn tēbēl běḥokmātô*), employing Hiphil-KWN as in Job 28:27b. In Job 38:37, Yhwh queries, "Who has counted out the clouds by wisdom?" (*mî-yěsappēr šěḥāqîm běḥokmâ*), employing Piel-SPR, just as in Job 28:27a. In both of these cases, it is the elements of creation that God either "counts" or "fixes." The language of firmly establishing the physical elements of creation permeates ancient Near Eastern and OT creation accounts.[535] In addition to its use in connection with the world in Jer 10:12 (= 51:15), Hiphil-KWN is used of the earth (Jer 33:2; Ps 65:10; cf. Polel in Isa 45:18), the mountains (Ps 65:7), and the sun (Ps 74:16). Ultimately, both "establishing" (Hiphil-KWN) and "counting out" (Piel-SPR) participate of the same metaphor of the divine creation-act as the work of a builder or artisan. This interpretation is clearly represented in the Gk. version of Ben Sira: "It is he who created her; he saw her and took her measure; he poured her out upon all his works" (NRSV). As Roland Murphy notes, this commentary is particularly apt, since the LXX of Sir 1:9 and the LXX of Job 28:27a both reflect the verbs Rʾ H and SPR:[536]

LXX Sir 1:9: καὶ <u>εἶδεν</u> καὶ <u>ἐξηρίθμησεν</u> αὐτήν...
And he *saw* and *counted* it...

LXX Job 28:27a: τότε <u>εἶδεν</u> αὐτὴν καὶ <u>ἐξηγήσατο</u> αὐτήν...
Then he *saw* it and he *narrated* it...

Against Harris' interpretation, Ben Sira undoubtedly picks up on this material element in Job 28:27, emphasizing that God saw and counted out wisdom itself. Thus wisdom is also being "fixed" or set in place along with the elements of creation.

Yet the semantic elasticity of SPR and KWN in the line allows a subtle shift toward the non-material and the cognitive, peaking with the last word in v. 27, ḤQR. While Rʾ H, SPR, and KWN may initially be read as actions upon wisdom as a material object, undertaken from the outside, the verb ḤQR suggests a shift toward wisdom's inside, a mental probing of its inner extent. Wisdom becomes a three-dimensional space that is known now not as object, but as *subject*.

---

535 E.g., Ee. I. 71; IV. 144; V. 8, 62 et al.; *Palm and Tamarisk* (Emar version), line 2; Akk. prologue to *Enuma Anu Enlil*, line 3; *After Anu Had Engendered Heaven*, line 2.

536 Roland Murphy, "The Personification of Wisdom," in *Wisdom in Ancient Israel: Essays in Honour of J. A. Emerton* (eds. John Day, Robert P. Gordon, and H. G. M. Williamson; Cambridge: Cambridge University Press, 1995), 224. But see already Peters, *Das Buch Job*, 307-308.

ḤQR is used with reference to the wisdom traditions in the Book of Job (ḤQR in 5:27; 8:8; cf. also 32:11). In 5:27 and 32:11, the verb takes objects that are closely connected to wisdom. Eliphaz states, "Look, this is what we have examined..." (*hinnēh-zōʾt ḥăqārnûhā*). He speaks here of the friends' experience, which is the basis for their claims to wisdom (5:27). Elihu claims to have waited patiently to speak until his friends "had examined the issues" (*ʿad-taḥqĕrûn millîn*), specifically the issues concerning who has wisdom and insight (32:11). Prov 28:11 states that a poor but perceptive person can see through the rich who thinks he is wise (*wĕdal mēbîn yaḥqĕrennû*). Elsewhere in the Wisdom Literature, the verb is used of examining the integrity of a person or their case (Prov 18:17; Job 13:9; 29:16). And while the phrasing is nominal rather than verbal, it is the inability of humans to fathom the full extent or depth of God's wisdom that is expressed by the phrases *ʾên ḥēqer* or *lōʾ ḥēqer* throughout the OT (Isa 40:28; Job 5:9; 9:10; Ps 145:3). Remarkably, in Job 5:9 and 9:10, the verb ḤQR parallels SPR (*mispār*), where both have to do with fathoming the full extent of God's works.[537] Thus the statements concerning God's abilities to "count" (Piel-SPR) wisdom and to "probe" (ḤQR) it in v. 27 are positive correlates of the negative statements about human inability to "number" God's wisdom (*litbûnātô ʾên mispār*) or to understand its full extent (*ʾên ḥēqer litbûnātô*) in Ps 147:5 and Isa 40:28.[538]

Despite the fact that it is most commonly used in creation texts of the establishment of an element of creation, Hiphil-KWN may also be used of "determining the qualities or position of an object" within a circumscribed space.[539] In this respect, it has semantic overlap with the verb ḤQR in BH. As van Hecke points out, Hiphil-KWN occurs in 1 Sam 23:22, where it is used of determining a person's hiding place (*mĕqômô*),[540] and in Deut 19:3, where it is used of assessing the distance

---

537 van Hecke, "Searching for and Exploring Wisdom," 159.

538 Gordis, *The Book of Job*, 311. Harris' objection that wisdom is not present in either Ps 147:5 or Isa 40:28 because the word *ḥokmâ* is not used is misguided ("Wisdom or Creation?" 423 n. 13).

539 van Hecke, "Searching for and Exploring Wisdom," 160. Alternatively, Niccacci points Piel-KWN in Job 8:8, where it is used in the sense of "establish (by personal examination)." He thus translates *hēkîn* in Job 28:27 as "he examined" ("vagliò"), suggesting that RʾH and KWN ("saw" and "examined") function as the first of two pair of verbs, while SPR and ḤQR ("counted" and "searched out") function as the second pair ("Giobbe 28," 33).

540 The passage in 1 Sam 23:22 is textually problematic. Some Heb. MSS and Syr. read BYN instead of KWN. Presuming that KWN is the correct reading, note that Hiphil-KWN is there collocated with RʾH, as in Job 28:27a.

of a road (*derek*).[541] Both of these objects—*māqôm* and *derek*—are root metaphors in Job 28 (see esp. *derek* // *māqôm* in v. 23). Thus, in Job 28:27, the verb KWN may refer both to "founding" wisdom as a physical element of creation and to "finding" wisdom by determining its location within a circumscribed space.

SPR may be applied to mental activity metaphorically. While it is used in the Piel of counting the clouds in Job 38:37, the root also occurs in Job 5:9 and 9:10 in parallel with ḤQR of "counting up" (> "fathoming") God's works (see also Job 36:26).

Thus Harris' suggestion is not compelling.[542] Ultimately, wisdom and creation are inextricable, since creation was founded by the principles of wisdom, and it continues to be ordered on them. In v. 27, the poet uses language often employed to describe creation (Rʾ H, SPR, KWN), to portray wisdom as an entity that can be seen, counted out, determined, and probed, just as elsewhere in the poem, wisdom is pictured as residing in a place (vv. 12b, 13a [*ʿerkāh*], 20b, 23b) with a path leading to it (v. 23a), and even issuing from a source (v. 20a; cf. v. 1a).

SPR and KWN in v. 27 facilitate the transition from creation-acts by the divine artisan in vv. 25-26 to acts of mental cognition and perception, climaxing with the verb ḤQR in v. 27. God's ability to "number" wisdom (*waysappĕrāh*) and his ability to "probe" it (*ḥĕqārāh*) in Job 28:27 suggest his utter mastery over it by measuring both its outer and inner extent. Such knowledge of wisdom's inner extent is a far more intimate knowledge than mere external observation. As the emphatic adverb *gām* suggests, v. 27b presents God's ability to "probe" (ḤQR) wisdom as the most magnificent achievement in the poem. ḤQR in v. 27b echoes the language of v. 3a, where the human probes the borders of the world for the stone. However, the God's probing wisdom in v. 27 represents a wholly different conceptual model for the search for wisdom than that undertaken by the human in the first section.[543]

While ḤQR in v. 3 was used of searching an area for an object that symbolized wisdom, in v. 27 ḤQR is used of searching wisdom itself, where wisdom is conceptualized as a three-dimensional space. As James Aitken comments, "There is a development, therefore, from the

541 van Hecke, "Searching for and Exploring Wisdom," 160 n. 53.

542 Clines also points out that it would be strange for the poem to speak of wisdom, then switch to creation in v. 27, and back to the topic of wisdom in v. 28 (Clines, *Job 21-37*, 922).

543 van Hecke, "Searching for and Exploring Wisdom," 158-60.

searching for a physical object to the searching for a cognitive (although almost personalized) object by God."[544]

28a-b. ***and he said… understanding*** [*wayyōʾmer… bînâ*]: This verse is undoubtedly one of the most maligned in the Book of Job, for several reasons: (1) Morphology and Syntax: The verse begins with the *wāw*-relative form *wayyōʾmer*, which is most commonly an element of narrative. Some view it as an "editorial splice."[545] (2) Vocabulary: The term *ʾădōnāy* is a *hapax legomenon* in the Book of Job. (3) Theology: Many commentators view it as a pious formulation typical of a "conservative" or "traditional" wisdom school, reflected particularly in proverbial wisdom (e.g., Prov 1:7; 3:7; 9:10; 15:33). Houtsma even suggests that it is a citation of Prov 3:7 or 9:10.[546] (4) Thematic Inconsistency: It is often thought that v. 28 presents a different kind of wisdom than that presented in v. 27 and the poem as a whole and that this evidences too great a degree of inconsistency with the previous context to have been original to it.[547] Due to one or several of these considerations, numerous scholars delete it entirely.[548]

But this verse, as Geller has noted, has "been declared guilty without trial."[549] Carol Fontaine opines, "[T]his verse represents the heart of the book in its final form and may not be brushed aside."[550] Its authen-

---

544 Aitken, "Lexical Semantics," 122. See also van Hecke, "Searching for and Exploring Wisdom," 159-60.

545 Pope, *Job*, 206; see also Dhorme, *Book of Job*, 414; Driver and Gray, *Job*, 1:245; Hölscher, *Das Buch Hiob*, 70; Duhm, *Das Buch Hiob*, 136.

546 Houtsma, *Textkritische Studien*, 65.

547 E.g., Pope, *Job*, 206; Driver and Gray, *Job*, 1:244-45. Van Oorschot's view is an interesting variation on this theme. He agrees with most that v. 28 presents a very different conception of wisdom (wisdom as the fear of God) than that presented in vv. 1-27 (hidden, cosmic wisdom). Nonetheless, he states that »v. 28 nimmt keine Trivialisierung des Vorangegangenen im Sinne der traditionellen Weisheitstheologie vor« (»Hiob 28,« 187).

548 E.g., Hölscher, *Das Buch Hiob*, 70; Fohrer, *Das Buch Hiob*, 392 n. 28a; cf. Duhm, *Das Buch Hiob erklärt*, 137; Hesse, *Hiob*, 157 n. 177; Strauß, *Hiob 19,1-42,17*, 155.

549 Geller, " 'Where is Wisdom?' " 156. However, it is clear from his comments elsewhere in the essay that he believes v. 28 to have been added by a later editor who hoped "to distract other readers from the poem's unorthodox message" (ibid., 175).

550 Fontaine, "Wounded Hero on a Shaman's Quest: Job in the Context of Folk Literature," in *The Voice from the Whirlwind: Interpreting the Book of Job* (eds. Leo G. Perdue and W. Clark Gilpin; Nashville, Tenn.: Abingdon, 1992), 79.

Compare the comment of Norbert Peters: »Wer V. 28 aus Kap[itel] 28 entfernt, reißt das Herz aus dem Kapital heraus!« (*Das Buch Job*, 309). See also the discussion of De Wilde, who cites Peters (*Das Buch Hiob*, 278-79). Weiser suggests that the entire poem is governed by the idea of wisdom as something that remains a secret to God and inaccessible to humanity. He believes that v. 28 draws a perfectly logical conclu-

ticity has been either vigorously defended or at least seriously considered by other scholars.[551] Rowley states summarily, "It is a pity to rob the poem of its climax and to turn it into the expression of unrelieved agnosticism."[552] Clines asserts, "I cannot prove that v. 28 is original, but I see it as a failure of nerve to excise it because of its difficulty."[553] The question of the originality of the verse and its function within the poem must be considered carefully on philological, literary, and theological grounds.

Something that is not emphasized enough in this discussion is that v. 28 is attested in all the ancient MSS and in the ancient versions. If it is a later addition, it must have been added prior to the mid-1st century C.E., which is the latest date proposed for the *manuscript* of 11Q10, on the basis of its paleography.[554] However, the original composition may be dated even earlier, possibly to the latter half of the 2nd century B.C.E.[555] Verse 28 is likewise attested in OG, which was in circulation by 100 C.E., if not before.[556] While these considerations do not conclusively point to the originality of Job 28:28, it significantly narrows the time frame in which it would have been added by a later editor, if it is, in-

---

sion to the poem, even if the wisdom in view is practical, rather than secretive, wisdom (*Das Buch Hiob*, 198-99).

551 Terrien, *Job*, 195-96; Gordis, *The Book of Job*, 538-39; Rowley, *The Book of Job*, 185; Delitzsch, *Book of Job*, 2:112-14; Habel, *The Book of Job*, 392-93; and Andersen, *Job*, 229. Cf. Tur-Sinai, *The Book of Job*, 409; and Hartley, *The Book of Job*, 383-84 and nn. 1-3.

552 Rowley, *The Book of Job*, 185.

553 Clines, " 'The Fear of the Lord is Wisdom' " 76.

554 García Martínez, Tigchelaar, and van der Woude, *Qumran Cave 11.II*, 87. It is written in a formal Herodian script (thus ca. 37-70 C.E.).

555 Cook, "Aspects of Wisdom in the Texts of Job," 32-33, who cites Michael Sokoloff (*The Targum to Job from Qumran Cave XI*, 9) and E. Y. Kutscher ("The Language of the Genesis Apocryphon: A Preliminary Study," in *Aspects of the Dead Sea Scrolls* [ScrHier 4; eds. Chaim Rabin and Yigael Yadin; Jerusalem: The Magnes Press, 1958], 22). Stephen A. Kaufman would date it later, to the 1st century B.C.E., on grammatical grounds ("The Job Targum from Qumran," *JAOS* 93 [1973]: 327). Bruce Zuckerman attempts to date 11Q10 paleographically, based on mistakes in 11Q10 due to graphic similarity between letters in the script of its *Vorlage*. This yields a relative chronology that basically supports Kaufman's analysis that the MS of 11Q10 dates to 100 B.C.E. or a few decades later (Zuckerman, "The Date of 11Q Targum Job," 57-78). However, Adam van der Woude has more recently suggested the last decades of the 2nd century B.C.E. or a bit later ("Job, Targum of," 413). Takamitsu Muraoka dates it even earlier, between 250 and 150 B.C.E., and asserts that 11Q10 is Babylonian, not Palestinian, in origin ("The Aramaic of the Old Targum of Job from Qumran Cave XI," *JJS* 25 [1974]: 425-443).

556 Dhorme, *Book of Job*, cxcvi.

deed, secondary. This logic holds for the entire chapter, as well as for the order of the controversial third cycle of speeches.[557]

28aα. *and he said to the human* [*wayyōʾmer lāʾādām*]: Though WYQṬL forms are most commonly an element of narrative, they occur with surprising frequency in the poetic sections of Job. By my count, there are 167 WYQṬL forms outside of ch. 28 (vv. 27a, 28a) in the Book of Job, excluding the frame narrative. Sixty-one of these forms are in short narrative introductions to each character's speech (typically *wayyaʿan… wayyōʾmer*). This leaves 106 WYQṬL forms within the body of the poems themselves. Thus the WYQṬL form alone is not proof that Job 28:28 is inauthentic. In the current context, the form marks the next action in sequence after the verbs introduced by *ʾāz* in v. 27 (*ʾāz rāʾāh waysappĕrāh hĕkînāh wĕgam-ḥĕqārāh… wayyōʾmer*).[558] This has been noted also by Budde: »V. 28 ist nicht zu übersetzen: ›Zum Menschen aber sprach er u.s.w.‹, sondern ויאמר schliesst sich in umittelbarer Folge an die Verba von v. 27 an: ›Und sprach dann zum Menschen.‹ «[559]

Ken. 378 lacks *lāʾādām,* but its originality is not in doubt, since it is attested in every other Heb. MS and in all the ancient versions.[560] 11Q10 understands a plural addressee here with *lbny* [*ʾnšʾ*] but this is simply interpretive.[561]

There is some question as to whether *ʾādām* in Job 28:28 refers to humanity, to one human, or to the man Adam. Virtually all the major English translations understand it as an address to the human race, thus interpreting the definite article in *lāʾādām* as generic, marking a class (NJPS, JB, NJB NEB, KJV, NKJV, RSV, NRSV, NAS, NAB, NIV, TNIV, ESV; see *IBHS* §13.5.1f). But why would God suddenly address the entire human race at the end of this poem?

It is possible also that God here addresses the human who was the subject of the first section (*ʾĕnôš*, v. 13) as a corrective to the attempts at gaining wisdom which have been displayed in the brash actions em-

557 See John Gray, "The Massoretic Text of the Book of Job, the Targum and the Septuagint Version in Light of the Qumran Targum (11Qtarg Job)," *ZAW* 86 (1974): 331-50. Compare Fitzmyer, who states, "Thus this targum of Job gives us an ancient form of the Book of Job that agrees in large part with the structure and build-up of the Hebrew text, as we know it in the MT" ("Some Observations on the Targum of Job from Qumran Cave XI," 508-509).

558 In fact, all the versions interpret the Heb. in this way (see Zuckerman, "The Process of Translation in 11QtgJob," 468).

559 Budde, *Das Buch Hiob*, 163.

560 Kennicott, *Vetus Testamentum Hebraicum*, 2:506.

561 Strauß, however, follows 11Q10 with »zum Menschen« (*Hiob 19,1-42,17*, 131, 133 n. 28b).

bodied in the poem's first section (esp. vv. 3-11). But if this human subject is in view, why did the poet not repeat the term *ʾĕnôš* in v. 28?

Tur-Sinai suggests that *hāʾādām* in v. 28 refers to the first human, Adam.[562] This view is particularly attractive in light of the temporal framework set up by the poet in vv. 25-27, which moves backward in time to distant days in which God engaged in creative acts of chaos-ordering. Verse 28 is also set during this time frame. Immediately following these skillful acts of building and ordering, God turns to address "the first man," Adam.

The view that "the human" in v. 28 refers to the first man also finds support in the Book of Job. In Job 15:7-9, Eliphaz ironically asks Job if he was the "first man born" (*rīʾšôn ʾādām*) who has "listened in on the secret council of God." This represents an ideal, especially with regard to the knowledge of wisdom, just as ante-diluvian knowledge of wisdom brought by the *apkallu* was idealized in the Mesopotamian traditions.[563] In 31:33, Job himself pleads, "Did I cover over my transgressions like Adam...?"

As the implied author of the poem in Job 28, v. 28 is both from the mouth of Job and addressed *to* Job (since Job is reporting God's speech). So how does Job employ these words purported to have come from God himself? It is quite possible that Job claims antiquity by taking on the persona of the "first man" in response to Eliphaz's rhetoric in 15:7. After constructing a parable of his friends' failed search for wisdom from the tradition in Job 28:1-11, he appeals to his friends' own means of legitimating authority through antiquity,[564] but he outstrips them. As the first human, he now has unrivalled claim to antiquity, and thus also unparalleled access to wisdom.

28aα-b.*"Behold, awe of the Lord... to turn from evil..."* [*hēn yirʾat ʾădōnāy... wĕsûr mērāʿ...*]: Neither Ken. 76 nor Syr. reflect *hēn* (Syr. may simply leave it untranslated), but it is attested in all the other Heb. MSS

562 He believes that ch. 28 "seems to stem from an elaborate poetical account of the Creation and the first steps of man" (Tur-Sinai, *The Book of Job*, 409; cf. ibid., 395). See also Jean Lévêque, "L'argument de la création dans le livre de Job," in *La Création dans l'Orient Ancien* (LD 127; Congrès de l'ACFEB, Lille [1985]; ed. F. Blanquart; Paris: Cerf, 1987), 280.

563 See, e.g., SB Gilg. XI. 9-204 in George, *BGE*, 1:702-17.

564 As Norman Habel states, for the friends, "ultimate authority and truth is primordial" ("Appeal to Ancient Tradition as a Literary Form," *ZAW* 88 [1976]: 267). For passages in which the friends appeal to traditional wisdom passed down from their ancestors, see 5:27 (Eliphaz); 8:8-13 (Bildad); and 15:17-18 (Eliphaz). Habel lists the following non-Joban passages as possible quotations from the tradition: 2:4; 4:7, 17; 5:2, 6, 7, 17; 8:11-12; 11:6b, 12; 15:14; 20:5; 22:12 (ibid., 253 n. 4).

and ancient versions.[565] The discourse marker *hēn* serves the same semantic and syntactical functions as its allomorph, *hinnēh*. It is a focus particle, pointing to the content of the sentence that follows. It may also be used when a speaker presents him- or herself, as in the case of Job 28:28, where it marks God's self-presentation.[566]

Heb. *ʾădōnāy* is a *hapax legomenon* in the Book of Job, and v. 28 as a whole has been held suspect for this reason. Elsewhere in the Book of Job, *ʾēl*, *ʾĕlôah*, *šadday*, *ʾĕlōhîm*, and *yhwh* are used, but never *ʾădōnāy*.[567] *ʾĕlōhîm* was used of God only five verses earlier in v. 23a.

One hundred and two (perhaps 104) Heb. MSS read *yhwh* instead of *ʾădōnāy*.[568] This is also reflected invariably in Tg., where the DN is marked with *yyy*. Four others read the compound name *yhwh ʾdny*.[569] Heb. *ʾădōnāy* is lacking altogether in Ken. 475 and 573.[570]

One would expect the DN *yhwh* to be collocated with *yirʾat* instead of *ʾădōnāy*, since the phrase *yirʾat yhwh* occurs 21 times in the OT.[571] In light of this fact, it is tempting to read with the 100 or so Heb. MSS that read *yhwh*. However, the phrases *yirʾat ʾĕlōhîm* (Gen 20:11; 2 Sam 23:3; Neh 5:9, 15; cf. also *wîrēʾ ʾĕlōhîm* in Job 1:1, and *yĕrēʾ ʾĕlōhîm* in Job 1:8; 2:3) and *yirʾat šadday* (Job 6:14) are also attested in the OT. Though reading *yhwh* here would provide a more typical phrase in the OT, it would not result in a more typical DN in the Joban dialogues. The DN *yhwh* is common enough for the epilogue and prologue, where it occurs 23 times. But it only occurs 6 times in the MT of the dialogues: five times in the God speeches and once in Job 12:9. Yet it is quite possible that the original reading in 12:9 was the far more common *ʾĕlôah*, as *ʾĕlôah* is attested in seven Heb. MSS.[572] This would relegate all occurrences of *yhwh* in the Book of Job to the God speeches.

Gordis and Terrien suggest that the reading *ʾădōnāy* reveals the Jewish tendency to substitute a euphemism for the tetragrammaton.[573] In other words, what is typically the perpetual *Qere* has in this case become the *Ketib*. From this, Gordis concludes that the 100 or so MSS that

---

565 Kennicott, *Vetus Testamentum Hebraicum*, 2:506.

566 For all the above on *hēn* / *hinnēh*, see van der Merwe, Naudé, and Kroeze, *A Biblical Hebrew Reference Grammar*, 328-30.

567 For figures and a discussion, see Driver and Gray, *Job*, 1:xxxv-xxxvi, and 232 n. 1.

568 Kennicott, *Vetus Testamentum Hebraicum*, 2:506.

569 Ibid. (MSS 168, 206, 242, 321).

570 Ibid.

571 *yirʾat yhwh*: Prov 1:7, 29; 2:5; 8:13; 9:10; 10:27; 14:26, 27; 15:16, 33; 16:6; 19:23; 22:4; 23:17; Isa 11:2, 3; 33:6; Ps 19:10; 111:10; 34:11; 2 Chr 19:9.

572 Driver and Gray, *Job*, 1:xxxv; ibid., 2:77

573 Gordis, *The Book of Job*, 538; Terrien, *Job*, 195. Compare Driver and Gray, *Job*, 2:198; and Budde, *Das Buch Hiob*, 163.

read *yhwh* in Job 28:28 are leveling to the more usual form.[574] An alternative view, proposed by Bickell and Beer, is that the original text read YRʾTY (cf. *yirʾātî* in Job 4:6; 22:4; Jer 32:40), and that later tradents took this as an abbreviation for *yirʾat yhwh,* which they changed to the perpetual *Qere yirʾat ʾădōnāy*.[575]

Even so, the reading *yirʾat ʾădōnāy* is supported by the majority of MSS, and one may consider this phrasing original to the book. If this is the case, Job 28:28 joins Ezek 13:9; 23:49; 24:24; and 28:24 as the only places in the OT where *ʾădōnāy* comes from the mouth of God.[576] Delitzsch records a total of 134 instances in the OT where *ʾădōnāy* is the *Ketib* and not the perpetual *Qere*.[577]

The occurrence of the phrasing *yirʾat ʾădōnāy... wĕsûr mērāʿ* in Job 28:28 unmistakeably recalls the descriptions of Job in the prose prologue where Job is said to be one who "fears God and turns from evil" (*wîrēʾ ʾĕlōhîm wĕsār mērāʿ*, 1:1; *yĕrēʾ ʾĕlōhîm wĕsār mērāʿ*, 1:8; 2:3). This literary connection is surely relevant for the interpretation Job 28, which climaxes with God's equating this very behavior with wisdom and understanding.

Recently David Clines has contributed to recovering the emotive aspect of the "fear of God," suggesting that human dread at God's awesomeness is the sense of the term (denotation), while ethical or cultic responses to this visceral reaction are the phrase's reference (or connotation).[578] Clines' emphasis on the non-rational, emotive aspect of the fear of God is on target, and it re-habilitates a crucial element of this concept that has often been lacking in previous scholarly treatment.[579]

On the other hand, Bruce Waltke, taking his starting point from Rudolf Otto's study, *Das Heilige,* holds together both the non-rational (including fear, love, and trust) and rational (moral conduct) aspects

---

574 Gordis, *The Book of Job,* 539.

575 Beer, *Der Text des Buches Hiob,* 183. See the discussions in Peters, *Das Buch Job,* 310; and De Wilde, *Das Buch Hiob,* 278.

576 Budde, *Das Buch Hiob,* 137; Driver and Gray, *Job* 2:198.

577 Delitzsch, *Book of Job,* 2:113

578 Clines, " 'The Fear of the Lord is Wisdom' " 64, 69-70; idem, *Job 21-37,* 924.

579 Note also the essay of Mayer I Gruber, "Fear, Anxiety and Reverence in Akkadian, Biblical Hebrew and Other North-West Semitic Languages," *VT* 40 (1990): 411-22, in which he suggests that both Heb. YRʾ and Akk. *palāḫu* can be understood in either the sense "to revere" or "to be anxious" (see esp. p. 420). In another essay, Gruber glosses *yirʾat ʾădōnāy* in Job 28:28 as "Devotion to the Lord" ("Human and Divine Wisdom in the Book of Job," in *Boundaries of the Ancient Near Eastern World: A Tribute to Cyrus Gordon* [eds. Meir Lubetski, Claire Gottlieb and Sharon Keller; JSOTSup 273; Sheffield: Sheffield Academic, 1998], 98).

without subordinating one to the other.[580] He states, "At one and the same time it signifies non-rational, numinous fear combined with love and trust, both of which are schematized by moral uprightness. In some texts the non-rational predominates, in others the rational; but 'awe' of God characterizes its core."[581] Despite some differences, Waltke and Clines together make a convincing case that the "awe" of God is at the core of this phrase.

580 Bruce K. Waltke, "The Fear of the Lord: The Foundation for a Relationship with God," in *Alive to God: Studies in Spirituality Presented to James Houston* (eds. J. I. Packer and Loren Wilkinson; Downer's Grove, Ill.: Intervarsity, 1992), 17-33; Rudolf Otto, *The Idea of the Holy: An Inquiry into the Non-Rational Factor in the Idea of the Divine and its Relation to the Rational* (trans. John W. Harvey; London: Oxford University Press, 1936). Originally published as *Das Heilige: über das Irrationale in der Idee des Göttlichen und sein Verhältnis zum Rationalen* (Breslau: Trewendt und Granier, 1923).

581 Waltke, "The Fear of the Lord," 30.

Chapter Five: The "Structured Commentary" in Job 28:15-19

5.1 Translation

15 {Fine gold cannot be given in its place.
Silver cannot be weighed for its purchase price.
16 It cannot be paid for with the gold of Ophir,
with precious carnelian or lapis-lazuli.
17 Neither gold nor glass can be estimated against it.
Ornaments of pure gold are not its exchange.
18 Neither pearls nor rock crystal should be mentioned.
A sack of wisdom is more precious than corals.
19 Topaz stones of Cush cannot be estimated against it.
It cannot be paid for with pure gold.}

5.2 Vocalized Text

15 {*lōʾ-yuttan sāgûr taḥtêhā*
wĕlōʾ yiššāqēl kesep mĕḥîrāh
16 *lōʾ-tĕsulleh bĕketem ʾôpîr*
bĕšōham yāqār wĕsappîr
17 *lōʾ-yaʿarkennāh zāhāb ûzĕkôkît*
ûtĕmûrātāh kĕlî-pāz
18 *rāʾmôt wĕgābîš lōʾ yizzākēr*
ûmešek ḥokmâ mippĕnînîm
19 *lōʾ-yaʿarkennāh piṭdat-kûš*
bĕketem ṭāhôr lōʾ tĕsulleh}

5.3 Discussion

The function of vv. 15-19 in the poem is disputed. While Geller considers them to be a "digression from [the poem's] main topic,"[1] Gordis goes so far as to say that they are "indispensible on the grounds both of content and of the form."[2] The position taken in this study is closer to that of Geller, and in what follows I offer my rationale for considering these lines to be an exegetical interpolation—in fact the earliest commentary on the poem in Job 28—which was subsequently incorporated into the canonical edition.

As noted in ch. 4, vv. 14-19 are lacking in both OG and 11Q10, and this common lacuna is very likely more than coincidental (see discussion of vv. 14a-19b in ch. 4.3). Yet appeal to textual attestation alone can be misleading. As G. Thomas Tanselle has aptly argued, text criticism is ultimately governed by an aesthetic rationale, since texts of literary works are reconstructed on the basis of some literary standard that the critic has in mind.[3] As he states, "[A]ny text that a textual critic produces is itself the product of literary criticism, reflecting a particular aesthetic position and thus a particular approach to what textual 'correctness' consists of."[4] Such aesthetic judgment is naturally open to dispute, and I do not wish to be dogmatic about the position I take here. Nevertheless, it is appropriate to lay out some of my reasoning for excluding vv. 15-19 from my reconstruction of the wisdom poem in Job 28.

The canonical poem in Job 28 is governed by two primary semantic fields: area (a spatial metaphor) and value (a social metaphor).[5] Spatial metaphors pervade the bulk of the poem, as both a human and a divine explorer probe wisdom's "source," "place," "path," and "abode." The metaphor of value is limited to vv. 15-19, which focus, by contrast, on wisdom's *cost*. Vocabulary of the marketplace is dominant: gold, silver, and precious objects may not be "given," "weighed," "paid for," "estimated," or "exchanged."

The poem's basic contrast in the search for wisdom is presented in diptych: human royal expedition (vv. 1-11) versus divine cosmic building works (vv. 23-27). Both metaphors fall within the poem's spatial semantic field. Furthermore, these two sections hinge upon a group of

---

1 Geller, " 'Where is Wisdom?' " 175. See also the discussion of Budde, who considers the verses to be a secondary interpolation (*Das Buch Hiob*, 160).

2 Gordis, *The Book of Job*, 537.

3 Tanselle, *A Rationale of Textual Criticism*.

4 Ibid., 35.

5 Müllner, »Der Ort des Verstehens,« 63-65.

rhetorical questions in which wisdom's source, place, and abode are likewise prominent (vv. 12-14, 20-22). In my estimation, then, Geller is correct that vv. 15-19 are "secondary to the main line of poetic logic."[6] The extended reflection on wisdom's *cost* in these lines seems to be a digression from the poem's dominant concern with wisdom's *place*.

Job 28:15-19 is best understood against ancient Near Eastern merchant accounts. A Neo-Babylonian account from the reign of Nabonidus illuminates the basis of their rhetoric:

295 minas of copper from Yamana .... at 1 mina 38 ⅓ shekels,
55 minas of lapis lazuli .... at 36 ⅔ shekels,
152 minas of *ṭumânu*-fibers .... at 1 mina 42 shekels,
233 minas of alum from Egypt .... at 1 mina 17 ⅔ shekels,
32 minas 20 shekels of *inzaḫurētu*-dye .... at 48 ½ shekels,
130 minas of iron from Yamana .... at 32 ½ shekels,
257 minas of iron from Lebanon .... at 42 ⅔ shekels.[7]

While this consignment text gives the silver value of each entry, Job 28:15-19 repeatedly states that wisdom's value has no commercial standard—be it gold, silver, or precious ornaments. In seeking to exhaust the possibilities of any commodity that might be offered as payment for wisdom, these lines engage in a sort of *Listenwissenschaft*, an encyclopedic, if tedious, organization of knowledge (see also Ezek 27:12-24; Isa 3:18-23).[8] Verses 15-19 may be seen as an attempt to enumerate "every precious thing" (see v. 10b) to which wisdom cannot be compared.

The view that these lines may be understood as an adaptation of a merchant's account is strengthened by their high concentration of foreign words, which contributes to the metaphorical projection of commerce with distant, exotic lands. *Ketem* (vv. 16a, 19b) and *ʾôpîr* both appear to be Egyptian loan words, possibly referencing loci in or around ancient Egypt (though *ketem* was likely loaned into Egyptian from

6 Geller, " 'Where is Wisdom?' " 175.

7 YOS 6 168. Translation of A. Leo Oppenheim, "Essay on Overland Trade in the First Millennium B.C.," *JCS* 21 (1967): 237. On merchants, money, and trade in the ancient Near East, note especially Christopher R. Monroe, "Money and Trade," in *A Companion to the Ancient Near East* (ed. Daniel C. Snell; BCAW; Malden, Mass., Oxford, England, and Carlton, Victoria: Blackwell Publishing, 2005), 171-183; and Daniel C. Snell, "Methods of Exchange and Coinage in Ancient Western Asia," in *CANE* 3:1487-1496. See also the helpful discussion of Old Assyrian trade and the merchant outpost at Kanesh in Van De Mieroop, *A History of the Ancient Near East*, 89-93.

8 See Baldauf, »Menschliches Können und göttliche Weisheit,« 63. For a brief but helpful discussion of *Listenwissenschaft*, see van der Toorn, *Scribal Culture*, 118-125, and 313 nn. 38-42.

Sumerian). The connection of gold with Egypt would not be surprising, given that Egyptian gold mines were known throughout the ancient Near East from at least 3000 B.C.E.[9] *Kûš* in v. 19a also refers to a locus around Egypt. *Mĕḥîr* in v. 15b is an Akkadian loan word, as is *zĕkôkît* in v. 17a, and possibly *šōham* in v. 16b. The etymology of *piṭdâ* in v. 19a may be Sanskrit.[10]

These projections of foreign lands are carried through in the translations of the ancient versions, where the translators of the Heb. are themselves often dependent upon foreign loan words. The Tg. and Vg. are particularly dependent upon Gk. terms, and the translator of Syh. likewise remains content with Gk. glosses for words he does not understand. Syh. also connects Gk. ⁎ὄνυχι in v. 16 (translating Heb. *šōham*) to Arabia with the marginal comment: "onyx is the great stone of Ṭēmāʾ." Tg. translates *kesep* in v. 15b with *symʾ*, from Persian *saim*.

The language of vv. 15-19 is entirely "realistic," in contrast to the dialectic between more realistic and more figurative meanings in vv. 1-14, 20-27. Verses 15-19 also lack any cosmic overtones such as those attached to the human search in Section One (vv. 3-11) or the speech of Deep, Sea, Destruction, and Death in Section Two (vv. 14, 22). Befitting their thorough "realism," the literary structure of vv. 15-19 also exhibits a formality uncharacteristic of the remaining lines of the poem, as vv. 16-19 are arranged in a chiastic pattern A : B : C :: C : B : A with "paid for" : "pure gold" : "estimated" :: "estimated" : "pure gold" : "paid for."[11]

As with proverb collections, Job 28:15-19 strikes one as being "additive and aggregative,"[12] and its rhetoric seems to have been influenced by similar motifs on the high value of wisdom in proverbial texts such as Prov 3:14-15:[13]

> Her trade value is greater than that of silver,
> her yield more than gold.
> She is more precious than corals;
> All desirable things[14] cannot equal her.

9 Snell, *Life in the Ancient Near East*, 25.

10 However, Powels considers this unlikely (»Indische Lehnwörter in der Bibel,« 198).

11 Ceresko, *Job 29-31 in the Light of Northwest Semitic*, 152.

12 van der Toorn, *Scribal Culture*, 119.

13 Clines rightly points out, however, that "[N]ever in Proverbs is the *impossibility* of buying wisdom with silver and gold a theme, as it is here" (*Job 21-37*, 918).

14 Reading *ḥăpāṣîm* for MT's *ḥăpāṣêkā*, following LXX. See discussion in Michael V. Fox, *Proverbs 1-9: A New Translation with Introduction and Commentary* (AB 18A; New York: Doubleday, 2000), 156-157 and 379.

Indeed, the epigrammatic flavor of vv. 15-19 may indicate that their author perceived the proverbial structure already present in Job 28:1a, 12a, and 28aβ, and expanded it.

On the basis of the foregoing textual and literary observations, I would suggest that Job 28:15-19 was an exegetical interpolation into the body of the poem that was added in the context of a new edition.[15] Cuneiform literature offers a prime example of such expansion in the SB Gilg. epic.[16] The case of biblical literature is different, since we lack earlier editions like the Sum. and OB predecessors to the SB Gilg. epic. However, lacunae in the ancient versions—such the absence of MT's vv. 14-19 in OG and 11Q10—may provide such evidence indirectly.[17] Beyond this, arguments for intratextual expansions in the OT rest solely on internal literary criteria.[18]

One relevant literary criterion is the *Wiederaufnahme*, which is a repetitive resumption.[19] Van der Toorn describes it thus: "Where an expansion causes an interruption in the flow of the text, the movement resumes with a repetition of the words found just before the expansion; the inserted text is thereby bracketed by two phrases that are very similar if not identical."[20] Following this line of thinking, the nearly exact repetition of the poem's "refrain" in vv. 12 and 20 may be evidence of such bracketing in Job 28, with v. 20—or perhaps vv. 20-22—signaling the interpolation of new material in-between.[21]

This small structured commentary in vv. 15-19 was facilitated by the focus on precious metals and stones in Section One (vv. 1-3, 6, 10-11) and by *ʿerkāh* in v. 13a, interpreted as "its price" (see *its abode* in ch. 4.3). The typical word pair silver // gold in v. 1 is matched in v. 15 by a

15 On exegetical additions, or interpolations, see Emanuel Tov, *Textual Criticism of the Hebrew Bible* (2d rev. ed.; Minneapolis: Fortress; Assen: Royal Van Gorcum, 2001), 276, 281-284. On expansions in biblical and ancient Near Eastern literature in general, see especially van der Toorn, *Scribal Culture*, 125-32.

16 van der Toorn, *Scribal Culture*, 126-27; Jeffrey H. Tigay, *The Evolution of the Gilgamesh Epic* (Philadelphia, Pa.: University of Pennsylvania Press, 1982); and idem, "The Evolution of the Pentateuchal Narratives in the Light of the Evolution of the *Gilgamesh Epic*," in *Empirical Models for Biblical Criticism* (ed. Jeffrey H. Tigay; Philadelphia, Pa.: University of Pennsylvania Press, 1985), 21-52.

17 See the cautious comments of Tov, *Textual Criticism*, 278-79 n. 65.

18 Ibid., 281-282; van der Toorn, *Scribal Culture*, 130.

19 Curt Kuhl, »Die ›Wiederaufnahme‹—ein literarkritisches Prinzip?« *ZAW* 64 (1952): 1-11.

20 van der Toorn, *Scribal Culture*, 130.

21 Cf. Geller, " 'Where is Wisdom?' " 182 n. 35.

synonymous pair in reverse order: fine gold // silver.[22] ʿRK is also a *Leitwort* in vv. 15-19, occurring in v. 17a and 19a. The motifs of weighing as a method of payment might also anticipate "weights" and "measures" in Section Three (v. 25), even though the sense there is architectural.

These lines make up a clearly-defined unit. In addition to their chiastic construction, vv. 15-19 are bound together by the unabated repetition of *lōʾ*, which occurs seven times in five lines. It is repeated in each line at the borders of the passage (vv. 15a, b; vv. 19a, b). But in the middle couplets, it is gapped in the second line (vv. 16b, 17b, 18b). These verses are shot through with vocabulary for "gold." Three words are used: *sāgûr* (v. 15a [MT *sĕgôr*]), *zāhāb* (v. 17a), and *ketem* (vv. 16a [*ketem ʾôpîr*], 19b [*ketem ṭāhôr*]). The verb *tĕsulleh* occurs in vv. 16a and 19b, forming an *inclusio* around vv. 16-19, as does *ketem*. Likewise, *yaʿarkennāh* is a theme-word, appearing in vv. 17a and 19a and underlining an economy in which payment was made by weight and number (also *yiššākēl* in v. 15b).[23] Much of the remaining vocabulary in these lines denote various ornaments, which also functioned as a form of currency in the ancient world (note esp. *kĕlî* in v. 17b, indicating "ornaments").[24]

5.4 Commentary on Job 28:15-19

15a. ***Fine gold cannot be given in its place*** [*lōʾ-yuttan sāgûr taḥtêhā*; MT *sĕgôr*]: The versions differ in their interpretations of what seems to be the same consonantal text. Both LXX and Aq read MT's Qal passive *yuttan* as the active *yittēn* (Th ⁎δώσει).[25] However, the daughter ver-

22 Elwolde, "Non-Contiguous Parallelism," 111.

23 King and Stager, *Life in Biblical Israel*, 194.

24 Ibid., 276. See, for example, the OA letter in which Taram-Kubi writes to her husband, Innaya, who is an Assyrian merchant working in Kanesh in central Anatolia: "Tell Innaya; Taram-Kubi says: 'You wrote to me as follows: "Keep the bracelets and the rings that you have; they will be needed to buy food." It is true that you send me half a pound of gold through Ili-bani, but where are the bracelets that you have left behind?' " (Translation of Van De Mieroop, *A History of the Ancient Near East*, 92, after Céline Michel, *Correspondance des marchands de Kanish* [Paris: Cerf, 2001], 466).

25 See Joüon §58a for a discussion of how the old Gp forms relate to the Dp and Hp stems. In the prefix conjugation, "Proto-Semitic" **yuqtal(u)* developed into the primitive Heb. *yuqṭal*, which is preserved in BH and is identical to the Hp *yuqṭal*. Since √NTN has no active form in the H-stem, *yuttan* should be considered a Gp form (i.e., Qal passive). See already Canaanite *yu-da-an* and related forms (with suffixes) in the El-Amarna letters (e.g., EA 89:58).

sions translate with the passive voice (OL *non dabitur*; Syh. *lʾ ytl*), along with Vg. (*non dabitur*), Syr. (*lʾ mtyhb*), and Tg. (*lʾ ytyhb*).

The interpretation of Heb. SGWR (or perhaps SGR; MT *sĕgôr*) caused the versions more trouble.[26] LXX translates with "a closed place" (*συγκλεισμόν; also Syh. *ḥbwšʾ*). Aq reads similarly with "a shutting up" (ἀπόκλειστον). Jerome's OL, however, reads "shut up gold" (*aurum conclusum* [where *conclusum* is marked with an obelus]). About three years later, in 390, Jerome would change this reading to *aurum obrizum* ("pure gold") in the Vg., employing a loan word from the Gk. adjective ὄβρυζον ("pure"), which is used in Gk. literature to modify χρυσίον.[27] Tg. translates in a similar fashion with "refined gold" (*dhb snyn*), using the same root that rendered ZQQ in v. 1b. Syr. translates with *dhb*.

The form *sĕgôr* occurs only one other time in the OT—Hos 13:8—in the phrase *wĕʾeqraʿ sĕgôr libbām*, which NJPS aptly translates, "[I will] rip open the casing of their hearts." However, the form *sāgûr* occurs 7 times in the OT, where it modifies *zāhāb* (see *zāhāb sāgûr* in 1 Kgs 6:20, 21; 7:49, 50; 10:21; 2 Chr 4:20, 22; 9:20). The consonantal SGWR in Job 28:15 (MT *sĕgôr*) may be re-pointed to *sāgûr*, as an abbreviation for the phrase *zāhāb sāgûr*, just as *ʾôpîr* is used as an abbreviation for *ketem ʾôpîr* in Job 22:24. Such an interpretation is supported by Akk. evidence in which the root SGR / SKR also modifies gold (*ḫurāṣu sagru* or *ḫurāṣu sakru*). *CAD* suggests that the meaning of the root in this use has to do with heating, and thereby purifying, gold.[28] Alternatively, Manfred Görg has proposed that the term here means "rolled gold" (»Goldblech«), being a technical loan word from Eg. *sqr*, which has to do with beating gold into thin sheets.[29] But Erman and Grapow suggest that Heb. *sĕgôr* is cognate to Eg. *sgr* (»Verschluss«), not *sqr*.[30]

It is possible that the notion of purity or refinement found in Vg. and Tg. is simply a semantic extension of the gold's being hidden or

---

26 Ken. MSS 3, 82, 260, and 264 preserve the more conservative, and likely more original, consonantal text with SGR (*Vetus Testamentum Hebraicum*, 2:506).

27 Liddell and Scott, *A Greek-English Lexicon*, 1196, s.v.; Note also that Tg. uses a loanword into Aram. based on the same Gk. word (*ʾwbryzwn*) to translate MT's *pāz* in v. 17b (Tg. 1).

28 *CAD* S, 217, s.v. *sekru* A and 213-14, s.v. *sekēru* B. See also references cited in *AHw* 2:1003, s.v. *sagru*. Von Soden glosses it as "a gold alloy" (»eine Goldlegierung«).

29 Manfred Görg, »Ein Ausdruck der Goldschmiedekunst im Alten Testament,« *BZ* N. F. 28 (1984): 253-55. He is followed by Strauß, *Hiob 19,1-42,17*, 148. See Adolf Erman and Hermann Grapow, *Wörterbuch der Ägyptischen Sprache* (7 vols.; Leipzig: J. C. Hinrichs, 1926-31), 4:306 s.v.; and Raymond O. Faulkner, *A Concise Dictionary of Middle Egyptian* (Oxford: The Griffith Institute, 1962), 250 s.v.

30 Erman and Grapow, *Wörterbuch der Ägyptischen Sprache*, 4:319, s.v.

closed up, a more basic meaning of Heb. SGR. Delitzsch, however, suggests that "shut up" should be understood in the sense of "compressed, unmixed [gold]."[31] Alternatively, one could understand the term as used in 1 Kgs 6:20, 21; 7:49, 50; 10:21; 2 Chr 4:20, 22; 9:20 to be derived from a homonymous root meaning "to heat, refine" corresponding to Akk. *sekēru* B.[32] In this case one could translate the term here as "refined/fine (gold)."[33] Based on the Akk. semantic evidence, this meaning is to be preferred,[34] and MT's should be re-pointed as *sāgûr* as an abbreviation for the phrase *zāhāb sāgûr* (see also *BHK*, *BHS*).[35] The literary argument for this reading is strong as well. In v. 15, *sāgûr* (MT *sĕgôr*) is parallel to *kesep*, which reprises the parallelism of *kesep* // *zāhāb* in v. 1.

15b. ***Silver cannot be weighed for its purchase price*** [*wĕlōʾ yiššāqēl kesep mĕḥîrāh*]: The root ŠQL, which is used elsewhere in the OT in the Niphal with reference to weighing out silver or gold for payment (see Ezr 8:33), could possibly be understood as "to be taken, to be removed," in accord with the meanings of a homonymous ŠQL in cognate languages such as Off. Aram., Akk., Syr., and Mand.[36] However, this does not yield good sense in this context. In ancient Near Eastern commerce, ŠQL basically meant "to pay."[37] "Weighing" seems to be its only use in the OT, and the metaphor of measuring out or lining up wisdom against other precious objects dominates vv. 15-19 (see *tĕsulleh* in vv. 16a, 19b; *yaʿarkennāh* in vv. 17a, 19a).

Heb. *mĕḥîr* seems to be a loan word from Akk. *maḫīru*, "purchase, purchase price," from the verbal root *maḫāru*, "to accept, buy, sell, do business."[38] The meaning of Heb. *mĕḥîr* is nonetheless quite evident

---

31 Delitzsch, *Book of Job*, 2:106.

32 See Clines, who interprets the verb accordingly. He cites Arab. *sajara* as a cognate, but not Akk. *sekēru* (*Job 21-37*, 902 n. 15b).

33 *CAD* S, 213-14, s.v. *sekēru* B.

34 This is not to say, however, that BH *sĕgôr* or *sāgûr* are Akk. loan words. See the discussion of Paul V. Mankowski, *Akkadian Loanwords in Biblical Hebrew* (HSS 47; ed. Lawrence E. Stager; Winona Lake, Ind.: Eisenbrauns, 2000), 107-108

35 So also *Pope*, Job, 204; De Wilde, *Das Buch Hiob*, 274. This is also suggested by Beer (*Der Text des Buches Hiob*, 180); Duhm (*Das Buch Hiob erklärt*, 136); and Budde (*Das Buch Hiob*, 160) without recourse to Akkadian.

36 See evidence in *HALOT* 4:1642, s.v. ŠQL.

37 Wolfram von Soden, *The Ancient Orient: An Introduction to the Study of the Ancient Near East* (trans. Donald Schley; Grand Rapids, Mich.: Eerdmans, 1994), 124. Originally published as *Einführung in die Altorientalistik* (Darmstadt: Wissenschaftliche Buchgesellschaft, 1985).

38 *HALOT* 2:568-69, s.v. *mĕḥîr* I; *CAD* M/1, 92-98, s.v. *maḫīru*; and ibid., 50-71, s.v. *maḫāru*. It is likely that Eg. *mḫrw* / *mḫrw* is borrowed from Akkadian. For a brief discussion, see Mankowski, *Akkadian Loanwords*, 92 and n. 322.

from its uses in the OT, where it means "equivalent value, purchase price, money."[39] Before the invention of coinage by the Lydians in about 625 B.C.E., precious metals—especially silver—were weighed out or measured as forms of payment.[40]

16a. ***It cannot be paid for with the gold of Ophir*** [*lōʾ-tĕsulleh bĕketem ʾôpîr*]: While all the versions seem to be reading the same consonantal text, there are some differences in interpretation. The Gk. traditions are divided on how to interpret *tĕsulleh*. On the one hand, LXX (⁎οὐ συμβασταχθήσεται), Syh. (*lʾ ttṭʿn*), and Sym (οὐκ ἀντιδοθήσεται) understand the notion of comparison, weighing, or exchange (thus interpreting √SLH = √SLʾ). On the other hand, OL (*erit deteriora*) and Aq (οὐκ ἀναβληθήσεται) seem to read from √SLH I ("to treat as worthless" [Qal]; "to throw away" [Piel]).[41] Syr., Vg., and Tg. all concur with LXX, Syh., and Sym in translating √SLH as equivalent to √SLʾ. One Ken. MS reads *tĕsulleʾ* with final *ʾālep*.[42] Fohrer points to the OSA verb ŚLʾ, meaning "to pay" and the related substantive *ślʾm*, meaning "tribute."[43] Budde, on the other hand, suggests that it should be related to BH SLL ("to pile up" [Qal]; "to cherish" [Pilpel]).[44] In accord with LXX, Syh., Sym, Syr., Vg., and Tg., the root SLH functions as a byform of SLʾ here and in v. 19b. The Pual of SLʾ is used in a similar sense in Lam 4:2 with *paz*.

Heb. *ketem* is probably an Eg. loan word from *ktmt*.[45] In the Egyptian literature, *ktmt* is used of a kind of gold that is found in Nubia.[46] However, the Egyptian itself may be a loan word from Sum. ku-dim, which came into Akk. as *kutimmu*, meaning "goldsmith, silversmith."[47] Thus while Heb. *ketem* was most likely borrowed through Egyptian, its origins may, in fact, be Sumerian. The term occurs elsewhere in the OT

---

39 *HALOT* 2:569, s.v. *mĕḥîr* I.

40 Snell, *Life in the Ancient Near East*, 24, 106-107, 128-29; von Soden, *Ancient Orient*, 123-24.

41 Tur-Sinai also suggests reading from SLH I, explaining that "[W]isdom will not be mingled, alloyed even with the gold of Ophir, for gold is worthless like dross in comparison with it" (*The Book of Job*, 404).

42 MS 250 (Kennicott, *Vetus Testamentum Hebraicum*, 2:506).

43 Fohrer, *Das Buch Hiob*, 391 n. 16 a.

44 Budde, *Das Buch Hiob*, 160; cf. Peters, *Das Buch Job*, 303. See *HALOT* 2:757, s.v.

45 Lambdin, "Egyptian Loan Words in the Old Testament," 151-52.

46 Erman and Grapow, *Wörterbuch der Ägyptischen Sprache*, 5:145, s.v. *ktm.t*.

47 Ibid., 5:152. See also *CAD* K, 608-609, s.v. *kutimmu*. *Contra* Dhorme, who thinks that Heb. *ketem* should be related to Akk. *katāmu*, "to cover" (*Book of Job*, 408). Delitzsch would also relate *ketem* to Heb. *kātam* and Arab. *katama*, which he glosses "*occulere*" ("to cover;" *Book of Job*, 2:106).

in Job 28:19; 31:24; Ps 25:12; Song 5:11; Dan 10:5; and Lam 4:1. The phrase *ketem ʾôpîr* also occurs in Isa 13:12, Ps 45:10, and 4Q491c 1:11 (*ktm ʾwpyrym*). In Isa 13:12 and in 4Q491c 1:11 it parallels *paz*, and its scarcity is emphasized (see also *paz* in Job 28:17b). A similar phrase, *zhb ʾpr*, is found in an 8th-century ostracon from Tell Qasile, as well as in 1 Chr 29:4 and Sir 7:18.[48] The phrase "works of Ophir" also apparently refers to gold or treasure in 4Q405 23 ii 9 (*mʿśy ʾwpyrym*). Other OT texts mention gold coming from Ophir or ships going to Ophir to acquire gold (1 Kgs 9:28; 10:11; 22:49; 2 Chr 8:18; 9:10). In every case but one, this is to acquire gold for the building of Solomon's temple.

The locus of Ophir is problematic. It is connected with Yoqtan and Havilah in the Table of Nations in Gen 10:29 (see also 1 Chr 1:23). Locations in India, South Arabia, East Africa, and South Africa have also been proposed. Dhorme considers Arabia most likely on the basis of Gen 10:29 and Gen 2:11-12.[49] But in his study of Ophir, Vassilios Christidès distinguishes between *two* Ophirs—Yoqtan's Ophir and Solomon's Ophir—concluding that Yoqtan's Ophir is to be located in southern Arabia.[50]

The versions are not much help in detecting the locus of Ophir in Job 28:16. Most simply transliterate *ʾôpîr*. Sym renders the whole phrase *ketem ʾôpîr* as "chief-ranking gold" (χρυσίον πρωτεῖον). Vg. guesses with "the dyed colors of India" (*tinctis Indiae coloribus*), which may be a synecdoche for colored garments from India.[51]

The Egyptian loan words and place names in our text support a locus in or near Egypt. Even if this is not to be understood in realistic terms, it seems that Egypt is *à propos* as a metaphorical projection in this section. Cush is mentioned in v. 19a (*kuš*), which was originally a district south of the second Nile cataract, though the term would eventually be used to refer to all of Upper Nubia.[52] This meshes perfectly with the fact that Eg. *ktmt* ("gold"), appearing in Job 28:16 as *ketem ʾôpîr*, is typically said to have been found in the land of Nubia in the Egyptian literature.[53] Nubia is located just south of Upper Egypt below Elephantine and Aswan, though the border between Nubia and Egypt was not

---

48 *HI*, 403-404 (*Qas* 2).

49 Dhorme, *Book of Job*, 408. See also discussion in King and Stager, *Life in Biblical Israel*, 170-71, 183.

50 Vassilios Christidès, "L'énigma d'Ophir," *RB* (1970): 240-47.

51 Peters, *Das Buch Job*, 303.

52 Timothy Kendall, "Kush," in *The Oxford Encyclopedia of Ancient Egypt* (ed. Donald B. Redford; 3 vols.; Oxford: Oxford University Press, 2001), 2:250.

53 Erman and Grapow, *Wörterbuch der Ägyptischen Sprache*, 5:145, s.v. *ktm.t*.

always clear.[54] Finally, the orthography in LXX^B and LXX^S may also be suggestive of an Egyptian locus. LXX^B,S read Σωφίϱ as opposed to Ωφίϱ in LXX^A, which may reflect Egyptianized Greek by prefixing Eg. /s/ (used as a prefix in place names) to Ωφίϱ (> Σωφίϱ).[55]

16b. ***with precious carnelian or lapis-lazuli*** [*bĕšōham yāqār wĕsappîr*]: The exact identification of Heb. *šōham* is difficult, but it is most likely carnelian, based on the Akk. substantive *sāmtu* A, meaning "a red stone, mostly designating carnelian," related to the verbal root *sâmu*, "to become red."[56] This meaning may also be applied to Ug. *šmt*, which Lete and Sanmartín gloss as "reddish shade, carnelian."[57]

The versions in Job 28:16b translate with several different terms. LXX reads ⁎ὄνυχι, though a few other traditions render with σαϱδονυχίῳ.[58] OL and Syh. follow LXX with *onice* and *ᵓnwkywn*. Syh. also glosses this in the margin with ONΥXION, with an additional explanation that "onyx is the great stone of Ṭēmāᵓ." However, Vg. translates with *lapidi sardonycho* ("the stone of sardonyx"), employing a Gk. loan word from σαϱδόνυξ. However, Syr. translates with *brwlᵓ* ("beryl [stones]"), and is followed by Tg., which reads *byrwlyn*, both loan words from Gk. βηϱύλλιον. All of these renderings are found in the Gk. translations of *šōham* elsewhere in the LXX.[59] Though the diversity of interpretations in the ancient versions does not contribute to a singular interpretation of the term, "carnelian" seems the best translation in Job 28:16.

Carnelian and lapis lazuli were long prized in the ancient Near East and were in many cases obtainable only as imports. Highly prized carnelian beads from the Indus Valley and lapis lazuli from Afghanistan were imported from Elam in the mid-third millennium and begin to appear then in archaeological contexts in Babylonia.[60] The two often are

54 Derek A. Welsby, "Nubia," in *The Oxford Encyclopedia of Ancient Egypt* (ed. Donald B. Redford; 3 vols.; Oxford: Oxford University Press, 2001), 2:551.

55 Delitzsch, *Book of Job*, 2:106-107.

56 *CAD* S, 121-24, s.v. *sāmtu* A, and ibid., 131-32, s.v. *sâmu*. However, Ephraim Speiser disputes this identification ("The Rivers of Paradise," in *"I Studied Inscriptions from Before the Flood": Ancient Near Eastern, Literary, and Linguistic Approaches to Genesis 1-11* [eds. Richard S. Hess and David Toshio Tsumura; SBTS 4; ed. David W. Baker; Winona Lake, Ind.: Eisenbrauns, 1994], 181. Originally published in *Festschrift Johannes Friedrich zum 65. Geburtstag am 27. August 1958 gewidmet* [ed. A. Moortgat et al.; Heidelberg: Carl Winter, 1959], 473-85).

57 *DUL*, 2:831, s.v.

58 Field, *Origenis Hexaplorum quae supersunt*, 2:50.

59 For evidence, see *HALOT* 4:1424, s.v. *šōham* I.

60 Van De Mieroop, *A History of the Ancient Near East*, 51; Snell, *Life in the Ancient Near East*, 23.

named together in Canaanite textile lists for deities[61] and in Mesopotamian mythic and epic texts. A noteworthy example of the latter is Gilgamesh's journey beyond Mt. Mashu, where he stumbles upon a magical garden, where trees bear carnelian (^{na4}*sāmtu* (GUG)) and lapis-lazuli (^{na4}*uqnû* (ZA.GÌN)).[62]

Heb. *šōham* occurs 10 times outside our passage in the OT (Gen 2:12; Exod 25:7; 28:9, 20; 35:9, 27; 39:6, 13; Ezek 28:13; 1 Chr 29:2). In Gen 2:12, it is said to be found in the land of Havilah. It occurs together with *sappîr* in descriptions of the priestly breastplate in Exod 28:18-20 and 39:11-13, as well as in Ezek 28:11, where both describe Eden, the garden of God. See discussion of *sappîr*, "lapis-lazuli," under *a place of lapis is its stones* in ch. 4.3.

17a. ***Neither gold nor glass can be estimated against it*** [*lōʾ yaʿarkennāh zāhāb ûzĕkôkît*; MT *yaʿarkennâ*]: Despite the fact that the *mappîq* is lacking in the final *hê* of *yaʿarkennāh*, the letter is certainly consonantal (see also v. 19a). The *mappîq* is often lost in the 3fs pronominal suffix (GKC §91e, 58g, 23k), as noted with MT's *mimmennāh* in Job 28:5a (see *A land from which food springs forth* in ch. 4.3).

The verb ʿRK has to do with arranging, setting in order, lining up, etc. As is evident from the Heb. substantive *ʿērek*, this "lining up" may be used of assessing value (see Lev 27:15, 19; 2 Kgs 23:35; 4Q159 ii 6), and such seems to be the case in Job 28:17. This meaning is also found with nouns in Punic (*ʿrk*$_2$, *ʿrk*$_1$) and in Ug. (*ʿrk* (I)).[63] The singular number of the verb suggests that *zāhāb* and *zĕkôkît* are itemized ("Neither gold nor glass"), not grouped together ("gold and glass"). The same is true with *rāʾmôt* and *gābîš* with the singular verb *yizzākēr* in v. 18a. Blommerde correctly points out that the 3fs suffix here and in v. 19a is datival.[64]

Heb. *zĕkôkît* is a *hapax legomenon* in the OT. Its meaning is relatively certain, however, based on Semitic cognates and on the translations of the ancient versions. LXX translates with ∗ὕαλος ("crystal"), while OL renders *vitrum* ("glass"). Syh. translates with the Aramaic cognate *zgwgtʾ*, having the same meaning. Other Gk. sources read κρύσταλλος

---

61 *CTU* 4.168 and 3.182. See also the mythic text *CTU* 1.23. Citations in *DUL*, 2:831, s.v. *šmt*.

62 See SB Gilg. IX.173-75 in George, *BGE*, 1:672-73. Dhorme also notes that these two occur together in the *Descent of Ishtar into the Netherworld* (*Book of Job*, 409).

63 *DNWSI*, 887-88, s.v. *ʿrk*$_2$ ("evaluation"); and ibid., 888, s.v. *ʿrkh*$_1$ ("estimate, valuation"); *DUL*, 1:182, s.v. *ʿrk* (I) ("bookkeeping account, list, fiscal evaluation").

64 Blommerde, *Northwest Semitic Grammar and Job*, 8, 107. See Joüon §125ba.

διαφανής ("transparent crystal").[65] Vg. (*vitrum*) and Syr. (*zgwgyt*ʾ) translate the same way as the daughter versions of LXX, while Tg. 1 translates similarly with *ʾsplyd*ʾ ("cut glass"). Tg. 2 uses the cognate *zkwkyt*ʾ.

Cognates are attested in numerous dialects of Aram., including Syr., Mand., and Jewish Palestinian Aram., all meaning "glass." One also finds Arab. *zajāj* and Akk. *zakakātu*. Based on the study of Fränkel, Driver and Gray suggest that the Arab. is a loan from the Aram.[66] *HALOT* suggests that the Aram. is itself a loan from the Akk., which is no doubt correct.[67] Thus, the Akk. evidence is primary.[68] In its attestations in SB, *zakakatu* seems to refer to a glaze or glass that was the color of lapis-lazuli (i.e., blue).[69] Garber and Funk note that opaque glass in various colors was found in Egyptian remains dating from the third millennium. These were "used as a substitute for precious stones, especially in inlaying of ornaments and utensils."[70]

17b. *Ornaments of pure gold are not its exchange* [*ûtĕmûrātāh kĕlî-pāz*]: The noun *tĕmûrâ* only occurs 5 times outside of our passage in the OT, 2 of these being in the Book of Job (Job 15:31; 20:18; Lev 27:10, 33; Ruth 4:7; see also *tmwr* in Sir 3:14; 4:10).[71] It may refer to a substituted item or, more abstractly, to value connected with that item. While LXX translates the Heb. substantive with a noun (*τὸ ἄλλαγμα αὐτῆς ["its exchange"]), Sym renders for sense with a related verb, ἀντικαταλλαγήσεται ("it will not be exchanged"), rightly supposing the gapping of *lō*ʾ in the second line of the couplet.[72] Jerome's rendering in the Vg. is similar with *non commutabuntur* ("nor will they be exchanged"). Tg^{C,S}, and numerous other MSS reflect MT's nominal construction with *pyrwgh* ("its exchange;" Tg. 1). Syr. here begins to be freer and seems to add phrases in vv. 17-18, perhaps dividing the consonantal Heb. text differently than MT.

Johannes de Rossi also notes 11 Heb. MSS that read *kĕlê* rather than *kĕlî*.[73] This may be inconsequential, however, since MT's *kĕlî* may be

65 Field, *Origenis Hexaplorum quae supersunt*, 2:50.

66 See Driver and Gray, *Job*, 2:196, and citation there.

67 *HALOT* 1:269, s.v. *zĕkôkît*.

68 See Mankowski, *Akkadian Loanwords*, 52-54.

69 *CAD* Z, 15, s.v. *zakakatu*.

70 Garber and Funk, "Jewels and Precious Stones," *IDB* 2:901. See also Gordis, *The Book of Job*, 309; and the helpful discussion in De Wilde, *Das Buch Hiob*, 275.

71 For the Heb. text of Ben Sira, see Vattioni, *Ecclesiastico*, 17, 21.

72 Ken. MS 153 reads *lō*ʾ in the second line. Though it is the correct interpretation, its textual authenticity is doubtful (*Vetus Testamentum Hebraicum*, 2:506).

73 de Rossi, *Variae Lectiones*, 4:123.

interpreted as a non-conventional collective (*IBHS* §7.2.1d).[74] In fact, LXX (*σκεύη), Sym (σκεύεσι), Vg. (*vasa*), and Tg. 1 (*mʾny*) all interpret *kĕlî* in this fashion. Heb. *kĕlî* may have the sense "ornament" or "finery," as in Exod 3:22 and Isa 61:10.[75]

Heb. *paz* occurs outside our passage only 7 other times in the OT (Isa 13:12; Ps 19:11; 21:4; Prov 8:19; Song 5:11, 15; Lam 4:2; but see also Sir 30:15). It is parallel to *zāhāb* here and in Ps 19:11. It also occurs with *zāhāb* in Ps 119:127 and with *ḥārûṣ* in Prov 8:19, where the syntax suggests a heightening from these terms to *paz*. Thus *paz* in that context seems to surpass both *zāhāb* and *ḥārûṣ* in value, though the parallelism in Isa 13:12 (// *ketem ʾôpîr*) and its use together with *ketem* in Song 5:11 suggests that it may be equivalent to or inferior to *ketem*.[76] The meaning "fine gold" is secure, and is found also in later Heb. and Aram.[77] Ug. *pḏ* may also have this meaning.[78]

18a. ***Neither pearls nor rock crystal should be mentioned*** [*rāʾmôt wĕgābîš lōʾ yizzākēr*]: The meaning of *rāʾmôt* is uncertain. It occurs only 2 other times in the OT, in Ezek 27:16 and Prov 24:7. In the Ezekiel passage, *rāʾmôt* is said to have been traded to Tyre from Edom.[79] In Prov 24:7, √RʾM may be understood to be a byform or dialectical variant of √RWM (see also *rāʾămâ* in Zech 14:10), or the text may be corrupt.[80] Most of the versions understand *rāʾmôt* in Job 28:18 to be related to RWM, an identification possibly facilitated by the orthography preserved in Ken. MSS 170 and 259 (*rāmôt*).[81] LXX translates with *μετέωρα ("high places"), while Sym translates similarly with ὑψηλὰ ("cultic high places;" preserved in Syh. as *rmtʾ*). Vg. and OL both translate with *excelsa* ("high things"). But Tg. reads *sndlnyn* ("sardonyx"), a corruption of Gk. σαρδόνυξ, σαρδόνυχος.[82] Syr. translates with *ṭbʿʾ* ("signet gems"). The translator of LXX-Ezek 27:16 was unsure about the

74 Cf. Driver and Gray, *Job*, 2:196.

75 *HALOT* 2:479, s.v.

76 Cf. Dhorme, *Book of Job*, 409.

77 See Jastrow, *Dictionary*, 2:1149-50, s.v. *pāz* and ibid., s.v. *pĕzôzāʾ*, *pîzûzāʾ*.

78 *DUL*, 2:664, s.v.

79 Reading *ʾĕdōm* with 25 Heb. MSS and the translations of Aq and Sym over against MT, which reads *ʾăram*, ("Aram"), due to graphic confusion between *rêš* and *dālet* in the Aramaic square script. It also seems possible, however, that Pabuli's "Udum" in the Kirta narrative is in view, but one can only speculate, since identification of this place is uncertain.

80 *HALOT* 3:1163, s.v. RʾM, suggests that this root is an Aramaic spelling of Heb. RWM due to dialectical variation.

81 Kennicott, *Vetus Testamentum Hebraicum*, 2:506.

82 Jastrow, *Dictionary*, 2:1005, s.v. *sandalkôn*.

meaning of the term in that context and so simply transcribed it as Ραμωθ. However, Vg. there translated with the anachronistic *sericum* ("silk").

Aside from the ancient versions, there are two main interpretations of *rā'môt*: "coral" or "pearls."[83] The possible Ug. cognate, *rimt*, is probably best translated "corals" in that literature, but its meaning is uncertain.[84] Rashi interprets Heb. *rā'môt* as "precious stones in the sea."[85] In his *Book of Roots*, David Kimchi glosses "coral" for *rā'môt* (אלמוגים or קורל).[86] Steven Byington, however, argues on the basis of Ezekiel's geographical notations that *rā'môt* means "pearls" and not "red coral" or "black coral."[87] Either "pearls" or "corals" for *rā'môt* would fit the context in Job 28:18a. The parallel *pĕnînîm* in v. 18b suggests something from the sea, though *pĕnînîm*, too, has been interpreted as both "pearls" and "coral." Delitzsch may be correct that "the ancient appellations of these precious things that belong to the sea are... blended."[88] Yet given the fact that *pĕnînîm* are described as "red" (*'ādĕmû*) in Lam 4:7, *pĕnînîm* seems to denote "corals," while *rā'môt* means "pearls." This distinction can be upheld in Job 28:18.

---

83 However, Arab. *ra'mat*, translated as "sea shells," has also been invoked to clarify Heb. *rā'môt*. Julius Wellhausen, *Reste arabischen Heidentums* (2d ed.; Berlin: G. Reimer, 1897), 163; See citations in *DUL*, 2:274, s.v.; *HALOT* 3:1164, s.v. *rā'môt* I.

84 The meaning "corals" is suggested by the immediately preceding context in *CTU* 1.3 iii 1-2. Here Anat "beautifies herself with murex, [Which] comes [from a thousand acres] in the sea" (*CTU* 1.3 iii 1-2; translation of Mark Smith, "The Baal Cycle," 109). Fohrer interprets it as a piece of jewelry worn on the breast (»Brustschmuck;« *Das Buch Hiob*, 391 n. 18a), as does Pope (*Job*, 204). However, *DUL* glosses it as " 'zither,' as a 'loved' object" (2:724, s.v.). The comments of Mark Smith, following Jonas Greenfield, reflect the same line of thought. He offers the reasonable suggestion that it is "Perhaps a stringed musical instrument in the shape of a bull's head" (hence *rimt* related to *rumm*, 'bulls' or 'buffalo') ("The Baal Cycle," 167 n. 56). He thus translates *CTU* 1.3 iii 4-5: "[She takes her harp in her hand,] / [P]uts the lyre to her breast," where *knr* // *rimt* ("The Baal Cycle," 109). As an alternative explanation for the meaning "coral" for Ug. *rimt* and its relation to *rumm*, note Delitzsch's comments about Heb. *rā'môt* which suggest that √R'M was applied to corals since the ancients thought they looked like wild oxen horns (Delitzsch, *Book of Job*, 2:109 n. 2). The same could be said, perhaps, for Ug. *rimt*. See also the context in which *rimt* occurs in *CTU* 1.7:22 and *CTU* 1.101:17.

85 A. J. Rosenberg, ed., *The Book of Job: A New Translation* (Judaica Books of the Holy Writings; New York: The Judaica Press, 1989), 146-147.

86 *Sepher Ha Shorashim* (Venice: n.pub., 1746), 221, s.v. RWM.

87 Steven T. Byington, "Hebrew Marginalia III," *JBL* 64 (1945): 340-41.

88 Delitzsch, *Book of Job*, 2:108. Similarly Gustav Hölscher, who cites Arab. evidence: »Im orientalischen Sprachgebrauch werden übrigens Korallen und Perlen oft verwechselt« (*Das Buch Hiob*, 73). Note also the comments of Norbert Peters: »Die Unterschied ist nicht eben groß, wenn man an Perlen aus durchbohrten runden Korallenstückchen denkt« (*Das Buch Job*, 304).

Heb. *gābîš* is a *hapax legomenon* in the OT, though Heb. *ʾelgābîš* is attested 3 times in Ezekiel (Ezek 13:11, 13; 38:22), where it clearly signifies "hail stones" or "lumps of ice."[89] Akk. *gamēsu* is used for precious stones or pendants, while *algamešu* may signify a soft stone, more specifically steatite.[90] However, *al-gu-MES* in one Akk. text seems to be used for a piece of jewelry.[91] The Ug. *hapax legomenon algbṯ* seems to be used of stones in general in *CTU* 4.158:15.[92]

Delitzsch helpfully points out that the ancients often used the same terms for glass and crystal and that they also seemed to believe that crystal was a product of the cold.[93] This is suggested by Pliny's account in his *Historia Naturalis*: "A cause to the contrary to the one mentioned is responsible for creating rock-crystal, for this is hardened by excessively intense freezing… that it is a kind of ice is certain."[94] The semantic range of Gk. κρύσταλλος ("ice" and "rock-crystal") also suggests this belief. Thus a meaning such as "crystal" or "glass" for *gābîš* in Job 28:18 would not be a surprising in light of the fact that *ʾelgābîš* means "ice" in its three occurrences in Ezekiel. In fact, *gābîš* is translated "crystal" in numerous Tg. MSS, which read *pyrwṣyn* or *byrwṣyn*.[95]

The Gk. translator does not understand the Heb. term and thus transliterates with γαβίς. However, Sym (ὑπερηρμένα; Syh. marg. *mʿlytʾ*) and Vg. (*eminentia*) translate as "lofty things," understanding *gābîš* to be related to Heb. *gābaš*, meaning "to be high, piled up."[96] Syr. seems to understand it as "beads" (*ḥwmrʾ*), while Tg[S,M] read "beryl" (*byrwryn*), from Gk. βηρύλλιον.

Heb. *yizzākēr* in this context is best interpreted in the sense of "to be named" or even "to be praised," both common in the Niphal.[97] In this respect, ZKR here is used in a similar fashion to Akk. *zakāru* A, "to invoke, declare, utter," etc.[98] As in v. 17a, the singular verb requires itemizing *rāʾmôt* and *gābîš* rather than treating them as a compound subject.

---

89 *HALOT* 1:51, s.v.

90 *CAD* G, 32, s.v. *gamēsu* and *CAD* A/1, 337-38, s.v. *algamešu*.

91 *CAD* A/1, 338, s.v. *algamešu*.

92 *DUL*, 1:54-55, s.v.

93 Delitzsch, *Book of Job*, 2:108.

94 Pliny, *Natural History* (10 vols.; LCL; Cambridge: Harvard University Press, 1938-1962), 37.9.23 (trans. D. E. Eichholz).

95 See Jastrow, *Dictionary*, 1:166, s.v. **birûṣîn*.

96 Ibid., 1:209, s.v. Dhorme suggests, rather, that Vg. and Sym connect it with Heb. GB, GBʿ (*Book of Job*, 409). But a derivation from *gābaš* seems more likely.

97 Compare the remarks of Clines, *Job 21-37*, 903 n. 18c.

98 *HALOT* 1:269-71, s.v. ZKR I; *CAD* Z, 16-22, s.v. *zakāru* A.

18b. ***A sack of wisdom is more precious than corals*** [*ûmešek ḥokmâ mippĕnînîm*]: The nominal form *mešek* occurs only here and in Ps 126:6. Unfortunately, its meaning in the Psalter is not very clear and thus cannot contribute conclusively to a discussion of *mešek* in Job 28:18. The verbal root MŠK occurs throughout the OT, however, with the sense "to pull, draw, drag." It may also mean "to grasp" (see Eccl 2:3). The Gk. translator, in fact, interprets MŠK in Job 28:18 as a finite verb (or an infc.) with ⁎ἕλκυσον ("he drew"), as does Vg. with *trahitur* ("is dragged"). Aq reflects MTQ rather than MŠK with γλυκύ ("sweet"). Only Tg. reads a substantive with *ngdʾ* ("load, freight"). It is difficult to say how Syr. translates *mešek* or if it does at all.

Driver and Gray translate *mešek* as "acquisition" in Job 28:18, and they suggest that the notion of preciousness is central there and in Ps 126:6. They propose that its use in Job 28:18 may allude to dragging out pearls from the sea.[99] Cohen has also suggested the translation "acquisition," though without mention of possible allusions to dragging the sea for pearls.[100] This meaning is also proffered by Niccacci and others.[101] Like Driver and Gray, Beer sees a possible connection to fishing out pearls in v. 18, and he offers the translation: »Fischen.«[102]

However, Yahuda believes that the word in our passage signifies a bracelet. He bases this on Arab. *masak*, which describes "arm bracelets or anklets made from amber or ivory pellets," and on wisdom's comparison with expensive jewelry in the OT and other Semitic literature (cf. Prov 1:9; 3:22; 6:21).[103] Yahuda thus translates v. 18b: »Ein Armband von Weisheit ist kostbarer als [ein solcher] von Perlen.«[104] However, he makes no comment about *mešek* in Ps 126:6.

HALOT glosses *mešek* with "leather pouch," citing cognates in several Aram. dialects, Arab., Akk., and Eg. which relate to skin or leather.[105] The root MŠK meaning "skin" or "pelt" is also attested in inscriptions in Off. Aram. and Palmyrene Aram.[106] The meaning "(leather) pouch" is certainly possible in Ps 126:6, and the editors of *HALOT* suggest the same understanding in Job 28:18. Köhler also trans-

---

99 Driver and Gray, *Job*, 1:214; 2:196.

100 Cohen, "Studies in Hebrew Lexicography," *AJSL* 40/3 (1924): 175.

101 Niccacci, "Giobbe 28," 31-32 and n. 17.

102 Beer, *Der Text des Buches Hiob*, 181.

103 Yahuda, »Hapax Legomena im Alten Testament,« 704 (»die aus Bernstein- oder Elfenbeinkügelchen hergestellten Arm- oder Fussspangen«).

104 Ibid.

105 *HALOT* 2:646, s.v. *mešek* I. See also Ludwig Köhler, »Hebräische Vokabeln II,« *ZAW* 55 (1937): 162, for comparative evidence.

106 *DNWSI* 2:700, s.v. *mšk*₁.

lates "leather bag" in both OT texts, suggesting that this meaning is ultimately derived from the verbal *māšak*, meaning "to pull, drag."[107] Thus: "to pull off" > "pulled off skin" > "leather (pouch)."

In the context of Job 28:15-19, any of the proposed meanings may be fitting. The context provided by the terms *rāʾmôt* and *pĕnînîm* in v. 18, both of which are found in the sea, suggests the possibility of understanding *mešek* in Job 28:18 as an allusion to dragging the ocean for pearls or pulling out corals.[108] This physical act may be abstracted to "acquisition," as Driver and Gray suggest.[109] However, it is best to understand the term here to mean "sack, bag," as suggested by *HALOT* and supported by the inscriptional evidence in cognate languages. This meaning is also fitting in Ps 126:6. The expression "a sack of wisdom" in Job 28:18 participates in the metaphor of value which dominates vv. 15-19, portraying wisdom as an object which can be weighed and measured as a form of payment.

Both Th and Vg. had difficulty with *pĕnînîm*. Th reads ⁎ἐσώτατα ("innermost things"), a Gk. word related to ἔσωθεν, which sometimes renders *mippĕnîmâ* (lit. "within") in the LXX (3 Kgdms 6:19; 2 Chr 3:4; see also 3 Kgdms 6:30 and Ezek 41:3, where ἐσώτερος, ἐσώτατος translates *pĕnîmâ*).[110] In the most conservative orthography, the consonantal text of MT would have been MPNNM. With the haplography of a *nûn*, the text would have been MPNM, possibly interpreted as *mippĕnīmā*, which would explain LXX's otherwise odd translation. Heb. *mippĕnîmâ* is connected to descriptions of the innermost room of the temple in 1 Kgs 6:19, 21, etc. Vg. also reads in this fashion with *de occultis* ("from obscurity"). Syh. explains its translation of the LXX (*hlyn dsgy gwyn*; "those things which are very internal") with a marginal gloss: *ʿwmqʾ* ("depth"). Aq, however, reflects Heb. *pĕnînîm* with τὰ περίβλεπτα ("distinguished things").[111] Tg. supports MT with *mrglyyn*, meaning "gems, jewels, pearls" (cf. Gk. μαργαρίτης).

---

107 Köhler, »Hebräische Vokabeln II,« 162.

108 Gary Martin offers the interesting possibility that the term *mešek* is used to conjure up the difficulty of the process of gathering pearl-producing oysters and of extracting pearls from them ("Elihu and the Third Cycle in the Book of Job," 192).

109 Still more meanings have been offered. Rowley's "price" seems to be related to the explanation of Driver and Gray for "acquisition" (*The Book of Job*, 183). De Wilde also suggests "worth" or "price," positing that these meanings may be derived from the sphere of 'pulling in' a profit from the point of view of a salesperson (*Das Buch Hiob*, 276). Ehrlich suggests "attraction" (»die Anziehung;« *Randglossen*, 6:292). Dhorme translates "extraction" (*Book of Job*, 409).

110 Hatch and Redpath, *A Concordance to the Septuagint*, 559, s.v. ἔσωθεν and ἐσώτερος, ἐσώτατος.

111 Ziegler, *Beiträge zum griecheschen Iob*, 60.

Heb. *pěnînîm* occurs 5 times outside of this passage in the OT (Prov 3:15 [*Qere*]; 8:11; 20:15; 31:10; Lam 4:7; but see also Sir 7:19; 30:15; 31:6). In two cases, wisdom is said to be more valuable than *pěnînîm* (Prov 3:15 [*Qere*]; 8:11). In Prov 20:15, "lips of knowledge" are said to be a more valuable object than gold or "much *pěnînîm*." In Prov 31:10, it is the "valiant woman" instead of wisdom who is more precious than *pěnînîm*. Lam 4:7 suggests that *pěnînîm* are red (*ʾāděmû*), and on that basis *pěnînîm* are probably best interpreted as "corals."

19a. ***Topaz stones of Cush cannot be estimated against it*** [*lōʾ-yaʿarkennāh piṭdat-kûš;* MT *yaʿarkennâ*]: On *yaʿarkennāh,* see discussion under *Neither gold nor glass can be estimated against it* in v. 17a. Heb. *piṭdâ* only occurs 3 times outside of our passage (Exod 28:17; 39:10; Ezek 28:13). It is sometimes translated as "chrysolite" (NJPS, NRSV), though LXX and Vg. suggest "topaz" (*τοπάζιον; *topazius*).[112] The Gk. semantic evidence could be misleading, however, if Delitzsch is correct that *piṭdâ* is derived from τόπαζ by transposition of consonants.[113] Alternatively, both Köhler and Pope have suggested that this word may ultimately have its origins in Sanskrit. That *piṭdâ* is a foreign loan word is suggested in part by the non-Semitic phonetic structure in which *ṭêt* and *dālet* occur in immediate succession.[114] While Pope believes it is ultimately to be derived from Sanskrit *tapas,* meaning "heat, fire,"[115] Köhler and others associate BH *piṭdâ* with Sanskrit words for "yellow."[116] However, Sylvia Powels denies its Indian origin.[117]

The *dālet* in *piṭdâ* lacks the expected *dāgēš* if the preceding *šěwāʾ* marks the close of the first syllable. On this basis, one could argue that the *ḥîreq* in the first syllable is long /ī/, and that the word was pronounced *pīṭědâ*. In light of the fact that it is very likely a non-Semitic loan word, one cannot be certain. But in its two occurrences in the Samaritan Pentateuch, which employs the internal *matres lectionis yôd* and

112 It may be, however, that what was called "topaz" in ancient times is now called "chrysolite," as suggested by De Wilde (*Das Buch Hiob*, 276).

113 Delitzsch, *Book of Job*, 2:109.

114 Powels, »Indische Lehnwörter,« 197.

115 Pope suggests that the Gk. τοπάζιον was derived from Sanskrit *tapas* (*Job*, 204). But he also seems to imply that the Heb. was borrowed from the Gk., not the Sanskrit (cf. Delitzsch, *Book of Job*, 2:109).

116 Köhler points to Sanskrit *pîta*, meaning "yellow" (»Hebräische Vokabeln II,« 169). Cf. *BDB*, 809, s.v.; De Wilde, *Das Buch Hiob*, 276. Hölscher (*Das Buch Hiob*, 71) and Peters (*Das Buch Job*, 304) also cite Sanskrit *pîtâšman*, meaning "yellow stone."

117 Powels, »Indische Lehnwörter,« 198.

wāw much more frequently than MT, the orthography is *pṭdh*, not *pyṭdh*.[118]

An alternative explanation is that the *ḥîreq* is short and that the *šĕwāʾ* may be explained as the "medium *šĕwāʾ*" which marks a vowel that was once pronounced but has now disappeared. This, however, is dubious. The existence of the so-called "medium *šĕwāʾ*" is still very questionable. Furthermore, this rule would only apply to a Semitic word. It seems best to assume the pronunciation *piṭdâ* with a short /i/, where the *dālet* has become spirantized from an original plosive (see GKC §10d).

Syr. again reflects a garbled text or, more likely, "midrashic" exegesis, as it translated the phrase *piṭdat-kûš* at least two times.[119] It first translates Heb. *piṭdâ* with *mrgnytʾ* ("pearls"), but it is also clear that *pdtʾ* ("ephod") is a phonological play on the Heb. as well. The latter translation may perhaps be explained by the fact that *piṭdâ* is listed among the stones in the priestly breastplate in Exod 28:17; 39:10. Tg. translates *piṭdâ* as green or yellow pearls (*mrglʾ yrqʾ*), which fits Pliny's remarks about the nature of *peridot* in *Historia Naturalis*.[120] If Eichholz is correct that "Oriental topaz seems to be included under *Chrysolithi*,"[121] then one could translate Heb. *piṭdâ* either as "chrysolite" or as "topaz," though "topaz" finds more support in the ancient versions (LXX, Vg.).

The linking of *piṭdâ* with *kûš* in Job 28:19 suggests a locus around Egypt. Pliny mentions sources that suggest "Topazos" to be the name of an island in the Red Sea.[122] Pope suggests the island of Zabarqad.[123] Cush was originally a district south of the second Nile cataract, though it eventually came to designate of Upper Nubia. LXX and Vg. suggest Ethiopia (Αἰθιοπίας; *Aethiopia*).

---

118 On the character of the Samaritan Pentateuch, see Bruce K. Waltke, "Samaritan Pentateuch," *ABD* 5:936-38. Text in Abraham Tal, *The Samaritan Pentateuch, Edited According to MS 6 (C) of the Shekhem Synagogue* (Texts and Studies in the Hebrew Language and Related Subjects 8; ed. Aron Dotan; Tel Aviv: Tel Aviv University 1994). My thanks to Bruce Waltke for a helpful discussion on Samaritan orthography.

119 See Szpek, "On the Influence of the Targum," 154 n. 56; Beer, *Der Text des Buches Hiob*, 182. For double translations in the Peshitta to Job, see Rignell, "Notes on the Peshiṭta of the Book of Job," 101-102, 104; Szpek, *Translation Technique*, 153-160. On double translations in Job 28 in particular, see Baumann, »Die Verwendbarkeit der Pešita,« (1899), 20; and Rignell, *The Peshitta to the Book of Job*, 221-223.

120 See also Garber and Funk, "Jewels and Precious Stones," *IDB* 2:902.

121 Pliny, *Natural History*, 10:250 note c. (Eichholz, LCL).

122 Ibid., 37.32.107-110.

123 Pope, *Job*, 204.

19b. ***It cannot be paid for with pure gold*** [*bĕketem ṭāhôr lōʾ tĕsulleh*]: For a discussion of *ketem* and *tĕsulleh*, see *It cannot be paid for with the gold of Ophir* in v. 16a. Vg. again guesses at *ketem* with *tincturae* ("color, dye"). While Sym translated *tĕsulleh* in v. 16a with ἀντιδιδόναι, he translates here with ἀντιτίθημι, though the sense is essentially the same. Tg^{M} contains a variant reading re-asserting the impossibility that a person could find wisdom with a low price and that one who does not guard it will be broken like glass. This variant is found after v. 17 in Tg^{L}.

Chapter Six: Conclusions

Bishop Lowth commented in his lecture on the poetry of Job: "Such a diversity of opinions has prevailed in the learned world concerning the nature and design of the Poem of Job, that the only point in which commentators seem to agree, is the extreme obscurity of the subject."[1] In the modern period, at least, that has been no less true of Job 28, which, as Newsom points out, is one of the most contested parts of the book.[2] This study, however, has made strides toward solving some of its perceived difficulties in several key areas, which I summarize here.

6.1 Poetic Language in Job 28

Upon consideration of its poetic strategies, it is not difficult to see how the poem has earned its reputation as "one of the most exquisite poetic compositions of the entire Bible."[3] The piece is image-driven, and its poet seems particularly attentive to diction, choosing words to maximize effect, and often creating semantic and phonological puns.[4] The dense rhetoric—especially evident in Section One—depends upon both "realistic" and "figurative" planes of meaning that may be interpreted in different ways in reading and re-reading the poem. This literal-metaphorical dialectic intermittently draws the reader down from the literal surface into the deeper symbolic and cosmic connotations of the poem's rich language. At the climax of the first section, the figurative

---

1 Robert Lowth, "Lecture XXXII: Of the Poem of Job," in *Lectures on the Sacred Poetry of the Hebrews* (trans. G. Gregory; 2 vols.; London: J. Johnson, 1787), 345. Originally published as *De sacra poesi Hebraeorum: praelectiones academicae Oxonii habitae: subjicitur Metricae Harianae brevis confutatio, et Oratio Crewiana : notas et epimetra adiecit Ioannes David Michaelis* (Göttingen: Pockwizil and Barmeier, 1758).

2 Newsom, "Re-considering Job," 162.

3 Newsom, "The Book of Job," 528.

4 While this description is particularly fitting for Job 28, in some respects it is characteristic of Biblical verse in general, which is typically lyric. Lacking the more expansive and continuous features of narrative poetry, Biblical Hebrew lyric is typified by a "smallness of scale" that is resultingly "tropologically dense." On all this, see F. W. Dobbs-Allsopp, "The Psalms and Lyric Verse," in *The Evolution of Rationality: Interdisciplinary Essays in Honor of J. Wentzel van Huyssteen* (ed. F. LeRon Shults; Grand Rapids, Mich., and Cambridge, U.K.: Eerdmans, 2006), 346-79.

swallows up the realistic senses which dominate it early on (vv. 10-11). Once the reader has made the symbolic connections between precious objects in the watery navel of the earth and deep wisdom, the association is quickly broken in v. 12, where the poem's rhetoric suggests that wisdom is clearly something *other than* what has been grasped by the human in v. 11. In Sections Two and Three, the poem operates almost entirely in the cosmic realm, where God, Death, and the Deep comment upon the search for wisdom and its accessibility. In these sections, the poem begins to re-define true wisdom, which God reveals from a thunderstorm in v. 28.

6.2 The Conceptual Background(s) of the Poem

It is often asserted that Job 28:1-11 presents "[o]ne of the most elaborate descriptions of prospecting and mining technology from the ancient Near East."[5] In this study, however, I have offered a fresh interpretive model for these lines. The metaphors of Section One are best understood against literature extolling the deeds of ancient Mesopotamian kings, who journey to the edges of the world in hopes of becoming the "first discoverer" of precious treasure. The more historically rooted Akkadian royal inscriptions serve as analogues to the realistic plane of meaning in Section One, while the more universal Mesopotamian epic traditions—especially the standard version of Gilgamesh—serve as analogues to its symbolic plane. Informed by ideological construals of space and Mesopotamian cosmic geography, Section One of Job 28 may be seen to have a predominantly horizontal, rather than vertical, focus. This reading challenges the widespread supposition that vv. 1-11 are primarily concerned with mining technology.

The royal expedition figured in Section One is set in diptych with divine cosmic building works in Section Three (vv. 23-27). Both of these large-scale metaphors participate in the poem's spatial semantic field. God's seeing wisdom during the creation of the cosmos is best interpreted against Mesopotamian royal inscriptions in which the king and his scholars survey building sites for the ancient ground plan of the temples which they re-built. Wisdom is the ancient plan of the cosmos and the foundation deposit which symbolizes the stability of the world.

5 Coogan, "The Goddess Wisdom," 206. See also the comments of Eveline J. van der Steen: "Job 28 is an extensive and detailed description of the various aspects of mining" ("Mining," *NIDB* 4:91).

6.3 The Subject of Verses 3-11

It has been very common in the modern period to understand the subject of the first section of the poem (esp. vv. 3-11) as human. In the last several decades, however, some scholars have returned to a view traceable to 100 B.C.E. or before by understanding God as the subject of the first section (and thus, the entire poem).

However, the reading presented in this study supports the conclusion that the subject of Section One is a human whose exploits in expedition are set against the architectural expertise of the divine Craftsman in the Section Three. The divine imagery in the first section of the poem is intentionally incongruous to its subject, drawing attention to the explorer's superhuman feats and simultaneously highlighting those feats as a transgression of divinely established boundaries. Gilgamesh's role as a "boundary-crosser" who accomplishes feats proper only to the gods provides an analogue to the similar accomplishments of a human in Job 28 on a quest for cosmic wisdom. The undetermined subject in v. 3 ("he") creates intentional ambiguity so as to allow its audience (both within the Book of Job and outside of it) to be drawn into that world, filling the role of this unnamed explorer, and thus drawing conclusions about their own relation to the trope of searching out wisdom presented there.

6.4 The Integrity and Structure of the Poem

There has been a strong bias in modern critical scholarship against the integrity of the poem, most of which is without textual support in the ancient versions. The most common target is the conclusion in v. 28, which is often excised as a pious moral platitude. The originality of other sections has been questioned as well. Some scholars have gone so far as to offer extensive re-arrangements of the lines to restore what they believe to have been the original order of the composition.[6] Others would understand Job 28 as having been pieced together from originally separate poems.

6 See the brief but helpful survey in Norman H. Snaith, *The Book of Job: Its Origin and Purpose* (SBT^2 11; eds. C. F. D. Moule et al.; Naperville, Ill.: Allenson, 1968), 65-66. Clear examples of this approach may be seen in the commentaries of Karl Budde (*Das Buch Hiob*) Bernhard Duhm (*Das Buch Hiob erklärt*), and Georg Fohrer (*Das Buch Hiob*) though these are merely representative of a widespread tendency. For a catalogue of scholarly positions through 1971, see Appendix III in Martin, "Elihu and the Third Cycle in the Book of Job," 268-69.

This study supports the general notion set forth by Westermann that portions of the poem may have grown out of a proverb.[7] The whole poem is framed upon vv. 1a, 12a, and 28aβ: "There is indeed a source for silver… / But wisdom—where is it found? / …awe of the Lord, *that* is wisdom…" The reading presented here suggests that the interrelation between the pieces of the poem is far too complex and multi-faceted to suppose that it is substantially the patch-work of an editor. Though such complexity cannot with certainty be attributed to one original author, it is difficult to believe that the poetic genius displayed in the poem's imagery, rhetoric, and structure could have been constructed from originally disparate pieces composed by other authors. Re-arranging or deleting portions of the poem without textual support creates far more problems than it solves, and it often reflects inadequate engagement with the poem according to its own aesthetic logic. On the whole, the poem should be interpreted as a unified composition whose present order is original.

The only exception to this position is vv. 15-19, which are suspect both textually and literarily. Here the metaphor of *cost* is dominant, whereas the remainder of the poem is concerned with wisdom's *place*. These verses are best viewed as a small structured commentary which was an exegetical interpolation into the original poem, even if their author correctly perceived the poem's proverbial character.

Contrary to predominant scholarly opinion, v. 28 is a crucial conclusion to the poem as a whole, and it is almost certainly original to it. Beyond completing the poem's proverbial structure, the triplet is a signal of poetic closure. The "awe of the Lord," of which the second line speaks, is perfectly fitting in the context of divine self-disclosure from a thunderstorm.

6.5 Wisdom in Job 28

It is somewhat commonplace to view Job 28 as an extended meditation on the nature of wisdom in the Book of Job. Some scholars believe that wisdom is either personified or hypostatized in the poem. However, this interpretation has no solid base; rather, it is Deep, Sea, Death, and Destruction who are personified so that they can declare their ignorance about wisdom's place.

---

7 Westermann, *Aufbau*, 130. However, contrary to the explanation offered in this study, Westermann believes that the proverb originally consisted of a question (v. 12 = v. 20) and an answer (v. 23 [positive]; v. 13 = v. 21 [negative]).

Carol Newsom has outlined the diverse conceptualizations of wisdom in Job 28, suggesting something like a process of objectification, abstraction, and reification.[8] My own reading supports the conclusions that she draws. While the first section conceptualizes wisdom as an object that may be sought out in the earth, the second section serves to subvert this metaphor and highlight its inadequacy. The third section works to re-construct a more adequate figuring of wisdom by reflecting on God's relation to it in the creative process. While the metaphors applied to wisdom in Section Three still conceptualize wisdom as object in some sense (vv. 23, 27), it is now more intimately tied up with creative action (see esp. vv. 25-26). Yet this conceptualization is not the poem's final trope. The use of flexible diction in vv. 26-27 anticipates another shift toward a heavily moral definition in v. 28. While the behavioral and attitudinal presentation of wisdom in the poem's conclusion is not of a wholly different kind than the wisdom presented in vv. 25-27, it is still undoubtedly a reification and re-definition. The poem as a whole, then, begins by objectifying wisdom in Section One, dissociates wisdom from such objectification and increasingly abstracts it in Sections Two and Three, and finally reifies it in actions by which humans participate in just world-ordering in its conclusion (v. 28). It is thus best to think in terms of several different, if related, conceptualizations of wisdom in Job 28. If one wishes to generalize about the theology of wisdom in Job 28, all of these conceptualizations—and the process by which wisdom moves from one to the next—must be taken into account.

6.6 The Genre of Job 28

Job 28 has been classified according to various generic forms. Most typically, it is called the "Hymn to Wisdom," even though formal hymnic features are largely absent.[9] Otherwise, it is given some descriptor borrowed from music or theater that reflects scholars' puzzlement over

---

8 Newsom, "Dialogue and Allegorical Hermeneutics," 303-304. She also gives some attention to this in her commentary ("The Book of Job," 533) and in her monograph (*Moral Imaginations*, 179-82).

9 The only part of the poem that comes close to hymnody is the (implicit) praise of God for his knowledge of wisdom's place in 28:23-27. Fokkelman calls ch. 28 an "anti-hymn" (*Reading Biblical Poetry*, 132). Compare also the "hymnic fragments" in Job's speeches to this point in the Poem (Job 9:5-13; 10:8-13; 12:13-25; 26:5-14), as well as those in the speeches of Eliphaz (5:9-16), Zophar (11:7-11), Bildad (25:2-6), and Elihu (e.g., 37:1-13). On hymnic material in the dialogues, see Alison Lo, *Job 28 as Rhetoric*, 133-152.

its function in the book: "intermezzo,"[10] "cadenza,"[11] "bridge,"[12] "fermata,"[13] or, especially, "interlude."[14] The reading of Job 28 offered here suggests that the poem is a metaphorical pastiche which draws upon and alters various kinds of material found throughout the ancient Near East: the royal expedition of the "first discoverer" (vv. 1-11), the royal survey of a temple site (vv. 23-27), and, in its canonical version, the merchant's account (vv. 15-19). All these are stretched across a proverbial frame (vv. 1a, 12a, 28aβ).

Carol Newsom has made the case that in Job 28 "one encounters a distinctive genre—the "speculative wisdom poem"—which is part of a larger world of wisdom literature."[15] She observes that, like Prov 8; Sir 1, 24; Bar 3:9-4:4; and possibly *1 Enoch* 42, the poem in Job 28 is concerned with the search for transcendent wisdom.[16] As do many of those texts, Job 28 describes this search using the trope of seeking and finding, creation imagery, and ethical statements, all with a didactic quality.[17] As monologic expressions of truth, these "speculative wisdom" texts systematize, unify, and abstract,[18] brokering meta-categories of wisdom and understanding from the standpoint of a traditional and coherent worldview.[19]

Despite some clear differences between Job 28 and the other biblical and pseudepigraphical texts to which Newsom compares it,[20] I believe

---

10 Fiddes, " 'Where Shall Wisdom Be Found?' " 186. He also calls it a "chorus" (ibid.).

11 Hoffman, *A Blemished Perfection*, 282.

12 Hartley, *Job*, 373; cf. Lo, *Job 28 as Rhetoric*, 49.

13 Westermann, *Aufbau*, 133. Somewhat similarly, Balentine calls it a "soliloquy"—an interior musing spoken aloud—which serves as "a resting place within the book's drama" (*Job*, 416-17).

14 Schökel and Sícre Díaz, *Job*, 394; Andersen, Job, 223-24. It is also called a "meditation," which likewise suggests its difference from what surrounds it (Driver and Gray, *Job*, 1:233; Janzen, *Job*, 187).

15 Newsom, *Moral Imaginations*, 171-73.

16 Ibid.

17 See the shared elements she lists in ibid., 172.

18 Idem, "Job as Polyphonic Text," 90.

19 Newsom, *Moral Imaginations*, 26, 172-73. Compare also her description of "didactic (narrative) literature" in ibid., 41-47.

20 For example, Job 28 does not praise wisdom as does Prov 8 and Sir 24, but it queries about wisdom's place (cf. Sir 1; Bar 3). Further, the comparison with Bar 3-4 and *1 Enoch* 42 is slightly problematized by the fact that these texts are dependent upon the Joban poem. In this connection, note Gerhard von Rad's comments about Job 28: »Was nun die Lehre dieses Lehrgedichtes anlangt, so sollte man bei dem Vergleich mit den übrigen Weisheitstexten (Prov 8, Sir 24 u. a.) zurückhaltend sein.« (*Weisheit in Israel*, 194). See also the brief comparisons of Job 28 with Prov 8; Sir 1, 24; Bar 3:9-4:4; 4 Macc and Wis; *1 Enoch* 42; and 11QPs[a] 18:5-15 (=11Q5; Ps 154; SyrPs 2) in Mar-

it is useful to speak of Job 28 as participating in a broader genre of poems concerned with the quest for wisdom.[21] The significance of this genre, however, is ultimately a question of use. One must consider the poem's *force as discourse*, which may be different from what it *says*.[22] In my view, the speaker of Job 28 utters this poem not because it reflects his own traditional and philosophical reflection on transcendent wisdom, but to take on this mode of conception in order to highlight its inadequacy.[23] In short, it is an overturning of convention within the frame of that convention.[24] This is not a poem praising wisdom, immanent or transcendent. Rather, it critiques the modes by which "sages" like Job's friends seek out wisdom, and it ultimately commends Job's moral character (see 1:1, 8; 2:3), equating it with wisdom and understanding (28:28).

The subtle and complex use of traditional material is discernable in every portion of the book.[25] Furthermore, there are numerous instances

---

kus Witte, *Vom Leiden zur Lehre*, 206-211. On the reception of Job 28 in Bar 3:9-4:4, see Odil Hannes Steck, »Israels Gott statt anderer Götter – Israels Gesetz statt fremder Weisheit: Beobachtungen zur Rezeption von Hi 28 in Bar 3,9-4,4,« in *»Wer ist wie du, HERR, unter den Göttern?«: Studien zur Theologie und Religionsgeschichte Israels für Otto Kaiser zum 70. Geburtstag* (eds. Ingo Kottsieper, Jürgen van Oorschot, Diethard Römheld, and Harald Martin Wahl; Göttingen: Vandenhoeck & Ruprecht, 1994), 457-71.

21 I do have some reservations, however, about the designation of the genre as "speculative." This seems to imply that the speaker of Job 28 is engaging in a sort of philosophical muse.

22 See the comments of Eagleton (*How to Read a Poem*, 90), who echoes the insights of speech-act theory in his distinction between force and meaning, or "doing" and "saying."

23 Newsom rightly acknowledges that "Genres are not tight classificatory systems" (*Moral Imaginations*, 172) and that genres can be invoked in heuristic fashion, regardless of the author's original intent ("Dramaturgy and the Book of Job," 393). Nevertheless, her polyphonic reading of the Book of Job tends to equate certain ways of conceiving the world ("moral imaginations") with distinct literary genres. For a response, see briefly Raymond C. Van Leeuwen, review of Carol A. Newsom, *The Book of Job: A Contest of Moral Imaginations*, *Int* 58 (2004): 185-86; idem, "Cosmos, Temple, House," 79.

24 See Mary Kinzie, *Poet's Guide to Poetry*, 27-28. She adduces the example of Shakespeare's Sonnet 110 in which he employs the sonnet form not to express longsuffering devotion to a lost lover (as is typical of a sonnet), but, rather, fretful dissatisfaction with his failings in that arena.

25 On the prose tale, see D. J. A. Clines, "False Naivety in the Prologue to Job," *HAR* 9 (1985): 127-36; and Alan Cooper, "Reading and Misreading the Prologue to Job," *JSOT* 46 (1990): 67-79. On Job's soliloquies, note the comment of Leo G. Perdue on Job 3: "In Job 3 the sage-hero has transformed a lament into a soliloquy of curse and death" ("Job's Assault on Creation," *HAR* [1987]: 312). J. J. M. Roberts points out how Job uses a legal metaphor in unconventional ways in Job 31 and thereby "exploit[s] ambiguities and logical weaknesses in the traditional legal metaphors" ("Job's Sum-

throughout the Book of Job in which Job problematizes ancient Israelite religious traditions (see, e.g., Job 7:17-18 and cf. Ps 8:5;[26] Job 3:4 and cf. Gen 1:3). The subversion of genre in particular has been a prominent focus in Joban scholarship since the studies of Katharine Dell and Bruce Zuckerman in 1991.[27] As Greenstein has pointed out, the Book of Job

---

mons to Yahweh: The Exploitation of a Legal Metaphor," *ResQ* 16 [1974]: 165). Regarding the wisdom dialogues, Frank Polak has pointed out that several of Job's speeches, such as those in chs. 12, 16-17, and 26, "satirize the wisdom style" ("On Prose and Poetry in the Book of Job," *JANESCU* 24 [1996]: 90). Note Edward Greenstein's comments on ch. 12 in particular: "Job reacts to Zophar's sadistic enthusiasm with characteristic irony. Mocking Zophar's pseudo-wisdom (chap. 12), Job goes on to mimic him and boldly to announce that he will sue the deity" ("A Forensic Understanding of the Speech from the Whirlwind," in *Texts, Temples, and Traditions: A Tribute to Menahem Haran* [ed. M. V. Fox et al.; Winona Lake, Ind.: Eisenbrauns, 1996], 243). On irony in the Yhwh speeches, see J. Gerald Janzen, "The Place of the Book of Job in the History of Israel's Religion," in *Ancient Israelite Religion: Essays in Honor of Frank Moore Cross* (eds. Patrick D. Miller, Jr., Paul D. Hanson, and S. Dean McBride; Philadelphia, Pa.: Fortress, 1987), 523-37. Janzen asserts that irony is one of the major rhetorical means by which the Joban poet transforms the Israelite religious tradition (ibid., 530). Dirk Geeraerts also highlights the use of humor and irony in the Book of Job, and he points in particular to Job 38-41 as an ironic text ("Caught in a Web of Irony: Job and His Embarrassed God," in *Job 28: Cognition in Context* [ed. Ellen van Wolde; BI 64; eds. Rolf Rendtorff and R. Alan Culpepper; Leiden and Boston: Brill, 2003], 37-56). He states, "Both microstructurally and macrostructurally ... humor and irony seem to play an important role in the construction of the Book of Job" (ibid., 43).

26 On Job 7:17-18 and Ps 8:5, see briefly P.-E. Dion, "Formulaic Language in the Book of Job: International Background and Ironical Distortions," *SR* 16 (1987): 190-191; also Michael Fishbane, "The Book of Job and Inner-biblical Discourse," in *The Voice from the Whirlwind: Interpreting the Book of Job* (eds. Leo G. Perdue and W. Clark Gilpin; Nashville, Tenn.: Abingdon, 1992), 87-90; and Christian Frevel » ›Eine kleine Theologie der Menschenwürde‹: Ps 8 und seine Rezeption im Buch Ijob,« in *Das Manna Fällt auch Heute Noch: Beiträge zur Geschichte und Theologie des Alten, Ersten Testaments. Festschrift für Erich Zenger* (eds. Frank-Lothar Hossfeld and Ludger Schwienhorst-Schönberger; HBS 44. eds; Hans-Josef Klauck and Erich Zenger; Freiburg, Basel, Wien, Barcelona, Rome, and New York: Herder, 2004), 244-72. Raymond Van Leeuwen, however, is very cautious about the connection. See his "Psalm 8.5 and Job 7.17-18: A Mistaken Scholarly Commonplace?" in *The World of the Arameans I: Biblical Studies in Honour of Paul-Eugène Dion* (eds. P.M. Michèle Daviau, John W. Wevers, and Michael Weigl; JSOTSup 324; Sheffield: Sheffield Academic Press, 2001), 205-215.

27 Zuckerman states, "[P]arody is not simply an aspect of the Poem but is instead the very essence of what the Poem actually is" (*Job the Silent*, 136). Zuckerman does not apply this to Job 28, however. He believes, to the contrary, that ch. 28 was one of the several supplements added to the original parodic composition by later tradents who did not perceive its nature correctly.

Building on the work of Georg Fohrer, Dell suggests that the Book of Job both misuses and re-uses conventional forms (*Job as Sceptical Literature*, 110) and that deliberate misuse is so pervasive that the best genre for the book is "parody"—a formal

overturns generic and rhetorical expectations. Job "is to be read as parodic and subversive and ironic."[28] Moshe Greenberg goes so far as to suggest that the "subversion of tradition" is the *hallmark* of the author of the Book of Job.[29]

That Job 28 may be something other than a straightforward use of traditional forms is, in fact, suggested by the surrounding context. The poem is bound by two sections in chs. 27 and 29-31, both introduced as *mĕšālîm*: "Again Job took up his *māšāl* and said…" The use of this formula in Job 29:1 is especially striking, since it implies that what has gone before—Job 28 in the received text—is also a *māšāl*.

The term *māšāl* in these instances is typically translated as "discourse,"[30] "theme,"[31] or the like. However, *māšāl* is rarely so functionally bland in the OT,[32] being used instead of didactic aphorisms, riddles, allegories, parables, and taunts.[33] The translation of the Vulgate, followed by KJV, is more on the mark with "parable."

Māšāl marks a function more than a genre, and "its meaning is fluid, being contingent... on context."[34] It is polysemic and opaque, and it draws on numerous genres to create an extended metaphor which poses a riddle requiring solution.[35] In this vein, Susan Niditch has suggested that Job 27, 29, and 30 are imaginative illustrations—didactic word pictures which make a point arising from experience and obser-

---

description that meshes with the skeptical content of Job (ibid., 148). Like Zuckerman, Dell does not apply this to Job 28, which she understands as a later addition (ibid., 138, 196-97). See also her brief discussion of genre issues in Job in "Reviewing Recent Research on the Wisdom Literature," *ExpTim* 119/6 (2008): 266.

28 Greenstein, "Writing a Commentary on the Book of Job," n.p.

29 Moshe Greenberg, "Job," in *The Literary Guide to the Bible* (eds. Robert Alter and Frank Kermode; Cambridge, Mass.: Belknap, 1987), 297 (emphasis mine).

30 See *HALOT* 2:648 s.v.; JB, RSV, NRSV, NAS, NEB, NIV, TNIV.

31 So NJPS, NAB.

32 A perusal of the glosses Klyne Snodgrass gives for both *māšāl* I and *māšal* I in BH demonstrates clearly how unusual the meaning "discourse" or the like would be for *māšāl* in Job 27:1 and 29:1 in light of its meanings elsewhere. See his *Stories with Intent: A Comprehensive Guide to the Parables of Jesus* (Grand Rapids, Mich., and Cambridge, U.K.: Eerdmans, 2008), 570-71.

33 See the basic uses listed in *HALOT* 2:648, s.v. *māšāl* I, as well as the discussion of K.-M. Beyse, "מָשָׁל," *TDOT* 9: 64-67; and Gerald Wilson, "מָשָׁל," *NIDOTTE* 4:1134-36. Note *māšāl* I in Job 13:12 ("proverbs, utterances"); *māšal* I in Job 17:6 (G "to be a byword") and 30:19 (HtD "to be like something"); and *mōšel* in Job 41:25 ("equal, similarity").

34 Stephen Curkpatrick, "Between *Mashal* and Parable: 'Likeness' as a Metonymic Enigma," *HBT* 24 (2002): 59.

35 Ibid., 70; Polk, "Paradigms, Parables, and *Mĕšālîm*," 572.

vation.[36] Following Timothy Polk, she highlights the important participatory aspect of these *měšālîm*. The points which they make depend upon drawing their audience into the extended metaphor to force them to reflect on their experience in relation to the truth or integrity of that created world.[37] I would suggest that the same can be said of Job 28. But in order to develop the suggestion that Job 28 is a *māšāl*, it is necessary to give still more attention to how the chapter functions in its canonical context.

6.7 The Place and Function of Job 28 in the Book of Job

At the outset of this study, I suggested that questions about the place and function of ch. 28 in the Book of Job must be informed above all by a deep reading of the poem itself. I would like now to offer a prospectus (building on the brief interpretation at the end of ch. 3.8) about how the reading presented in this study might affect those larger literary questions. While the sketch offered here should be adequate for that purpose, what follows—and, to some extent, the comments on genre in ch. 6.6—should be fleshed out with further study.

The view that Job 28 presents a parable or a riddle is not completely novel. In 1956, Claus Westermann suggested that Job 28 was a riddle, and this view has been picked up with some alteration by Paul Fiddes, Yair Hoffman, and David Clines.[38] Westermann's generic rubric was largely conditioned by his form-critical judgment that the poem was an expanded proverb. Clines, who bases his judgment more on his perception of the poem's rhetoric than on form-critical categories, suggests that Job 28 is best understood as "instruction [which] takes the form of an *extended riddle*."[39]

---

36 Niditch, "Folklore and Wisdom: *Mashal* as an Ethnic Genre," in idem, *Folklore and the Hebrew Bible* (Guides to Biblical Scholarship: Old Testament Series; Minneapolis, Minn.: Fortress, 1993), 85.

37 See especially Polk, "Paradigms, Parables, and *Měšālîm*," 572-73. Also note Gerald Wilson's comments: "The contexts in Job are difficult and the meaning of *māšāl* less than certain, but it may be that some aspect of warning or admonition characterizes those passages as well" ("מֹשֶׁל," *NIDOTTE* 4:1135).

38 Westermann, *Aufbau*, 130: »Rätselwort« (first edition published in 1956); Fiddes, " 'Where Shall Wisdom Be Found?' " 172; Hoffman, *A Blemished Perfection*, 279; Clines, *Job 21-37*, 906, 911, 923.

39 Clines, *Job 21-37*, 906 (italics his).

Remarkably, however, none has pointed to the superscription in Job 29:1 which, in fact, commends this view by suggesting that what precedes it is a *māšāl*. This oversight is undoubtedly connected to the fact that most scholars deny that the poem is original to the book, many of them suggesting that it reflects the author's or editor's own judgment on the state of the dialogues at this point. Others go so far as to attribute Job 28 to Bildad, Eliphaz, Zophar, Elihu, or Yhwh.[40] The British literary critic I. A. Richards even assigned the chapter to Satan at the end of his play, *Job's Comforting*.[41]

The conclusions that Job 28 is out of place and that it cannot be read as Job's speech depend heavily upon an interpretation of the poem as an interlude, meditative hymn, or some kind of speculative reflection that does not fit within the heated and self-destructing third cycle of dialogues. Though the questions of genre and tone are not the only important considerations, other judgments about the supposed traditional theology of the bulk of the poem and the seeming incongruity of the poem's message with Job's disturbed internal reality often flow from these *prima facie* suppositions about the conventions by which the meaning of ch. 28 operates. In short, most scholars do not orient themselves toward Job 28 as a poem that may, in fact, *subvert* convention.

Understanding Job 28 as a parabolic subversion of the trope of the search for wisdom raises new possibilities for reading the poem in its canonical context. Rather than reflecting the poet's (or some other author's) views on the nature of transcendent wisdom, Job 28 serves to turn the "wisdom expedition" theme back on the friends (who have repeatedly claimed their connection with wisdom through the tradition) in order to underscore the futility of their search.[42] As Greenstein points out, "The main source of knowledge for the companions is... the traditional wisdom that tends to take the form of proverbs and epigrams."[43] Not coincidentally, the vocabulary often tied up with their search for traditional wisdom is that of "probing," the same word which is thematic in Job 28 (ḤQR in 28:3, 27; see also 5:27; 8:8; 32:11). Throughout the dialogues, Job refutes the friends with personal experience and with their own "traditional" wisdom. In the latter case, he

40 For a helpful catalogue of opinions through 1971, see Martin, "Elihu and the Third Cycle in the Book of Job," 265-67.

41 *Internal Colloquies: Poems and Plays of I. A. Richards* (New York: Harcourt Brace Jovanovich, 1958), 324-25.

42 See also Newsom, *Moral Imaginations*, 179.

43 Greenstein, " 'On My Skin and in My Flesh' " 64. See also Habel, "Appeal to Ancient Tradition," 253-272; and the helpful qualifications of Newsom, *Moral Imaginations*, 87.

does so "both to demonstrate that he is no less versed in it than his colleagues and in order to hold it up to criticism."[44] As Greenstein points out, "Job's use of proverbs and other traditional wisdom is nearly the opposite in purpose of his friends."[45]

The first section of Job 28 is Job's parody of the friends' exploration of the tradition, through which they, like ancient Mesopotamian kings, have sought to join the ranks of rulers and sages of old by becoming widsom's "first discoverer." To disabuse them of their hubris, Sections Two and Three emphasize the inaccessibility of the wisdom they claim to know. Section Three connects wisdom with divine world-ordering, but it ends by emphasizing the accessibility of wisdom, at least to those who "fear God and turn from evil." In that final turn, Job recounts God's speech to the first human as if he himself had fulfilled Eliphaz's challenge issued in 15:7-8 by "listening in on council of God." Not coincidentally, wisdom, as v. 28 states, belongs to someone precisely like Job (cf. 1:1, 8; 2:3). The ironic force of the poem's conclusion in Job's mouth cannot be missed for its seemingly traditional content. As the implied author of ch. 28, Job has out-traditioned the traditionalists. While his friends have done violence to the very order that they claim to uphold, Job finally reverts to an orderly symbolic universe that rewards his own moral strengths by affording him wisdom. Now reinstated as a sage,[46] Job becomes the only one engaged in the debate who is truly wise.

But Job's lesson to his friends in ch. 28 becomes God's lesson to Job in chs. 38-39, which employ remarkably similar imagery (see 38:4-7, 16-18, 19-21, 24-27, 33-38, 39-41). Rather than using the indirection of a parable, God interrogates Job directly, from the storm wind. He queries in 38:16-18:

16 Have you gone to the sources of the sea (*nibkê-yām*),
 or have you walked in the depths of the deep (*ḥēqer tĕhôm*)?
17 Have the gates of death been revealed to you?
 Have you seen the gates of deep darkness (*ṣalmāwet*)?
18 Have you examined (*hitbōnantā*) the breadth of the earth?
 Tell me, if you know it all!

44 Greenstein, " 'On My Skin and in My Flesh' " 69.

45 Ibid., 70.

46 See the comments of Brevard Childs, *Introduction to the Old Testament as Scripture* (Philadelphia, Pa.: Fortress, 1979), 542.

Like his friends, Job can make no claim to have reached the source of wisdom through such an epic journey.[47] Nor can he speak, as God challenges him to do, "as the First Man of primal times who was privy to the deliberations of the heavenly council."[48] His attempt to identify his own righteousness with true wisdom, even if only a rhetorical tact to silence his opponents, is an egregious error. In the end, Job must relinquish all claims to understanding and recognize his place among those like his friends for whom wisdom can remain only a rumor.

---

47 See Newsom, "The Book of Job," 603, on the journey motif in these lines and its cosmic geography. Note also how the temple-building imagery in 38:4-7 overlaps with that in 28:23-27.

48 Habel, "Appeal to Ancient Tradition," 268.

Selected Bibliography

Abusch, Tzvi. "The Development and Meaning of the Epic of Gilgamesh: An Interpretive Essay." *Journal of the American Oriental Society* 121 (2001): 614-22.

Aejmelaeus, Anneli. "Function and Interpretation of כי in Biblical Hebrew." *Journal of Biblical Literature* 105 (1986): 193-209.

Aitken, James K. "Lexical Semantics and the Cultural Context of Knowledge in Job 28, Illustrated by the Meaning of *ḥāqar*." Pages 119-138 in *Job 28: Cognition in Context*. Edited by Ellen van Wolde. Biblical Interpretation 64. Edited by R. Alan Culpepper and Rolf Rendtorff. Leiden: E. J. Brill, 2003.

Albertz, Rainer. "The Sage and Pious Wisdom in the Book of Job: The Friends' Perspective." Pages 243-61 in *The Sage in Israel and the Ancient Near East*. Translated by Leo G. Perdue. Edited by John G. Gammie and Leo G. Perdue. Winona Lake, Ind.: Eisenbrauns, 1990.

Albright, W. F. "The Mouth of the Rivers." *The American Journal of Semitic Languages and Literatures* 35 (1919): 161-95.

Alexander, Philip S. "Targum, Targumim." Pages 320-331 in Volume 6 of *Anchor Bible Dictionary*. Edited by D. N. Freedman. 6 volumes. New York: Doubleday, 1992.

Alster, Bendt. "The Paradigmatic Character of Mesopotamian Heroes." *Revue d'assyriologie et archaeologie orientale* 68 (1974): 49-60.

Alter, Robert. *The Art of Biblical Poetry*. New York: Basic Books, 1985.

______. "The Characteristics of Ancient Hebrew Poetry." Pages 611-24 in *The Literary Guide to the Bible*. Edited by Robert Alter and Frank Kermode. Cambridge, Mass.: The Belknap Press of Harvard University, 1987.

______. *The Pleasures of Reading in an Ideological Age*. New York: Simon and Schuster, 1989.

Andersen, Frances I. *Job*. Tyndale Old Testament Commentaries. London: Inter-Varsity, 1976.

Anderson, Gary A. "The Cosmic Mountain: Eden and Its Early Interpreters in Syriac Christianity." Pages 187-224 in *Genesis 1-3 in the History of Exegesis: Intrigue in the Garden*. Studies in Women and Religion 27. Edited by Gregory Allen Robbins. Lewiston and Queenston: The Edwin Mellen Press, 1988.

Aquinas, Thomas. *The Literal Exposition on Job: A Scriptural Commentary Concerning Providence*. The American Academy of Religion Classics in Religious Studies 7. Translated by Anthony Damico. Edited by Carl A. Raschke. Interpretive essay and notes by Martin D. Yaffe. Atlanta, Ga.: Scholars, 1989.

Auden, Wystan Hugh. "Making, Knowing, and Judging." Pages 31-60 in *The Dyer's Hand and Other Essays*. New York: Vintage International, 1989. Originally an inaugural lecture delivered before the University of Oxford on 11 June 1956, as Oxford Professor of Poetry.

Baldauf, Christfried. »Menschliches Können und göttliche Weisheit in Hiob 28.« *Theologische Versuche* 13 (1983): 57-68.

Balentine, Samuel E. *Job*. Smyth & Helwys Bible Commentary 10. Macon, Ga.: Smyth & Helwys, 2006.

Bandstra, Barry. "The Syntax of the Particle *ky* in Biblical Hebrew and Ugaritic." Ph.D. diss., Yale University, 1982.

Barr, James. "Hebrew Orthography and the Book of Job." *Journal of Semitic Studies* 30 (1985): 1-33.

______. "Philology and Exegesis: Some General Remarks, with Illustrations from Job." Pages 39-61 in *Questions disputes d'Ancien Testament: Méthode et théologie. XXIIIe session des Journées Bibliques de Louvain*. Edited by C. Brekelmans. Bibliotheca ephemeridum theologicarum lovaniensium 33. Leuven: Leuven University Press, 1974.

Barthes, Roland. *The Pleasure of the Text*. Translated by Richard Miller with a note on the text by Richard Howard. New York: Hill and Wang, 1975.

Barton, George A. "The Composition of Job 24-30." *Journal of Biblical Literature* 30 (1911): 66-77.

Baumann, Eberhard. »Die Verwendbarkeit der Pešita zum Buche Ijob für die Textkritik.« *Zeitschrift für die alttestamentliche Wissenschaft* 19 (1899): 15-95.

______. »Die Verwendbarkeit der Pešita zum Buche Ijob für die Textkritik.« *Zeitschrift für die alttestamentliche Wissenschaft* 20 (1900): 177-224.

Beaulieu, Paul-Alain. *The Reign of Nabonidus, King of Babylon, 556-539 B.C.* Yale Near Eastern Researches 10. Edited by W. W. Hallo et al. New Haven and London: Yale University Press, 1989.

______. "The Social and Intellectual Setting of Babylonian Wisdom Literature." Pages 3-20 in *Wisdom Literature in Mesopotamia and Israel*. Edited by Richard J. Clifford. Society of Biblical Literature Symposium Series 36. Edited by Christopher R. Matthews. Atlanta, Ga.: Society of Biblical Literature, 2007.

Beer, Georg. *Der Text des Buches Hiob untersucht*. Marburg: N. G. Elwertsche Verlagsbuchhandlung, 1897.

Berlin, Adele. "Ethnopoetry and the Enmerkar Epics." *Journal of the American Oriental Society* 103 (1983): 17-24.

______. "On Reading Biblical Poetry: The Role of Metaphor." Pages 25-36 in *Congress Volume, Cambridge 1995*. Edited by J. A. Emerton. Vetus Testamentum Supplements 66. Leiden, New York, and Köln, 1997.

Black, Jeremy. *Reading Sumerian Poetry*. Ithaca, NY: Cornell University Press, 1998.

______, G. Cunningham, J. Ebeling, E. Flückiger-Hawker, E. Robson, J. Taylor, and G. Zólyomi. *The Electronic Text Corpus of Sumerian Literature*. Online: http://etcsl.orinst.ox.ac.uk/. Oxford, 1998–2006.

______, Graham Cunningham, Eleanor Robson, and Gábor Zólyomi. *The Literature of Ancient Sumer*. Oxford: Oxford University Press, 2004.

Blenkinsopp, Joseph. "Gilgamesh and Adam: Wisdom through Experience in *Gilgamesh* and in the Biblical Story of the Man, the Woman, and the Snake." Pages 85-101 in *Treasures Old and New: Essays in the Theology of the Pentateuch*. Grand Rapids, Mich.: Eerdmans, 2004.

Blommerde, Anton. *Northwest Semitic Grammar and Job*. Biblica et orientalia 22. Rome: Pontifical Biblical Institute, 1969.

Borger, Riekele. *Die Inschriften Asarhaddons König von Assyrien*. Archiv für Orientforschung: Beiheft 9. Edited by Ernst Weidner. Graz: Ernst Weidner, et al., 1956.

Bottéro, Jean. "Intelligence and the Technical Function of Power: Enki/Ea." Pages 323-50 in *Mesopotamia: Writing, Reasoning, and the Gods*. Translated by Zainab Bahrani and Marc van de Mieroop. Chicago and London: University of Chicago, 1992. Originally published as "L'intelligence et la function technique du pouvior: Enki/ Éa—pour donner une idée de la systémique du pantheon." Pages 102-111 in Volume 2 of *Dictionnaire des Mythologies*. 2 vols. Edited by Yves Bonnefoy. Paris: Flammarion, 1981.

Brooks, Cleanth. "The Heresy of Paraphrase." Pages 192-214 in *The Well Wrought Urn: Studies in the Structure of Poetry*. San Diego, New York, and London: Harcourt Brace, 1942.

Brown, Francis, Samuel R. Driver, and Charles A. Briggs, eds. *A Hebrew and English Lexicon of the Old Testament, with an Appendix Containing the Biblical Aramaic. Based on the Lexicon of William Gesenius as Translated by Edward Robinson*. Oxford: Clarendon, 1907.

Brownlee, William. "The Cosmic Role of Angels in the 11Q Targum of Job." *Journal for the Study of Judaism* 8 (1977): 83-84.

Buccellati, Giorgio. "On Poetry—Theirs and Ours." Pages 105-34 in *Lingering Over Words: Studies in Ancient Near Eastern Literature in Honor of William L. Moran*. Edited by Tzvi Abusch, John Huehnergard, and Piotr Steinkeller. Harvard Semitic Studies 37. Atlanta, Ga.: Scholars, 1990.

______. "Wisdom and Not: The Case of Mesopotamia." *Journal of the American Oriental Society* 101 (1981): 35-47.

Budde, Karl. *Das Buch Hiob*. Handkommentar zum Alten Testament 2/1. Göttingen: Vandenhoeck & Ruprecht, 1896.

______. »Die Capitel 27 und 28 des Buches Hiob.« *Zeitschrift für die alttestamentliche Wissenschaft* 2 (1882): 193-274.

Byington, Steven T. "Hebrew Marginalia II: Job 28." *Journal of Biblical Literature* 61 (1942): 205-207.

______. "Hebrew Marginalia III." *Journal of Biblical Literature* 64 (1945): 340-41.

Calvin, John. *Sermons on Job. 16th-17th Century Facsimile Edition*. Edinburgh: Banner of Truth, 1993. Original published 1574.

Caspari, C. P. *Das Buch Hiob (1,1 – 38, 16) in Hieronymous's Übersetzung aus der alexandrinischen Version*. Christiania: A. W. Brøggers Bogtrykkeri, 1893.

Cavigneaux, Antoine. »Lexikalische Listen.« Pages 609-41 in Volume 6 of *Reallexikon der Assyriologie und vorderasiatischen Archäologie*. 11 volumes, incomplete. Edited by Erich Ebeling et al. Berlin: de Gruyter, 1928—.

Ceresko, Anthony. *Job 29-31 in the Light of Northwest Semitic: A Translation and Philological Commentary*. Biblica et orientalia 36. Rome: Biblical Institute Press, 1980.

Ceriani, Antonio Maria. *Codex Syro-Hexaplaris Ambrosianus, photolithographice editus*. Monumenta Sacra et Profana 7. Florence and London: Mediolani, Impensis Bibliothecae Ambrosianae, 1874.

Charlesworth, James H. "Bashan, Symbology, Haplography, and Theology in Psalm 68." Pages 351-372 *David and Zion: Biblical Studies in Honor of J. J. M. Roberts*. Edited by Bernhard F. Batto and Kathryn L. Roberts. Winona Lake, Ind.: Eisenbrauns, 2004.

Christidès, Vassilios. "L'énigma d'Ophir." *Revue biblique* (1970): 240-47.

Claassen, W. T. "Speaker-Oriented Functions of *Kî* in Biblical Hebrew." *Journal of Northwest Semitic Languages* 11 (1983): 29-46

Clifford, Richard J. *Creation Accounts in the Ancient Near East and in the Bible*. Catholic Biblical Quarterly Monograph Series 26. Edited by Michael Barré. Washington, D.C.: The Catholic Biblical Association of America, 1994.

______. *The Cosmic Mountain in Canaan and the Old Testament*. Harvard Semitic Monographs 4. Cambridge, Mass.: Harvard University Press, 1972.

Clines, D. J. A., ed. *Dictionary of Classical Hebrew*. 6 volumes (incomplete). Sheffield: Sheffield Academic Press, 1993-

______. "False Naivety in the Prologue to Job." *Hebrew Annual Review* 9 (1985): 127-36.

______. *Job 1-20*. Word Biblical Commentary 17. Dallas, Tex.: Word, 1989.

______. *Job 21-37*. Word Biblical Commentary 18A. Nashville, Tenn.: Thomas Nelson, 2006.

______. "Putting Elihu in his Place: A Proposal for the Relocation of Job 32-37." *Journal for the Study of the Old Testament* 29 (2004): 243-53.

______. " 'The Fear of the Lord is Wisdom' (Job 28:28): A Semantic and Contextual Study." Pages 57-92 in *Job 28: Cognition in Context*. Edited by Ellen van Wolde. Biblical Interpretation 64. Edited by R. Alan Culpepper and Rolf Rendtorff. Leiden and Boston: Brill, 2003.

Cohen, A. "Studies in Hebrew Lexicography." *American Journal of Semitic Languages and Literature* 40/3 (1924): 153-85.

Cohen, Chaim. "The Meaning of צלמות 'Darkness': A Study in Philological Method." Pages 287-309 in *Texts, Temples, and Traditions: A Tribute to Menahem Haran*. Edited by Michal V. Fox et al. Winona Lake, Ind.: Eisenbrauns, 1996.

Collon, Dominique. *First Impressions: Cylinder Seals in the Ancient Near East*. Revised Edition. London: British Museum Press, 2005.

Coogan, Michael D. "The Goddess Wisdom—'Where Can She Be Found?': Literary Reflexes of Popular Religion." Pages 203-209 in *Ki Baruch hu: Ancient Near Eastern, Biblical and Judaic Studies in Honor of Baruch A. Levine*. Edited by R. Chazon, W. W. Hallo, and L. H. Schiffman. Winona Lake, Ind.: Eisenbrauns, 1999.

Cook, Johann. "Aspects of Wisdom in the Texts of Job (Chapter 28)—*Vorlage(n)* and/or translator(s)?" *Old Testament Essays* 5 (1992): 26-45.

Cooper, Alan. "Narrative Theory and the Book of Job." *Studies in Religion* 11 (1982): 35-44.

______. "Reading and Misreading the Prologue to Job." *Journal for the Study of the Old Testament* 46 (1990): 67-79.

Cox, Claude E. "Methodological Issues in the Exegesis of LXX Job." Pages 79-89 in *VI Congress of the International Organization for Septuagint and Cognate Studies, Jerusalem 1986*. Edited by Claude E. Cox. Society of Biblical Literature Septuagint and Cognate Studies 23. Atlanta, Ga.: Scholars, 1987.

Craigie, Peter C. "Job and Ugaritic Studies." Pages 28-35 in *Studies in the Book of Job: Papers Presented at the Forty-ninth Annual Meeting of the Canadian Society of Biblical Studies, May 1981*. Edited by Walter E. Aufrecht. Studies in Religion Supplements 16. Waterloo, Ontario: Wilfrid Laurier University Press / Canadian Corporation for Studies in Religion, 1985.

Crenshaw, James. "Job." Pages 331-355 in *The Oxford Bible Commentary*. Edited by John Barton and John Muddiman. Oxford and New York: Oxford University Press, 2001.

Cross, Frank Moore. *Canaanite Myth and Hebrew Epic*. Cambridge, Mass., and London: Harvard University Press, 1973.

______. "The Development of the Jewish Scripts." Pages 170-264 in *The Bible and the Ancient Near East: Essays in Honor of William Foxwell Albright*. Edited by G. Ernest Wright. Garden City, NY: Doubleday, 1961.

_____. "The Papyri and their Historical Implications." Pages 17-29 in *Discoveries in the Wâdī ʾed-Dâliyeh*. Edited by P. W. Lapp and N. L. Lapp. Annual of the American Schools of Oriental Research 41. Edited by Delbert R. Hillers. Cambridge, Mass.: American Schools of Oriental Research, 1974.

Cunchillos, J.-L., J.-P. Vita, and J.-Á. Zamora, with R. Cervigón. *A Concordance of Ugaritic Words*. 5 volumes. Translated by A. Lacadena and A. Castro. Piscataway, NJ: Gorgias Press, 2003.

Curkpatrick, Stephen. "Between *Mashal* and Parable: 'Likeness' as a Metonymic Enigma." *Horizons in Biblical Theology* 24 (2002): 58-71.

Dahood, Mitchell J. "Chiasmus in Job: A Text-Critical and Philological Criterion." Pages 119-130 in *A Light Unto My Path: Old Testament Studies in Honor of Jacob M. Myers*. Gettysburg Theological Studies 4. Edited by Howard N. Bream, Ralph D. Heim, and Carey A. Moore. Philadelphia, Pa.: Temple University Press, 1974.

______. "Hebrew-Ugaritic Lexicography VII." *Biblica* 50 (1969): 337-356.

______. "Northwest Semitic Philology and Job." Pages 55-74 in *The Bible in Current Catholic Thought*. Edited by J. L. McKenzie. New York: Herder and Herder, 1962.

Dalley, Stephanie. *Myths from Mesopotamia: Creation, the Flood, Gilgamesh, and Others*. Revised edition. Oxford: Oxford University Press, 2000.

Damrosch, David. *The Buried Book: The Loss and Rediscovery of the Great Epic of Gilgamesh*. New York: Henry Holt and Company, 2006.

______. *The Narrative Covenant: Transformations of Genre in the Growth of Biblical Literature*. Ithaca, NY: Cornell University Press, 1987.

Delitzsch, Franz. *A Biblical Commentary on the Book of Job*. 2 vols. Translated by Francis Bolton. Edinburgh: T & T Clark, 1966. Originally published as *Biblischer Commentar über die poetischen Bücher des Alten Testaments, 2. Band: Das Buch Iob*. Leipzig: Dörffling and Franke, 1876.

Dell, Katharine. "Plumbing the Depths of Earth: Job 28 and Deep Ecology." Pages 116-25 in *The Earth Story in Wisdom Traditions*. Edited by Norman C. Habel and Shirley Wurst. The Earth Bible 3. Sheffield: Sheffield Academic Press, 2001.

______. "Reviewing Recent Research on the Wisdom Literature." *Expository Times* 119/6 (2008): 261-269.

______. *The Book of Job as Sceptical Literature*. Beihefte zur Zeitschrift für die alttestamentliche Wissenschaft 197. Berlin and New York: Walter de Gruyter, 1991.

Dever, William G. "Timnaᶜ." Pages 217-18 in Volume 5 of *The Oxford Encyclopedia of the Ancient Near East*. Edited by Eric M. Meyers. New York and Oxford: Oxford University Press, 1997.

De Wilde, A. *Das Buch Hiob: eingeleitet, übersetzt und erläutert. Oudtestamentische Studiën* 22. Edited by A. S. van der Woude. Leiden: E.J. Brill, 1981.

Dhorme, Édouard. *A Commentary on the Book of Job*. Translated by Harold Knight. Nashville, Tenn.: Thomas Nelson, 1984. Originally published as *Le Livre de Job*. Études Bibliques. Paris: J. Gabalda, 1926.

______. "Les Chapitres XXV-XXVIII du Livre de Job." *Revue biblique* 33 (1924): 343-56.

Dick, Michael B. "Job xxviii 4: A New Translation." *Vetus Testamentum* 29 (1979): 216-21.

______. "The Neo-Assyrian Royal Lion Hunt and Yahweh's Answer to Job." *Journal of Biblical Literature* 125 (2006): 243-70.

Dietrich, Manfred, Oswald Loretz, and Joaquín Sanmartín. *The Cuneiform Alphabetic Texts from Ugarit, Ras Ibn Hani and Other Places*. Abhandlungen zur Literatur Alt-Syren-Palästinas und Mesopotamiens 8. Münster: Ugarit-Verlag, 1995.

Dobbs-Allsopp, F. W. "Poetry, Hebrew." Pages 550-558 in Volume 4 of *The New Interpreter's Dictionary of the Bible*. Edited by K. D. Sakenfeld. 5 vols. Nashville, Tenn.: Abingdon, 2006-2009.

______. "The Psalms and Lyric Verse." Pages 346-79 in *The Evolution of Rationality: Interdisciplinary Essays in Honor of J. Wentzel van Huyssteen*. Edited by F. LeRon Shults. Grand Rapids, Mich., and Cambridge, U.K.: Eerdmans, 2006.

______., J. J. M. Roberts, C. L. Seow, and R. E. Whitaker. *Hebrew Inscriptions: Texts from the Biblical Period of the Monarchy, with Concordance*. New Haven: Yale University Press, 2004.

Donner, Herbert and Wolfgang Röllig. *Kanaanäische und aramäische Inschriften*. 3 vols. Wiesbaden: Otto Harrassowitz, 1962-64.

Driver, G. R. "Birds in the Old Testament: I. Birds in Law." *Palestine Exploration Quarterly* 87 (1955): 5-20.

______. "Birds in the Old Testament: II. Birds in Life." *Palestine Exploration Quarterly* 87 (1955): 129-40.

______. "Hebrew Notes." *Vetus Testamentum* 1 (1951): 241-50.

______. "Problems in Job." *American Journal of Semitic Languages and Literatures* 52/3 (April 1936): 72-93.

Driver, Samuel Rolles and George Buchanan Gray. *A Critical and Exegetical Commentary on the Book of Job*. 2 vols. International Critical Commentary. Edinburgh: T & T Clark, 1921.

Duhm, Bernhard. *Das Buch Hiob erklärt*. Kurzer Hand-Commentar zum Alten Testament XVI. Freiburg im Breisgau: J. C. B. Mohr, 1897.

Eagleton, Terry. *How to Read a Poem*. Malden, Mass.; Oxford, UK; and Carlton, Victoria: Blackwell, 2007.

Ehrlich, Arnold B. *Randglossen zur Hebräischen Bibel. Textkritisches, Sprachliches, und Sachliches. Sechster Band: Psalmen, Sprüche, und Hiob*. Leipzig: J. C. Hinrichs, 1918.

Elliger, K. and W. Rudolph, eds. *Biblia Hebraica Stuttgartensia*. 5th, corrected edition. Stuttgart: Deutsche Bibelgesellschaft, 1997.

Ellis, Richard S. *Foundation Deposits in Ancient Mesopotamia*. Yale Near Eastern Researches 2. Edited by W. W. Hallo et al. New Haven and London: Yale University Press, 1968.

Elwolde, John F. "Non-Contiguous Parallelism as a Key to Literary Structure and Lexical Meaning in Job 28." Pages 103-118 in *Job 28: Cognition in Context*. Edited by E. van Wolde. Biblical Interpretation 64. Edited by R. Alan Culpepper and Rolf Rendtorff. Leiden and Boston: E. J. Brill, 2003.

______. "The Use of Arabic in Hebrew Lexicography: Whence? Whither?, and Why?" Pages 369-75 in *William Robertson Smith: Essays in Reassessment*. Edited by W. Johnstone. Journal for the Study of the Old Testament: Supplement Series 189. Sheffield, U.K.: Sheffield Academic Press, 1995.

Emerton, John A. "Was There an Epicene Pronoun *hūʾ* in Early Hebrew?" *Journal of Semitic Studies* 45 (2000): 267-76.

Erman, Adolf and Hermann Grapow. *Wörterbuch der Ägyptischen Sprache*. 7 vols. Leipzig: J. C. Hinrichs, 1926-31.

Falkenstein, Adam and Wolfram von Soden. *Sumerische und akkadische Hymnen und Gebete*. Zürich and Stuttgart: Artemis-Verlag, 1953.

Faulkner, Raymond O. *A Concise Dictionary of Middle Egyptian*. Oxford: The Griffith Institute, 1962.

Favaro, Sabrina. *Voyages et voyageurs à l'époque néo-assyrienne*. State Archives of Assyria Studies 18. Helsinki: The Neo-Assyrian Text Corpus Project of the University of Helsinki, 2007.

Fedrizzi, Pio. *Giobbe*. La Sacra Bibbia: Antico Testamento. Edited by Salvatore Garofalo. Rome and Turin: Marietti, 1972.

Fiddes, Paul S. " 'Where Shall Wisdom be Found?': Job 28 as a Riddle for Ancient and Modern Readers." Pages 171-90 in *After the Exile: Essays in Honour of Rex Mason*. Edited by John Barton and David J. Reimer. Macon, Ga.: Mercer University Press, 1996.

Field, Frederick. *Origenis Hexaplorum quae supersunt: sive, Veterum interpretum graecorum in totum Vetus Testamentum fragmenta: post Flaminium, Nobilium, Drusium, et Montefalconium, adhibita etiam versione syro-hexapalri*. 2 vols. Oxford: Oxford University Press, 1875.

Fitzmyer, Joseph. "Some Observations on the Targum of Job from Qumran Cave XI." *Catholic Biblical Quarterly* 36 (1974): 503-524.

Fohrer, Georg. *Das Buch Hiob*. Kommentar zum Alten Testament 16. Gütersloh: Gerd Mohn, 1963.

Fokkelman, Jan P. *Major Poems of the Hebrew Bible: At the Interface of Prosody and Structural Analysis, Volume IV: Job 15-42*. Translated by Ch. E. Smit. Studia semitica neederlandica 47. Edited by W. J. van Bekkum et al. Assen, The Netherlands: Van Gorcum, 2004.

______. *Reading Biblical Poetry: An Introductory Guide*. Louisville and London: Westminster John Knox Press, 2001.

Fontaine, Carol. "Wounded Hero on a Shaman's Quest: Job in the Context of Folk Literature." Pages 70-85 in *The Voice from the Whirlwind: Interpreting the Book of Job* Edited by Leo G. Perdue and W. Clark Gilpin. Nashville, Tenn.: Abingdon, 1992.

Foster, Benjamin R. *Before the Muses: An Anthology of Akkadian Literature*. 3d ed. Bethesda, Md.: CDL Press, 2005.

______. *The Epic of Gilgamesh: A New Translation, Analogues, Criticism*. New York and London: W. W. Norton & Company, 2001.

Fox, Michael V. "Job the Pious." *Zeitschrift für die alttestamentliche Wissenschaft* 117 (2005): 351-66.

______. *Proverbs 1-9: A New Translation with Introduction and Commentary*. Anchor Bible 18A. New York, London, Toronto, Sydney, and Auckland: Doubleday, 2000.

______. "Words for Wisdom." *Zeitschrift für Althebraistik* 6 (1993): 149-69.

Franke, Sabina. "Kings of Akkad: Sargon and Naram-Sin." Translated by Andrew Baumann. Pages 831-41 in Volume 2 of *Civilizations of the Ancient Near East*. 4 vols. Edited by Jack Sasson. New York: Scribners, 1995.

Freedman, David Noel. "Orthographic Peculiarities in the Book of Job." *Eretz Israel* 9 (1969): 35*-44*.

Frost, Robert. "Education by Poetry." Pages 33-46 in *Selected Prose of Robert Frost*. Edited by Hyde Cox and Edward Connery Lathem. New York, Chicago, and San Francisco: Holt, Rinehart, and Winston, 1966. Originally delivered at Amherst College and subsequently revised for publication in the *Amherst Graduates' Quarterly* (February 1931).

______. "The Constant Symbol." Pages 23-29 in *Selected Prose of Robert Frost*. Edited by Hyde Cox and Edward Connery Lathem. New York, Chicago, and San Francisco: Holt, Rinehart and Winston, 1966. First published in *The Atlantic Monthly*, October 1946.

Futato, Mark D. "Sense Relation in the 'Rain' Domain of the Old Testament." Pages 83-97 in *Imagery and Imagination in Biblical Literature: Essays in Honor of Aloysius Fitzgerald, F.S.C.* Edited by Lawrence Boadt and Mark S. Smith. Catholic Biblical Quarterly Monograph Series 32. Washington, D.C.: The Catholic Biblical Association of America, 2001.

Gailey, James Herbert. "Jerome's Latin Version of Job from the Greek, Chapters 1-26: Its Text, Character, and Provenance." Th.D. diss., Princeton Theological Seminary, 1945.

______. *Jerome's Latin Version of Job from the Greek, Chapters 1-26: Its Text, Character, and Provenance. An Abstract of a Dissertation Submitted in Partial Fulfillment of the Requirements for the Degree of Doctor of Theology, Princeton Theological Seminary, Princeton, New Jersey*. Princeton Seminary Pamphlet Series; Princeton, NJ: Committee on Publications, 1948.

Galter, Hannes D. *Der Gott Ea/Enki in der akkadischen Überlieferung. Eine Bestandsaufnahme des vorhanden Materials*. Dissertationen der Karl-Franzens-Universität Graz 58. Graz: Verlag für die Technische Universität Graz, 1983.

Garber, P. L. and R. W. Funk. "Jewels and Precious Stones." Pages 898-205 in Volume 2 of *Interpreter's Dictionary of the Bible*. 4 vols. Edited by G. A. Buttrick. Nashville, Tenn: Abingdon, 1962.

Gard, Donald H. "The Concept of Job's Character According to the Greek Translator of the Hebrew Text." *Journal of Biblical Literature* 72 (1953): 182-86.

______. "The Concept of the Future Life According to the Greek Translator of the Book of Job." *Journal of Biblical Literature* 73 (1954): 137-143.

Geeraerts, Dirk. "Caught in a Web of Irony: Job and His Embarrassed God." Pages 37-56 in *Job 28: Cognition in Context*. Edited by Ellen van Wolde; Biblical Interpretation 64. Edited by R. Alan Culpepper and Rolf Rendtorff. Leiden and Boston: Brill, 2003.

Gehman, Henry S. "The Theological Approach of the Greek Translator of Job 1-15." *Journal of Biblical Literature* 68 (1949): 231-40.

Geller, Stephen A. "Hebrew Prosody and Poetics: I. Biblical." Pages 509-11 in *The New Princeton Encyclopedia of Poetry and Poetics*. Edited by Alex Preminger and T. V. F. Brogan. New York: MJF Books, 1993.

______. "Nature's Answer: The Meaning of the Book of Job in its Intellectual Context." Pages 109-132 in *Judaism and Ecology: Created World and Revealed Word*. Edited by Hava Tirosh-Samuelson. Publications of the Center for the Study of World Religions, Harvard Divinity School. Edited by Lawrence E. Sullivan. Religions of the World and Ecology. Edited by Mary Evelyn Tucker and John Grim. Cambridge, Mass.: Harvard University Press, 2002.

______. *Sacred Enigmas: Literary Religion in the Hebrew Bible*. London and New York: Routledge, 1996.

______. "The Language and Imagery in Psalm 114." Pages 179-194 in *Lingering Over Words: Studies in Ancient Near Eastern Literature in Honor of William L. Moran*. Edited by Tzvi Abusch, John Huehnergard, and Piotr Steinkeller. Harvard Semitic Studies 37. Atlanta, Ga.: Scholars, 1990.

______. "Theory and Method in the Study of Biblical Poetry." *Jewish Quarterly Review* 73 (1982): 65-77.

______. "Through Windows and Mirrors into the Bible: History, Literature, and Language in the Study of the Text." Pages 3-40 in *A Sense of Text. The Art of Language in the Study of Biblical Literature: Papers from the Symposium at the Dropsie College for Hebrew and Cognate Learning, May 11, 1982*. Edited by Stephen A. Geller. *Jewish Quarterly Review* Supplement 1982. Winona Lake, Ind.: Distributed for the Dropsie College by Eisenbrauns, 1983.

______. " 'Where is Wisdom?': A Literary Study of Job 28 in its Settings." Pages 155-188 in *Judaic Perspectives on Ancient Israel*. Edited by J. Neusner, B. Levine, and E. Frerichs. Philadelphia, Pa.: Fortress, 1987.

Gentry, Peter John. *The Asterisked Materials in the Greek Job*. Society of Biblical Literature Septuagint and Cognate Studies 38. Atlanta, Ga.: Scholars, 1995.

______. "The Place of Theodotion-Job in the Textual History of the Septuagint." Pages 199-230 in *Origen's Hexapla and Fragments: Papers presented at the Rich Seminar on the Hexapla, Oxford Centre for Hebrew and Jewish Studies, 25th July–3rd August 1994*. Edited by Alison Salvesen. Texte und Studien zum Antiken Judentum 58. Edited by Martin Hengel and Peter Schäfer. Tübingen: Mohr Siebeck, 1998.

George, Andrew R. *The Babylonian Gilgamesh Epic. Introduction, Critical Edition, and Cuneiform Texts*. 2 vols. Oxford: Oxford University Press, 2003.

______. *The Epic of Gilgamesh: The Babylonian Epic Poem and Other Texts in Akkadian and Sumerian*. London: Penguin Books, 1999.

______. "The Epic of Gilgameš: Thoughts on Genre and Meaning." Pages 37-65 in *Gilgameš and the World of Assyria. Proceedings of the Conference held at Mandelbaum House, The University of Sydney, 21-23 July 2004*. Edited by Joseph Azize and Noel Weeks. Ancient Near Eastern Studies: Supplement 21. Edited by Antonio Sagona and Claudia Sagona. Leuven, Paris, and Dudley, Mass.: Peeters, 2007.

Gerardi, Pamela. "Epigraphs and Assyrian Palace Reliefs: The Development of the Epigraphic Text." *Journal of Cuneiform Studies* 40 (1988): 1-35.

Gerleman, Gillis. *Studies in the Septuagint, I. Book of Job*. Lunds universitets årsskrift, neue Folge 1. Volume 43/2. Lund: C. W. K. Gleerup, 1946.

Gibson, John C. L. *Textbook of Syrian Semitic Inscriptions*. 3 vols. Oxford: Clarendon, 1971-1982.

Gioia, Dana. "Can Poetry Matter?" *Atlantic Monthly* 267/5 (May 1991): 94-105.

Glassner, J.-J. "Sargon 'roi du combat'." *Revue d'assyriologie et d'archéologie orientale* 79 (1985): 115-126.

Goatly, Andrew. *The Language of Metaphors*. London and New York: Routledge, 1997.

Gold, Sally L. Review of David Shepherd, *Targum and Translation: A Reconsideration of the Qumran Aramaic Version of Job*. *Hebrew Studies* 46 (2005): 430-33.

Good, Edwin M. *In Turns of Tempest: A Reading of Job, with a Translation*. Stanford: Stanford University Press, 1990.

Gordis, Robert. "The Asseverative Kaph in Ugaritic and Hebrew." *Journal of the American Oriental Society* 63 (1943): 176-78.

______. *The Book of Job: Commentary, New Translation, and Special Studies*. New York: Jewish Theological Seminary of America, 1978.

______. *The Book of God and Man: A Study of Job*. Chicago and London: The University of Chicago Press, 1965.

Gordon, Cyrus. *Ugaritic Textbook: Glossary, Indices*. Analecta orientalia 38. Rome: Pontifical Biblical Institute, 1965. Revised reprint 1998.

Görg, Manfred. »Ein Ausdruck der Goldschmiedekunst im Alten Testament.« *Biblische Zeitschrift*, neue Folge 28 (1984): 250-55.

Goshen-Gottstein, Moshe H. *The Aleppo Codex. Provided with massoretic notes and pointed by Aaron Ben Asher. The Codex Considered authoritative by Maimonides. Part One: Plates*. Jerusalem: Magnes, 1976.

______. "The Aleppo Codex and the Rise of the Massoretic Bible Text." *Biblical Archaeologist* 42/3 (Summer 1979): 145-163.

______. "The Authenticity of the Aleppo Codex." *Textus* 1 (1960): 17-58.

Grabbe, Lester L. *Comparative Philology and the Text of Job: A Study in Methodology*. Society of Biblical Literature Dissertation Series 34. Edited by Howard C. Kee and Douglas A. Knight. Missoula, Mont.: Scholars Press / The Society of Biblical Literature, 1977.

Grätz, H. H. »Die Integrität der Kapitel 27 und 28 im Hiob.« *Monatschrift für Geschichte und Wissenschaft des Judentums* 21 (1872): 241-50.

______. *Emendationes in plerosque Sacrae Scripturae Veteris Testamenti Libros*. 3 fascicles. Breslau: Schlesische Buchdruckerei, 1892.

Gray, John. "The Massoretic Text of the Book of Job, the Targum and the Septuagint Version in Light of the Qumran Targum (11Qtarg Job)." *Zeitschrift für die alttestamentliche Wissenschaft* 86 (1974): 331-50.

Grayson, A. Kirk. *Assyrian Rulers of the Early First Millennium BC I (1114-859 B.C.)*. Royal Inscriptions of Mesopotamia, Assyrian Periods 2. Edited by A. Kirk Grayson et al. Toronto, Buffalo, and London: University of Toronto Press, 1991.

______. *Assyrian Rulers of the Early First Millennium BC II (858-745 B.C.)*. Royal Inscriptions of Mesopotamia, Assyrian Periods 3. Edited by A. Kirk Grayson et al. Toronto, Buffalo, and London: University of Toronto Press, 1996.

Greenberg, Moshe. "Job." Pages 283-304 in *The Literary Guide to the Bible*. Edited by Robert Alter and Frank Kermode. Cambridge, Mass.: The Belknap Press of Harvard University, 1987.

Greenstein, Edward L. "A Forensic Understanding of the Speech from the Whirlwind." Pages 241-58 in *Texts, Temples, and Traditions: A Tribute to Menahem Haran*. Edited by M. V. Fox et al. Winona Lake, Ind.: Eisenbrauns, 1996.

______. "Aspects of Biblical Poetry." *Jewish Book Annual* 44 (1986-1987): 33-42.

______. "Features of Language in the Poetry of Job." Pages 81-96 in *Das Buch Hiob und seine Interpretationen. Beiträge zum Hiob-Symposium auf dem Monte Verità von 14.-19. August 2005*. Edited by Thomas Krüger et al. Abhandlungen zur Theologie des Alten und Neuen Testaments 88. Edited by Erhard Blum et al. Zürich: Theologischer Verlag Zürich, 2007.

______. "Kirta." Pages 9-48 in *Ugaritic Narrative Poetry*. Edited by Simon B. Parker. Society of Biblical Literature Writings from the Ancient World 9. Atlanta, Ga.: Scholars, 1997.

______. " 'On My Skin and in My Flesh': Personal Experience as a Source of Knowledge in the Book of Job." Pages 63-77 in *Bringing the Hidden to Light: The Process of Interpretation. Studies in Honor of Stephen A. Geller*. Edited by Kathryn F. Kravitz and Diane M. Sharon. Winona, Lake, Ind.: The Jewish Theological Seminary and Eisenbrauns, 2007.

______. "On the Prefixed Preterite in Biblical Hebrew." *Hebrew Studies* (1988): 7-17.

______. "Some Remarks on Metaphors in the Book of Job." Paper presented at the annual meeting of the SBL. Atlanta, Ga., November 2003.

______. "The Job of Translating Job." Pages 119-123 in *Essays in Biblical Method and Translation*. Brown Judaic Studies 92. Edited by Jacob Neusner, et al. Atlanta, Ga.: Scholars Press, 1989.

______."The Language of Job and its Poetic Function." *Journal of Biblical Literature* 122 (2003): 651-66.

______. "The Poem on Wisdom in Job 28 in its Conceptual and Literary Contexts." Pages 253-80 in *Job 28: Cognition in Context*. Edited by Ellen van Wolde. Biblical Interpretation 64. Edited by R. Alan Culpepper and Rolf Rendtorff. Leiden and Boston: E. J. Brill, 2003.

______. "The Poetic Use of Akkadian in the Book of Job." Paper presented at the annual meeting of the SBL. Boston, Mass., 24 November 2008.

______. "Theories of Modern Bible Translation." Pages 85-118 in *Essays in Biblical Method and Translation*. Brown Judaic Studies 92. Edited by Jacob Neusner, et al. Atlanta, Ga.: Scholars Press, 1989.

______. "Writing a Commentary on the Book of Job." Paper presented at the annual meeting of the SBL. Philadelphia, Pa., 22 November 2005.

Gruber, Mayer I. "Fear, Anxiety and Reverence in Akkadian, Biblical Hebrew and Other North-West Semitic Languages." *Vetus Testamentum* 40 (1990): 411-22.

______. "Human and Divine Wisdom in the Book of Job." Pages 88-102 in *Boundaries of the Ancient Near Eastern World: A Tribute to Cyrus H. Gordon*. Edited by Meir Lubetski, Claire Gottlieb and Sharon Keller. Journal for the Study of the Old Testament: Supplement Series 273. Sheffield: Sheffield Academic Press, 1998.

Guillaume, A. *Studies in the Book of Job with a New Translation*. Edited by John MacDonald. Annual of the Leeds University Oriental Society Supplement 2. Leiden: Brill, 1968.

Gunter, Ann C. "Materials, Technology, and Techniques in Artistic Production." Pages 1539-1552 in Volume 3 of *Civilizations of the Ancient Near East*. 4 vols. Edited by Jack Sasson. New York: Scribners, 1995.

Habel, Norman C. "Appeal to Ancient Tradition as a Literary Form." *Zeitschrift für die alttestamentliche Wissenschaft* 88 (1976): 253-272.

______. *The Book of Job: A Commentary*. Old Testament Library. Philadelphia, Pa.: Westminster, 1985.

______. "The Implications of God's Discovering Wisdom in Earth." Pages 281-98 in *Job 28: Cognition in Context*. Edited by Ellen van Wolde. Biblical Interpretation Series 64. Edited by R. Alan Culpepper and Rolff Rendtorff. Leiden and Boston: Brill, 2003.

Hadley, Judith M. "Wisdom and the Goddess." Pages 234-43 in *Wisdom in Ancient Israel: Essays in Honour of J. A. Emerton*. Edited by John Day, Robert P. Gordon, and H. G. M. Williamson. Cambridge: Cambridge University Press, 1995.

Hallo, W. W. and K. Lawson Younger, Jr., eds. *The Context of Scripture: Canonical Compositions, Monumental Inscriptions, and Archival Documents from the Biblical World*. 3 vols. Leiden and Boston: Brill, 2003.

Harris, Scott L. "Wisdom or Creation? A New Interpretation of Job xxviii 27." *Vetus Testamentum* 33 (1983): 419-27.

Hatch, Edwin and Henry A. Redpath. *A Concordance to the Septuagint and the Other Greek Versions of the Old Testament (Including the Apocryphal Books)*. 2d ed. Grand Rapids: Baker, 1991.

Hartley, John E. *The Book of Job*. New International Commentary on the Old Testament. Grand Rapids, Mich.: Eerdmans, 1988.

Heaney, Seamus. "The Impact of Translation." Pages 36-44 in *The Government of the Tongue: Selected Prose 1978-1987*. New York: The Noonday Press/Farrar, Straus and Giroux, 1988. Originally a contribution to the 1986 conference of the English Institute and printed in the *Yale Review*.

______. "The Redress of Poetry." Pages 1-16 in *The Redress of Poetry*. New York: The Noonday Press/Farrar, Straus, and Giroux, 1995. Originally delivered on 24 October 1989 as Oxford Professor of Poetry.

Heater, Jr., Homer. *A Septuagint Translation Technique in the Book of Job*. Catholic Biblical Quarterly Monograph Series 11. Washington, DC: The Catholic Biblical Association of America, 1982.

Hecke, Pierre van. "Are People Walking After or Before God?: On the Metaphorical Use of הלךְ אחרי and הלךְ לפני." *Orientalia lovaniensia periodica* 30 (1999): 37-71.

______. "Pastoral Metaphors in the Hebrew Bible and in its Ancient Near Eastern Context." Pages 200-217 in *The Old Testament in Its World. Oudtestamentische Studiën* 52. Edited by Robert P. Gordon and Johannes C. de Moor. Leiden and Boston: Brill, 2005.

______. "Searching for and Exploring Wisdom: A Cognitive Semantic Approach to the Hebrew Verb *ḥāqar* in Job 28." Pages 139-162 in *Job 28: Cognition in Context*. Edited by Ellen van Wolde. Biblical Interpretation 64. Edited by R. Alan Culpepper and Rolf Rendtorff. Leiden and Boston: Brill, 2003.

______. "Shepherds and Linguists: A Cognitive-Linguistic Approach to the Metaphor 'God is Shepherd' in Gen 48,15 and Context." Pages 479-93 in *Studies in the Book of Genesis: Literature, Redaction, and History*. Edited by A. Wénin. Bibliotheca ephemeridum theologicarum lovaniensium 155. Leuven: Leuven University Press, 2001.

Hecker, Karl. *Untersuchungen zur akkadischen Epik*. Alter Orient und Altes Testament 8. Edited by Kurt Bergerhof, Manfried Dietrich, and Oswald Loretz. Kevelaer: Butzon and Bercker. Neukirchen-Vluyn: Neukirchener, 1974.

Hess, Richard S. "Adam, Father, He: Gender Issues in Bible Translation." *The Bible Translator* 56 (2005): 144-53.

Hillers, Delbert R. "Dust: Some Aspects of Old Testament Imagery." Pages 105-109 in *Love and Death in the Ancient Near East: Essays in Honor of Marvin H. Pope*. Edited by John H. Marks and Robert M. Good; Guilford, Conn.: Four Quarters Publishing Company, 1987.

Hoffman, Yair. *A Blemished Perfection: The Book of Job in Context*. Translated by J. Chipman. Journal for the Study of the Old Testament: Supplement Series 213. Edited by David J. A. Clines and Philip R. Davies. Sheffield: Sheffield Academic Press, 1996. Originally published as *Sh'lemut p'gumah: sefer Iyyob we-riqᶜo*. Biblical Encyclopedia Library 12. Jerusalem and Tel Aviv: Bailik and Hayim Rosenburg, Tel Aviv University, 1995.

Hoftijzer, J. and K. Jongeling. *Dictionary of the North-West Semitic Inscriptions*. 2 vols. Handbuch der Orientalistik 1/21. Leiden, New York, Köln: E. J. Brill, 1995.

Hölscher, Gustav. *Das Buch Hiob*. 2d edition. Handbuch zum Alten Testament 17. Edited by Otto Eissfeldt. Tübingen: Mohr (Siebeck), 1952.

Horowitz, Wayne. *Mesopotamian Cosmic Geography*. Mesopotamian Civilizations 8. Edited by Jerrold S. Cooper. Winona Lake, Ind.: Eisenbrauns, 1998.

Hurowitz, Victor (Avigdor). *I Have Build You an Exalted House: Temple Building in the Bible in Light of Mesopotamian and Northwest Semitic Writings*. Journal for the Study of the Old Testament: Supplement Series 115. American Schools of Oriental Research Monograph Series 5. Edited by David J. A. Clines et al. Sheffield: Sheffield Academic Press, 1992.

Houtsma, Martijn Theodor. *Textkritische Studien zum Alten Testament I: Das Buch Hiob*. Leiden: E. J. Brill, 1925.

Hulsbosch, Ansfridus "Sagesse créatrice et éducatrice. I. Job 28." *Augustinianum* 1 (1961): 217-35.

Hurvitz, Avi. "Hebrew and Aramaic in the Biblical Period: The Problem of 'Aramaisms' in Linguistic Research on the Hebrew Bible." Pages 24-37 in *Biblical Hebrew: Studies in Chronology and Typology*. Edited by Ian Young. Journal for the Study of the Old Testament: Supplement Series 369. Edited by D. J. A. Clines et al. London and New York: T & T Clark, 2003.

______. "The Chronological Significance of 'Aramaisms' in Biblical Hebrew." *Israel Exploration Journal* 18 (1968): 234-40.

Jacobsen, Thorkild. "The Gilgamesh Epic: Romantic and Tragic Vision." Pages 231-49 in *Lingering Over Words: Studies in Ancient Near Eastern Literature in Honor of William L. Moran*. Edited by Tzvi Abusch, John Huehnergard, and Piotr Steinkeller. Harvard Semitic Studies 37. Atlanta, Ga.: Scholars Press, 1990.

______. *The Harps that Once...: Sumerian Poetry in Translation*. New Haven and London: Yale University Press, 1987.

______. *The Treasures of Darkness. A History of Mesopotamian Religion*. New Haven and London: Yale University Press, 1976.

Janzen, J. Gerald. *Job*. Interpretation: A Bible Commentary for Teaching and Preaching. Edited by James Mays. Atlanta: John Knox Press, 1985.

_______. "The Place of the Book of Job in the History of Israel's Religion." Pages 523-537 in *Ancient Israelite Religion: Essays in Honor of Frank Moore Cross*. Edited by Patrick D. Miller, Jr., Paul D. Hanson, and S. Dean McBride. Philadelphia, Pa.: Fortress, 1987.

Jastrow, Marcus. *A Dictionary of the Targumim, the Talmud Babli and Yerushalmi, and the Midrashic Literature*. 2 vols. London: Luzac; New York: G. Putnam's Sons, 1903.

Joüon, Paul. *A Grammar of Biblical Hebrew*. Translated and revised by Takamitsu Muraoka. 2 volumes. Subsidia biblica 14/1-2. Rome, 1991.

______. "Notes philologiques sur le texte hébreu de Job 1, 5; 9, 35; 12, 21; 28, 1; 28, 27; 29, 14." *Biblica* 11 (1930): 322-24.

Kamp, Albert. "World Building in Job 28: A Case of Conceptual Logic." Pages 307-320 in *Job 28: Cognition in Context*. Edited by Ellen van Wolde. Biblical Interpretation 64. Edited by R. Alan Culpepper and Rolf Rendtorff. Leiden and Boston: Brill, 2003.

Kaufman, Stephen A. "The Job Targum from Qumran." *Journal of the American Oriental Society* 93 (1973): 317-27.

Kautzsch, Emil. *Gesenius' Hebrew Grammar, as edited and enlarged by the late E. Kautzsch.* Second English edition revised in Accordance with the twenty-eighth German edition (1909) by A. E. Cowley. Oxford: Clarendon, 1910.
Kennicott, Benjamin. *Vetus Testamentum Hebraicum cum Variis Lectionibus.* 2 vols. Oxford: Clarendon, 1776-80.
Kimchi, David. *Sefer Ha Shorashim.* Venice: n.pub., 1746.
King, Philip J. and Lawrence E. Stager. *Life in Biblical Israel.* Library of Ancient Israel. Edited by Douglas A. Knight. Louisville, Ky.: Westminster John Knox, 2001.
Kinzie, Mary. *A Poet's Guide to Poetry.* Chicago, Ill.: University of Chicago, 1997.
Kittel, Rudolf, editor. *Biblia Hebraica.* 3d edition. Stuttgart: Württembergische Bibelanstalt, 1937.
Knudtzon, J. A. *Die El-Amarna-Tafeln.* 2 vols. Leipzig: J. C. Hinrichs, 1915.
Köhler, Ludwig. »Hebräische Vokabeln II.« *Zeitschrift für die alttestamentliche Wissenschaft* 55 (1937): 161-174.
______, Walter Baumgartner, and J. Jacob Stamm. *The Hebrew and Aramaic Lexicon of the Old Testament.* Translated and edited under the supervision of Mervin E. J. Richardson. 5 vols. Leiden, 1994-1999.
Kovacs, Maureen Gallery. *The Epic of Gilgamesh. Translated, with an Introduction and Notes.* Stanford, Ca.: Stanford University Press, 1985.
Kramer, Samuel Noah, and John Maier. *Myths of Enki, the Crafty God.* New York and Oxford: Oxford University Press, 1989.
Kuhl, Curt. »Die ›Wiederaufnahme‹—ein literarkritisches Prinzip?« *Zeitschrift für die alttestamentliche Wissenschaft* 64 (1952): 1-11.
______. »Neuere Literarkritik des Buches Hiob.« *Theologische Rundschau,* neue Folge 21 (1953): 257-317.
Kutz, Karl V. "The Old Greek of Job: A Study in Early Biblical Exegesis." Ph.D. diss., University of Wisconsin-Madison, 1997.
______. "Characterization in the Old Greek of Job." Pages 345-55 in *Seeking Out the Wisdom of the Ancients: Essays Offered to Honor Michael V. Fox on the Occasion of his Sixty-Fifth Birthday.* Edited by Ronald L. Troxel, Kelvin G. Friebel, and Dennis R. Magary. Winona Lake, Ind.: Eisenbrauns, 2005.

Lagarde, Paul de. *Hagiographa Chaldaice.* Leipzig: B. G. Teubner, 1873.
Lakoff, George and Mark Johnson, *Metaphors We Live By.* Chicago and London: University of Chicago Press, 1980.
Lambdin, Thomas O. "Egyptian Loan Words in the Old Testament." *Journal of the American Oriental Society* 73 (1953): 145-55.
Lambert, W. G. "The Sultantepe Tablets: VIII. Shalmaneser in Ararat." *Anatolian Studies* 11 (1981): 143-158.
Langdon, Stephen. *Die Neubabylonischen Königsinschriften.* Translated by Rudolf Zehnpfund. Vorderasiatische Bibliothek 4. Leipzig: J. C. Hinrichs, 1912.
Lange, N. R. M. de. "Some New Fragments of Aquila on Malachi and Job?" *Vetus Testamentum* 30 (1980): 291-94.
Lete, Gregorio del Olmo and Joaquín Sanmartín, *A Dictionary of the Ugaritic Language in the Alphabetic Tradition.* 2d, revised edition. 2 vols. Handbuch der Orientalistik 67. Edited and Translated by Wilfred G. E. Watson. Leiden and Boston: Brill, 2004.

Levenson, Jon D. *Sinai and Zion. An Entry into the Jewish Bible.* San Francisco: Harper, 1985.

______. *Creation and the Persistence of Evil: The Jewish Drama of Divine Omnipotence.* Princeton, NJ: Princeton University Press, 1988.

Lévêque, Jean. *Job et son Dieu: Essai d'exégèse et le théologie biblique.* 2 vols. *Études bibliques.* Paris: Gabalda, 1970.

______. "L'argument de la création dans le livre de Job." Pages 261-299 in *La Création dans l'Orient Ancien.* Lectio Divina 127. Congrès de l'ACFEB, Lille [1985]. Edited by F. Blanquart. Paris: Cerf, 1987.

Lewis, C. S. *A Preface to Paradise Lost.* London: Oxford University Press, 1942.

______. "Bluspels and Flalansferes: A Semantic Nightmare." Pages 251-65 in *Selected Literary Essays.* Edited by Walter Hooper. Cambridge, U.K.: Cambridge University Press, 1969.

______. *Studies in Words.* 2d edition. Cambridge, New York, and Melbourne: Cambridge University Press, 1960.

Lewis, Theodore J. "*CT* 13.33-34 and Ezekiel 32: Lion-Dragon Myths." *Journal of the American Oriental Society* 116 (1996): 28-47.

______. *Cults of the Dead in Ancient Israel and Ugarit.* Harvard Semitic Monographs 39. Atlanta, Ga.: Scholars Press, 1989.

Ley, Julius. *Das Buch Hiob nach seinem Inhalt, seiner Kunstgestaltung und religiösen Bedeutung.* Halle: Verlag der Buchhandlung des Waisenhauses, 1903.

Liddell, Henry George and Robert Scott. *A Greek-English Lexicon.* Oxford: Clarendon, 1996.

Lindenberger, James M. *The Aramaic Proverbs of Ahiqar.* Baltimore and London: The Johns Hopkins University Press, 1983.

Lipiński, Edward. "Éa, Kothar et El." *Ugarit-Forschungen* 20 (1988):137-143.

Lisowski, Gerhard. *Konkordanz zum Hebräischen Alten Testament: nach dem von Paul Kahle in der Biblia Hebraica edidit Rudolf Kittel besorgten Masoretischen Text: unter verantwortlicher Mitwirkung von Leonard Rost.* 3d edition. Edited by Hans Peter Rüger. Stuttgart: Deutsche Bibelgesellschaft, 1993. Previously published 1958, 1966.

Liverani, Mario. "The Deeds of Ancient Mesopotamian Kings." Pages 2353-2366 in Volume 4 of *Civilizations of the Ancient Near East.* 4 vols. Edited by Jack Sasson. New York: Scribners, 1995.

Lo, Alison. *Job 28 as Rhetoric: An Analysis of Job 28 in the Context of Job 22-31.* Vetus Testamentum Supplements 97. Edited by Hans M. Barstad et al. Leiden and Boston, Brill, 2003.

Löhr, Max. »Job c. 28.« Pages 67-70 in *Oriental Studies Published in Commemoration of the Fortieth Anniversary (1883-1923) of Paul Haupt as Director of the Oriental Seminary of the Johns Hopkins University, Baltimore, MD.* Baltimore, Md.: Johns Hopkins University Press, 1926.

Louden, Bruce. "The Gods in Epic, or the Divine Economy." Pages 90-104 in *A Companion to Ancient Epic.* Edited by John Miles Foley. Malden, Mass.; Oxford; and Carlton, Victoria: Blackwell, 2005.

Lowth, Robert. "Lecture XXXII: Of the Poem of Job." Pages 345-85 in Volume 2 of *Lectures on the Sacred Poetry of the Hebrews*. Translated by G. Gregory. 2 vols. London: J. Johnson, 1787. Originally published as *De sacra poesi Hebraeorum: praelectiones academicae Oxonii habitae: subjicitur Metricae Harianae brevis confutatio, et Oratio Crewiana: notas et epimetra adiecit Ioannes David Michaelis*. Göttingen: Pockwizil and Barmeier, 1758.

Luckenbill, Daniel David. *Ancient Records of Assyria and Babylonia*. 2 vols. Chicago: University of Chicago Press, 1927.

Lugt, Pieter van der. *Rhetorical Criticism and the Poetry of the Book of Job*. *Oudtestamentische Studiën* 32. Edited by A. S. van der Woude. Leiden, New York, and Köln: E. J. Brill, 1995.

______. "The Form and Function of the Refrains in Job 28: Some Comments Relating to the 'Strophic' Structure of Hebrew Poetry." Pages 265-293 in *The Structural Analysis of Biblical and Canaanite Poetry*. Journal for the Study of the Old Testament: Supplement Series 74. Edited by Willem van der Meer and Johannes C. de Moor. Sheffield: Sheffield Academic Press, 1988.

McKane, William. "Benjamin Kennicott: An Eighteenth-Century Researcher." *Journal of Theological Studies* 28 (1977): 445-64.

______. "The Theology of the Book of Job and Chapter 28 in Particular." Pages 711-22 in *Gott und Mensch im Dialog: Festschrift für Otto Kaiser zum 80. Geburtstag*. Edited by Markus Witte. Beihefte zur Zeitschrift für die alttestamentliche Wissenschaft 345/II. Berlin and New York: Walter de Gruyter, 2004.

Mankowski, Paul V. *Akkadian Loanwords in Biblical Hebrew*. Harvard Semitic Studies 47. Edited by Lawrence E. Stager. Winona Lake, Ind.: Eisenbrauns, 2000.

Marcos, Natalio Fernández. "The Septuagint Reading of the Book of Job." Pages 251-66 in *The Book of Job*. Edited by W. A. M. Beuken. Bibliotheca ephemeridum theologicarum lovaniensium 114. Leuven: Leuven University Press, 1994.

Mangan, Céline. "The Interpretation of Job in the Targums." Pages 267-80 in *The Book of Job*. Edited by W.A.M. Beuken. Bibliotheca ephemeridum theologicarum lovaniensium 114. Leuven: Leuven University Press, 1994.

______. "The Targum of Job. Translated with a Critical Introduction, Apparatus, and Notes." *The Aramaic Bible: The Targums of Job, Proverbs, and Qohelet*. The Aramaic Bible 15. Edited by Kevin Cathcart, Michael Maher, and Martin MacNamara. Collegeville, Minn.: Liturgical Press, 1991.

Martin, Gary W. "Elihu and the Third Cycle in the Book of Job." Ph.D. diss, Princeton University, 1972.

Martínez, Florentino García, Eibert J. C. Tigchelaar, and Adam S. van der Woude. *Qumran Cave 11/2 (11Q2-18, 11Q20-31)*. Discoveries in the Judean Desert XXIII. Oxford: Clarendon, 1998.

Maul, Stefan. *Das Gilgamesch-epos: Neu übersetzt und kommentiert*. Münich: C. H. Beck, 2005.

Mayer, Walter. »Sargons Feldzug gegen Urartu – 714 v. Chr. Text und Übersetzung.« *Mitteilungen der Deutschen Orient-Gesellschaft zu Berlin* 115 (1983): 65-132.

Merino, Luis Díez. "Manuscritos del Targum de Job." *Henoch* 4 (1982): 41-64.

______. *Targum de Job: Edición Principe del Ms. Villa-Amil n. 5 de Alfonso de Zamora*. Bibliotheca Hispana Biblica 8. Madrid: Consejo Superior de Investigaciones Cientificas, Instituto "Francisco Suarez," 1984.

Merwe, Christo H. J. van der, Jackie A. Naudé, and Jan H. Kroeze. *A Biblical Hebrew Reference Grammar*. Biblical Languages: Hebrew 3. Edited by Stanley E. Porter and Richard S. Hess. Sheffield: Sheffield Academic Press, 1999.

Michel, Walter. "ṢLMWT, 'Deep Darkness' or 'Shadow of Death'?" *Biblical Research* 29 (1984): 5-20.

______. "The Ugaritic Texts and the Mythological Expressions in the Book of Job." Ph.D. diss., University of Wisconsin-Madison, 1970.

Miller, Jr., Patrick D. "Meter, Parallelism, and Tropes: The Search for Poetic Style." *Journal for the Study of the Old Testament* 28 (1984): 99-106.

Monroe, Christopher M. "Money and Trade." Pages 171-183 in *A Companion to the Ancient Near East*. Edited by Daniel C. Snell. Blackwell Companions to the Ancient World: Ancient History. Malden, Mass., Oxford, England, and Carlton, Victoria: Blackwell, 2005.

Moran, William L. "The Gilgamesh Epic: A Masterpiece from Ancient Mesopotamia." Pages 2327-2336 in Volume 4 of *Civilizations of the Ancient Near East*. 4 vols. Edited by Jack Sasson. New York: Scribners, 1995.

______. "The Hebrew Language in its Northwest Semitic Background." Pages 54-72 in *The Bible and the Ancient Near East: Essays in Honor of William Foxwell Albright*. Edited by G. Ernest Wright; Garden City, NY: Doubleday, 1961.

Mowinckel, Sigmund. "שׁחל." Pages 95-103 in *Hebrew and Semitic Studies Presented to Godfrey Rolles Driver*. Edited by D. Winton Thomas and W. D. McHardy. Oxford: Clarendon, 1963.

Muhly, James D. "Mining and Metalwork in Ancient Western Asia." Pages 1501-1522 in Volume 3 of *Civilizations of the Ancient Near East*. 4 vols. Edited by Jack Sasson. New York: Scribners, 1995.

Muilenburg, James. "The Linguistic and Rhetorical Usages of the Particle כי in the Old Testament." *Hebrew Union College Annual* 32 (1961): 135-60.

Müller, Hans-Peter. *Das Hiobproblem: Seine Stellung und Entstehung im Alten Orient und im Alten Testament*. Erträge der Forschung 84. Darmstadt: Wissenschaftliche Buchgesellschaft, 1978.

Müllner, Ilse. »Der Ort des Verstehens: Ijob 28 als Erkenntnisdiskussion des Ijobbuchs.« Pages 57-83 in *Das Buch Ijob: Gesamtdeutungen—Einzeltexte—Zentrale Themen*. Edited by Theodor Seidl and Stephanie Ernst. Österreichische Biblische Studien 31. Edited by Georg Braulik. Frankfurt am Main: Peter Lang, 2007.

Muraoka, Takamitsu. *Emphatic Words and Structures in Biblical Hebrew*. Jerusalem: Magnes; Leiden: E. J. Brill, 1985.

______. "The Aramaic of the Old Targum of Job from Qumran Cave XI." *Journal of Jewish Studies* 25 (1974): 425-443.

______. "Words of Cognition in Job 28: Hebrew and Greek." Pages 93-102 in *Job 28: Cognition in Context*. Edited by Ellen van Wolde. Biblical Interpretation 64. Edited by R. Alan Culpepper and Rolf Rendtorff. Leiden and Boston: Brill, 2003.

Murphy, Roland E. "The Personification of Wisdom." Pages 222-233 in *Wisdom in Ancient Israel: Essays in Honour of J. A. Emerton*. Edited by John Day, Robert P. Gordon, and H. G. M. Williamson. Cambridge: Cambridge University Press, 1995.

Newsom, Carol A. "Bakhtin, the Bible, and Dialogic Truth." *Journal of Religion* 76 (1996): 290-306.

______. "Dialogue and Allegorical Hermeneutics in Job 28:28." Pages 299-306 in *Job 28: Cognition in Context*. Edited by Ellen van Wolde. Biblical Interpretation 64. Edited by R. Alan Culpepper and Rolf Rendtorff. Leiden and Boston: Brill, 2003.

______. "Job, Book of." Pages 412-413 in Volume One of *Encyclopedia of the Dead Sea* Scrolls. 2 vols. Edited by Lawrence H. Schiffmann and James A. Vanderkam. Oxford: Oxford University Press, 2000.

______. "Re-considering Job." *Currents in Biblical Research* 5 (2007): 155-182.

______. *The Book of Job: A Contest of Moral Imaginations*. Oxford and New York: Oxford University Press, 2003.

______. "The Book of Job: Introduction Commentary, and Reflections." Pages 319-637 in *The New Interpreter's Bible, Volume IV: 1 & 2 Maccabees; Introduction to Hebrew Poetry; Job; Psalms*. Edited by Leander Keck et al. Nashville, Tenn.: Abingdon, 1996.

______. "The Book of Job as Polyphonic Text." *Journal for the Study of the Old Testament* 97 (2002): 87-108.

______. "The Moral Sense of Nature: Ethics in the Light of God's Speech." *Princeton Seminary Bulletin*, new series 15 (1994): 9-27.

Niccacci, Alviero. "Analysing Biblical Hebrew Poetry." *Journal for the Study of the Old Testament* 74 (1997): 77-93.

______. "Giobbe 28." *Studii biblici Franciscani liber annus* 31 (1981): 29-58.

______. "The Biblical Hebrew Verbal System in Poetry." Pages 247-268 in *Biblical Hebrew in its Northwest Semitic Setting: Typological and Historical Perspectives*. Edited by Steven E. Fassberg and Avi Hurvitz. Publication of the Institute for Advanced Studies 1. Jerusalem: The Hebrew University Magnes Press; Winona Lake, Ind.: Eisenbrauns, 2006.

Niditch, Susan. "Folklore and Wisdom: *Mashal* as an Ethnic Genre." Pages 67-87 in idem, *Folklore and the Hebrew Bible*. Guides to Biblical Scholarship: Old Testament Series. Minneapolis, Minn.: Fortress, 1993.

Noegel, Scott B. "Mesopotamian Epic." Pages 233-245 in *A Companion to Ancient Epic*. Edited by John Miles Foley. Malden, Mass.; Oxford; and Carlton, Victoria: Blackwell, 2005.

Nougayrol, Jean, et al., eds. *Ugaritica V: Nouveaux texts accadiens, hourrites et ugaritiques des archives et bibliothèques privées d'Ugarit; commentaries des texts historiques, première partie*. Mission de Ras Shamra 16. Paris: Imprimerie Nationale, 1968.

Oorschot, Jürgen van. »Hiob 28: Verborgene Weisheit und die Furcht Gottes als Überwindung einer Generalisierten חכמה.« Pages 183-201 in *The Book of Job*. Edited by W.A.M. Beuken. Bibliotheca ephemeridum theologicarum lovaniensium 114. Leuven: Leuven University Press, 1994.

Oppenheim, A. Leo. "Essay on Overland Trade in the First Millennium B.C." *Journal of Cuneiform Studies* 21 (1967): 236-254.

Orlinsky, Harry. "Studies in the Septuagint of the Book of Job. Chapter I: An Analytical Survey of Previous Studies." *Hebrew Union College Annual* 28 (1957): 53-74.

______. "Studies in the Septuagint of the Book of Job. Chapter II: The Character of the Septuagint Translation of the Book of Job." *Hebrew Union College Annual* 29 (1958): 229-71.

______. "Studies in the Septuagint of the Book of Job. Chapter III: On the Matter of Anthropomorphisms, Anthropopathisms, and Euphemisms." *Hebrew Union College Annual* 30 (1959): 153-67

______. "Studies in the Septuagint of the Book of Job. Chapter III.B.: Anthropopathisms." *Hebrew Union College Annual* 32 (1961): 239-68.

______. "Studies in the Septuagint of the Book of Job. Chapter IV: The Present State of the Greek Text of Job." *Hebrew Union College Annual* 33 (1962): 119-51.

______. "Studies in the Septuagint of the book of Job. Chapter V: The Hebrew *Vorlage* of the Septuagint of Job: A. The Text and Script." *Hebrew Union College Annual* 35 (1964): 57-78.

______. "Studies in the Septuagint of the Book of Job. Chapter V.: The Hebrew *Vorlage* of the Septuagint of Job: B. The Kethib and the Qere." *Hebrew Union College Annual* 36 (1966): 37-47.

______. "The Septuagint as Holy Writ and the Philosophy of the Translators." *Hebrew Union College Annual* 46 (1975): 89-114.

Pardee, Dennis. Review of Josef Tropper, *Ugaritische Grammatik*. *Archiv für Orientforschung* online version 50 (2003/2004): 1-404.

Payne Smith, J. (Mrs. Margoliouth), editor. *A Compendious Syriac Dictionary*. Founded upon the *Thesaurus Syriacus* by R. Payne Smith. Oxford: Clarendon, 1903.

Perdue, Leo G. "Cosmology and the Social Order in the Wisdom Tradition." Pages 457-478 in *The Sage in Israel and the Ancient Near East*. Edited by John G. Gammie and Leo G. Perdue. Winona Lake, Ind.: Eisenbrauns, 1990.

______. "Job's Assault on Creation." *Hebrew Annual Review* (1987): 295-315.

______. "Wisdom in the Book of Job." Pages 73-98 in *In Search of Wisdom: Essays in Memory of John G. Gammie*. Edited by Leo G. Perdue, Bernard Brandon Scott, and William Johnston Wiseman. Louisville, Ky: Westminster John Knox, 1993.

Peters, Norbert. *Das Buch Job übersetzt und erklärt*. Exegetisches Handbuch zum Alten Testament 21. Edited by Alfons Schulz-Breslau. Münster in Westfalia: Verlag der Aschendorffschen Verlagsbuchhandlung, 1928.

Pinches, Theophilus Goldridge. "Hymns to Pap-due-garra." Pages 63-86 in *Journal of the Royal Asiatic Society Centenary Supplement, 1924*. London: The Royal Asiatic Society of Great Britain and Ireland, 1924.

Pliny, *Natural History*. Edited by Eicholz. 10 vols. Loeb Classical Library. Cambridge: Harvard University Press, 1938-1962.
Ploeg, J. P. M. van der and A. S. van der Woude (with the collaboration of B. Jongeling). *Le Targum de Job de la Grotte XI de Qumrân*. Leiden: E. J. Brill, 1971.
Polak, Frank. "On Prose and Poetry in the Book of Job." *Journal of the Ancient Near Eastern Society of Columbia University* 24 (1996): 61-97.
Polk, Timothy. "Paradigms, Parables, and *Měšālîm*: On Reading the *Māšāl* in Scripture." *Catholic Biblical Quarterly* 45 (1983): 564-583.
Pope, Marvin H. *El in the Ugaritic Texts*. Vetus Testamentum Supplements 2. Leiden: E. J. Brill, 1955.
______. *Job, Translated with an Introduction and Notes*. 3d edition. Anchor Bible 15. Garden City, NY: Doubleday and Company, 1973.
______. " 'Pleonastic' Wāw Before Nouns in Ugaritic and Hebrew." *Journal of the American Oriental Society* 73 (1953): 95-98.
Powels, Sylvia. »Indische Lehnwörter in der Bibel.« *Zeitschrift für Althebraistik* 5 (1992): 186-200.
Propp, William Henry. *Water in the Wilderness: A Biblical Motif and its Mythological Background*. Harvard Semitic Monographs 40. Edited by Frank Moore Cross. Atlanta, Ga.: Scholars Press, 1987.

Rad, Gerhard von. *Weisheit in Israel*. Neukirchen-Vluyn: Neukirchener, 1970.
Rahlfs, Alfred. *Septuaginta, Id est Vetus Testamentum graece iuxta LXX interpretes*. Stuttgart: Deutsche Bibelgesellschaft, 1935.
Reddy, M. Prakasa. "The Book of Job—A Reconstruction." *Zeitschrift für die alttestamentliche Wissenschaft* 90 (1978): 59-94.
Regnier, A. "La Distribution des Chapitres 25-28 du Livre de Job." *Revue biblique* 33 (1924): 186-200.
Reichert, Victor E. *Job. Hebrew Text & English Translation with an Introduction and Commentary*. Soncino Books of the Bible. Edited by A. Cohen. London, Jerusalem, and New York: The Soncino Press, 1946.
Reider, Joseph. *An Index to Aquila*. Completed and revised by Nigel Turner. Vetus Testamentum Supplements 12. Edited by G. W. Anderson et al. Leiden: E. J. Brill, 1966.
______. "Contributions to the Scriptural Text." *Hebrew Union College Annual* 24 (1952/53): 85-106.
______. "Etymological Studies in Biblical Hebrew." *Vetus Testamentum* 2 (1952): 113-30.
Rendsburg, Gary A. "A New Look at Penteteuchal *HWʾ*." *Biblica* 63 (1982): 351-69.
______. "Hebrew Philological Notes (II)." *Hebrew Studies* 42 (2001): 187-95.
Renz, Johannes, and Wolfgang Röllig. *Handbuch der Althebräischen Epigraphik*. 3 vols. Darmstadt: Wissenschaftliche Buchgesellschaft, 1995-2003.
Revard, Stella P. "Epic: I. History." Pages 361-75 in *The New Princeton Encyclopedia of Poetry and Poetics*. Edited by Alex Preminger and T. V. F. Brogan. New York: MJF Books, 1993.
Rignell, L. G. "Notes on the Peshiṭta of the Book of Job." *Annual of the Swedish Theological Institute* 9 (1973): 98-106.

______. *The Old Testament in Syriac According to the Peshiṭta Version*. Edited on behalf of the International Organization for the Study of the Old Testament by The Peshiṭta Institute, Leiden. Part II, fascicle 1a. Leiden: E. J. Brill, 1982.

______. *The Peshitta to the Book of Job, Critically Investigated with Introduction, Translation, Commentary, and Summary*. Edited by Karl-Erik Rignell. Kristianstad: Monitor, 1994.

Roberts, J. J. M. "Job's Summons to Yahweh: The Exploitation of a Legal Metaphor." *Restoration Quarterly* 16 (1974): 159-65.

______. "*NIŠKAḤTÎ ... MILLĒB*, Ps. xxxi 13." *Vetus Testamentum* 25 (1975): 797-800.

Rossi, Johannes B. de. *Variae Lectiones Veteris Testamenti ex Immensa MSS*. Parma: Ex Regio Typographeo, 1784.

Roth, Martha T. *Law Collections from Mesopotamia and Asia Minor*. 2d edition. With a Contribution by Harry A. Hoffner, Jr. Edited by Piotr Michalowski. SBLWAW 6. Edited by Simon B. Parker. Atlanta, Ga.: Scholars, 1997.

______. et al, editors. *The Assyrian Dictionary of the Oriental Institute of the University of Chicago*. Chicago, 1956-.

Rowley, H. H. *The Book of Job*. Revised Edition. New Century Bible. Grand Rapids, Mich.: Eerdmans, 1976.

Russell, H. F. "Shalmaneser's Campaign to Urartu in 856 B.C. and the Historical Geography of Eastern Anatolia According to the Assyrian Sources." *Anatolian Studies* 34 (1984): 171-201.

Sasson, Jack M. "Comparative Observations on the Near Eastern Epic Traditions." Pages 215-232 in *A Companion to Ancient Epic*. Edited by John Miles Foley. Malden, Mass., Oxford, UK, and Carlton, Victoria: Blackwell, 2005.

Sawyer, John F. A. "The Authorship and Structure of the Book of Job." Pages 253-57 in *Studia Biblica 1978: I. Papers on Old Testament and Related Themes*. Sixth International Congress on Biblical Studies, Oxford 3-7 April 1978. Edited by E. A. Livingstone. Journal for the Study of the Old Testament: Supplement Series 11. Sheffield: JSOT Press, 1979.

Schmid, H. H. "Creation, Righteousness, and Salvation: 'Creation Theology' as the Broad Horizon of Biblical Theology." Pages 102-117 in *Creation in the Old Testament*. Translated by B. Anderson and Dan G. Johnson. Issues in Religion and Theology 6. Edited by B. Anderson. Philadelphia: Fortress, 1984. Originally published in *Zeitschrift für Theologie und Kirche* 70 (1973): 1-19.

______. *Gerechtigkeit als Weltordnung*. Beiträge zur historischen Theologie 40. Tübingen: Mohr Siebeck, 1968.

Schökel, Luis Alonso. *A Manual of Hebrew Poetics. Subsidia Biblica* 11. Rome: Pontifical Biblical Institute, 1988.

______. and J. L. Sicre Díaz. *Job: Comentario teológico y literario*. Nueva Biblia Española. Madrid: Ediciones Cristiandad, 1983.

Schoors, Anton. "The Particle כִּי." Pages 240-276 in *Remembering all the way...: A collection of Old Testament studies published on the occasion of the fortieth anniversary of the Oudtestamentisch Werkgezelschap in Nederland. Oudtestamentische Studiën* 11. Edited by A. S. van der Woude, et al. Leiden: Brill, 1981.

Schulz-Flügel, Eva. "The Latin Old Testament Tradition." Pages 642-62 in Volume I.1 of *Hebrew Bible / Old Testament: Its History of Interpretation*. Edited by Magne Saebø. 2 vols. Göttingen: Vandenhoeck and Ruprecht, 1996.

Scurlock, Jo Ann. "Death and the Afterlife in Ancient Mesopotamian Thought." Pages 1883-1894 in Volume 3 of *Civilizations of the Ancient Near East*. 4 vols. Edited by Jack Sasson. New York: Scribners, 1995.

Seow, C. L. "The Orthography of Job and its Poetic Effects." Paper presented at the annual meeting of the SBL. Boston, Mass., 24 November 2008.

Settlemire, Clara Catherine. "The Meaning, Importance, and Original Position of Job 28." Ph.D. diss., Drew University, 1969.

______. "The Original Position of Job 28." Pages 287-317 in *The Answers Lie Below: Essays in Honor of Lawrence Edmund Toombs*. Edited by Henry O. Thompson. Lanham, New York, and London: University Press of America, 1984.

Shepherd, David. *Targum and Translation: A Reconsideration of the Qumran Aramaic Version of Job*. Edited by W.J. van Bekkum et al. Studia semitica neederlandica 45. Assen, The Netherlands: Van Gorcum, 2004.

______. "Will the Real Targum Please Stand Up?: Translation and Coordination in the Ancient Aramaic Versions of Job." *Journal of Jewish Studies* 51 (2000): 88-116.

Skehan, Patrick W., Eugene Ulrich, and Judith E. Sanderson, eds. *Qumran Cave 4/IV: Palaeo-Hebrew and Greek Biblical Manuscripts*. Discoveries in the Judean Desert 9. Oxford: Clarendon, 1992.

Sivan, Daniel. *A Grammar of the Ugaritic Language*. Handbuch der Orientalistik 28. Leiden, New York, and Köln: E. J. Brill, 1997.

Sjöberg, Åke, Erle Leichty, and Steve Tinney. The Pennsylvania Sumerian Dictionary Project. Online: http://psd.museum.upenn.edu/epsd/index.html.

Smith, Barbara Herrnstein. *Poetic Closure: A Study of How Poems End*. Chicago and London: The University of Chicago Press, 1968.

Smith, Mark S. "The Baal Cycle." Pages 81-176 in *Ugaritic Narrative Poetry*. Edited by Simon B. Parker. Society of Biblical Literature Writings from the Ancient World 9. Atlanta, Ga.: Scholars Press, 1997.

______. *The Origins of Biblical Monotheism: Israel's Polytheistic Background and the Ugaritic Texts*. Oxford and New York: Oxford University Press, 2001.

Snaith, Norman H. *The Book of Job: Its Origin and Purpose*. Studies in Biblical Theology, second series. Edited by C. F. D. Moule et al. Naperville, Ill.: Allenson, 1968.

Snell, Daniel C. *Life in the Ancient Near East*. New Haven and London: Yale University Press, 1997.

______. "Methods of Exchange and Coinage in Ancient Western Asia." Pages 1487-1497 in Volume 3 of of *Civilizations of the Ancient Near East*. 4 vols. Edited by Jack Sasson. New York: Scribners, 1995.

Snodgrass, Klyne. *Stories with Intent: A Comprehensive Guide to the Parables of Jesus*. Grand Rapids, Mich., and Cambridge, U.K.: Eerdmans, 2008.

Soden, Wolfram von. *Akkadisches Handwörterbuch*. 3 vols. Wiesbaden: Otto Harrasowitz, 1965-81.

______. »Kleine Beiträge zum Ugaritischen und Hebräischen.« Pages 291-300 in *Hebräische Wortforschung. Festschrift zum 80. Geburtstag von Walter Baumgartner*. Vetus Testamentum Supplements 16. Edited by G. W. Anderson et al. Leiden: E. J. Brill, 1967.

Sokoloff, Michael. *A Dictionary of Jewish Palestinian Aramaic of the Byzantine Period*. Second Edition. Ramat-Gan, Israel: Bar-Ilan University Press; Baltimore, Md.: The Johns Hopkins University Press, 2002.

______. *The Targum to Job from Qumran Cave XI*. Ramat-Gan, Israel: Bar-Ilan University Press, 1974.

Stager, Lawrence E. "Jerusalem and the Garden of Eden." *Eretz Israel* 26 (1999): 183*-194*.

______. "Jerusalem as Eden." *Biblical Archaeology Review* 26/3 (May-June, 2000): 36-47, 66.

Stec, David M. The *Text of the Targum of Job: An Introduction and Critical Edition*. Arbeiten zur Geschichte des antiken Judentums und des Urchristentums 20. Leiden, New York, and Köln: E. J. Brill, 1994.

Steen, Eveline J. van der. "Mining." Pages 91-92 in Volume 4 of *The New Interpreter's Dictionary of the Bible*. Edited by K. D. Sakenfeld. 5 vols. Nashville, Tenn.: Abingdon, 2006-2009.

Stevens, Wallace. "Adagia." Pages 184-202 in *Opus Posthumous*. Revised, enlarged, and corrected edition. Edited by Milton J. Bates. New York: Vintage Books, 1990. Originally published 1957.

______. "Poetry and Meaning." Pages 249-50 in *Opus Posthumous*. Revised, enlarged, and corrected edition. Edited by Milton J. Bates. New York: Vintage Books, 1990. Originally published 1957.

Strauß, Hans. *Hiob 19,1-42,7*. Biblischer Kommentar, Altes Testament 16/2. Edited by M. Noth and H. W. Wolff. Neukirchen-Vluyn: Neukirchen Verlag, 2000.

Strawn, Brent A. *What is Stronger than a Lion?: Leonine Image and Metaphor in the Hebrew Bible and the Ancient Near East*. Orbis Biblicus et Orientalis 212; Fribourg: Academic Press; Göttingen: Vandenhoeck and Ruprecht, 2005.

Sutcliffe, E. F. "The Clouds as Water-Carriers in Hebrew Thought." *Vetus Testamentum* 3 (1953): 99-103.

Sweet, Ronald F. G. "The Sage in Akkadian Literature: A Philological Study." Pages 45-65 in *The Sage in Israel and the Ancient Near East*. Edited by John G. Gammie and Leo G. Perdue. Winona Lake, Ind.: Eisenbrauns, 1990.

Szpek, Heidi M. "An Observation on the Peshiṭta's Translation of *ŠDY* in Job." *Vetus Testamentum* 47 (1997): 550-53.

______. *Translation Technique in the Peshitta to Job: A Model for Evaluating a Text with Documentation from the Peshitta to Job*. Society of Biblical Literature Dissertation Series 137. Edited by David L. Petersen. Atlanta, Ga.: Scholars, 1992.

______. "On the Influence of the Septuagint on the Peshitta." *Catholic Biblical Quarterly* 60 (1998): 251-266.

______. "On the Influence of the Targum on the Peshitta to Job." Pages 142-158 in *Targum Studies, Volume Two: Targum and Peshitta*. Edited by Paul V. M. Flesher. South Florida Studies in the History of Judaism. Edited by Jacob Neusner. Atlanta, Ga.: Scholars and University of South Florida, 1998.

Talon, Philippe. *The Standard Babylonian Creation Myth Enūma Eliš: Introduction, Cuneiform Text, Transliteration, and Sign List with a Translation and Glossary in French*. State Archives of Assyria Cuneiform Texts 4. Helsinki: The Neo-Assyrian Text Corpus Project, 2005.

Tanselle, G. Thomas. *A Rationale of Textual Criticism*. Philadelphia: University of Pennsylvania Press, 1989.

Terrien, Samuel. "Fear." Pages 256-260 in Volume 2 of *The Interpreter's Dictionary of the Bible: An Illustrated Encyclopedia*. Edited by G. A. Buttrick. 4 vols. Nashville, Tenn.: Abingdon, 1962.

______. *Job*. Commentaire de l'ancien Testament XIII. Neuchâtel: Delachaux & Niestlé, 1963.

Thomas, D. Winton. "צַלְמָוֶת in the Old Testament." *Journal of Semitic Studies* 7 (1962): 191-200.

Thompson, R. Campbell. *Cuneiform Texts from Babylonian Tablets, &c. in the British Museum. Part XVIII*. London: Trustees of the British Museum, 1904.

Thureau-Dangin, François. *Die Sumerischen und Akkadischen Königsinschriften*. Vorderasiatische Bibliothek 1/1. Leipzig: J. C. Hinrichs, 1907.

______. *Rituels accadiens*. Paris: E. Leroux, 1921.

______. *Une relation de la huitème campagne de Sargon (714 av. J.-C.)*. Musée du Louvre—Département des antiquités orientales. Paris: Paul Geuthner, 1912.

Toorn, Karel van der. *Scribal Culture and the Making of the Hebrew Bible*. Cambridge, Mass., and London: Harvard University Press, 2007.

______. "Why Wisdom Became a Secret: On Wisdom as a Written Genre." Pages 21-32 in *Wisdom Literature in Mesopotamia and Israel*. Edited by Richard J. Clifford. Society of Biblical Literature Symposium Series 36. Edited by Christopher R. Matthews. Atlanta, Ga.: Society of Biblical Literature, 2007.

Torczyner, Harry. *Das Buch Hiob. Eine Kritische Analyse des Überlieferten Hiobtextes*. Wien and Berlin: R. Löwit Verlag, 1920. (see also s.v. Tur-Sinai)

Tournay, R. "L'Ordre primitif des Chapitres XXIV-XXVIII du Livre de Job." *Revue biblique* 64 (1957): 321-34.

Tov, Emanuel. *Textual Criticism of the Hebrew Bible*. 2d, revised edition. Minneapolis, Minn.: Fortress; Assen: Royal Van Gorcum, 2001.

Tromp, Nicholas J. *Primitive Conceptions of Death and the Nether World in the Old Testament*. Biblica et Orientalia 21. Rome: Pontifical Biblical Institute, 1969.

Tropper, Josef. *Ugaritische Grammatik*. Alter Orient und Altes Testament 273. Münster: Ugarit-Verlag, 2000.

Tsamodi, Yosef. "The Wisdom Hymn (Job 28): Its Place in the Book of Job." *Beit Mikra* 28 (1982-83): 268-77 (in Hebrew).

Tur-Sinai, N. H. *The Book of Job*. Revised edition. Jerusalem: Kiryat Sepher, 1967. (see also s.v. Torczyner)

Van De Mieroop, Marc. *A History of the Ancient Near East, ca. 3000-323 BC*. Blackwell History of the Ancient World. Malden, Mass.; Oxford, UK; and Carlton, Victoria: Blackwell, 2004.

Van Leeuwen, Raymond C. "A Technical Metallurgical Usage of יצא." *Zeitschrift für die alttestamentliche Wissenschaft* 98 (1986): 112-13.

______. "Cosmos, Temple, House: Building and Wisdom in Mesopotamia and Israel." Pages 67-92 in *Wisdom Literature in Mesopotamia and Israel*. Edited by Richard J. Clifford. Society of Biblical Literature Symposium Series 36. Edited by Christopher R. Matthews. Atlanta, Ga.: Society of Biblical Literature, 2007.

______. "In Praise of Proverbs." Pages 308-327 in *Pledges of Jubilee: Essays in Honor of Calvin G. Seerveld*. Edited by Lambert Zuidervaart and Henry Luttikhuizen. Grand Rapids, Mich.: Eerdmans, 1995.

Vanstiphout, Herman. *Epics of Sumerian Kings: The Matter of Aratta*. Edited by Jerrold S. Cooper. Society of Biblical Literature Writings from the Ancient World 20. Atlanta, Ga.: 2003.

Vattioni, Francesco. *Ecclesiastico: Testo ebraico con apparato critico e versioni greca, latina e siriaca*. Pubblicazioni del Seminario di Semitistica: Texts 1. Edited by Giovanni Garbini. Naples: Oriental Institute of Naples, 1968.

Vaux, Roland de. *Ancient Israel: Its Life and Institutions*. Translated by John McHugh. London: Darton, Longman, and Todd, 1961. Originally published as *Les institutions de l'Ancien Testament*. 2 vols. Paris: Cerf, 1958.

Wallace, Howard. "Eden, Garden of." Pages 281-83 in Volume 2 of *Anchor Bible Dictionary*. Edited by D. N. Freedman. 6 vols. New York: Doubleday, 1992.

______. "Garden of God." Pages 906-907 in Volume 2 of *Anchor Bible Dictionary*. Edited by D. N. Freedman. 6 vols. New York: Doubleday, 1992.

Waltke, Bruce K. "The Fear of the Lord: The Foundation for a Relationship with God." Pages 17-33 in *Alive to God: Studies in Spirituality Presented to James Houston*. Edited by J. I. Packer and Loren Wilkinson. Downers Grove, Ill.: Intervarsity, 1992.

______. and Michael P. O'Connor. *An Introduction to Biblical Hebrew Syntax*. Winona Lake, Ind.: Eisenbrauns, 1990.

Walton, John H. *Ancient Near Eastern Thought and the Old Testament: Introducing the Conceptual World of the Hebrew Bible*. Grand Rapids, Mich.: Baker Academic, 2006.

Waterman, Leroy. "Note on Job 28 4." *Journal of Biblical Literature* 71 (1952): 167-70.

Watson, Wilfred G. E. *Classical Hebrew Poetry: A Guide to Its Techniques*. Edinburgh: T&T Clark, 2005. Originally published in Journal for the Study of the Old Testament: Supplement Series 26. Sheffield: JSOT Press, 1984.

Weber, R., ed. *Biblia Sacra Iuxta Vulgatam Versionem. Tomus I: Genesis-Psalmi*. 3d, corrected edition. 2 vols. Stuttgart: Deutsche Bibelgesellschaft, 1985.

Weiser, Artur. *Das Buch Hiob übersetzt und erklärt*. Göttingen: Vandenhoeck and Ruprecht, 1951.

Wendland, Ernst. " 'Where in the world can *wisdom* be found?' [Job 28:12, 20]: A textual and contextual survey of Job 28 in relation to its communicative setting, ancient [ANE] and modern [Africa]." *Journal for Semitics* 12 (2003): 1-33.

Westenholz, Joan Goodnick. "Heroes of Akkad." *Journal of the American Oriental Society* 103 (1983): 327-36.

______. *Legends of the Kings of Akkade: The Texts*. Mesopotamian Civilizations 7. Edited by Jerrold S. Cooper. Winona Lake, Ind.: Eisenbrauns, 1997.

Westermann, Claus. *Der Aufbau des Buches Hiob. Mit eine Einführung in die neuere Hiobforschung von Jürgen Kegler*. 2d, expanded edition. Calwer Theologische Monographien: Reihe A, Bibelwissenschaft, 6. Edited by Peter Stuhlmacher and Claus Westermann. Stuttgart: Calwer Verlag, 1977. First edition published as *Der Aufbau des Buches Hiob*. Beiträge zur historischen Theologie 23. Tübingen: Mohr Siebeck, 1956.

Whybray, Norman. *Job*. Readings: A New Biblical Commentary. Edited by John Jarick. Sheffield: Sheffield Academic Press, 1998.

Wiggermann, F. A. M. "mušḫuššu." Pages 455-62 in Volume 8 of *Reallexikon der Assyriologie und vorderasiatischen Archäologie*. 11 volumes, incomplete. Edited by Erich Ebeling et al. Berlin: de Gruyter, 1928-.

______. "Tišpak, His Seal, and the Dragon *mušḫuššu*." Pages 117-133 in *To the Euphrates and Beyond: Archaeological Studies in Honour of Maurits N. van Loon*. Edited by O. Haex et al. Rotterdam: Balkema, 1989.

Williams, R. J. *Hebrew Syntax: An Outline*. Toronto: University of Toronto Press, 1967.

Wilson, Gerald. *Job*. New International Biblical Commentary 10. Edited by Robert L. Hubbard, Jr., and Roberts K. Johnston. Peabody, Mass.: Hendrickson; Milton Keynes, U.K.: Paternoster, 2007.

______. "משל." Pages 1134-36 in Volume 2 of *New International Dictionary of Old Testament Theology and Exegesis*. Edited by W. A. VanGemeren. 5 vols. Grand Rapids, Mich.: Zondervan, 1997.

Witte, Markus. *Vom Leiden zur Lehre: Der dritte Redegang (Hiob 21-27) und die Redaktionsgeschichte des Hiobbuches*. Beihefte zur Zeitschrift für die alttestamentliche Wissenschaft 230. Edited by Otto Kaiser. Berlin and New York: Walter de Gruyter, 1994.

______. "The Greek Book of Job." Pages 33-54 in *Das Buch Hiob und seine Interpretationen. Beiträge zum Hiob-Symposium auf dem Monte Verità von 14.-19. August 2005*. Edited by Thomas Krüger et al. Abhandlungen zur Theologie des Alten und Neuen Testaments 88. Edited by Erhard Blum et al. Zürich: Theologischer Verlag Zürich, 2007.

Wolde, Ellen van. "Wisdom, Who Can Find It?: A Non-Cognitive and Cognitive Study of Job 28:1-11." Pages 1-36 in *Job 28: Cognition in Context*. Edited by Ellen van Wolde. Biblical Interpretation 64. Edited by R. Alan Culpepper and Rolf Rendtorff. Leiden and Boston: Brill, 2003.

Wolfers, David. *Deep Things Out of Darkness. The Book of Job: Essays and a New English Translation*. Grand Rapids, Mich.: Eerdmans, 1995.

______. "The Stone of Deepest Darkness: A Mineralogical Mystery (Job XXVIII)." *Vetus Testamentum* 44 (1994): 274-276.

______. "The Volcano in Job 28." *Jewish Bible Quarterly* 18 (1989-90): 234-40.

Woude, Adam S. van der. "Job, Targum of." Pages 413-414 in Volume 1 of *Encyclopedia of the Dead Sea* Scrolls. 2 vols. Edited by Lawrence H. Schiffmann and James A. Vanderkam. Oxford: Oxford University Press, 2000.

Yahuda, A. S. »Hapax Legomena im Alten Testament.« *Jewish Quarterly Review* 15 (1902-1903): 698-714.

Zerafa, Peter Paul. *The Wisdom of God in the Book of Job*. Studia Universitatis S. Thomae in Urbe 8. Rome: Herder, 1978.

Ziegler, Joseph. *Beiträge zum griechischen Iob*. Göttingen: Vandenhoeck & Ruprecht, 1985.

______. *Iob*. Septuaginta: Vetus Testamentum Graecum. Auctoritate Academiea Scientiarum Gottingensis editum. XI/4. Göttingen: Vandenhoeck & Ruprecht, 1982.

Zimmerman, Ruben. »Homo Sapiens Ignorans: Hiob 28 als Bestandteil der ursprünglichen Hiobdichtung.« *Biblische Notizen* 74 (1994): 80-100.

Zuckerman, Bruce. "Job, Targums of." Pages 868-69 in Volume 3 of *Anchor Bible Dictionary*. Edited by D. N. Freedman. 6 vols. New York: Doubleday, 1992.

______. *Job the Silent: A Study in Historical Counterpoint*. New York and Oxford: Oxford University Press, 1991.

______. "The Date of 11Q Targum Job: A Paleographic Consideration of its Vorlage." *Journal for the Study of the Pseudepigrapha* 1 (1987): 57-78.

______. "The Process of Translation in 11QtgJob: A Preliminary Study." Ph.D. diss., Yale University, 1980.

______. "Two Examples of Editorial Modification in 11QtgJob." Pages 269-74 in *Biblical and Near Eastern Studies: Essays in Honor of William Sanford LaSor*. Edited by Gary Tuttle. Grand Rapids, Mich.: Eerdmans, 1978.

Index of Ancient Texts

Biblical Texts

Old Testament

8	16, 174, 180, 237
8:10-11	63, 174
8:11	229
8:17	90
8:18	174
8:18-21	63
8:19	174, 224
8:21	174
8:22-31	94n286, 188
8:24	94n284
8:27	94n284, 180, 194
8:28	94n284, 180
8:29	94n284, 194
8:30	94n284
9	174, 180
9:10	204
10:11	63
13:14	63
14:12	40, 62
14:27	63
15:11	184, 185
15:33	204
16:16	63
16:25	40, 62
18:4	63
18:17	202
20:15	62, 166
24:3-4	192
24:7	224
25:20	154
26:7	141
26:13	155
27:20	184, 185
28:11	202
31:10	229
31:19	162
31:20	180

Ecclesiastes

7:12	63
7:25	168
10:9	126

Song of Songs

1:6	149
5:11	220, 224
5:14	146
5:15	224

Isaiah

3:18-23	213
7:11	168
11:15	73
13:12	220, 224
14	88n265
14:8	74
15:1	122, 123, 186
17:4	141, 142
18:6	149
19:6	141, 142
25:8	184
28:16	132
30:8	194
30:33	136
37:24	74
38:14	141
40:12	94, 192, 193
40:12-14	94n286
40:28	202
41:5	190
41:18	123
46:11	149
49:16	194
50:7	159, 160
51:10	168, 180
54:5	73
54:10	119
54:11	146
54:11-12	63n142, 132
58:8	165
58:11	123
61:10	224
63:13	180
66:16	135

Jeremiah

2:31	48
4:7	54
5:6	54
5:22	194
9:9	154
9:20	184

10:12 201
12:8 54
12:9 149
13:23 145
17:16 123
20:5 166
32:40 209
49:18 139
49:19 54
49:33 139
50:40 139
50:44 54
51:15 201
51:53 119

Lamentations
2:3 51
2:4 51
4:1 132, 220
4:2 224
4:7 146, 225, 229

Ezekiel
1:4 160
1:26 132, 146
1:27 160
4:1 194
8:2 145, 160
10:1 132, 146
13:9 209
13:11 226
13:13 226
22:25 166
23:14 194
23:49 209
24:24 209
26:19 180
27:12-24 213
27:16 (LXX) 224
27:22 166
27:34 168
28:2 88n265
28:2-10 88n265
28:11 222
28:12-13 83
28:12-14 51
28:12-19 88n265
28:13 83, 146, 166, 222, 229
28:13-14 63, 76
28:14 51, 132, 145
28:16 132, 145
31:3-17 85
31:4 180
31:6 183
31:13 183
31:14 76
31:15 180
32:2 158
32:4 183
38:20 183
38:22 226
39:4 149
39:14 130
41:3 228
47:1-12 83

Daniel
2:22 87
2:35 165
2:45 165
9:25 123
10:5 220
10:6 145
11:38 166
11:42 161

Hosea
2:20 183
4:3 183
5:14 155, 156
6:3 123
13:7 155, 156
13:8 217
13:14 184
14:9 176

Joel
4:18 83

Amos
3:4 54

5:19 158

Jonah
2:6 179, 180
2:6-7 82, 162
2:7 143
3:4 144

Micah
1:4 135
3:3 125
5:1 124
5:7 54
6:7 136
7:17 78

Nahum
1:5 162

Habbakuk
2:5 184
3:6 162
3:9 73, 83
3:10 179, 180

Zechariah
8:6 119
9:3 77
9:16 132
10:1 196
14:8 83
14:10 224

New Testament

Matthew
10:16 78

Revelation
21:11-12 63n142
21:18-21 63n142

Apocrypha and Septuagint

Baruch
3 237n20
3:9-4:4 16, 237
3:29 184n449
3:37-4:4 14
5:7 164

3 Kingdoms
6:19 228
6:30 228

Sirach
1 16, 237
1:9 201
3:14 (Heb) 223
4 174, 180
4:10 (Heb) 223
6 174, 180
7:18 220
7:19 229
16:23 (Heb) 191n486
16:25 191n486
24 16, 174, 180, 237
30:15 224, 229
31:6 229
35:20 (Heb) 196
35:24 198
35:26 196
40:13 (Heb) 198
40:13 198
43:31 199
51 174, 180

Wisdom of Solomon
8 174, 180

Non-Biblical Texts

Akkadian

Adapa 92n275

Assurbanipal Inscriptions
A-B NW Palace 55

Babylonian Map of the World (BM 92687; Westenholz)
obv., 5′ 80
obv., 5′-8′ 79n220
rev., 8′ 54

Babylonian Theodicy (Lambert)
line 57 66n152

Code of Hammurabi (Roth)
xlix 98-113 86n255

Cuneiform Texts from the British Museum (CT)
13 33-34 157
16 46 84n247
18 29 65

El-Amarna (Knudtzon)
16 77n209
19 77n209
85:35 42n61
86:33 42n61
89:58 216n25
288:6 123n115

Enuma Anu Enlil (prologue)
Line 3 201n535

Enuma Elish (Talon)
I. 1, 7, 9 94n284
I. 3-5 180n432
I. 71 201n535
I. 80 96n294
IV. 141-44 96
IV. 142-43 193
IV. 143 94
IV. 144 201n535
V. 8 201n535
V. 62 201n535
V. 119 84n244

Esarhaddon Inscriptions (Borger)
Annals frag. f, rev. 4-7 55n108
AsBbA rev.:30-33 53
AsBbA rev.:36 53n100, 58n121
AsBbE obv.:14 58n121
K. 2801 145n235
Nineveh A iv.46-48 48n82
Nineveh A iv.47 52n97
Nineveh A iv.57 52n97
Nineveh A iv.53-60 55n107

Etana (Neo-Assyrian version)
III. 102 92n276
III. 139 92n276

Gilgamesh epic (George)

Old Babylonian
A2207, line 38′ 74n197
IM, line 18 74n197
Nippur school tablet 80n225
VA+BM iv 10-11 69n170

Middle Babylonian
Boghazköy obv., i 15′-17′ 81n232

Standard Babylonian
I. 1 37, 65n150, 98n306
I. 1-2 64
I. 1-8 87n260
I. 1-28 65
I. 3 37, 65n150, 98n306
I. 6-8 64
I.7-8 85n251
I. 9 102
I. 10 36, 66
I. 11-22 102
I.19 98n308

Aramaic

Dead Sea Scrolls

Index of Authors